Edward B. Eastwick

The Gulistan

Or, Rose-garden of Shekh Muslihud-din Sadi of Shiraz

Edward B. Eastwick

The Gulistan
Or, Rose-garden of Shekh Muslihud-din Sadi of Shiraz

ISBN/EAN: 9783337075071

Printed in Europe, USA, Canada, Australia, Japan

Cover: Foto ©ninafisch / pixelio.de

More available books at **www.hansebooks.com**

THE GULISTĀN;

OR,

ROSE-GARDEN,

OF

SHEKH MUṢLIḤU'D-DĪN SĀDĪ OF SHĪRĀZ,

TRANSLATED

FOR THE FIRST TIME INTO PROSE AND VERSE, WITH AN INTRODUCTORY
PREFACE, AND A LIFE OF THE AUTHOR, FROM THE ĀTISH KADAH,

BY

EDWARD B. EASTWICK, C.B., M.A., F.R.S., M.R.A.S.,

OF MERTON COLLEGE, OXFORD ; MEMBER OF THE ASIATIC SOCIETIES
OF PARIS AND BOMBAY; AND FORMERLY PROFESSOR OF ORIENTAL
LANGUAGES AND LIBRARIAN IN THE EAST INDIA COLLEGE,
HAILEYBURY.

SECOND EDITION.

LONDON:
TRÜBNER & CO., LUDGATE HILL.
1880.
[All rights reserved.]

STEPHEN AUSTIN AND SONS, PRINTERS, HERTFORD.

PREFACE TO THE SECOND EDITION.

THE FIRST EDITION of my translation of the Gulistān was published by Mr. Stephen Austin, of Hertford, in 1852. A new edition has been frequently called for, and negociations have been more than once entered into for re-printing it, but my time has been too much occupied to allow of their being brought to a satisfactory result. The former edition was an "edition de luxe," and the high price at which it sold put it out of the reach of many, who, it is hoped, will purchase it in its present form. The extraordinary popularity of the work in the East, and its intrinsic merits, may well lead to the expectation that it will find a place in all public libraries. It may be added that the translation has been carefully read through and compared with the original by an Indian gentleman, who is a profound Persian scholar, and possesses at the same time a complete mastery of English, and who has expressed himself satisfied with this version of the most famous work of the immortal Sâdī.

EDWARD B. EASTWICK.

London, *May 27th*, 1880.

PREFACE.

The Gulistān of Sādī has attained a popularity in the East which, perhaps, has never been reached by any European work in this Western world. The school-boy lisps out his first lessons in it; the man of learning quotes it; and a vast number of its expressions have become proverbial. When we consider, indeed, the time at which it was written—the first half of the thirteenth century— a time when gross darkness brooded over Europe, at least—darkness which might have been, but, alas! was not felt—the justness of many of its sentiments, and the glorious views of the Divine attributes contained in it, are truly remarkable. Thus, in the beginning of the Preface, the Unity, the unapproachable majesty, the omnipotence, the long-suffering, and the goodness of God, are nobly set forth. The vanity of worldly pursuits, and the true vocation of man, are everywhere insisted upon:

"The world, my brother! will abide with none,
 By the world's Maker let thy heart be won." (p. 24.)

In Sādī's code of morals, mercy and charity are not restricted, as by some bigoted Muḥammadans, to true believers:

> "*All Adam's race* are members of one frame;
> Since all, at first, from the same essence came.
> If thou feel'st not for others' misery,
> A son of Adam is no name for thee." (p. 38.)

Evil, it is said, should be requited with good, thus:

> "Whenever then
> Thy enemy thee slanders absent, thou
> To his face applaud him." (p. 57.)

and:

> "Shew kindness even to thy foes." (p. 67.)

See also the story of the Khalīfah Hārūn's son (p. 67); and of the recluse (p. 76):

> "The men of God's true faith, I've heard,
> Grieve not the hearts e'en of their foes.
> When will this station be conferred
> On thee, who dost thy friends oppose?"

Sādi not only preached the duty of contentment and resignation, but practised what he preached. In a life prolonged to nearly twice the ordinary period allotted to man, he shewed his contempt for riches, which he might easily have amassed, but which, when showered on him by the great, he devoted to pious purposes; being minded that:

> "The poor man's patience better is than gold." (p. 99.)

Thus, when the Prime Minister of Hulaku Khān sent him a present of 50,000 dīnārs, he expended it in erecting a house for travellers, near Shirāz. But it will be sufficient for those who would form a just estimate of Sādi to peruse his works, especially the IIIrd and VIIIth books of the Gulistān, which set forth his good sense, humility, and cheerful resignation to the Supreme will, in the clearest light. Of the history of his long and useful life we, unfortunately, know but little; and that little is comprised in the notice of him which is here subjoined from the Ātish Kadah. Ross, however, with much diligence and acuteness, has drawn from his works themselves some other interesting particulars relating to him. It appears that his father's name was Ābdu'llāh, and that he was descended from Ālī, the son-in-law of Muḥammad; but that, nevertheless, his father held no higher office than some petty situation under the Dīwān. From Būstān, II. 2, it appears that he lost his father when but a child; while, from the 6th Story of the VIth Chapter of the Gulistān, we learn that his mother survived to a later period. He was educated at the Nizāmiah College at Baghdād, where he held an Idrār, or fellowship (Būstān, VII. 14), and was instructed in science by the learned Abū'l-farj-bin-Jauzī (Gulistān, II. 20), and in theology by Ābdu'l-Ḳādir Gīlānī, with whom he made his first pilgrimage to Makkah. This pilgrimage he repeated no less than fourteen times. It is to his residence at Baghdād—where Arabic, as he tells us in the IIIrd Chapter of the Gulistān, was spoken with great purity—that we, perhaps, owe the profusion of Arabic verses and sentences which are scattered through his works. He had, however, scarce reached his mid-career when that imperial city was taken and sacked by the Tartar Hulaku, with a prodigious massacre of the inhabitants; on which occasion he gave expression to his regrets in a Ḳaṣīdah, or elegy.

Sādī was twice married. Of his first nuptials, at

Aleppo, we have a most amusing account in the 31st Story of the IInd Chapter of the Gulistān. His enforced labour with a gang of Jews in the fosse of Tripolis was not likely to increase his good opinion of the Christian sect; for it appears from that story, that his taskmasters, the Crusaders, had not made him prisoner in war, but while practising religious austerities in the desert; and he, therefore, certainly deserved more lenient treatment. Whatever might, however, have been Sâdi's opinion of Christians[a]—and it certainly was not very favourable— he speaks with reverence of their Lord, as he does also of St. John the Baptist. Thus, in his Badīya, he says, "It is the breath of Jesus, for in that fresh breath and verdure the dead earth is reviving:" and, in the Gulistān, II. 10, we find Sâdī engaged in devotion at the tomb of John the Baptist, of which he says—

"The poor, the rich, alike must here adore;
The wealthier they, their need is here the more."

where it is to be remarked that his prayers were offered only to the Deity; but he knelt at the tomb, supposing, with other Muḥammadans and Roman Catholics, that it was not only allowable, but salutary, to entreat the intercession of holy men.

Sâdi married a second time at Sanāā, the capital of Yaman; and, in the Būstān, IX. 25, pours out his regrets for the loss of his only son. His notices of the female sex are, in general, not very laudatory, and his

---

[a] *Vide* Chapter III. Story 21:

"A Christian's well may not be pure, 'tis true,
'Twill do to wash the carcase of a Jew."

opinions on this head seem to have strengthened as he grew in years. Ross mentions Europe, Barbary, Abyssinia, Egypt, Syria, Palestine, Armenia, Asia Minor, Arabia, Persia, Tartary, Afghānistān, and India, as the countries in which he travelled; and Kœmpfer, who visited Shīrāz A.D. 1686, tells us that he had been in Egypt and Italy; and that, to his knowledge of Oriental tongues, he had even superadded an acquaintance with Latin, and, in particular, had diligently studied Seneca. Sâdī himself informs us that he was at Dihlī during the reign of Uglamish, who died A.H. 653 = A.D. 1255, and there exist some verses in the Urdū dialect which he is said, but perhaps without much reason, to have composed. Jāmī supposes that the beautiful youth whom Sâdī encountered at Kashgarh, and who is mentioned in the 17th story of the Vth chapter of the Gulistān,[b] was the famous poet of Dihlī, Amīr Khusrau; and it is certain that it was owing to the eulogies of Khusrau that Sâdī was invited by Sultān Muhammad to Multān, where that prince offered to found a monastery for him.

Sâdī seems to have spent the latter part of his life in retirement. He died on the evening of Friday, in the month of Shawwāl, A.H. 690 = A.D. 1291, says Daulat Shāh, and was buried near Shīrāz. Kœmpfer, in 1686, and Colonel Franklin, in 1787, visited his tomb, and the latter mentions it as being "just in the state it was in when Sâdī was buried." In person, Sâdī was, as Ross conjectures, of a mean appearance, low of stature, spare and slim. In the picture which Colonel Franklin saw of him, near his tomb, he is represented as wearing the

---

[b] Ross's Translation.

khirkah, or long blue gown of the darwesh, with a staff in his hand.

The great beauty of Sâdî's style is its elegant simplicity. In wit he is not inferior to Horace, whom he also resembles in his "curiosa verborum felicitas." Of his works the Gulistān may be ranked first. The numerous translations of his writings shew that his merits have not been altogether unappreciated even in these Western regions. George Gentius has the credit of first making known to European readers the Gulistān, by his "Rosarium Politicum," published at Amsterdam, A.D. 1651, of which it is sufficient to observe that it exhibits, along with the energy, all the roughness of a pioneer. A century and a half elapsed between the appearance of this Latin translation and the English one of Gladwin, which, though deserving of much commendation, is somewhat too free;[c] as are also those of Dumoulin, published at Calcutta in 1807, and of Lee, published in London in 1827. In

---

[c] Thus, at p. 53, l. 11, of my edition of the Persian text, اگر مستوجب عقوبتم *agar mustaujib-i ukūbatam*, is translated by Gladwin, " Shouldst Thou doom me to punishment ;" and p. 55, l. 14, اینقدر بس که روی در خلقست *īn kadr bas kih rūi dar khalkast*, "This is sufficient with a mortal face," which is very incorrect. At p. 76, l. 10, he renders ز موری *za mūrī*, "to an ant," which, as well as being incorrect, destroys the sense. At p. 79, l. 18, اتفاق می سازم *ittifāk mī sāzam* is rendered, "I am reflecting"! At p. 80, l. 13, از نهیب برد عجوز *az nahīb-i bard-i ʿajūz*, is translated by "in the depth of winter." At p. 147, l. 10, for سود سرمایه عمرم *sūd-i sarmāyah-i ʿumram*, we find "the chief comfort of my life." At p. 149, l. 10, he omits an entire line.

TRANSLATOR'S PREFACE. xiii

1823 Mr. James Ross, a retired civilian, published a new translation,[d] which he dedicated, by permission, to

[d] At p. 18, l. 12, of the Persian preface (my edition), Ross translates مخل بندم ولي نه در بوستان *nakhl bandam walī nah dar būstān,* " I am a gardener, but not in a garden,"—where he appears to me to lose the whole pith of the sentence, viz., the implied comparison between the flowers of an artificial flower-maker and those of nature. At p. 7, l. 16, we find نسل و تبار *nasl wa tabār* rendered, in Ross, " The tree of their wickedness,"—where he evidently mistakes the Arabic word for the Persian. At p. 12, l. 10, كه سلطان بلشكر كند سروري *kih Sulṭān ba lashkar kunad sarwarī* is rendered, " For a king with an army constitutes a principality,"—which is altogether wide of the obvious meaning that " A king rules through his troops." At l. 17, in the same page, we find پادشاهي كه طرح ظلم فكند, *pādshāhī kih ṭarḥ ẓulm fikanad,* " A king that can anyhow be accessory to tyranny,"—where the obvious meaning of طرح *ṭarḥ,* " le fondement," as Semelet rightly translates it, is overlooked, though so clearly shewn by the use of پاي *pāe* in the next line. At p. 20, l. 4, Ross strangely mistakes رعايت *riāyat* for رعيت *raīyat,* and renders در رعايتِ مملكتِ سستي كردي *dar riāyat-i mamlakat sustī kardī,* " was easy with the yeomanry in collecting revenue " ! In the same line both he and Semelet wrongly translate پيشين *pīshīn,* " ancient," whereas it is evident from the sequel of the story that the king was cotemporary with Sādī, who knew one of his soldiers, and the word should, therefore, be rendered " former." At p. 23, l. 19, Ross gives a new sense to حرامي *ḥarāmī,* " revenue-embezzler." At p. 25, l. 16, Ross translates مُشار اليه بالبنان و معتمد عليه عند الاعيان *mushārun ilaihi b'ilbanān wa mutamad alaihi ăndu'l-āiyān,* " Towards whom all turned for counsel, and upon whom all eyes rested their hope,"—which does not

the Chairman and Court of Directors of the East India
Company, and which he especially informs us was in-

contain a single word of the original, for even اعیان *aiyán*
cannot here be rendered "eyes." In the last line of the same
page, Ross renders تاریکی *táríkí*, "Chaos," completely and
most gratuitously destroying the beautiful metaphor. At p. 28,
l. 20, we have a tolerable instance of a free translation; حاکم را
این سخن پسندیده آمد *hákim-rá ín sukhan pasandídah ámad*,
"When the prince heard this sentiment he subscribed to its
omnipotence"! The two first lines in p. 29 are sadly mis-
translated,

چو کعبه قبلهٔ حاجت شد از دیار بعید
روند خلق بدیدارش از بسی فرسنگ

Chú kábah kiblah-i hájat shud az diyár-i baíd,
Rawand khalk ba-dídárash az basí farsang.

which he renders thus, "When the fane of the Cablah at
Mecca became their object from a far-distant land, pilgrims
would hurry on to visit it from many farsangs." The Kâbah
it is needless to remark, is the Black Temple at Mecca,
and the Kiblah is the place to which people turn in prayer.
قبله *Kiblah*, therefore, should here be taken with *hájat*,
with which it is connected by an *izáfah*, and the از دیار بعید
az diyár-i baíd as evidently belongs to روند *rawand*, from which
it should not be separated by a stop. At p. 31, l. 7, 8, the
complet is so translated as to become quite unmeaning. At
p. 32, l. 13, Ross translates ملک بر آن لشکری خشم گرفت
malik bar án lashkarí khishm girift, "The sovereign let loose
the army of his wrath"—a mistake which it is hardly possible
to imagine a mere beginner would make. Gladwin rightly
translates the sentence in his curt, free manner, "the king

tended to be literal, and thereby useful to the Students of the East India College. He prefixed to it a very

being displeased;" and Semelet, who reads برو *bar-ū* for بر آن لشكري *bar ān lashkarī*, renders it "le roi se met en colère contre lui." At p. 34, l. 6, همچنان در فكر آن بيتم كه گفت *hamchunān dar fikr-i ān baitam kih guft*, where بيتم *baitam* is for بيت هستم *bait hastam*, as Gladwin and Semelet rightly take it, whereas Ross renders it "applicable to which is that stanza of mine." At p. 38, l. 7, Ross renders بحيف *ba-ḥaif* "at a low price," instead of "by force," and he also mistakes the sense of بطرح *ba-ṭarḥ*. At p. 41, l. 10, گرچه نعمت بفر دولت اوست *garchich ni'mat ba-far-i daulat-i ūst*, is translated, "Though it be for their benefit that his glory is exalted"—a sense which can in no way be extracted from the words. At p. 41, l. 13, Ross renders مراورا از بندگان بسياهي بخشيد *marūrā az bandagān ba-siyāhī bakhshīd*, "he *forced* her upon a negro," a strange sense of بخشيدن *bakhshīdan*. At p. 53, l. 10, Ross translates حصا *ḥaṣa*, in defiance of the dictionary and of the other translations, "the black stone," instead of "pebbles," as Gladwin rightly renders it. In the next line he translates مستوجب *mustaujib*, "doomed," for "deserving." At p. 55, l. 14, he translates روي در خلقست *rūī dar khalḳast*, "this much is sufficient that it has a threadbare hood!"—a translation so amazing that one must suppose he read the passage differently, though it stands so in Gentius, whose text he professed to follow. At p. 57, l. 16, Ross has evidently misunderstood the sentence, چيزي نكردي كه بكار آيد *chīzī na kardī kih bakār āyad*,—which he renders, "that nothing be omitted that can serve a purpose." At p. 61, l. 10, Ross gives a ridiculous version of خامان مجلس در جوش *khāmān-i majlis dar jūsh*, "and the rawest of the assembly bubbled in unison."

valuable essay on the works and character of Sádī; but, of his Translation, I regret to say that I cannot speak in terms of unqualified praise. In 1828, M. Semelet published the Persian text of the Gulistān in Paris, and six years afterwards, a most excellent Translation, to which the first place must undoubtedly be assigned;º while Gladwin's version occupies the second; that of Ross, the third; and that of Gentius, the fourth.

At p. 64, l. 7, سر و پا برهنه *sar o pā barahnah* is rendered, "naked from head to foot," instead of "with bare head and feet." At p. 64, l. 15, Ross translates ببالینش *ba-bālīnash*, "to his *bier*," instead of "pillow." At p. 69, l. 2, بدست این مطرب *ba-dast-i īn muṭrib* is rendered, "in the hand of this minstrel," instead of "by means of this musician." At p. 74, l. 7, Ross translates حبوب *hubūb*, "zephyr"! and, at p. 76, l. 3, هني *hani-a*, "immense;" and l. 9, گور *gūr*, "an elk." At p. 95, l. 8, Ross renders صف *ṣaff*, "group." At p. 102, l. 6, تعرض سؤال *taârruẓ-i suāl*, "prostitution of begging." At p. 109, l. 18, گدائي دول *gadāī haul* is rendered, "an importunate mendicant." At p. 178, l. 14, لقمه ادرار فروشند *lukmah-i idrār farāshand* is rendered, "that they may entitle themselves to the bread of charity." At least ten times this number of inaccuracies might have been noticed, but these will be sufficient to show how unsafe a guide Ross proves himself as a translator.

º I have found but very few passages in which it appears to me that M. Semelet has failed to give the sense of the original. One is in Chap. I. (p. 4, l. 13), where he renders سري *sarī*, "le premier;" and line 17 of the same page, where درشتي *durushtī*, is rendered "la masse." At p. 34, l. 7, he renders یپبانی, "un gardien de chameaux." At p. 162, l. 14. فلاح *falāh*, is translated "le paysan." There are some other inadvertencies, which will be found referred to in the notes.

For the publication of the present Translation, the only apology that seems requisite is the fact that those of Gladwin and Ross have long been out of print. Moreover, if the Eastern saying be true that

هر لفظ سعدي *har lafz-i Sádí,*
هفتاد و دو معني *haftád wa dú máni.*

"Each word of Sádí has seventy-two meanings," there is room for a septuagint of translators. There is, however, another ground on which the Translation now offered to the public may claim notice, that it is, I believe, the first attempt, on anything like an extensive[f] scale, to render Persian poetry into English verse. Ross, in his Introductory Essay, asserts, in the words of Cowper, that "it is impossible to give, in rhyme, a just translation of any ancient poetry of Greece or Rome, and still less (here he means "still more" impossible) of Arabic and Persian." It will be for the Oriental scholar to judge how far I have departed from the true meaning of the original in putting it into English verse. For myself, I can only say I have not knowingly allowed myself any license except on very few occasions, on each of which I have excused myself in a note. I have also endeavoured to make the metre correspond in some degree to that of the Persian, and I have uniformly

---

[f] Atkinson has published some spirited versions extracted from the Sháh-námah; but I speak here of a continuous work. I do not mention Miss Costello's "Rose Garden of Persia," which is merely a translation from the French, and exhibits about as much of the originals as Moore's "Lalla Rookh," that is, nothing but a certain Oriental tone and gilding.

done my best to preserve the play upon words which occurs so often, and which is accounted such a beauty in the East.

I have only further to add that, to mark the Arabic passages, italics have been adopted; and that where I have had occasion to insert any explanation, the words employed are enclosed in brackets.

EDWARD B. EASTWICK.

HAILEYBURY COLLEGE,
October 1st, 1852.

LIFE OF SÀDÌ.

SHEKH MUSLIHU'D-DĪN, surnamed Sâdī, is the most eloquent of writers, and the wittiest author of either modern or ancient times, and one of the four monarchs of eloquence and style. In the opinion of this humble individual (the author of the Ātish Kadah) no one has appeared since the first rise of Persian Poetry who can claim a superior place to Firdausī of Tūs, Nizāmī of Kum, Anwarī of Abīward, and Shekh Sâdī. In short, all I could say of the qualities which adorned his mind and heart, and of his perfections, displayed and secret, would not amount to the thousandth part of the reality, or be more than a trifling indication of the whole. In accordance with this, my master, the august and felicitous Mīr Saiyid Ālī Mushtāk, used to call Sâdī the "Nightingale of a Thousand Songs," intending to express that in every branch of poetry he displayed the perfection of genius. In a word, I used to busy myself with reflecting, whether in the revolutions of Time there had ever been a period, when men of learning were more lightly esteemed than at present; or, with reference to the want of appreciation evinced by the generation in which we live, whether bards were ever more undervalued than now? until I saw it mentioned in a Biography that a number of Poets once questioned Muḥammad Hamkar (Praise be to God! the like of him does not exist in these days) as to the comparative excellence of Sâdī and Imāmī of Herāt. He answered them with this verse,

"Not to Imāmī's strain,
Can I or Sâdī e'er attain!"

On reading this, I returned thanks to God that this age is guiltless of such folly as this. Men of sense will be alive to the disgraceful injustice of such a sentence, though as to himself Muḥammad Hamkar pronounced rightly. It is quite true that Imāmī is a far superior poet to the author of the verse quoted above, but there is not the shadow of a pretence for comparing him with the illustrious Sâdī, nor is there a single person save the three great poets whose names are given above, who can be placed in the same rank. With relation to the preceding anecdote a stanza occurred to me as I was composing the life of Sâdī, which perhaps is not altogether devoid of point, and which I will here set down.

One said, "The palm of merit has been given
 To Imām of Herāt, o'er Sâdī, by
Muḥammad Hamkar;—what think'st thou?" "Good
 Heaven!
How much does Hamkar[a] herein err!" said I.

Sâdī is said to have been a disciple of Shekh Shahā-

[a] There is a play on the words "Hamkar" and سِتَمکر, "unjust," which cannot be preserved in English.

bu'd-dín; and Daulat Shah[b] writes that he lived to the age of one hundred and twenty years; and that after his tenth year he spent thirty years in various countries in acquiring learning, and thirty years more in travelling and making himself practically acquainted with things, and thirty years more in the environs of Shīrāz, in a spot which for beauty equals the Garden of Paradise; where men of learning and eminence resorted to him, and where he employed himself in devotion. Here he was supplied with delicious viands by his disciples, and it was his wont after satisfying his hunger to wrap up what was left and suspend it in a basket, and the wood-cutters who used to cut bushes in the neighbourhood of Shīrāz took these fragments away. One day, a person, by way of experiment, disguised himself as a wood-cutter and went to the place where the fragments were. On reaching towards them, his arm became stiff and remained stretched out. He cried out, "O Shekh! come to my aid!" Sâdī replied, "If this be the dress of a bush-cutter, where are the scars on thy hands and feet? or if thou art a robber, where is thy strong arm and firm heart that without a wound or pain thou makest these outcries?" He then prayed for him and the man was healed.

They also relate that a devout person of Shīrāz saw in a dream that the angels in heaven were moved, and that the cherubs were singing softly the poetry of Shekh Sâdī, and said that "this couplet of Sâdī is worth the praises and hymns of angel-worship for a whole

[b] The name of the author of a celebrated Biography of Learned Men.

year." When he awoke, he went to Sádi and found him with ecstatic fervour reciting this couplet,

To pious minds each verdant leaf displays,
A volume teeming with th' Almighty's praise.

The devotee related to Sádi the vision before mentioned, and besought him to pray in his behalf.

The repartees of Sádi are numberless; nor is it requisite to recount what is known to all. Once in his travels he arrived at Tabrīz, where he learnt on inquiry after Khwājah Hamām,[c] that he had a son of great beauty and accomplishments; and that he guarded him from acquaintance with strangers with the most scrupulous care, insomuch that he took him to the private baths. Sádi went to the bath on the day that the Khwājah had fixed to come, and concealed himself in a corner until he arrived with his son; when laying aside his mantle, he stepped in. Khwājah was displeased when he saw him, and seating his son behind him, he asked Sádi, whence he came? and what was his profession? Sádi replied that he came from the fair land of Shīrāz; and that he was a poet. Khwājah said, "Holy God! in this country the men of Shīrāz are more plentiful than dogs!" "It is just the reverse in my country," replied Sádi, "for there the men of Tabrīz are less[d] than dogs." There happened to be there a vessel of water. Khwājah said, "It is strange,

[c] Name of a famous poet.
[d] The wit lies in the double sense of کمتر *kamtar*, which means "fewer"—answering to بیشتر *bishtar*—"more numerous," and also "inferior."

the people of Shīrāz are bald-headed like the bottom of this vessel." "Stranger still," replied Sâdī, turning up the cup, "the heads of the people of Tabrīz are as empty as the mouth[e] of this." "Prithee," rejoined Khwājah with a discomfited look, "Do they ever quote the poems of Hamām in Shīrāz?" "Yes," answered Sâdī, and he then repeated this concluding verse of one of Hamām's odes,

"Hamām divides[f] me from my love—one day
 That veil, I hope, will be removed away."

Khwājah said, "I conjecture that thou art Shekh Sâdī? for to no one else belongs such quickness." Sâdī answered in the affirmative; on which Khwājah kissed his hand, and made his son pay his respects, and took his illustrious visitor home with him, where he showed him every attention for some time—"Would that I too had been with them!"[g]

I have repeatedly perused the writings of this poet, whose whole works deserve to be transcribed here. Some extracts, however, of his elegies, odes, didactic poems and facetiæ, which appear to me to possess the most perfect beauty, are all that I am able to extract; and I shall quote this one passage from his prose writings,

---

[e] I have changed this repartee a little, at the risk of losing somewhat of its point.

[f] Hamām was sitting between his son and Sâdī. In the original sense, a Ṣūfīistic one, a veil is said to be between Hamām and his beloved one, i.e. God.

[g] This is an exclamation of the author, and is to be found in the Ḳur'ān.

though I have not admitted any other prose extract from any writer into this book:

"They asked a philosopher, 'Who should be called fortunate, and who unfortunate?' He replied, 'He is to be called fortunate, who sowed and reaped; and he must be reckoned unfortunate, who died and left [what he possessed without enjoying it.]'"

The rest of his sayings, full of wisdom as they are, must be sought in the Gulistān, to which the reader is referred.

Sádī flourished in the reign of Sád Atābak, whence his name of Sádī, and he died in Shīrāz, in the year 691 A.H. (This is the date according to D'Herbelot, but according to Daulat Sháh, 690, see p. xi.)

A LIST OF THE WRITINGS OF SÁDÍ.

AS ENUMERATED BY ROSS.

1 to 6.—Risālah; or Treatise.
7.—Gulistān.
8.—Būstān.
9.—Arabian Kasāids.
10.—Persian Kasāids.
11.—Marāsī; or Dirges.
12.—Mixed Poems, Persian and Arabic.
13.—Poems, with recurring lines.
14.—Plain Ghazals.
15.—Rhetorical Ghazals.
16.—Works written in later life.
17.—Writings in earlier life.
18.—Poems addressed to Shamsu'd-dīn.
19 —Fragments.
20.—Facetiæ.
21.—Tetrastichs.
22.—Distichs.

I boast not the stock of my own excellence;
But hold forth my hand, like a beggar, for pence.
I have heard in the day of hope and of fear,[a]
God's mercy the good and the sinner will spare:
If thou, too, herein seest faults, be it thine
Like thy Maker to act; like Him be benign.

Būstān of Sādī.

---

[a] That is, in the day of resurrection.

PREFACE.

IN THE NAME OF GOD, THE MERCIFUL, THE COMPASSIONATE!

PRAISE be to God! (May he be honoured and glorified!) whose worship is the means of drawing closer to Him, and in giving thanks to whom is involved an increase of benefits. Every breath which is inhaled prolongs life, and when respired exhilarates the frame. In every breath therefore two blessings are contained, and for every blessing a separate thanksgiving is due.

COUPLETS.

Whose hands suffice? whose voices may
The tribute of His praises pay?
O! ye of David's line! His praises sing,[1]
For few are grateful found to him [their King.]

STANZA.

Best for the slave his fault to own,
And seek for pardon at God's throne:
For none can hope to pay aright
A homage worthy of his might.
   The raindrops of his mercy, shed
   On all, descend unlimited,
   His bounteous store for all is spread.
Dark though their sins may be, He does not rend
   The veil that clokes His creatures' shame;
Nor stays His bounty, though they oft offend,
   [But aye continueth the same.]

---

[1] This is a quotation from the Ḳur'ān; Chap. xxxiv., v. 12.

STANZA.

All-Gracious One! who, from Thy hidden store,
On Guebre[2] dost, and Pagan, alms bestow!
When will Thy mercies crown Thy friends no more?
Thou, who with love regardest e'en Thy foe!

He biddeth His chamberlain, the morning breeze, spread out the emerald carpet [of the earth,] and commandeth His nurses, the vernal clouds, to foster in earth's cradle the tender herbage, [*lit.*, "the daughters of the grass"] and clotheth the trees with a garment of green leaves, and at the approach of spring crowneth the young branches with wreaths of blossoms; and by His power the juice of the cane becometh exquisite honey, and the date-seed, by His nurture, a lofty tree.

STANZA.

Cloud and wind, and sun and sky,
Labour all harmoniously,
That while they thee with food supply,
Thou mayst not eat unthankfully.[3]
Since all are busied and intent for thee,
Justice forbids that thou a rebel be.

It is a tradition of the Chief of Created Beings, and the Most Glorious of Existences, the Mercy[4] of the Universe, the Purest of Mankind, and the Complement of Time's Circle, Muḥammad Muṣṭafa (On whom be blessing and peace!)

COUPLET.

Gracious Prophet! intercessor! worthy of obedience, thou!
Beautiful, of mien majestic, comely, and of smiling brow.

---

[2] Byron has Anglicised the word "Guebre," and it seems more euphonious than گبر *Gabar*, or Moore's "Gheber."

[3] بغفلت مخوری *ba-ghaflat na-kh'uri*, "thou shouldst not eat carelessly," or according to Gladwin, "in neglect." This must mean "carelessly with reference to God," *i.e.* "unthankfully."

[4] That is, "means of obtaining mercy from God for all creatures."

COUPLET.

To the wall of the faithful what sorrow, when pillared [securely] on thee?
What terror where Núḥ[5] is the pilot, though rages the storm-driven sea?

VERSE.

All perfect he, and therefore won
His lofty place, and [like a sun]
His beauty lighted up the night.
Fair are his virtues all, and bright.
Let peace and benediction be
On him and his posterity!

[The tradition is] that whenever one of his sinful servants in affliction lifteth up the hands of penitence in the court of the glorious and Most High God, in the hope of being heard; the Most High God regardeth him not; again he supplicateth Him, again God turneth from him; again humbly and piteously he beseecheth Him; [then] God Most High (Praise be to Him!) saith, "*O my angels, verily I am ashamed by reason of my servant, and he hath no God but myself; therefore of a surety I pardon him,*"[6] that is to say, "I have answered his prayer and accomplished his desire, since I am ashamed because of his much entreaty and supplication."

COUPLET.

God's condescension and his mercy see!
His servant sinneth, and ashamed is He!

The devout dwellers at the temple of His glory confess the faultiness of their worship saying, "*We have not worshipped Thee as Thou oughtest to be worshipped!*" and those who would describe the appearance of His beauty are amazed and say, "*We have not known Thee as Thou oughtest to be known.*"

---

[5] Núḥ is the Oriental form of the name of the Prophet Noah.

[6] These words being in Arabic, an explanation of them is afterwards given in Persian, introduced by "that is to say."

STANZA.

If one His praise of me would learn,
What of the traceless can the tongueless tell?
Lovers[7] are killed by those they love so well;
No voices from the slain return.

STORY.

A devout personage had bowed his head on the breast of contemplation, and was immersed in the ocean of the divine presence. When he came back to himself from that state, one of his companions sportively asked him— "From that flower-garden where thou wast, what miraculous gift hast thou brought for us?" He replied, "I intended to fill my lap as soon as I should reach the rose-trees, and bring presents for my companions. When I arrived there the fragrance of the roses so intoxicated me that the skirt of my robe slipped from my hands."

VERSE.

O bird of morn![8] love of the moth be taught;
Consumed it dies nor utters e'en a cry!
Pretended searchers! of this true love nought
Know ye,—who know tell not their mystery.
O loftier than all thought,
Conception, fancy, or surmise!

---

[7] The soul and the Deity are often, by Oriental writers, imaged by the lover and his beloved one.

[8] The nightingale is so called as singing in the morning twilight. Gladwin reads اى مرغ سحر *ai murgh-i saḥr*, and translates, "O bird of the desert!" and in my edition of the Text I unfortunately retained this reading, which, however, I now think incorrect, and prefer reading with M. Semelet, اى مرغ سحر *ai murgh-i saḥar*, "O bird of the morning!" The comparison is this, that as the nightingale, for all its warblings, is not so true a lover as the moth, which perishes in the brilliance it adores without a sigh; so the truly devout are not those who speak of their devotion, but those who are wrapt into silent ecstacy.

> All vainly Thou art sought,
> [Too high for feeble man's emprise.]
> Past is our festive day,[9]
> And reached at length life's latest span;
> Thy dues are yet to pay,
> The firstlings of Thy praise by man.

RECITAL OF THE GLORIOUS QUALITIES OF THE MONARCH OF THE TRUE FAITH (MAY GOD MAKE CLEAR ITS DEMONSTRATION[10]) ABŪ-BAKR-BIN-SĀD-BIN-ZANGĪ.[11]

The fair report of Sâdī, which is celebrated by the general[12] voice; and the fame of his sayings, which has travelled the whole surface[13] of the earth; and the loved reed,[14] which imparts his discourse, and which they devour like honey; and the manner in which men carry off the scraps of his writing, as though they were gold leaf[15]—are not to be ascribed to the perfection of his own excellence or eloquence, but [to this, that] the Lord of

---

[9] Life is finely compared by Oriental writers to an entertainment which is succeeded by the darkness and silence of night.

[10] Gladwin has a different reading, where the benediction refers to the king, "may God perpetuate his reign!"

[11] بن *Bin* signifies "son of."

[12] Literally, "which has fallen into the mouths of the common people." So the Latin "volitare per ora virûm."

[13] Richardson's Dictionary makes بسيط *basīṭ* an adjective only, but in this passage it is evidently a substantive.

[14] The Oriental قلم *kalam* (calamus) or pen is, as every one knows, a reed. This leads to various poetical fantasies. Thus Maulavī Rūmī,

> "Hear the reed's complaining wail!
> Hear it tell its mournful tale!
> Torn from the spot it loved so well,
> Its grief, its sighs our tears compel."

[15] This expression may also mean "bills of exchange." Gladwin so translates it. Others think it means a diploma of honour, amongst whom is M. Semelet.

the Earth, the Axis of the Revolution of Time, the Successor of Sulaimān, the Defender of the People of the True Faith, the Puissant King of Kings, the Great Atābak[16] Muzaffaru'd-dīn Abū-bakr-bin-Sâd-bin-Zangī, God's shadow on earth *(O God! approve him and his desires!)* has regarded him with extreme condescension and bestowed on him lavish commendation, and evinced a sincere regard for him. Of a verity, from attachment to him, all people, both high and low, have become favourably inclined towards me, *since men adopt the sentiments of their kings.*[17]

QUATRAIN.

Since to my lowliness thou didst with favour turn,
  My track is clearer than the sun's bright beam.
Though in thy servant all might every fault discern;
  When kings approve, e'en vices virtues seem.

VERSE.

'Twas in the bath, a piece of perfumed clay
Came from my loved one's hands to mine, one day.
"Art thou then musk or ambergris?" I said;
"That by thy scent my soul is ravished?"
"Not so," it answered, "worthless earth was I,
But long I kept the rose's company;
Thus near, its perfect fragrance to me came,
Else I'm but earth, the worthless and the same."[18]

---

[16] اتابک *Atābak* is a Turkish word signifying "father of the prince." It was originally applied to a prime minister or great noble of state. It afterwards became the title of a dynasty of Persian kings, originally Turkumāns, who reigned from 1148 to 1264 A.D. To the sixth of these, Sâd-bin-Zangī, Sâdī dedicates his "Gulistān." He reigned thirty-five years, and died A.D. 1259.

[17] A quotation from the Kur'ān.

[18] By this simile, which in the original is of exquisite beauty, Sâdī would express his own unworthiness, and the estimation imparted to him by the King's favour.

Lord! for the Faithful's sake his life renew,
Double the guerdon to his virtues due,
Exalt his friends', his nobles' dignity,
And those destroy, who hate him or defy;
As in the Ḳur'ān's verse, Thy will be done,
Protect, O God! his kingdom and his son.

VERSE.

Happy in truth the world through him—may he
Be happy! and may Heaven-sent victory,
Like a proud banner, him o'ercanopy!
He is the root, then may the tree be blest! [19]
Fairest are aye the plants whose seed is best.

May the most High and Holy God preserve to the day of resurrection the fair territory of Shirāz in the security of peace through the awe inspired by its just rulers, and the magnanimous spirit of its sagacious superintendents!

VERSE.

Knowest thou not in distant lands,
   Why I made a long delay?
I, through fear of Turkish bands,
   Left my home and fled away.
Earth was ravelled by those bands
   Like an Æthiop's hair; and they,
Slaughter-seeking, stretched their hands,
   Human wolves, towards the prey.
Men like angels dwelt within,[20]
   Lion-warriors roamed around.
Back I came, how changed the scene!
   Nought but peacefulness I found:
Tigers though they late had been,
   Changed their fierceness, fettered, bound.

---

[19] The State is here compared to a tree, of which the King is the root.

[20] "Within," *i.e.*, in the city of Shirāz, then one of the most populous on earth. The surrounding districts were suffering from an irruption of savage Turks.

Thus in former times I saw,
  Filled with tumult, trouble, pain,
Earth uncurbed by rule or law.
  But strife owned our monarch's reign,
  Heard Atābak's name with awe,
  Heard, and all was peace again.[21]

VERSE.

The clime of Fārs[22] dreads not Time's baneful hand,
While one like thee, God's Shadow, rules the land.
None at this day can shew on earth's wide breast,
A haven, like thy gate, of peace and rest.
'Tis thine to guard the poor : a grateful sense
Is due from us—from God thy recompense.
Lord! shield the land of Fārs from faction's storm,
Long as winds blow, or earth retains its form.

CAUSE OF WRITING THE "GULISTĀN."

One night I was reflecting on times gone by and regretting my wasted life; and I pierced the stony mansion of my heart with the diamond of my tears, and recited these couplets applicable to my state.

DISTICHS.

One breath of life each moment flies,
A small remainder meets my eyes.
Sleeper! whose fifty years are gone,
Be these five[23] days at least thy own.
Shame on the dull, departed dead,
Whose task is left unfinished;

---

[21] I have been obliged to render these last three lines very freely. There is in them, however, nothing to delay the student.

[22] Fārs is that province of Persia of which Shīrāz is the capital.

[23] This is an indefinite number, used to express any short period.

In vain for them the drum was beat,
Which warns us of man's last retreat.
Sweet sleep upon the parting-day [24]
Holds back the traveller from the way.
Each comer a new house erects,
Departs,—the house its lord rejects.
The next one forms the same conceit;
This mansion none shall ere complete.
Hold not as friend this comrade light,
With one so false no friendship plight.
Since good and bad alike must fall,
He's blest who bears away the ball.[25]
Send to thy tomb an ample store;[26]
None will it bring—then send before.
   Like snow is life in July's sun,
   Little remains; and is there one
   To boast himself and vaunt thereon?[27]
With empty hand thou hast sought the mart;
I fear thou wilt with thy turban part.[28]
Who eat their corn while yet 'tis green,
At the true harvest can but glean.
To Sâdī's counsel let thy soul give heed,
This is the way—be manful and proceed.

[24] These verses may seem unconnected, but they are not more so than in the original; the rendering is most close.

[25] This is an allusion to the game of *chaugān*, which is a sort of tennis played on horseback. He who bears off the ball is the winner.

[26] Of good deeds—which are here compared to the provisions for a journey.

[27] This is somewhat freely translated. Gladwin reads خـرِّ هنـوز; *ghirah hanūz*, and translates, "Art thou yet slothful?" I prefer reading و خواجه غـرِّ هنـوز; *wa khwājah gharrah hanūz*;—literally "and my gentleman is still boastful."

[28] "Thou hast" and "thou wilt" must be here read, for the sake of the metre, as one syllable. It is frequently impossible to avoid stiffness and other faults in the versification, that the literal translation may be preserved.

After deliberating on this subject I thought it advisable that I should take my seat in retirement and gather under me my robe, withdrawing from society, and wash the tablet of my memory from vain words, nor speak idly in future.

COUPLET.

Better who sits in nooks, deaf, speechless, idle,
Than he who knows not his own tongue to bridle.

At length one of my friends who was my comrade in the camel-litter[29] and my closet-companion[30] entered my door according to old custom. Notwithstanding all the cheerfulness and hilarity which he displayed, and his spreading out the carpet of affection, I returned him no answer, nor lifted up my head from the knee of devotion. He was pained, and looking towards me said,

STANZA.

Now that the power of utterance is thine,
Speak, O my brother! kindly, happily,
To-morrow's message bids thee life resign,
Then art thou silent of necessity.

One of those attached to me [*i.e.*, a kinsman *or* a servant] informed him regarding this circumstance, saying, "Such an one [*i.e.*, Sádí] has made a resolution and fixed determination to pass the rest of his life in the world as a devotee, and embrace silence. If thou canst, take thy way, and choose the path of retreat.[31]

---

[29] The كَجَاوَهْ *kajāwah* is nothing more than two panniers slung one on each side a camel, and each containing a traveller; who of course would prefer a friend as his *vis-à-vis* in such a situation. The expression then means simply a comrade in travel.

[30] As we should say "a bosom-friend."

[31] Gladwin understands this as an exhortation to adopt a similar abnegation of the world. I cannot agree with this opinion, and think that the speaker simply desired Sádí's friend to withdraw if he could make up his mind to leave him (اَگَر تَوانی *agar tawāni* "if thou art able").

He replied, "By the glory of the Highest, and by our ancient friendship! I will not breathe nor stir a step until he hath spoken according to his wonted custom, and in his usual manner: for to distress friends is folly, but the expiation of an oath is easy.[32] It is contrary to rational procedure and opposed to the opinion of sages, that the Zū'l-fakār[33] of Ālī should remain in its scabbard, or the tongue of Sâdī [silent] in his mouth.

STANZA.

What is the tongue in mouth of mortals?—say!
'Tis but the key that opens wisdom's door:
While that is closed who may conjecture,—pray?
If thou sell'st jewels or the pedlar's store?

STANZA.

Silence is mannerly, so deem the wise,
But in the fitting time use language free;
Blindness of judgment just in two things lies,
To speak unwished, not speak unseasonably.

In brief, I had not the power to refrain from conversing with him, and I thought it uncourteous to avert my face from conference with him, for he was an agreeable companion and a sincere friend.

COUPLET.

When thou contendest, choose an enemy[34]
Whom thou mayst vanquish or whom thou canst fly.

[32] The non-observance of a rash oath is expiated by fasting three days, or by feeding and clothing ten poor persons, or by setting one captive free.

[33] Zū'l-fakār was the name of a two-edged sword which Muḥammad pretended to have received from the Angel Gabriel; and which he bequeathed to his son-in-law Ālī. The author of the Ḳāmūs says that it was the sword of Ās-bin-Munabbih, an unbeliever, who was slain at the battle of Badr.

[34] In these lines lie some difficulties well descanted on by M. Semelet, but which require but a word here. The words در ستیز *dar sitīz* may be translated "in strife," in which case

By the mandate of necessity I spoke, and we went out for recreation, it being the season of spring, when the asperity of winter was mitigated, and the time of the roses' rich display had arrived.

COUPLET.

Vestments green upon the trees
　Like the [costly] garments seeming,
Which at Íd's festivities
　Rich men wear [all gaily gleaming.]

STANZA.

'Twas Urdabihisht's first day, the Jalālian[35] month of spring,
From the pulpits of the branches slight we heard the bulbuls[36] sing
The red red branches were be-gemmed with pearls of glistening dew,
Like moisture on an angry beauty's cheek, a cheek of rosy hue.

[So time passed] till one night[37] it happened that I was walking at a late hour in a flower-garden with one of my friends.[37] The spot was blithe and pleasing, and

supply ببین *babīn* before the next line; or spite of the dictionaries, those words may perhaps mean "try for one," "choose," in which case there is no ellipse. گزیر *guzīr* can hardly mean "aid," here—the "du secours" of M. de Sacy; but rather "a means of success," the چارہ *chārah* of Castell.

[35] Jalālu'd-dīn, King of Persia, began to reign A.H. 475 = 1082 A.D. His æra dates from that year. Urdabihisht is the second month of the Jalālian year, and corresponds with our April.

[36] The bulbul, it is almost unnecessary to say, is the nightingale.

[37] I must confess that I think the sense would be greatly improved if we could get rid of با یکی از دوستان *bā yakī az dūstān*, and read شب را *shab-rā* for تا شبی *tā shabī*, in which case it would be the same friend who persuaded Sádī to give up his

the trees intertwined there charmingly. You would have said that fragments of enamel were sprinkled on the ground, and that the necklace of the Pleiades was suspended from the vines that grew there.

STANZA.

A garden where the murmuring rill was heard;
While from the trees sang each melodious bird;
That, with the many-coloured tulip bright,
These, with their various fruits the eye delight.
The whispering breeze beneath the branches' shade,
Of bending flowers a motley carpet made.

In the morning, when the inclination to return prevailed over our wish to stay,[38] I saw that he had gathered his lap full of roses, and fragrant herbs, and hyacinths, and sweet basil, [with which] he was setting out for the city. I said, "To the rose of the flower-garden there is, as you know, no continuance; nor is there faith in the promise[39] of the rose garden: and the sages have said that we should not fix our affections on that which has no endurance." He said, "What then is my course?" I replied, "For the recreation of the beholders and the gratification of those who are present, I am able to compose a book, 'the Garden of Roses,' whose leaves the rude hand of the blast of autumn cannot affect; and the blitheness of whose spring the revolution of time cannot change into the disorder of the waning year.

taciturnity, that walked with him at night, and received the promise of the "Gulistán."

[38] Every line of Sádí is said to have هفتاد و دو معنی *haftād wa dū mānī*, "seventy-two meanings," and this sentence may fairly be thought to have a different meaning from the one given in the text. It may be rendered, "the desire to return, in order to repose, prevailed with us."

[39] I prefer translating عهد *ahd* thus. Gladwin translates it "continuance;" and M. Semelet renders it by "la saison."

DISTICHS.

What use to thee that flower-vase of thine?
Thou would'st have rose-leaves; take then, rather, mine.
Those roses but five days or six will bloom;
This garden ne'er will yield to winter's gloom."

As soon as I had pronounced these words, he cast the flowers from his lap, and took hold of the skirt of my garment, [saying] "*When the generous promise, they perform.*" It befel that in a few days a chapter or two were entered in my note-book, on the advantages of society,[10] and the rules of conversation,[11] in a style that may be useful to orators, and augment the eloquence of letter-writers.[12] In short, the rose of the flower-garden still continued to bloom, when the book of the "Rose Garden" was finished. It will, however, be then really perfected when it is approved and condescendingly perused[13] at the court of the King, the Asylum of the

---

[10] The seventh chapter, در تأثیر تربیت *dar tāsīr-i tarbiyat*. Ross translates معاشرة، *muāsharat*, "education," which is hardly defensible. It means rather "enjoyable intercourse."

[11] The eighth chapter, در آداب صحبت *dar ādāb-i ṣuḥbat*.

[12] Richardson's Dictionary is silent as to this word مترسلان *mutarassilān*.

[13] A string of titles separates the latter part of this sentence, which I have somewhat freely translated, from the پسندیده آید *pasandīdah āyad*, "it is approved." The more literal rendering would be, "It will, however, be really complete when it shall have been approved at the court of the King, the Asylum of the World," etc., "and [when] he shall have condescended to peruse it with the benign glance of imperial favour." Owing to the length of the titles, the passage is rather involved, and all the translators appear to me to deal unfairly by it. Ross and Gladwin both omit to translate ابو بکر بن سعد بن زنگی *Abū-bakr-bin-Sad-bin-Zangī*; whence it would almost seem that they overlooked the circumstance that the Sád-bin-Atābak was the son of Abū-bakr, who was the son of a former Sád, and who admitted the second Sád to reign jointly with himself.

world, the Shadow of the Creator, and the Light of the
Bounty of the All-provider, *the Treasury of the Age,
the Retreat*[44] *of true Religion, the Aided by Heaven, the
Triumphant over his Enemies, the Victorious Arm of
the Empire, the Lamp of the excelling Faith, the Beauty
of Mankind, the Glory of Islām, Sâd, the son of the Most
Puissant King of Kings, Master of attending Nations, Lord
of the Kings of Arabia and Persia, Sovereign of Land
and Sea, Heir to the Throne of* Sulaimān, *Atābak the
Great, Muzaffaru'd-dīn Abū-bakr-bin-Sâd-bin-Zangī :* (May
God most High perpetuate the good fortune of both, and
prosper all their righteous undertakings !)

VERSE.

If the imperial favour should it grace,
  'Twill rival China's[45] paintings, Arjang's pictured leaf.[46]
Ne'er with chagrin can it o'ercloud the face ;
  For the rose garden[47] is no place for grief,
    And its fair preface bears, impressed by fame,
    Great Sâd Abū-bakr-Sâd-bin-Zangī's name.

[44] كهف *Kahf* signifies "a cave," especially the cave in which the seven young Christians of Ephesus took refuge from the persecutions of the Emperor Decius. They are called the اصحاب كهف *ashāb-i kahf,* "lords of the cave."

[45] M. Semelet quotes Gentius as to a great city on the confines of India called Sina, and possessing an edifice adorned with paintings, to which he supposes allusion is here made. I should rather suppose that Chinese paintings were meant.

[46] Richardson's Dictionary tells us that Arjang is the name of the house of the painter Manes. M. Semelet holds it to mean a book of his ; and Ross translates the passage by "the picture-portfolio of Manī." Manī or Manes, the founder of the Manichæans, was a painter of wondrous skill, who lived in the reign of Shāhpur or Sapor, the son of Ardasīr Bābakān. He was burnt alive by order of Bahrām.

[47] An equivoque on the word Gulistān.

EULOGIUM OF THE MIGHTY NOBLE, FAKHRU'D-DĪN ABŪ-BAKR-BIN-ABŪ-NASR.

A second time the bride of my imagination, conscious of her want of beauty, lifts not up her head, nor raises the eye of despondency from the instep of bashfulness, and comes not forth adorned among the bevy of beauties, save when decked with the ornaments of the approbation of the mighty, wise, just, and divinely-supported Lord, the Victorious over his Foes, Prop of the Imperial Throne, Counsellor of State, Shelter of the Indigent, Asylum of the Poor, Patron of the Eminent, Friend of the Pure, Glory of the People of Fārs, Right-hand of the Empire, Prince of Favourites, Ornament of the State and of Religion, Succour of the True Faith and of the Faithful, Pillar of Kings and Princes; Abū-bakr-bin-Abū-nasr (May God prolong his life, increase his dignity, cause his breast to expand with joy, and double his reward! for he is extolled by the nobles of all quarters of the globe, and is an assemblage of all laudable qualities).

COUPLET.

When his kind care, protective, one defends,
Pious his sins become, his foemen, friends.

To each one of the other servants and attendants a separate duty is assigned; such that if in the performance of it they indulge in any negligence or sloth, they assuredly incur the liability of reproof, and expose themselves to rebuke; all save this tribe of Darweshes [of whom Sādi is one] from whom thanks are due for the benefits they receive from the great, and whom it behoves to recount the fair virtues [of their benefactors] and offer up prayers for their welfare:[8] and the per-

---

[8] Ross here and in several places renders خير *khair* by "charity." I cannot think it has this meaning in this place, where, if "alms" were intended, خيرات *khairāt* would, in my opinion, be used.

formance of such duties as these is better in absence than when present, for in the latter case it borders on ostentation, and in the former it is far from outward show and allied to acceptance with God.

VERSE.

Straight grew the sky's crook'd back[49] from that fair hour,
When the great mother, Time, produced a son like thee;
Signal that act of God's wise, gracious power,
In forming one who should to all a blessing be!
Lasting his fortune, whose fair name survives;
For after him, his memory shall by fame endure;
To thee the praise of learned men nought gives:
The soul-entrancing cheek needs not the toilette's[50] lure.

AN APOLOGY FOR THE OMISSION OF SERVICE, AND THE CAUSE OF SELECTING SECLUSION.

A faultiness and neglect which takes place in the assiduity of my service at the court of my lord arises à-propos to what a body of the sages of Hind said of the excellence of Buzurchimihr.[51] At length they were unable to discover any defect in him but this, that in utterance he was slow (that is,[52] delayed long), so that his hearers were obliged to wait a long time until he could explain himself. Buzurchimihr heard this and said, "It is better to be anxious what I shall say, than to suffer remorse for what I have said."

[49] However unpalateable to European taste, I am obliged to present this strange metaphor in all its marvellous monstrosity.

[50] Metre compels me to substitute the temple for the priestess. Instead of "toilette" it should be "tire-woman."

[51] Buzurchimihr was the prime minister of Nūshīrwān, king of Persia, in whose reign Muḥammad was born.

[52] The word here rendered "slow" is, in the text, Arabic, and is there explained in Persian to mean "delayed long." In English the latter expression becomes superfluous.

DISTICHS.

The well-taught orators,[53] the men of age,
 First ponder well and then their thoughts declare:
Waste not thy breath in thoughtless speech; if sage
 Thy counsel, slowness will it nought impair.
Reflect, then speak; and let thy utterance cease
Ere others say, " Enough ! " and bid thee " Peace ! "
Men by the power of speech the brutes excel,
The brutes surpass thee if thou speakest not well.

And more especially in the presence of the Eye[54] of Royalty (glorious be his victory !), which is the rallying point for the wise, and the centre where profound sages meet; if I should display boldness in pursuing the conversation I might be guilty of presumption, and should be producing my trumpery[55] before his incomparable Excellency; and a glass-bead were not worth a barley-corn in the jewellers' mart, and a lamp gives no light in the sun, and a lofty minaret shows low at the foot of mount Alwand.[56]

[53] سخن دان پرورده پیر کهن. M. Semelet connects the پیر کهن pīr-i kuhan with the پرورده parwardah, and translates it thus, " L'homme éloquent, instruit par un vieux maître," which may well be admitted among the seventy-two meanings of each sentence of the divine Sádī.

[54] This word (اصحاب) is in the plural, but the vazīr alone is meant. The expression, " Eye of the king," is, as is well known, one of the titles of a vazīr.

[55] Here is said to be an allusion to the Ḳur'ān, c. xii. v. 88. يَا اَيُّهَا ٱلْعَزِيزُ جِئْنَا بِبِضَاعَةٍ مُزْجَاةٍ yā aiyuhā'l ăzīzu ji'nā bi-bizāătin muzjātin, " O most excellent! we have come with little money;" where the brothers of Joseph are addressing him when about to buy corn.

[56] At eight or ten leagues to the east of Tehrān is the remarkable peak of Alwand, or Alburz, as the inhabitants of Tehrān call it. It is covered with eternal snow, and, according to Olivier, sometimes emits smoke.

DISTICHS.

He who exalts his neck with pride
Is girt with foes on every side;
Sâdî lies prostrate, free from care:
None of the fallen ere make war.
Reflection first, speech last of all,
The basement must precede the wall.
True, that the art of making flowers I know;
But shall I try it where real flow'rets grow?
A beauty I—but will my cheek look fair,
When they with Canaan's glory[57] me compare?

They said to the sage Luķmãn,[58] "From whom didst thou learn wisdom?" He replied, "From the blind, who advance not their feet till they have tried the ground." *Try the egress before you enter.*

HEMISTICH.

Try first your powers, and then try a wife.

---

[57] These lines require a little expansion, which I have given to them. Sâdî says, that though he may have a reputation for learning, it would appear altogether contemptible at the Court of the vazîr, himself so wise, and surrounded by such a galaxy of sages; just as a maker of artificial flowers would make himself ridiculous if he practised his art amid real flowers, or as an ordinary beauty would forfeit all pretensions to loveliness if compared with Joseph, the beauty of Canaan, whose charms, according to Musalmãn, were incomparable.

[58] Luķmãn, after whom the thirty-first chapter of the Ķur'ãn is called, is by some reckoned among the Prophets, and called the cousin of Job; and by others, the grand-nephew of Abraham; others say he was born in the time of David, and lived to that of Jonah; others, again, call him an Æthiopian slave, liberated by his master for his fidelity. His fables and maxims are celebrated in the East, and the Greeks probably borrowed their account of Æsop from his history.

VERSE.

Dauntless the cock in war, yet to what end
Shall he with brazen-taloned hawks contend?
Capturing the mouse the cat doth lionly;
Gauged with the leopard but a mouse is she!

Nevertheless, in reliance on the liberal disposition of the great, who conceal the faults of the humble, and use no endeavour to disclose the defects of their inferiors, I have inserted in this book, in a concise way, a few narratives of rare adventures, and traditions, and tales, and verses, and manners of ancient kings, and I have expended some portion of precious life upon it. Such was my motive for composing the Gulistān.

STANZA.

This verse instructive shall remain when I,
Scattered in dust, in several atoms lie;
In short, since in no mundane thing I see
The signs impressed of perpetuity,
This picture shall my sole memorial be;
Perhaps hereafter, for this pious task,
Some man of prayer for me too grace shall ask.

Mature consideration as to the arrangement of the Book, ordering of the chapters, and conciseness, made me[59] deem it expedient that this delicate Garden, and this densely wooded grove, should, like Paradise,[60] be divided into eight chapters, in order that it may become the less likely to fatigue.

[59] M. Semelet's reading دیدم *dīdam*, is perhaps better than the one here adopted, in which امعان نظر *imān-i naẓar* is made the nominative to دید *dīd*. I confess I should like to insert و *wa* before ایجاز *ijāz*.

[60] Here is an equivoque on the word بهشت *bihisht*, which means "Paradise," but with a little alteration becomes بهشت *ba-hasht*, "in eight." The Musalmān divide Paradise into eight regions.

LIST OF THE CHAPTERS.

CHAPTER
- I. On the Manners of Kings.
- II. On the Qualities of Darweshes.
- III. On the Excellence of Contentment.
- IV. On the Advantages of Taciturnity.
- V. On Love and Youth.
- VI. On Decrepitude and Old Age.
- VII. On the Effect of Education.
- VIII. On the Duties of Society.

DATE OF THE BOOK.

Six hundred six and fifty years had waned
From the famed Flight[61]; then when no sorrow pained
My heart, I sought these words, with truth impressed,
To say, and thus have said: to God belongs the rest.

[61] The flight of Muḥammad, the Æra by which the Musalmān reckon, took place on the 16th of July, 622. Consequently the date of the Gulistān is A.D. 1258.

CHAPTER I.

ON THE MANNERS OF KINGS.

Story I.

I have heard of a king who made a sign to put a captive to death. The hapless one, in a state of despair, began in the dialect he spoke[62] to abuse the monarch, and use opprobrious language; as they say, "Every one, who washes his hands of life, utters all he has in his heart."

COUPLET.
He that despairs, gives license to his tongue,
As cats by dogs o'erpressed rush madly on.

COUPLET.
The hand, when flight remains not, in despair
Will grasp the point[63] of the sharp scymitar.

The King asked, "What does he say?" One of the vazirs, who was of a good disposition,[64] said, "O my Lord! he says that [*Paradise, whose breadth equalleth the heavens and the earth, is prepared for the godly*], *who bridle their anger, and forgive men; for God loveth the*

---

[62] Literally, "he had." So also in Gaelic, "I have no English," for "I speak no English."

[63] M. Semelet translates سر *sar*, by "la poignée," which appears less correct. Sádi says, "In despair the naked hand will seize the point of a sword held by a foe." Ross and Gladwin render سر *sar* by "edge," which is rather ذباب *zubáb* or لب *lab*.

[64] Richardson's Dictionary very strangely omits this meaning of محضر *mahzar*.

beneficent."[65] The King had compassion upon him, and gave up the intention of [spilling] his blood. Another vazīr, who was his rival, said, "It beseems not such as we are to speak aught but truth in the august presence of kings. This person reviled the king, and spoke unbecomingly." At this speech the King frowned and said, "That untruth of his is more acceptable to me than this truth which thou hast spoken; for that inclined[66] towards a good purpose, and this to malevolence; and the sages have said, 'Well-intentioned falsehood is better than mischief-exciting truth.'"

COUPLETS.

Words which beguile thee, but thy heart make glad,
Outvalue truth which makes thy temper sad.
They by whose counsels kings are ruled, 'twere shame
If good in all they said were not their aim.

This maxim was inscribed over the vaulted entrance of Farīdūn's[67] palace.

---

[65] This is a quotation from the Ḳur'ān, c. iii. v. 134; and it is very essential to note this, as the vazīr can hardly be said to have told a falsehood in putting a text enjoining mercy into the mouth of the captive; at least, there is a shade of difference between this and inventing something out of his own head. This very text is said to have been quoted to Ḥasan, grandson of Muḥammad, when a slave threw something boiling hot over him. At the first sentence, Ḥasan replied, "I am not angry"; at the second, "I forgive you"; and at the conclusion, viz., "God loveth the beneficent," he added, "Since it is so I give you your liberty and four hundred pieces of silver."—*Vide* Sale's Koran, p. 47, Note D.

[66] M. Semelet seems to think that رُوی *rūī* is here used in an uncommon sense, but the literal translation is simply "its countenance was towards good,"—an easy metaphor.

[67] Farīdūn was the seventh king of the first dynasty of Persian kings. He overcame the tyrant Ẓaḥḥāḳ, and imprisoned him in the mountain Damāvend.

DISTICHS.

The world, my brother! will abide with none,
By the world's Maker let thy heart be won.
Rely not, nor repose on this world's gain,
For many a son like thee she has reared and slain.
What matters, when the spirit seeks to fly,
If on a throne or on bare earth we die?

STORY II.

One of the kings of Khurāsān[68] beheld, in a dream, Sultān Maḥmūd[69] Sabuktagīn, a hundred years after his death, when all his body had dissolved and become dust, save his eyes, which, as heretofore, moved in their sockets and saw. All the sages were at a loss for the interpretation of this, except a darwesh, who made his obeisance, and said, "His eyes still retain their sight, because his kingdom is in the possession of others."

VERSE.

Full many a chief of glorious name
    Beneath the ground now buried lies,
Yet not one token of his fame
    On earth's wide surface meets our eyes.
That aged form of life bereft,
    Which to earth's keeping they commit,
The soil devours; no bone is left,
    No trace remains to tell of it.
The glorious name of Nūshīrvān
    Lives in his deeds year after year.

[68] Khurāsān, according to Richardson's Dictionary, is the ancient Bactria, lying to the north of the Oxus, but at present it is used of Afghānistān, from the Bolān to Herāt, and the frontiers of Persia.

[69] Maḥmūd succeeded his father, Sabuktagīn, on the throne of Ghaznī, A.D. 997, and died after a reign of thirty-three years, and after he had conquered great part of Hindūstān, and taken the cities of Dihlī and Kanoj.

Do good, my friend! and look upon
This life as an occasion won
For acting well, ere yet we hear
Of thee, that thy career is done.

Story III.

I have heard of a prince who was of low stature and mean appearance, while his other brothers were tall and handsome. One day, his father surveyed him with loathing and contempt. The son had penetration enough to discover [his feelings], and said, "O my father! an intelligent dwarf is superior to an ignorant giant. Not every thing that is higher in stature is more valuable: '*The sheep is clean and the elephant unclean.*'

COUPLET.

Least of earth's mountain's is Sinai, yet all
In worth and rank with God beneath it fall.

STANZA.

Hast thou heard how the lean sage wittily
   A bloated fool's presumption stilled?
'The steed of Arab race, though slim he be,
   Transcends a stall with asses filled.'"

His sire laughed, and the Pillars of the State approved, and his brothers were mortally offended.

VERSE.

While a man's say is yet unsaid,
   His weakness, merits, none descry;
Think not each waste's untenanted:
   A sleeping tiger there may lie.

I have heard, that at that time a dangerous enemy to the King shewed himself. When the two armies encountered, the first person who galloped forward on the field of battle was that young prince, exclaiming,

STANZA.

I'm not he that, on the battle-day, my back will meet
 thy sight;
I'm one whose head thou'lt follow 'mid the dust and
 gory fight.
He must stake carelessly his blood who joins in war's
 grim strife;
Who flies in war risks carelessly his fellow-soldier's life.

He said this, and rushed on the hostile array; after overthrowing several veteran warriors he came back. As soon as he presented himself to his father, he kissed the ground of obedience[70] and said,

STANZA.

Thou who my stature didst with scorn survey,
 Think not that roughness marks the bold in war;
The slender courser in the battle-day
 Will the fat stall-fed ox outvalue far.

They relate that the host of the enemy was numerous, and this side fewer. A body of the latter prepared to fly; the young prince uttered a shout and said, "O men! exert yourselves, that ye may not be clothed in the dress of women." The horsemen were inspired by his words with increased ardour, and made a simultaneous charge. I have heard that on that day they obtained a victory over the enemy. The King kissed his head and his eyes and embraced him, and each day entertained a stronger regard for him until he made him his heir. His brothers envied him, and put poison in his food. His sister saw it from a window, and closed the casement sharply. The young prince, by his acuteness, understood her meaning, and drew back his hand from the food, and said, "It is impossible that men of merit should perish, and those who have none should occupy their places."

[70] This expression is a very common one. It simply means, "kissed the ground obediently."

COUPLET.

What though the phœnix from the world take flight,
'Neath the owl's shadow none will ere alight.

They acquainted the father with this circumstance. He sent for the brothers and gave them a fitting reproof. Afterwards he assigned to each a suitable portion of his dominions, so that faction subsided and discord was appeased. In relation to this[71] they have said, that "Ten darweshes may sleep under one blanket, but one country cannot contain two kings."

STANZA.

The man of God with half his loaf content,
To darweshes the remnant will present;
But though a king seven regions should subdue,
He'll still another conquest keep in view.

STORY IV.

A horde of Arabian robbers had fixed themselves on the summit of a mountain, and had stopped the passage of caravans, and the inhabitants of the country were in terror of their ambuscades, and the forces of the Sultān were repulsed by them, because they had possessed themselves of an inaccessible retreat in the crest of the mountain, and made it their refuge and place of abode. The governors of provinces in that direction took counsel as to the means of getting rid of the annoyance they

---

[71] Gladwin leaves the از اینجا‎ *az ínjā*, untranslated. M. Semelet translates it simply by "et." Ross inserts, "but the ferment was increased," as an explanation. Hence it appears to me that all the translators have missed the right meaning of the concluding passage, which I am of opinion is simply an explanation of how the discord subsided, viz.: because each brother had a separate kingdom allotted to him. To suppose, with Ross, that the discord increased, would give a singularly abrupt termination to the story.

occasioned, saying,[72] "If this band maintain themselves any time in this fashion, resistance to them will become impossible."

DISTICHS.

A single arm may now uptear
A tree if lately planted there;
But if it for a time you leave,
No engine could its roots upheave.
A spade may the young rill restrain,
Whose channel, swollen [by storms and rain]
The elephant attempts in vain.

They came to the decision[73] to depute a person to reconnoitre them: and these watched their opportunity until the robbers made a foray on a tribe and their hold was evacuated, when they despatched a small body of experienced veterans to conceal themselves in a defile of the mountain. At night, when the robbers returned, having accomplished their expedition, and brought back their spoil, they laid aside their arms and deposited their booty. The first enemy that attacked them was sleep.[74] As soon as a watch[75] of the night had passed—

COUPLET.

The solar orb sank down in night's thick gloom,
As, in the fish-maw, Jonas found a tomb.[76]

---

[72] I think M. Semelet has done well in supplying كه *kih* here, and should wish it to be supplied in my edition of the text.

[73] Literally, "the word was fixed on this," a Persianism which must be freely rendered.

[74] There should be a full stop at بود *búd*, and a comma at بگذشت *ba-guzasht*. M. Semelet's punctuation is preferable to that of my edition, which is copied from Gladwin's.

[75] That is, at nine o'clock, since the night is reckoned from six p.m., and each watch is of three hours' duration.

[76] This is certainly a strange comparison. It seems to me a simile with the slenderest possible thread of similarity.

The valiant men leapt forth from their ambuscade and bound the hands of all of them, one after the other, behind their backs. In the morning they brought them to the palace of the king. He gave a sign to put them all to death. It happened that among them was a stripling, the fruit of whose youthful prime was but just ripening, and the bloom of the rose-garden of whose cheek had just expanded. One of the vazírs kissed the foot of the king's throne, and bowed the face of intercession to the ground and said, "This child has not yet tasted the fruit of the garden of life, nor reaped enjoyment from the flower of his youth. I rely on the clemency and virtues of his Majesty, that he will oblige his slave by sparing his life." The King looked displeased at these words, and his lofty understanding did not approve them, and he said,

COUPLET.
" The good in vain their rays will pour
  On those whose hearts are bad at core.
T' instruct the base will fail at last,
  As walnuts on a dome you cast.[77]

It is better to cut off their race and tribe, and more advisable to extirpate them root and branch;[78] since, to extinguish a fire and to leave the embers, and to kill a serpent and preserve its young, are not the acts of wise men.

STANZA.
What though life's water from the clouds descend,
  Thou'lt ne'er pluck fruit from off the willow-bough;
Not on the base thy precious moments spend,
  Thou'lt ne'er taste sugar from the reed, I trow."

[77] If you throw walnuts on a dome they will fall down again, and perhaps on your own head; such is the meaning of this strange, but frequently occurring simile.

[78] Literally, "root and foundation," which corresponds to our expression as used in the text.

The vazīr heard these words, and, willing or not, assented to them, and extolled the excellence of the king's judgment and said, "What my lord *(may his dominion be eternal!)* has been pleased to say is the essence of truth: for had he been reared in the bond of the society of those evil persons he would have become one of them. However, your slave is in hopes that he will receive his education in the society of good men, and will adopt the character of the wise, since he is yet but a child, and the rebellious and perverse habits of those bandits have not fixed themselves in his nature; and in the traditions of the Prophet [it is said] "*There is no person born but assuredly he is begotten* [with a natural disposition] *to the faith of Islām; then his parents make a Jew of him, or a Christian, or a Magian.*

STANZA.

Lot's wife consorted with the unjust, and she
Quenched in her race the light of prophecy.
And the cave-sleepers'[79] dog sometime remained
With good men, and the rank of man attained."

When he had thus spoken, a number of the councillors of state united with him in intercession, so that the king abstained from shedding his blood and said, "I have spared his life, though I disapprove of it."

QUATRAIN.

Knowest thou what Zāl to valiant Rustam said?
Deem not thy foeman weak, without resource;
Full many a rill, from tiny springlet fed,
Sweeps off the camel in its onward course.

In short, the vazīr took the youth to his house and reared him delicately, and appointed a learned preceptor

---

[79] For an account of the Seven Sleepers who fell asleep in a cave near Ephesus in the reign of the Emperor Decius A.D. 253, and awoke A.D. 408, under that of Theodosius the Younger, *vide* the Kur'ān, c. 18, and M. Semelet's notes on this passage of the Gulistān.

to instruct him, who taught him elegant address and quickness in repartee, and all the manners fit for the service of kings, so that he was viewed with approbation by his compeers. At length the vazīr related somewhat of his abilities and good qualities to his Majesty the king, saying, "The instruction of the wise has produced an effect upon him, and has expelled from his disposition his former ignorance." The king smiled at these words and said,

COUPLET.

"The wolf's whelp will at last a wolf become,
  Though from his birth he finds with man a home."

After this, two years passed away, and a set of dissolute fellows in the quarter where he lived joined themselves to him, and formed a league with him, so that at a favourable opportunity he slew the vazīr with his two sons, and carried off an immense booty, and took the place of his father in the robber's cave, and became an avowed rebel. They acquainted the king. The king seized the hand of amazement with his teeth,[50] and said,

VERSE.

"Who can from faulty iron good swords frame?
  Teaching, O Sage! lends not the worthless worth.
The rain, whose bounteous nature's still the same,
  Gives flowers in gardens, thorns in salt land birth.
Salt ground will not the precious spikenard bear;
  Waste not thereon the seed of thy emprise:
Who benefits on evil men confer,
  Upon the good no less heap injuries."

STORY V.

I saw at the gate of the palace of Ughlamish[51] the son of an officer endowed with intellect, quickness of

---

[50] Orientals represent surprise by biting the fore-finger.

[51] Ughlamish was the son of the celebrated Tartar conqueror, Jangīz Khān, and reigned towards the year 656 of the Hijrah.

parts, understanding and sagacity beyond description. Even from the time of his childhood the signs of greatness were found on his forehead, and the rays of luminousness visible and distinct in his countenance, and many hearts were enamoured of him.

COUPLET.

And high above his head shone lustrously
The star of wisdom and of majesty.

In short, he became a favourite of the Sulṭān, for he possessed beauty of person and perfection of mind: and the sages have said, "Wealth consists in talent, not in goods; greatness, in understanding, not in age." His compeers grew envious of him, and accused him of treason, and used fruitless endeavours to put him to death.

HEMISTICH.

While friends are true what can the foe effect?

The king asked him, "What is the cause of their hostility towards you?" He replied, "I have satisfied all who are under the shadow of the royal dominion, except the envious, who cannot be contented, except by the waning of my good fortune. May the wealth and auspicious destiny of my lord remain perpetual!"

VERSE.

This can I do—inflict distress on none;
  Envy's its own distress—what can I there?
Perish, O envious one! for thus alone
  Canst thou escape from thy self-nurtured care.
The wretched long to witness the decay
  Of fortune's favours to the happier few:
But, though the bat be visionless by day,
  Can we for this a fault or failing view
In the sun's fount of light? 'T were better far
  A thousand of such eyes no vision knew,
Than the bright radiance of the sun to mar.

Story VI.

They relate of one of the kings of Persia, that he had extended the hand of oppression upon the property of his subjects, and had entered on a course of tyranny and injustice. The people were reduced to extremity by the snares of his cruelty, and from the anguish of his tyranny took the road of exile. As the people diminished, the resources of the State were impaired, and the treasury remained empty, and enemies pressed him on every side.

STANZA.

He who in adversity would succour have,
  Let him be generous while he rests secure.
Thou that reward'st him not, wilt lose thy slave,
    Though wearing now thy ring.[82] Wouldst thou secure
    The stranger as thy slave, be to him kind ;
    And by thy courtesy enslave his mind.

One day they read, in his presence, the book of the Shāh-nāmah, in the part which relates to the decline of the empire of Zaḥḥāk, and the reign of Farīdūn. The vazīr asked the king, saying, " Farīdūn possessed not treasure, territory, or troops ; in what manner was the kingdom secured in his favour ? " He replied, " Just as you have heard ; the people rallied round him from attachment to him, and gave him their support : he gained the kingdom." The vazīr rejoined, " O king ! since sovereignty is acquired by the people's resorting to one, why dost thou scatter the people from thee ? unless, indeed, thou dost not purpose to be a king."

COUPLET.

Since monarchs by their troops their States control,
Cherish thy host, O king ! with all thy soul.

---

[82] I have not translated بگوش *ba-gūsh*, "in the ear." The ring in the ear is the badge of servitude in the East.

The king asked, "What causes the soldiery and the people to rally round you?" He replied, "A king must be just, that they may resort to him, and merciful, that they may sit secure under the shadow of his greatness—and thou hast neither of these two qualities."

DISTICHS.

Kingcraft yokes not with tyranny:
The wolf cannot the shepherd be.
Tyrants who on their people fall,
Sap their own State's foundation-wall.

The counsel of the faithful vazīr suited not the king's temper. He ordered him to be bound and sent him to prison. No long time had elapsed when the sons of the king's uncle rose in revolt, and arrayed an army against him, and demanded the kingdom of their father. Numbers who had been driven to despair by his tyranny, and were dispersed, gathered round them and lent them their support, so that the kingdom passed from his hands.

STANZA.

The king who dares his subjects to oppress,
  In day of need will find his friend a foe—
A mighty one. Soothe, rather, and caress
  Thy people; and in war-time thou wilt know
No fear of foes; for a just potentate
The nation's self will be a host to guard the State.

Story VII.

A king was seated in a vessel with a Persian slave. The slave had never before beheld the sea, nor experienced the inconvenience of a ship.[1] He began to

---

[1] M. Semelet explains this as meaning of "sea-sickness;" but I think the context shews it has a more general meaning. It is evident the vessel was floating quietly along, so that when the slave was thrown in he was not swept away, but easily reached the rudder.

weep and bemoan himself, and a tremor pervaded his
frame. In spite of their endeavours to soothe him, he
would not be quieted. The comfort of the king was
disturbed by him; but they could not devise a remedy.
In the ship there was a philosopher,[54] who said, "If you
command, I will silence him." The king answered, "It
would be the greatest favour." The philosopher directed
them to cast the slave into the sea. He underwent
several submersions, and they then took him by the hair
and dragged him towards the ship. He clung to the
rudder of the vessel with both hands, and they then
pulled him on board again. When he had come on
board, he seated himself in a corner and kept quiet.
The king approved, and asked, "What was the secret of
this expedient?" The philosopher replied, "At first he
had not tasted the agony of drowning, and knew not the
value of the safety of a vessel. In the same manner a
person who is overtaken by calamity learns to value
a state of freedom from ill."[54]

STANZA.

Sated, thou wilt my barley-loaf repel.
 She whom I love ill-favoured seems to thee.
To Eden's Houris[55] Írāf would seem hell :
 Hell's inmates ask—they'll call it heavenly

COUPLET.

Wide is the space 'twixt him who clasps his love,
And him whose eyes watch for the door to move.[56]

---

[54] I think Ross and Gladwin, as also M. Semelet, wrong in rendering حکیم *ḥakīm*, "a physician;" to tally with which the two former translate عافیت *áfiyat*, by "health." M. Semelet, on the contrary, very properly gives "*incolumitas*" as its equivalent.

[55] For the Houris, *vide* Sale's Koran. p. 393 ; and for Írāf (or Purgatory), Sale, p. 111.

[56] In expectation of seeing his loved one come in.

Story VIII.

They said to Hurmuz Tājdār,[87] "What fault didst thou find in the vazīrs of thy father that thou didst command them to be imprisoned?" He replied, "I discovered no fault in them; but I saw that they had a boundless fear of me in their hearts, and that they had not entire confidence in my promise. I feared that through dread of injury to themselves they might attempt my destruction; wherefore I put into practice the maxim of the wise men who have said,

STANZA.

Thou who art wise, fear him who feareth thee,
   Though thou like him a hundred wouldst despise :
Seest thou not, how in last extremity,
   The cat will lacerate the leopard's eyes?
Hence, too, the snake the shepherd wounds; for he
   Dreads the raised stone and down-crushed agonies."

Story IX.

One of the Arabian kings was sick in his old age, and the hope of surviving was cut off. Suddenly a horseman entered the portal, and brought good tidings, saying, "By the auspicious fortune of my lord we have taken such a castle, and the enemies are made prisoners, and the troops and peasantry in that quarter are entirely reduced to obedience." When the king heard this speech he heaved a cold sigh, and said, "These joyful tidings are not for me, but for my enemies; that is, the heirs of my crown."

---

[87] Hurmuz Tājdār, or "the crown-wearer," was so called because, wishing to dispense justice on all occasions himself, without the intervention of others between himself and his subjects, he continually wore the crown, to denote his readiness to discharge his kingly functions. He was the son of Nūshīrvān, and his tutor, Buzurchimihr, has been already mentioned in the Preface.

STANZA.

In this fond hope, dear life, alas! has waned:
  That my heart's wish might not be wished in vain:
Hope, long delayed, is granted. Have I gained
  Aught?—Nay. Life spent returns not back again.

STANZA.

Death's hand has struck the signal-drum;
  Eyes! now obey your parting knell!
Hands, wrists, and arms, all members, come,
  And bid a mutual, long farewell!
Hope's foe, Death, has me seized at last;
  Once more, O friends! before me move;
In folly has my time been past:
  May my regrets your warning prove!

STORY X.

In a certain year I was engaged in devotion at the tomb of the Prophet Yahiya,[88] in the principal mosque of Damascus. It happened that one of the Arabian princes, who was notorious for his injustice, came as a pilgrim thither, performed his prayers, and asked [of God] what he stood in need of.

COUPLET.

The poor, the rich, alike must here adore:
The wealthier they, their need is here the more.

He then turned towards me and said, "On account of the generous character of darweshes, and the sincerity of their dealings, I ask you to give me the aid of your spirit, for I stand in dread of a powerful enemy." I

---

[88] St. John the Baptist, whose remains were said to be interred in a church at Damascus. After the conquest of Syria by the Musalmān, this church was converted into a mosque, and called the mosque of the tribe of Ummiyah.

replied, "Shew mercy[89] to thy weak subjects, that thou mayst not experience annoyance[89] from a puissant foe."

VERSE.

With the strong arm and giant grasp 'tis wrong
To crush the feeble, unresisting throng.
Who pities not the fallen, let him fear,
Lest, if he fall, no friendly hand be near.
Who sows ill actions and of blessing dreams,
Fosters vain phantasies and idly schemes.
Unstop thy ears, thy people's wants relieve,
If not, a day[90] shall come when all their rights receive.

DISTICHS.

All Adam's race are members of one frame;
Since all, at first, from the same essence came.
When by hard fortune one limb is oppressed,
The other members lose their wonted rest:
If thou feel'st not for others' misery,
A son of Adam is no name for thee.

Story XI.

A darwesh, whose prayers were accepted with God, made his appearance in Baghdād. They told this to Ḥajjāj-bin-Yūsuf,[91] who sent for him, and said, "Offer up a good prayer for me." The darwesh said, "O God! take away his life." "For God's sake!" asked he, "what prayer is this?" He replied, "It is a good prayer for thee, and for all Musalmān."

---

[89] There is here a rhyme in the words رحمت, raḥmat, and زحمت, zaḥmat, which cannot be preserved in English.

[90] That is, the day of resurrection.

[91] Ḥajjāj-bin-Yūsuf was the Governor of Arabian Irāḳ, under the Khalīfah Abd-ul-malik, A.H. 65. He was notorious for his oppression.

DISTICHS.

Oppressor! troubler of the poor!
How soon shall this thy mart [92] be o'er!
What good will empire be to thee?
Better thy death than tyranny.

Story XII.

An unjust king asked a religious man, "What sort of devotion is to be esteemed highest?" He replied, "For thee to sleep at noon,[93] in order that in this state thou mightest cease for an instant to oppress mankind."

STANZA.

A tyrant lay, his noontide slumber taking:
  Said I—'Tis best this scourge should sleeping lie;
And he whose sleep is better than his waking.
  'Tis best for such an evil one to die."

Story XIII.

I have heard of a prince who had turned night into day, and had drunk wine all night; and, in the height of his intoxication, uttered this couplet,

COUPLET.

"Of all my bright and gladsome moments the gladdest
  is this one;
When of good or ill I reck not, and I harbour fear of
  none."

A darwesh, entirely destitute of clothing, lay beneath his palace, outside, in the cold, and exclaimed,

---

[92] The termination of life is here, as often elsewhere, compared to the closing of a market.

[93] Ross renders it, "to sleep till noon." If any one prefers this rendering I have nothing to say against it, except that perhaps تا *tá* would be used in place of the *izáfat* were it correct. The noontide-sleep is customary in hot climates.

COUPLET.

"Thou with whom none may in success compare,
Grant thou art griefless; say, Have I no care?"

The king was pleased with this address. He held out from the window a purse containing a thousand dīnārs, and said, "O darwesh! hold thy lap." He replied, "Whence shall I get a lap, I who have not a garment?" The king's compassion for his wretched state increased; he added to the purse a rich robe, which he sent out to him. The darwesh, in a short time, spent and squandered that sum of money, and came back.

COUPLET.

Money abides not in the palm of those who careless live,[91]
Nor patience in the lover's heart, nor water in the sieve.

At a time when the king did not concern himself about him, they announced his state. He was displeased, and his countenance changed at this intelligence. And for this reason men of sagacity and experience have said, that it is requisite to beware of the violence and despotic temper of kings; since for the most part their high thoughts are engaged with the arduous affairs of State, and they will not endure the vulgar throng.

DISTICHS.

Let him not hope kings' favours, who omits
To watch the moment which his prayer befits.
Till thou observest the just time for speech
Do not by useless words thy cause impeach.

The king said, "Drive away this impudent and prodigal mendicant who, in so short a time, has dissipated such a treasure, and does not know that the royal treasury is to supply morsels to the poor, not feasts to the fraternity of devils."

"Wandering devotees, who have renounced the world and are, therefore, careless.

COUPLET.

The dolt, who in bright day sets up a camphor light,
Soon thou wilt see his lamp devoid of oil at night.

One of the vazīrs, who was a man of prudence, said, "O my lord! to such persons one ought to give an allowance, by instalments, of what is just enough for their support, that they may not become lavish in their expenses. But as to what thou commandest, namely, to treat him with violence, and to drive him away, it is not consonant with true generosity to make one expect favour and then to wound his spirit with disappointment."

COUPLET.

Ope not thyself the door of greediness;
But roughly it to close beseems thee less.

STANZA.

None see the Ḥijāz pilgrims, faint with thirst,
 Crowd to the margin of the briny sea:
Where'er the fountains of sweet water burst
 Their way; there men, and birds, and ants will be.

Story XIV.

One of the former kings showed remissness in protecting his dominions, and treated his army with severity. On the appearance of a powerful enemy, all turned their backs.

COUPLETS.

Soldiers, from whom the State withholds its gold,
Will from the scymitar their hands withhold.
What valour in war's ranks will he display,
Whose hand is empty on the reckoning day?

I had a friendship with one of those who had declined service. I reproached him and said, "He is base and unthankful, and vile and ungrateful, who, on a slight change of fortune, deserts his old master, and lays aside the obligations of favours received for years." He replied, "If I was to tell you [how matters stood] you would acquit me. Suppose my horse had no barley, and my saddle-cloth was in pawn; and one cannot valiantly risk one's life for a Sultān who is miserly to his soldiers."

COUPLET.

Give thy troops gold that for thee they may die;
Else they'll go seek a better destiny.

COUPLET.

The well-fed warrior will with ardour fight;
The starved will be as ardent in his flight.

STORY XV.

One of the vazīrs had been dismissed from office, and had entered the community of darweshes, and the blessed influence of their society took effect upon him, and his peace of mind was restored to him. The king's heart became again reconciled to him, and he offered him employment. The vazīr declined it, and said, "Discharge is better than charge."

QUATRAIN.

Those who in safety's quiet nook repose
    Have stopped the teeth of dogs and tongues of men;
    Far from the slander and the reach of foes,
        They tear their paper and destroy their pen.

The king said, "It is most certain that I have need of a man of consummate wisdom, who may be suitable for the councils of the State." He replied, "The sign of a man of consummate wisdom is not to engage in such matters."

COUPLET.

The Humā[95] is for this of birds the king :
It feeds on bones and hurts no living thing.

APOLOGUE.

They said to a lynx,[96] "How didst thou come to choose service in attending on the lion?" He replied, "Because I feed on the remains of his quarry, and pass my life in security from the malice of my enemies under the shelter of the awe which he inspires." They rejoined, "Now that thou hast come under the shadow of his protection, and avowest thy thankfulness for his favours; why dost thou not approach nearer, that he may include thee in the circle of his especial favourites, and reckon thee among his devoted adherents?" He replied, "I am not so secure from his violence."

COUPLET.

Though for a hundred years the Guebre feeds his flame,
Did he once fall therein, 'twould feed on him the same.

Sometimes it happens that the counsellor of his majesty the Sulṭān is rewarded with gold, and at another time, it may be that he loses his head; and the sages have said, "You ought to be on your guard against the changeableness of the temper of kings; for, sometimes they are displeased at a respectful salutation, and at other times they bestow dresses of honour in return for abuse :" and they have observed that, "Great facetious-

---

[95] The Humā is the Phœnix ; or, as D'Herbelôt tells us, a sort of eagle which feeds on bones, and is therefore called by the Persians Ustukhwān Kh'ur, the Ossifrage. This bird, from its not injuring other animals, is thought of happy augury, and from its name is derived the Persian adjective همايون humāyūn, "auspicious."

[96] The other translators avoid rendering this word, and call it the Siyāh Gūsh. The literal meaning is, "black ear."

ness is an accomplishment in courtiers; but a fault in wise men."

COUPLET.

To keep thy place and dignity be thine ;
To courtiers wit and pleasantry resign.

Story XVI.

One of my companions came to me with complaints of his ill-fortune, saying, "I have but little means of subsistence, and a large family, and I cannot support the burthen of poverty; it has frequently entered my head that I would go to another country, in order that, live how I may, no one may know of my welfare or the reverse.

COUPLET.

Full many a starving wight has slept[27] unknown ;
Full many a spirit fled that none bemoan.

Again, I am in dread of the rejoicing of my enemies, lest they should laugh scoffingly at me behind my back, and impute my exertions in behalf of my family to a want of humanity, and say,

STANZA.

See now, that wretch devoid of shame ! for him
　　Fair fortune's face will smile not, nor has smiled ;
Himself he pampers in each selfish whim,
　　And leaves his hardships to his wife and child.

And I know something, as you are aware, of the science of accounts ; if by your interest a means [of subsistence] could be afforded me, which might put me at ease, I should not be able to express my gratitude sufficiently to the end of my life." I replied, "O my friend ! the king's service has two sides to it,—hope of a livelihood, and terror for one's life ; and it is contrary

[27] Here used for "died."

to the opinion of the wise, through such a hope to expose oneself to such a fear.

STANZA.

None in the poor man's hut demand
Tax on his garden or his land.
Be thou content with toil and woe,
Or with thy entrails feed the crow."

He replied, "These words that thou hast spoken do not apply to my case, nor hast thou returned an answer to my question. Hast thou not heard what they have said: 'that the hand of every one who chooses to act dishonestly trembles in rendering the account'?"

COUPLET.

God favours those who follow the right way,
From a straight road I ne'er saw mortal stray.

"And the sages have said, 'Four kinds of persons are in deadly fear of four others: the brigand of the Sultān, and the thief of the watchman, and the adulterer of the informer, and the harlot of the superintendent of police:' and what fear have those of the settling, whose accounts are clear?"

STANZA.

Wouldst thou confine thy rival's power to harm
  Thee at discharge? then while thy trust remains,
Be not too free; none shall thee then alarm.
  'Tis the soiled raiment which, to cleanse from stains,
  Is struck on stones and asks the washer's pains.

I answered, "Applicable to thy case is the story of that fox which people saw running away in violent trepidation.[98] Some one said to him, 'What calamity has happened to cause thee so much alarm?' He replied, 'I have heard they are going to impress the camel.' They rejoined, 'O Shatter-brain! what connection has a camel with thee, and what resemblance hast thou to it?' He

[98] Literally, "falling and rising."

answered, 'Peace! for if the envious should, to serve their own ends, say, "This is a camel," and I should be taken, who would care about my release so as to inquire into my condition? and before the antidote is brought from Irāk, the person who is bitten by the snake may be dead.'[99] And in the same way thou possessest merit, and good faith, and piety, and uprightness; but the envious are in ambush, and the accusers are lurking in corners. If they should misrepresent thy fair qualities, and thou shouldest incur the king's displeasure and fall into disgrace, who would have power, in that situation of affairs, to speak for thee? I look upon it as thy best course to secure the kingdom of contentment, and to abandon the idea of preferment, since the wise have said,

COUPLET.

'Upon the sea 'tis true is boundless gain:
Wouldst thou be safe, upon the shore remain.'"

When my friend heard these words he was displeased, and his countenance was overcast, and he began to utter words which bore marks of his vexation, saying, "What judgment, and profit, and understanding, and knowledge is this? and the saying of the sages has turned out correct, in that they have said, 'Those are useful friends who continue so when we are in prison; for at our table all our enemies appear friends.'

STANZA.

Think not thy friend one who in fortune's hour
Boasts of his friendship and fraternity.
Him I call friend who sums up all his power
To aid thee in distress and misery."

[99] The تریاق *tiryāk* is an antidote against poison. Some think it is treacle; and others the bezoar-stone. Others would derive it from θήρ "a noxious beast," and ἀκέομαι "to heal." This sentence is a proverb in common use.

I saw that he was troubled, and that my advice was taken in bad part. I went to the president of finance,[100] and, in accordance with our former intimacy, I told him the case; in consequence of which he appointed my friend to some trifling office. Some time passed away; they saw the amenity of his disposition, and approved his excellent judgment. His affairs prospered, and he was appointed to a superior post; and in the same manner the star of his prosperity continued to ascend until he reached the summit of his desires, and became a confidential servant of his Majesty the Sultān, *and the pointed-at by men's fingers, and one in whom the ministers of State placed their confidence.* I rejoiced at his secure position and said,

COUPLET.

Have no doubts because of trouble nor be thou discomfited;
For the water of life's fountain[101] springeth from a gloomy bed.

COUPLET.

*Ah! ye brothers of misfortune! be not ye with grief oppressed,
Many are the secret mercies which with the All-bounteous rest.*

COUPLET.

Sit not sad because that Time a fitful aspect weareth;
Patience is most bitter, yet most sweet the fruit it beareth.

[100] ديوان *diwān* may, as M. Semelet remarks, have several meanings; but the one evidently intended here is what I have given; for Sâdī's friend, we are told, had a talent for accounts.

[101] Muḥammadans believe in a fountain of life, to taste one drop of which bestows immortality. They say that خضر Khiẓr, or Elias, who, they suppose, was the general of the first Alexander, discovered this fountain, and drank of it, and hence he can never die.

During this interval I happened to accompany a number of my friends on a journey to Ḥijāz.[102] When I returned from the pilgrimage to Makkah he came out two stages to meet me. I saw that his outward appearance was one of distress, and that he wore the garb of a darwesh. I said, "What is thy condition?" He replied, "Just as thou saidst: a party became envious of me, and accused me of disloyal conduct; and the king did not deign to inquire minutely into the explanation of the circumstances; and my former companions, and even my sincere friends, forbore to utter the truth, and forgot their long intimacy.

STANZA.

When one has fallen from high heaven's decree,
    The banded world will trample on his head;
Then fawn and fold their hands respectfully,
    When they behold his steps by fortune led.

In short, I was subjected to all kinds of tortures till within this week that the good tidings of the safety of the pilgrims[103] arrived, when they granted me release from grievous durance, with the confiscation of my hereditary estate." I said, "At that time thou wouldest not receive my suggestion, that the service of the king is like a sea-voyage, at once profitable and fraught with peril; where thou either wilt acquire a treasure, or perish amid the billows.

COUPLET.

Or with both hands the merchant shall one day embrace
    the gold;
Or by the waves his lifeless form shall on the strand be
    rolled."
I did not think it right to lacerate his mental wounds

---

[102] Arabia Petraea.
[103] The pilgrims to Makkah.

further, or to sprinkle them with salt. I confined myself to these two couplets and said,

STANZA.

"Knewest thou not that thou wouldst see the chains upon
   thy feet,
  When a deaf ear thou turnedst on the counsels of the
   wise?
If the torture of the sting thou canst not with courage
   meet,
  Place not thy finger in the hole where the sullen
   scorpion lies."

Story XVII.

Certain persons were associates of mine, whose external conduct was adorned with rectitude. A great personage entertained a strong opinion in their favour, and had settled a pension upon them. But one of them did an act which was unbecoming the character of a darwesh. The favour of that person was estranged, and their market was depreciated.[104] I wished to set my companions free as regarded their allowance, and resolved to wait on their patron. The porter would not suffer me to enter, and treated me with insolence. I excused him, in accordance with what they have said,

STANZA.

"To door of king, or minister, or peer,
  Draw thou not nigh unless with patrons girt;
For if a poor man at the gate appear,
  Warders his collar seize, and dogs his skirt."

As soon as the favourite attendants of that great man were informed of my condition, they brought me in with respect, and assigned me a place of distinction. However, I submissively seated myself lower, and said,

---

[104] That is, their supplies were cut off.

COUPLET.

"Permit me, a slave of low degree,
To sit among those who wait on thee."

He replied, "My God! my God! what room is there for this speech?"

COUPLET.

What though my head and eyelids thou shouldst press,
I'd bear thy love-airs for thy loveliness.

In short, I seated myself, and conversed on all subjects, till the circumstance of my friends' disgrace was introduced. I said,

STANZA.

"What did the Lord of past munificence
　See in his servants that he deemed them vile?
God's rule is boundless, and, with love immense,
　He notes our sins, but us sustains meanwhile."

These words were approved by the prince, and he ordered that they should make ready the means of maintenance for my friends, according to the former custom, and that they should make up to them the supplies which they would have received during the time their allowance was stopped. I returned thanks for this favour, and kissed the ground of obedience, and asked pardon for my boldness; and as I was departing I said these words,

STANZA.

"The Kâbah[105] is the place of answered prayer;
　Therefore, from many a league the pilgrim throngs
To view its fane; from distant lands repair
　The hurrying crowds. Thus, too, to thee belongs
Patience, with supplicants like me to bear;
　For none cast stones at trees save fruit be there."

---

[105] The temple at Makkah.

was offended, and observed, "This tribe of tatterdemalions is on a level with brutes." The vazīr said, "The king of earth's surface passed near thee; why didst thou not do him homage, and perform thy respects?" He replied, "Tell the king to look for service from one who expects favours from him, and let him also know that kings are for the protection of their subjects, not subjects for the service of kings: as they have said,

STANZA.

'Kings are but guardians, who the poor should keep;
  Though this world's goods wait on their diadem.
Not for the shepherd's welfare are the sheep:
  The shepherd rather is for pasturing them.

CONCLUDING STANZA.

To-day thou markest one flushed with success:
  Another sick with struggles 'gainst his fate:
Pause but a little while, the earth shall press
  His brain that did such plans erst meditate.
Lost is the difference of king and slave,
  At the approach of destiny's decree:
Should one upturn the ashes of the grave,
  Could he discern 'twixt wealth and poverty?'"

The discourse of the darwesh made a strong impression on the king. He said, "Ask a boon of me." The darwesh replied, "I request that thou wilt not again disturb me." On this the king rejoined, "Give me some piece of advice." He said,

STANZA.

"Now that thy hands retain these blessings, know—
  This wealth, these lands, from hand to hand must go."

STORY XXIX.

A vazīr went to Zū'l-nūn,[122] of Egypt, and requested the

[122] Gentius tells us that there were two Zū'l-nūns: one, the prophet Jonah, who lived about 862 B.C.; and the other,

aid of his prayers, saying, "I am day and night employed in the service of the Sultān, hoping for his favour, and dreading his wrath." Zū'l-nūn wept, and said, "If I had feared the Most High God as thou dost the Sultān, I should have been of the number of the just."

STANZA.

Could the holy darwesh cease from worldly joy and sorrow,
   On the sky his foot would be;
And the vazīr for himself angelic light would borrow,
   Served he God as royalty.[123]

Story XXX.

A king gave an order to put an innocent person to death. He said, "O king! for the anger which thou feelest against me, seek not thine own injury!" The king asked, "How so?" He replied, "I shall suffer this pang but for a moment, and the guilt of it will attach to thee for ever."

QUATRAIN.

Circling on, life's years have fled, as flies the breeze of morn;
   Sadness and mirth, and foul and fair, for aye have passed away.
Dream'st thou, tyrant! thou hast wreaked on me thy rage and scorn?
   The burthen from my neck has passed, on thine must ever stay.

Suban, who, being in a vessel, was accused of stealing a very valuable pearl, and invoked God's aid to establish his innocence, whereupon the pearl was discovered in a fish. The person here alluded to is Abū Fazl Suban bin Ibrāhīm, a celebrated Muḥammadan saint, chief of the Ṣūfīs, who died in Egypt, A.H. 245.

[123] There is a very elegant turn in the original, which cannot be imitated in English : مَلِكْ *malik* is "a king," and مَلَكْ *malak* "an angel."

This admonition of his operated advantageously on the king, and he forbore to shed his blood, and asked pardon of him.

Story XXXI.

The vazīrs of Nūshīrwān were consulting on a matter connected with State affairs, and each delivered his opinions in accordance with what he judged best. The king also took part in their deliberations. Buzurchimihr adopted the opinion of the king. The vazīrs said to him privately, "What superiority didst thou discern in the king's opinion above the counsels of so many sage persons?" He replied, "In that the end of the affair is unknown, and the opinions of all depend on the will of the Most High God, whether they turn out just or erroneous. Wherefore it is better to conform to the monarch's opinion, that, should it turn out unfavourably, our obsequiousness will secure us from his reproaches.

DISTICHS.

Opinions, differing from the king, to have :
Is your own hands in your own blood to lave.
Should he affirm the day to be the night,
Say you behold the moon and Pleiads' light."

Story XXXII.

A traveller[124] twisted his ringlets,[125] saying, "I am a

[124] In my edition, I read in accordance with four MSS. سِيَاحِي *saiyāḥī*, instead of the شَيَّادِي *shaiyādī*, which M. Semelet, Gladwin, and Ross prefer. The sense of the latter, "an impostor," is certainly more suitable to the context, but then it does not occur in the dictionaries, and is contrary to the MSS.

[125] This implies merely a swaggering air, as we say, "twirled his moustache." I do not believe that the descendants of Âlī have any particular way of wearing the hair, though there is a difference in their turbans and the colour of their clothes.

5

descendant of Álí," and entered the city along with the caravan from Ḥijāz, giving out that he had come from the pilgrimage to Makkah; and produced an idyl before the king, affirming it to be his own. One of the king's counsellors had that year returned from travelling. He said, "I saw him in Baṣrah,[126] at the festival of Azḥa;[127] how, then, can he have come from the pilgrimage to Makkah?" Another said, "His father was a Christian in Malāṭiyah;[128] how should he be a descendant of Álí?" His verses were found in the Dīwān[129] of Anvarī.[130] The king ordered him to be beaten and sent him away, saying, "Why hast thou uttered so many falsehoods?" He replied, "Lord of earth's surface! I will speak one word more, and if it be not true, I am worthy of any punishment that thou mayest command." The king inquired, "What is that?" He replied,

STANZA.

"Curds,[131] which to thee a poor man brings, will prove,
  Water, two cups; and buttermilk, one spoon.
Let not my idle tales thine anger move,
  For, from a traveller, lies thou'lt hear full soon."

[126] A seaport town in the Persian Gulf.

[127] The Íd, or festival of Azḥa, is held by the Muḥammadans on the tenth day of the month Zi'l-ḥajj, which is the last of the Musalmān year. It is celebrated in honour of the offering up of Ishmael by Abraham, for the Muḥammadans pretend that he, and not Isaac, was to be the sacrifice.—*Vide* Kānūn-i Islām, p. 226.

[128] Malta.

[129] A poem, consisting of a series of odes, of which the first class terminate with ا *a*, the second with ب *b*, and so on through the alphabet.

[130] A celebrated Persian poet, who died A.H. 577 = A.D. 1200. He was patronized by Sulṭān Sanjār, of the Saljuk family.

[131] This alludes to the practice in Persia of breakfasting on a cup of curds and bread, with a slice of cheese or melon.

The king laughed and said, "In thy life thou never saidst a truer word than this." He then commanded the usual allowance for descendants of the Prophet to be got ready for him.

Story XXXIII.

They have related that a certain vazīr was compassionate to his inferiors, and studied the welfare of all. It happened that he fell under the king's displeasure. All exerted themselves to obtain his release; and those who had the custody of him alleviated his punishment; and the other nobles spoke of his good qualities to the king, so that the king forgave his fault. A sage heard of this, and said,

STANZA.

"To gain thy friends' affection,
  Sell the garden of thy sire;
To give them food, protection,
  With thy goods go feed the fire.
Shew kindness even to thy foes;
  The dog's mouth with a morsel close."[132]

Story XXXIV.

One of the sons of Hārūnu'r-rashīd[133] came to his father in a passion, saying, "Such an officer's son has insulted me, by speaking abusively of my mother."

---

[132] I have been compelled to translate these lines freely, *metri causá*. The literal version is, for the third and fourth lines, "to cook the pot of thy well-wishers, it is better to burn all thy household furniture." The other lines are more literally rendered, save that each second line ends with a rhyming participle, which cannot be carried out in English.

[133] That is, "Hārūn the Just." He began to reign A.H. 170, and was the fifth Khallīfah of the house of Abbās. He sent presents to Charlemagne, and, like him, divided his empire among his three sons.

Hárún said to his nobles, "What should be the punishment of such a person?" One gave his voice for death, and another for the excision of his tongue, and another for the confiscation of his goods and banishment. Hárún said, "O my son! the generous part would be to pardon him, and if thou canst not, then do thou abuse his mother, but not so as to exceed the just limits of retaliation, for in that case we should become the aggressors."

STANZA.

They that with raging elephants make war
  Are not, so deem the wise, the truly brave;
But in real verity, the valiant are
  Those who, when angered, are not passion's slave.[131]

DISTICHS.

An ill-bred fellow once a man reviled,
  Who patient bore it, and replied, "Good friend!
Worse am I than by thee I could be styled,
  And better know how often I offend."

Story XXXV.

I was seated in a vessel along with some persons of distinction. A barge, which was in our wake, went down, and two brothers were plunged into the vortex. One of the great personages said to the boatman, "Save those two, and I will give thee a hundred dínárs." The boatman plunged into the water and rescued one. The other perished. I said, "He was destined not to survive, wherefore thou camest too late to get hold of him." The boatman laughed, and said, "What thou sayest is most true, and, besides, my mind was more set on saving this one, because once when I was exhausted in the desert he set me on his camel, and I had been flogged by the other in my childhood." I

---

[131] More literally, "do not speak intemperately."

replied, "*The Great God is righteous! for every one who does well benefits his own soul; and every one that sinneth, sinneth against himself.*"

STANZA.

Strive not to pain a single heart,
 Nor by that thorny pathway move.
But with the needy aye take part;
 To thee, too, this will succour prove.

STORY XXXVI.

There were two brothers, one of whom served the Sulṭān, and the other obtained his bread by his manual labour. Once on a time the rich one said to the poor one, "Why dost thou not serve the Sulṭān, by which thou mayst escape from thy toilsome work?" He replied, "Why dost thou not work in order to free thyself from the disgrace of being a servant? since the sages have said, 'It is better to eat barley bread, and sit on the ground, than to gird oneself with a golden girdle, and stand up to serve.'"

COUPLET.

Better from lime make mortar with thy hand,
Than before chiefs with folded arms to stand.

STANZA.

Life, precious life, has been in pondering spent
 On summer clothing and on winter food.
O glutton belly! let one loaf content
 Thee, rather than the back [in slavish mood]
Be to the ground in others' service bent.

STORY XXXVII.

A person brought to Nūshirwān the Just good news, saying, "God [may he be honoured and glorified!] has removed such and such an enemy of thine." He replied, "Hast thou heard at all that he will spare me?"

COUPLET.

In my foe's death, what joy is there for me?
For my life, too, cannot eternal be.

Story XXXVIII.

A council of wise men at the court of Kisra[135] was discussing a certain matter. Buzurchimihr was silent. They said, "Why dost thou not deliver thy opinion with us in this consultation?" He replied, "Vazīrs are like physicians: and the physican does not give medicine save to the sick. Wherefore, when I see that your opinion is right, it would not be wise for me to interfere therein with my voice."

STANZA.

Without my meddling, if a thing succeed,
For me to give advice therein, what need?
But if I see a blind man and a pit,
Why, then, I'm guilty if I silent sit.

Story XXXIX.

When Hārūnu'r-rashīd had conquered Egypt, he said, "In contradiction to that impious rebel[136] who, through pride of having Egypt for his kingdom, laid claim to divine honours, I will give this province to none but the lowest of my slaves." He had a black slave of great stupidity, whose name was Khuṣaib; on him he bestowed the land of Egypt. They say that his intellect and capacity were so limited that when a body of Egyptian cultivators complained to him that they had sown cotton on the banks of the Nile, and that, owing to an unseasonable fall of rain, it had been destroyed; he replied, "You

---

[135] Kisra or Chosroes, as the Arabs styled the Persian kings of the Sassanian race, is here used for Nūshīrwān.
[136] Pharaoh is here meant.

ought to sow wool, that it might not be swept away." A sage heard it and said,

DISTICHS.

"If with your wisdom grew your store,
The fool would be the truly poor;
But Heaven to the fool supplies
Such wealth as would amaze the wise."[137]

DISTICHS.

Fortune and wealth are not to merit given:
None can obtain them but by aid from Heaven.
In this world oft a marvel meets our eyes;
The undiscerning honoured, scorned the wise.
The alchymist expires with grief and pain,
And fools a treasure 'neath a shed obtain.

Story XL.

They had brought a Chinese girl, of surpassing beauty and loveliness, to an Arabian king. In a moment of intoxication he attempted to embrace her. The damsel resisted him. The king was enraged, and bestowed her on one of his slaves, who was a negro, and whose upper lip ascended above his nostrils, and whose lower lip hung down on his collar. His form was such that the demon Sakhr would have fled at his appearance.

COUPLET.

In him th' extreme of ugliness was found,
As beauty to all time fair Joseph crowned.

STANZA.

Not such his person that description can
  His hideous aspect typify;
The fetor [save us!] from him foully ran
  Like carrion sun-baked in July.

At that season the passions of the negro were roused,

---

[137] In the original it is "a hundred wise men."

and he was overpowered by lust. Agitated by desire he deflowered her. In the morning, the king sought for the girl and could not find her. They told him what had happened. He was incensed, and commanded that they should bind the negro and the girl fast together by their hands and feet, and cast them from the roof of the palace into the fosse. One of the vazīrs, who was of a benevolent disposition, bent down his face in intercession to the ground and said, "The negro is not to blame in this matter; for all your Majesty's slaves and attendants are accustomed to your royal bounty." The king said, "What great difference would it have made had he forborne to meddle with her for a night?" The vazīr replied, "Sire! hast thou not heard what they have said,

STANZA.

'When to a limpid fountain one parched with thirst
　　advances,
　Think not a raging elephant him would scare;
　Or, when alone, an infidel sees meat with famished
　　glances,
　Can reason think he'd pause for the fast-day there.'"
The king was pleased with this pleasantry, and said, "I give thee the negro; but what shall I do with the girl?" He replied, "Give the girl to the negro; for his leavings are fit only for himself."

STANZA.

　Never take him for thy friend
　　Who goes where it beseems him not:
　The purest water will offend
　　The thirstiest lips, if it be got
　From one whose breath is foul and hot.

STANZA.

　Ne'er will the orange from the Sultān's hand
　Once in the dunghill fallen, more there rest:
　Though thirsty, none will water e'er demand,
　　When ulcerated lips the jar have pressed.

Story XLI.

They said to Alexander of Rūm, "How didst thou conquer the eastern and western worlds, when former kings surpassed thee in treasures, and territory, and long life, and armies, and yet did not obtain such victories?" He replied, "By the aid of the Most High God. Whenever I subdued a country I did not oppress its inhabitants, and I never spoke disparagingly of its kings."

COUPLET.

Ne'er will he be called great among the wise,
Who to the truly great their name denies.

STANZA.

These are no more than trifles, swiftly sped,
    Fortune and throne, command and conquest—all.
Destroy not thou the good name of the dead,
    That thy fame, too, may last and never fall.

CHAPTER II.

ON THE QUALITIES OF DARWESHES.

Story I.

A person of distinction asked a holy man, "What sayest thou with regard to a certain devotee; for others have spoken sneeringly of him?" He replied, "In his outward conduct I discern no fault, and I know nothing of his secret defects."

STANZA.

When thou dost one in saintly vestments find,
Doubt not his goodness or his sanctity.
What though thou knowest not his inmost mind?
Not within doors need the Muḥtasib[138] pry.

Story II.

I once saw a darwesh, who, with his head resting on the threshold of the temple at Makkah, called the Kâbah, was weeping and saying, "O Thou merciful and compassionate One! Thou knowest what homage can be offered by a sinful and ignorant being worthy of thee!"[139]

---

[138] The Muḥtasib is the Muḥammadan superintendent of police, who prevents drunkenness, gaming, and other disorders; but, as appears from this passage, his business is rather to enforce external decency, than to suppress latent immorality.

[139] That is, "The homage of a sinful being cannot be worthy of God."

STANZA.

For my scant service I would pardon crave,
Since on obedience I can ground no claim.
Sinners, of sin repent; but those who have
Knowledge of the Most High, at pardon aim
For worthless worship [which they view with shame].

The pious seek the reward of their obedience, and merchants look for the price of their wares, and I, thy servant, have brought hope, not obedience, and have come to beg, not to traffic. "*Do unto me that which is worthy of Thee, and not that of which I am worthy.*"

COUPLET.

Whether Thou wilt slay or spare me, at Thy door my head
    I lay;
To the creature will belongs not, Thy commandment I
    obey.

STANZA.

A supplicant at Makkah's shrine who wept
    Full piteously and thus exclaimed, I saw;
"I ask Thee not my homage to accept,
    But through my sins Thy pen absolving draw."

Story III.

Ábdu'l-Kádir Gílání[140] laid his face on the pebbles in the sanctuary of the Kábah, and said, "O Lord! pardon me; but if I am deserving of punishment, raise me up at the resurrection blind, that I may not be ashamed in the sight of the righteous."

STANZA.

Humbly in dust I bow each day
    My face, with wakening memory,
O Thou! whom I forget not, say,
    Dost Thou bethink Thee e'er of me?

[140] This saintly personage was a celebrated Ṣúfí of Baghdád, under whom Sádí embraced the doctrine of the Mystics.

Story IV.

A thief entered the house of a recluse. However much he searched, he found nothing. He turned back sadly and in despair, and was observed by the holy man, who cast the blanket on which he slept in the way of the thief, that he might not be disappointed.

STANZA.

The men of God's true faith, I've heard,
  Grieve not the hearts e'en of their foes.
When will this station be conferred
  On thee who dost thy friends oppose?

The friendship of the pure-minded, whether in presence or absence, is not such that they will find fault with thee behind thy back, and die for thee in thy presence.

COUPLET.

Before thee like the lamb they gentle are:
Absent, than savage wolves more ruthless far.

COUPLET.

They who the faults of others bring to you.
Be sure they'll bear to others your faults too.

Story V.

Certain travellers had agreed to journey together, and to share their pains and pleasures. I wished to join them. They withheld their consent. I said, "It is inconsistent with the benevolent habits of the eminent to avert the countenance from the society of the lowly, and to decline to be of service to them; and I feel in myself such power of exertion and energy that in the service of men I should be an active friend, not a weight on their minds.

COUPLET.

What though I'm borne[141] *not in the camel throng,*
Yet will I strive to bear your loads along."

One of them said, "Let not thy heart be grieved at the answer thou hast received, for within the last few days, a thief came in the guise of a darwesh, and linked himself in the chain of our society."

COUPLET.

What know men of the wearer, though they know the
   dress full well?
The letter-writer only can the letter's purport tell.

Inasmuch as the state of darweshes is one of security,[142] they had no suspicion of his meddling propensities, and admitted him into companionship.

DISTICHS.

Rags are th' external sign of holiness;
Sufficient—for men judge by outward dress.
Strive to do well, and what thou pleasest, wear;
Thy head a crown, thine arm a flag[143] may bear.
Virtue lies not in sackcloth coarse and sad;
Be purely pious, and in satin clad:

---

[141] There is an attempt here at a pun in the words اكبِ, *rākib*, "I am riding," and حامل *ḥāmil*, "I am bearing."

[142] This word سلامت *salāmat*, is variously rendered. M. Semelet translates it by "une assurance"; Ross by "reverence"; Gladwin by "everywhere approved," renderings sufficiently free, one would think, and all of them objective. I prefer giving the word a subjective meaning, when it may take its natural signification and yet make good sense.

[143] M. Semelet, from a note of M. de Sacy, conjectures علم *ālam* to mean "a rich dress, worn by the great;" or, "a piece of rich stuff worn by kings on the left shoulder." Gladwin and Ross translate as above, and I am content to follow them.

True holiness consists in quitting vice,
The world and lust,—not dress;—let this suffice.
Let valiant men their breasts with iron plate:
Weapons of war ill suit the effeminate.

"In short, one day, we had journeyed till dusk, and slept for the night under a castle's walls. The graceless thief took up the water-pot of one of his comrades, saying that he was going for a necessary purpose, and went, in truth, to plunder.

COUPLET.

He'd fain with tattered garment for a darwesh pass,
And makes the Kabah's[144] pall the housings of an ass.

As soon as he had got out of sight of the darweshes he scaled a bastion,[145] and stole a casket. Before the day dawned, that dark-hearted one had got to a considerable distance, and his innocent companions were still asleep. In the morning they carried them all to the fortress and imprisoned them. From that day we have abjured society, and kept to the path of retirement, for, *in solitude there is safety.*"

STANZA.

When but one member of a tribe has done
   A foolish act, all bear alike disgrace,
Seest thou how in the mead one ox alone
   Will lead astray the whole herd of a place?

I said, "I thank God (may He be honoured and glorified!) that I have not remained excluded from the

---

[144] First the Khalīfahs, then the Sulṭāns of Egypt, and lastly those of Constantinople, have been in the habit of sending annually to Makkah a rich covering of brocade for the temple there, called the Kābah.

[145] I must confess I consider this reading unsatisfactory, and much prefer Dr. Sprenger's برخى رفت *bar<u>kh</u>ī haraft*, "he went a little distance." The Doctor has a misprint directly after: دجى for درجى *darjī*.

beneficial influences of the darweshes, although I have been deprived of their society, and I have derived profit from this story, and this advice will be useful to such as I am through the whole of life."

DISTICHS.

Be there but one rough person in their train,
For his misdeeds the wise will suffer pain.
Should you a cistern with rose-water fill,
A dog dropped in it would defile it still.

Story VI.

A religious recluse became the guest of a king. When they sate down to their meals, he ate less than his wont; and when they rose up to pray, he prayed longer than he was accustomed to, that they might have a greater opinion of his piety.

COUPLET.

O Arab! much I fear thou at Makkah's shrine wilt never be,
For the road that thou art going is the road to Tartary.

When he returned to his own abode he ordered the cloth to be laid that he might eat. He had a son possessed of a ready wit, who said, "O my father! didst thou eat nothing at the entertainment of the Sultān?" He replied, "I ate nothing in their sight to serve a purpose." The son rejoined, "Repeat thy prayers again, and make up for their omission, since thou hast done nothing that can serve any purpose."

STANZA.

Thy merits in thy palm thou dost display;
 Thy faults beneath thy arm from sight withhold.
What wilt thou purchase, vain one! in that day,
 The day of anguish, with thy feigned gold?[116]

[116] Literally, "Base silver or coin."

Story VII.

I remember that, in the time of my childhood, I was devout, and in the habit of keeping vigils, and eager to practise mortification and austerities. One night I sate up in attendance on my father, and did not close my eyes the whole night, and held the precious Kur'ān in my lap while the people around me slept. I said to my father, "Not one of these lifts up his head to perform a prayer.[147] They are so profoundly asleep that you would say they were dead." He replied, "Life of thy father! it were better if thou, too, wert asleep ; rather than thou shouldst be backbiting people."

STANZA.

Naught but themselves can vain pretenders mark,
   For conceit's curtain intercepts their view.
Did God illume that which in them is dark,
   Naught than themselves would wear a darker hue.[148]

Story VIII.

In a certain assembly they were extolling a person of eminence, and going to an extreme in praising his excellent qualities. He raised his head, and said, "I am that which I know myself to be."

COUPLET.

Thou who wouldst sum my virtues up, enough thou'lt find
In outward semblance ; to my secret failings blind.

---

[147] Literally, "A double prayer," "binæ precationes," as M. Semelet remarks, like "deux Pater et deux Avé."

[148] This translation is free. The nominative is throughout in the singular, and the last line is literally, "He would see no one more wretched than himself."

STANZA.

My person, in men's eyes, is fair to view;
But, for my inward faults, shame bows my head.
The peacock, lauded for his brilliant hue,
Is by his ugly feet discomfited.

STORY IX.

One of the holy men of Mount Lebanon, whose discourses were quoted, and whose miracles were celebrated throughout the country of Arabia, came to the principal mosque of Damascus, and was performing his ablutions on the side of the reservoir of the well. His foot slipped, and he fell into the basin, and got out of it with the greatest trouble. When prayers were finished, one of his companions said, "I have a difficulty." The Shekh inquired what it was. He replied, "I remember that thou didst walk on the surface of the western sea without wetting thy feet, and to-day thou wast within a hair's breadth of perishing in this water, of but one fathom depth; what is the meaning of this?" He bent his head in the lap of meditation, and after much reflection, raised it, and said, "Hast thou not heard that the Lord of the World, Muhammad Mustafa (may the blessing and peace of God be upon him!) said, '*I have a season with God, in which neither ministering angel, nor any prophet that has been sent, can vie with me,*' but he did not say that this season was perpetual. In such a time as he mentioned, he was wrapt beyond Gabriel and Michael; and, at another time, he was contented with Hafsah [149] and Zainab, for the vision of the pious is between effulgence and obscurity; at one moment He shews Himself, at another snatches Himself from our sight."

---

[149] These are the names of two of Muhammad's wives, of which the latter was a Jewess who poisoned him.

COUPLET.

Thou dost Thy face now shew and now conceal,
Thy worth enhancest, and inflam'st our zeal.

STANZA.

I'll with unintercepted gaze survey
Him whom I love, and, wildered, lose my way.
One while a flame He kindles—bright in vain,
For soon He quenches it with cooling rain;
'Tis thus thou seest me burnt, then drowned again.

STORY X.

VERSE.

To that bereaved father[150] one once said,
"Aged sire! on whose bright soul truth's light is shed,
From Egypt his coat's scent thy nostrils knew;
In Canaan's pit why was he hid from view?"
"My state," he said, "is like heaven's flashing light:
One moment shewn, the next concealed in night;
Now on the azure vault I sit supreme;
In darkness now my own feet hidden seem.
Did but the darwesh in one state abide,
He might himself from both worlds aye divide."[151]

STORY XI.

I once, in the principal mosque of Baálbak,[152] addressed a few words, by way of exhortation, to a frigid assembly,

---

[150] Jacob,—to the story of whose son Joseph, perpetual reference is made by the Musalmán.

[151] That is, he might attain re-union with the Deity.

[152] Baálbak, by the Greeks called Heliopolis, is a city now in ruins, situated at the foot of Anti-Libanus, in the direct route between Tyre and Palmyra, by traffic with which cities it greatly profited. The principal temple, which is of extraordinary size and beauty, seems to have been built by Antoninus Pius. It contains now but 1200 inhabitants.

whose hearts were dead, and who had not found the way from the material to the spiritual world. I saw that my speech made no impression on them, and that the flame of my ardour did not take effect on their green wood. I felt repugnance to continue instructing such mere animals, and to holding up a mirror in the district of the blind; however, the gate of my spiritual discourse continued open, and the chain of my address was prolonged in explanation of the verse, "*We are nearer to him than the jugular vein.*" [153] I had brought my discourse to this point, when I exclaimed,

STANZA.

"Not to myself am I so near as He,
  My friend; and stranger still, from Him I'm far.
What can I do? where tell this mystery?
  He's in our arms, yet we excluded are."

I was intoxicated with the spirit of this address, and the remainder of the cup was in my hands, when, a traveller passing by the assembly, my last words [154] made an impression upon him. He gave such an applauding shout that the others, in sympathy with him, joined in the excitement, and the most apathetic of the assembly shared his enthusiasm. I exclaimed, "Praise be to God! Those at a distance who have knowledge of Him are admitted into His presence, while those who are at hand, but are deprived of vision, are kept aloof."

---

[153] This verse of the Ḳur'ān occurs in ch. L., l. 27, of Sale's Translation.

[154] The translators, in my opinion, have missed the sense of دور *daur*, which I take to mean not "ondulation," according to M. Semelet, but "circle of the cup"; the metaphor being still kept up, and the last sentence being compared to the last time the cup is sent round.

STANZA.

Expect not from that speaker eloquence,
 Whose words his audience cannot value well.
With a wide field of willingness commence,
 Then will the orator the ball[155] propel.

Story XII.

One night, in the desert of Makkah, from excessive want of sleep, I was deprived of the power of proceeding. I reclined my head, and bade the camel-driver leave me alone.

STANZA.

What distance can the tired footman go,
 When Bactria's camel faints beneath the load?
In the same time that fat men meagre grow,
 The lean will perish on affliction's road.

The camel-driver said, "O brother! the sanctuary[156] is before thee, and the robber behind; if thou goest on, thou wilt obtain thy object; if thou sleepest, thou wilt die."

COUPLET.

Sweet is slumber in the desert under the acacia-tree,
 On the night when friends are marching, but it bodeth
   death to thee.

Story XIII.

I saw a devotee on the sea-shore, who had received a wound from a leopard, and had been for a long time thus

---

[155] There is an equivoque here which cannot be retained in English: گوی *gūī* signifies both "speech," and "the ball used in the game of Chaugān."

[156] There is a pun here, impossible to render in English, on the words حرم *ḥaram*, "sanctuary," and حرامي *ḥarāmī*, "a robber."

afflicted, but could obtain no relief from any medicine, and yet incessantly returned thanks to God Most High. They asked him, saying, "How is it that thou, who art suffering from this calamity, art returning thanks?" He replied, "Praise be to God! that I am suffering from a calamity, and not from a sin."

STANZA.

If that loved One should slay me cruelly,
Thou shouldst not say, e'en then, I feared to die.
I'd ask, What fault has Thy poor servant done?
'Tis for Thine anger that I grieve alone.

STORY XIV.

A darwesh, having some pressing occasion, stole a blanket from the house of a friend. The judge ordered his hand to be cut off. The owner of the blanket interceded for him, saying that he had pardoned him. The judge said, "I shall not desist from carrying out the law on account of thy intercession." He replied, "Thou hast spoken the truth, but it is not necessary to punish with amputation one who steals property dedicated to pious purposes, for *'the fakir does not possess anything, and is not possessed by any one.'* Whatever the darwesh possesses is for the benefit of the necessitous." The judge released him, and said, "Was the world too narrow for thee, that thou must steal nowhere but from the house of such a friend?" He replied, "My Lord! hast thou not heard the saying, 'Make a clean sweep in thy friend's house, but do not even knock at the door of thy enemies.'"

COUPLET.

Art thou distressed? yield not to weak despair;
Uncloak thy friends, but strip thy foemen bare.[157]

---

[157] Literally, "strip off their skins." The second sentiment does not agree with the first.

Story XV.

A king said to a holy man, "Dost thou ever remember me?" He replied, "Yes! whenever I forget my God."

COUPLET.

Those He repels, to every side direct
Their course—whom he invites, all else reject.

Story XVI.

A certain pious man in a dream beheld a king in paradise and a devotee in hell. He inquired, "What is the reason of the exaltation of the one, and the cause of the degradation of the other? for I had imagined just the reverse." They said, "That king is now in paradise owing to his friendship for darweshes, and this recluse is in hell through frequenting the presence of kings."

STANZA.

Of what avail is frock, or rosary,
  Or clouted garment? Keep thyself but free
From evil deeds, it will not need for thee
  To wear the cap of felt: a darwesh be
In heart, and wear the cap of Tartary.

Story XVII.

A man on foot, with bare head and bare feet, came from Kúfah[158] with the caravan proceeding to Hijáz, and

---

[158] Kúfah is a city on the Euphrates, four days' journey from Baghdád, and so near Basrah that the two towns are called the two Basrahs, or the two Kúfahs. The Persians assert that it was built by Húshang, the second king of the Píshdádyán, or second dynasty of Persia. Khondemír, however, affirms that it was founded by Sád, a general of the Khalífah Omar, A.H. 17. The first Abbásí Khalífah made it his capital, and it became so extensive that the Euphrates was called نهر كوف nahar-i Kúfah, "the river of Kúfah." The oldest Arabic characters are called Kúfic, from this city.

accompanied us. I looked at him, and saw that he was wholly unprovided with the supplies requisite for the journey. Nevertheless, he went on merrily, and said,

VERSE.

"I ride not on a camel, but am free from load and
    trammel;
To no subjects am I lord, and I fear no monarch's word;
I think not of the morrow, nor recall the gone-by sorrow,
Thus I breathe exempt from strife, and thus moves on my
    tranquil life."

One who rode on a camel said to him, "O darwesh! whither art thou going? turn back, or thou wilt perish from the hardships of the way." He did not listen, but entered the desert and proceeded on. When we reached "the palm-trees of Maḥmūd," fate overtook the rich man and he died. The darwesh approached his pillow, and said, "I have survived these hardships, and thou hast perished on the back of thy dromedary."

COUPLET.

A person wept the livelong night beside a sick man's bed:
When it dawned the sick was well, and the mourner, he
    was dead.

STANZA.

Fleet coursers oft have perished on the way,
    While the lame ass the stage has safely passed;
Oft have they laid the vigorous 'neath the clay,
    While the sore-wounded have revived at last.

Story XVIII.

A king sent an invitation to a religious man. The latter thought to himself, "I will take a medicine to make me look emaciated; perhaps it may increase the good opinion entertained of me." They relate that he swallowed deadly poison, and died.

STANZA.

He who, pistachio-like, all kernel seemed,
 An onion was; for fold on fold was there.
The saint who turns to man to be esteemed,
 Must on the Ḳiblah [159] turn his back in prayer.

COUPLET.

Who calls himself God's servant must forego
All else, and none besides his Maker know.

Story XIX.

In the country of the Greeks some banditti attacked a caravan, and carried off immense riches. The merchants made lamentations and outcries, and called upon God and the Prophet to intercede for them, without avail.

COUPLET.

When the dark-minded robber finds success,
What cares he for the caravan's distress?

The philosopher Luḳmān was among them. One of those who composed the caravan said, "Say some words of wisdom and admonition to them; perchance they may restore a portion of our goods; for it would be a pity that such wealth should be lost." Luḳmān said, "It would be a pity to address the words of wisdom to them."

---

[159] The Ḳiblah is the point to which men turn in prayer. This, among Jews and Christians, is Jerusalem; and when Muhammad first ordered his followers to turn to the temple at Makkah, it occasioned such discontent that he added a verse, to the effect that prayer is heard to whatever quarter the supplicant turns. However, Muḥammadans now all turn to Makkah when praying.

STANZA.

When rust deep-seated has consumed the steel,
  Its stain will never a new polish own.
Advice affects not those who cannot feel:
  A nail of iron cannot pierce a stone.

STANZA.

In prosperous days go seek out the distressed;
  The poor man's prayer can change misfortune's course.
Give when the beggar humbly makes request,
  Lest the oppressor take from thee by force.

Story XX.

However much the excellent Sheikh Shamsu'd-dín Abū'l-faraj-bin-Jauzí[160] commanded me to abandon music, and directed me towards retirement and solitude, the vigour of my youth prevailed, and sensual desires continued to crave. Maugre my will, I went some steps contrary to the advice of my preceptor, and enjoyed the delights of music and conviviality. When the admonitions of my master returned to my recollection, I used to exclaim,

COUPLET.

"E'en the Ḳāẓī would applaud us, could he of our
    party be;
Thou Muhtasib! quaff the wine-cup, and thou wilt the
    drunkard free."

Till one night I joined the assembly of a tribe, and saw amongst them a minstrel.

---

[160] Ross reads Abū'l-faraḥ, as I felt inclined to do; but Gladwin, Semelet, and Sprenger read Abū'l-faraj. He was Sâdī's preceptor, and was the son of an eminent poet and sage, who died A.H. 597.

COUPLET.

Thou'dst say that through his fiddle-bow thy arteries would burst,
Than tidings of thy father's death wouldst own his voice more curst.

The fingers of his friends were at one time stopping their ears, at another pressed on their lips, to bid him be silent.

VERSE.

We haste to music's sound with stirred and kindling breast,
But thou a minstrel art, whose silence pleases best.

COUPLET.

One solitary pleasure in thy strains we find,
'Tis when they cease, we go, and thou art left behind.

DISTICHS.

When my shocked ear that lutist's voice had riven,
Straight to my host I cried, "For love of heaven,
Or with the quicksilver stop my ear, I pray,
Or ope thy door and let me haste away."

However, for the sake of my friends, I accommodated myself to the circumstances, and passed the night until dawn in this distress.

STANZA.

Mū'azzin![161] why delay thy morning task?
Know'st thou not how much of the night is sped?
Wouldst know its length? it of my eyelids ask,
For ne'er has sleep its influence o'er them shed.

---

[161] I have here translated somewhat freely. Literally it is, "The mū'azzin raised his voice unseasonably; he knows not how much of the night is passed. Ask the length of the night of my eyelashes, for not one moment has sleep passed on my eyes." The mū'azzin is the summoner to prayer, or crier of the mosque. I am inclined to think that the free translation above represents what Sâdī really intended.

In the morning, by way of a blessing, I took my turban from my head, and some dīnārs [162] from my belt, and laid them before the minstrel, and embraced him, and returned him many thanks. My friends observed that the feeling I evinced towards him was contrary to what was usual, and ascribed it to the meanness of my understanding, and laughed at me privately. One of them extended the tongue of opposition, and began to reproach me, saying, "This thing thou hast done accords not with the character of the wise; thou hast given the tattered robe, which is the dress of darweshes, to such a musician as has never in his whole life had one diram [163] in his hand, nor a particle of gold on his drum.

DISTICHS.

Such minstrel (from this mansion far be he!)
As in one place none twice will ever see.
The moment that his strains his gullet leave,
The hairs upon his hearer's flesh upheave.
The sparrow flies from horror at his note;
Our brain he shatters, while he splits his throat."

I said, "It is advisable for you to shorten the tongue of reproach, for, to me, his miraculous powers have been clearly evinced." He replied, "Acquaint me with these circumstances, that we may approach him,[164] and ask forgiveness for the joke which has been passed." I replied, "It is by reason of this, because my preceptor

---

[162] The dīnār is nearly equal to a ducat or sequin, about nine shillings; but, according to the Ḳānūn-i Islām, only five.

[163] A silver coin, worth, according to some, twopence.

[164] Sprenger's reading of همچنین تقرّب نمائیم *hamchunīn takarrub numāīm*, seems better than همکنان تقرّب *hamkunān takarrub*. The iẓāfat under the ن *n*, of همکنان *hamkunān*, in my edition, is a misprint.

had repeatedly commanded me to give up music, and amply advised me, but his words had not entered the ear of my acceptance; to-night, however, my auspicious fortune and happy destiny conducted me to this monastery, where, by means of this musician, I have repented, vowing that I will never again betake myself to music [165] or conviviality."

STANZA.

When a sweet palate, mouth, lips, voice, we find,
  Singing or speaking, they'll enchant the heart;
Ushāḳ, Sifāhān, Hijāz,[166] all combined,
  From a vile minstrel's gullet pain impart.

STORY XXI.

They asked Luḳmān, "Of whom didst thou learn manners?" He replied, "From the unmannerly. Whatever I saw them do which I disapproved of, that I abstained from doing."

STANZA.

Not e'en in jest a playful word is said,
  But to the wise, 'twill prove a fruitful theme.
To fools, a hundred chapters may be read
  Of grave import; to them they'll jesting seem.

STORY XXII.

They relate that a religious man, in one night, would

---

[165] The سماع samā, appears to be "the circular ecstatic dance of darweshes." In my edition, a و wa is omitted between سماع samā, and مخالطة mukhālaṭat.

[166] The names of three favourite musical modes; and not even these, says Sādī, can please us if the musician be a bad one.

eat three pounds[167] of food, and before dawn go through the Ḳur'án in his devotions. A holy man heard of this, and said, "If he were to eat half a loaf, and go to sleep, he would be a much better man than he is."

STANZA.

Keep thou thy inward man from surfeit free,
That thou, therein, the light of heaven may see.
Art thou of wisdom void? 'tis that with bread
Thou 'rt to thy nostrils over-surfeited.

STORY XXIII.

The divine grace caused the lamp of mercy to shine on the path of one lost in sin, so that he entered the circle of men of piety. By the happy influence of the society of darweshes, and the sincerity of their prayers, his evil qualities were exchanged for good ones, and he withdrew his hand from sensuality; and, nevertheless, the tongue of calumniators was lengthened with regard to him, to the effect that he was, just as before, subject to the same habits, and that no confidence could be placed in his devotion and uprightness.

COUPLET.

By penitence thou mayst exempted be
From wrath divine : man's tongue thou canst not flee.

He was unable to endure the injustice of their tongues, and complained to the superior of his order, and said, "I am harassed by the tongues of men." His preceptor

---

[167] In my edition I read نیم من *nīm man*, "half a man," the *man* being, according to Chardin, 5 lb. 11 oz.: but the other editors, Sprenger, Semelet, etc., read ده من *dah man*, "ten *mans*," or 58 lb. 12 oz., which is surely ridiculous. In India, the "man" is = 40 sers, or 80 lbs., which would prove too much even for the appetites of these gentlemen.

wept, and said, "How canst thou return thanks for this blessing, that thou art better than they think thee?

STANZA.

How oft, sayest thou, malignant enemies
   Seek to find fault with wretched me!
What if to shed thy blood they furious rise,
   Or sit in changeless enmity?
Be thou but good, and ill-report despise:
   'Tis better thus than thou shouldst be
Bad whilst thou seemest good in others' eyes.

But, behold me, who am regarded by all as perfection, and yet am imperfection itself.

COUPLET.

Had but my deeds been like my words, ah! then,
I had[168] been numbered, too, with holy men.

COUPLET.

True, I may be from neighbours' eyes concealed:
God knows my acts, both secret and revealed.

STANZA.

I close the door before me against men,
   That my faults may not stand to them confessed:
Of what avail its bar 'gainst Thee, whose ken
   Sees both the hidden and the manifest!"

Story XXIV.

I complained to one of our elders that a certain person had testified against me that I had been guilty of mis-

---

[168] The بودمی *bûdamî*, read by Sprenger and Semelet at the end of the second line of this couplet, is much better than the مردمی *mardamî*, in my edition.

conduct.[169] He replied, "Put him to the blush by thy virtuous conversation."

VERSE.

Walk well, that he who would calumniate
Thee may naught evil find of which to prate;
For when the lute a faithful sound returns,
It from the minstrel's hand, what censure earns!

Story XXV.

They asked one of the Shekhs of Damascus, "What is the true state of Ṣūfiism?"[170] He replied, "Formerly they were a sect outwardly disturbed, but inwardly collected; and at this day they are a tribe outwardly collected and inwardly disturbed."

STANZA.

While ever roams from place to place thy heart,
No peacefulness in solitude thou'lt see;
Hast thou estates, wealth, rank, the trader's mart?
Be thy heart God's—this solitude may be.

Story XXVI.

I remember that one night we had travelled all night in a caravan, and in the morning slept on the edge of a

---

[169] Ross and Gladwin, it appears to me, mistranslate this sentence. Sprenger reads, که فلان بغسادِ من گواهی داد *kih fulān ba-fasād-i man gueāhī dād,* "That a certain person had borne witness to my misconduct," which is obviously not so good as the reading in the text.

[170] The Ṣūfīs are a sect of Muḥammadan mystics, whose opinions, with regard to the soul, the Deity, and creation, very much resemble the esoteric doctrines of the Brāhmaṇs. They look upon the soul as an emanation from the Deity, to be re-asorbed into its source, and regard that absorption as attainable by contemplation.

forest. A distracted person, who accompanied us on that journey, uttered a cry, and took the way to the wilderness, and did not rest for a moment. When it was day I said to him, "What state is this?" He replied, "I saw the nightingales engaged in pouring forth their plaintive strains from the trees, while the partridges uttered their cries from the mountains, the frogs from the water, and the beasts from the forests. I reflected that it would be ungrateful for me to slumber neglectful while all were engaged in praising God."

DISTICHS.

But yester morn, a bird with tender strain,
 My reason, patience, sense, endurance stole;
A comrade, one most near in friendship's chain,
 (Perhaps he heard th' outpourings of my soul),
Said, "My belief would ne'er have credited
 That a bird's voice could make thee thus distraught."
"It fits not well my state as man," I said,
 "That birds their God should praise, and I say nought."

STORY XXVII.

Once on a time, in travelling through Arabia Petræa, a company of devout youths shared my aspirations[171] and my journey. They used often to chant and repeat mystic verses; and there was a devotee *en route* with us, who thought unfavourably of the character of darweshes, and was ignorant of their distress. When we arrived at the palm-grove of the children of Hallāl, a dark youth came out of one of the Arab families, and raised a voice which might have drawn down the birds from the air. I saw

---

[171] There is rather a neat pun in the Persian here, which I have made a poor attempt to preserve. همدم *hamdam*, signifies "breathing together;" *i.e.*, "a friend;" همقدم *hamḳadam*, "stepping together"; *i.e.*, "a companion."

the camel of the devotee begin to caper, and it threw its rider, and ran off into the desert. I said, "O Shekh! it has moved a brute, does it not create any emotion in thee?"

VERSE.

Knowest thou what said the bird of morn, the nightingale, to me?
"What meanest thou that art unskilled in love's sweet mystery?
The camels, at the Arab's song, ecstatic are and gay;
Feel'st thou no pleasure, then thou art more brutish far than they!"

COUPLET.

When e'en the camels join in mirth and glee,
If men feel naught, then must they asses be.

COUPLET.

Before the blast the balsams[172] bend in the Arab's garden[173] lone;
Those tender shrubs their boughs incline; naught yields the hard firm stone.

DISTICHS.

All things thou seest still declare His praise;
The attentive heart can hear their secret lays.
Hymns to the rose the nightingale His name;
Each thorn's a tongue His marvels to proclaim.

Story XXVIII.

A king had reached the close of his life, and had no heir to succeed him. He made a will, that they should place the royal crown on the head of the first person who might enter the gates of the city in the morning,

---

[172] The بان *bān* is the myrobolan, whence is obtained the fine balsam, called Benjamin, or Benzoin.

[173] M. Semelet informs us that the حمى *ḥama* is the space enclosed by the nomadic Arab for his use.

and should confide the government to him. It happened that the first person who entered the city-gate was a beggar, who throughout his whole life had collected scrap after scrap, and sewn rag upon rag. The Pillars of the State, and ministers of the late king, executed his will, and bestowed on him the country and the treasure. The darwesh carried on the government for a time, when some of the great nobles turned their necks from obeying him, and the princes of the surrounding countries rose up on every side to oppose him, and arrayed their armies against him. In short, his troops and his subjects were thrown into confusion, and a portion of his territory departed from his possession. The darwesh was in a state of dejection at this circumstance, when one of his old friends, who was intimate with him in the time of his poverty, returned from a journey, and, finding him in this exalted position, said, "Thanks be to God (may He be honoured and glorified!) that thy lofty destiny has aided thee, and thy auspicious fortune has led thee on, so that thy rose has come forth from the thorn, and the thorn from thy foot, and thou hast arrived at this rank, '*surely with calamity comes rejoicing.*' [171]

COUPLET.

The bud now blossoms; withered now is found:
The tree now naked; now with leaves is crowned."

He replied, "O brother! condole with me; for there is no room for felicitation. When thou sawest me, I was distressed for bread, and now I have the troubles of a world upon me."

DISTICHS.

Have we no wordly gear—'tis grief and pain:
Have we it—then its charms our feet enchain.
Can we than this a plague more troublous find,
Which absent, present, still afflicts the mind?

[171] "After pain comes pleasure;" "Après la peine le plaisir."

STANZA.

Wouldst thou be rich, seek but content to gain;
  For this a treasure is that ne'er will harm.
If in thy lap some Dives riches rain,
  Let not thy heart with gratitude grow warm;[175]
For, by the wisest, I have oft been told,—
The poor man's patience better is than gold.

COUPLET.

A locust's leg, the poor ant's gift, is more
Than the wild ass dressed whole from Bahrām's [176] store.

Story XXIX.

A person had a friend who was filling the office of Diwān.[177] A long interval had passed without his happening to see him. Some one said, "It is a long time since thou sawest such a one." He replied, "Neither do I wish to see him." By chance one of the Diwān's people was there; he asked, "What fault has he committed that thou art indisposed to see him?" He answered, "There is no fault; but the time for seeing a Diwān is when he is discharged from his office."

STANZA.

While office lasts, amid the cares of place,
  The great can well dispense with friendship's train;
But in the day of sorrow and disgrace,
  They come for pity to their friends again.

---

[175] I have been obliged to render this line freely. Literally it is, "See that thou dost not regard his recompense."

[176] Bahrām, the sixth of that name, was a king of Persia, called Gūr, from his fondness for hunting the wild ass. This couplet is a sort of Oriental version of the widow's mite.

[177] Accountant-General, or superintendant of the imperial finances.

Story XXX.

Abū Hurairah[178] used every day to wait upon Muṣṭafā[179] (may the blessing and peace of God be upon him!). The latter said, "O Abū Hurairah! *visit me less often and thou wilt increase our friendship;*"[180] that is, "Come not every day, that our attachment may be augmented."

ANECDOTE IN ILLUSTRATION.

They said to a wise man, "Notwithstanding the kindly influence which the sun exerts, we have not heard that any one ever regarded it as a friend." He replied, "It is because we can see it every day except in winter, when it is concealed and beloved."

STANZA.

There is no harm in visiting a friend;
But not so oft that he should say, "Enough!"
If thou wilt thyself only reprehend,
Thou wilt not meet from others a rebuff.

Story XXXI.

Having become weary of the society of my friends at

---

[178] That is, "The father of the kitten." M. Semelet tells us Omar, who succeeded Abū-bakr as Khalīfah, was so called, because he always carried a kitten on his arm. It was a name given him by Muḥammad. But we are informed by the Kāmūs that the name is assigned, for no less than thirty different reasons, to Abdu'r-raḥmān bin Sakhr. Abulfeda says, "Præterea quoque postremum hunc obiit Abu-Horaira de cujus et nomine et genere certum non constat. Fuit perpetuus comes et famulus prophetæ, tantumque ejus dictorum factorumque retulit, ut multi sint qui ob immanem traditionum, quas edidit, numerum suspectum fraudis eum habeant." Page 375, ed. Reiskii.

[179] "Chosen," a name of Muḥammad.

[180] This last sentence is in Arabic, and therefore the Persian interpretation is immediately added.

Damascus, I set out for the wilderness of Jerusalem, and associated with the brutes, until I was made prisoner by the Franks, who set me to work along with Jews at digging in the fosse of Tripolis, till one of the principal men of Aleppo, between whom and myself a former intimacy had subsisted, passed that way and recognised me, and said, "What state is this? and how are you living?" I replied,

STANZA.

"From men to mountain and to wild I fled
   Myself to heavenly converse to betake ;
Conjecture now my state, that in a shed
   Of savages I must my dwelling make."

COUPLET.

Better to live in chains with those we love,
Than with the strange 'mid flow'rets gay to move.

He took compassion on my state, and with ten dinārs redeemed me from the bondage of the Franks, and took me along with him to Aleppo. He had a daughter, whom he united to me in the marriage-knot, with a portion of a hundred dinārs. As time went on, the girl turned out of a bad temper, quarrelsome and unruly. She began to give a loose to her tongue, and to disturb my happiness, as they have said,

DISTICHS.

"In a good man's house an evil wife
Is his hell above in this present life.
From a vixen wife protect us well,
Save us, O God! from the pains of hell."

At length she gave vent to reproaches, and said, "Art thou not he whom my father purchased from the Franks' prison for ten dinārs?" I replied, "Yes! he redeemed me with ten dinārs, and sold me into thy hands for a hundred."

DISTICHS.

I've heard that once a man of high degree
From a wolf's teeth and claws a lamb set free.
That night its throat he severed with a knife.
When thus complained the lamb's departing life,
"Thou from the wolf didst save me then, but now,
Too plainly I perceive the wolf art thou."

STORY XXXII.

A king asked a religious man how his precious time was passed. He replied, "I pass the whole night in prayer, and the morning in benedictions and necessary requirements; and all the day in regulating my expenses."[1] The king commanded that they should supply him with food enough for his support, in order that his mind might be relieved from the burthen of his family.

DISTICHS.

Thou who art fettered by thy family!
Must ne'er again thyself imagine free.
Care for thy sons, bread, raiment, and support,
Will drag thy footsteps back from heaven's court.
All day I must the just arrangements make;
To God, at night, myself in prayer betake.
Night comes; I would to prayer my thoughts confine,
But think, How shall my sons to-morrow dine?

---

[1] Semelet and Sprenger, and also Ross and Gladwin, read, instead of ملك, *malik*, ملك را مضمون اشارت عابد معلوم گشت. *malik-rā mazmūn-i ishārat-i ābid mālūm gasht*. "The king perceived the drift of the devotee's hint;" but I think it much better to omit this, and suppose that the king gave the allowance of his own free will, without its being asked for.

Story XXXIII.

One of the Syrian recluses had for years worshipped in the desert, and sustained life by feeding on the leaves of trees. The king of that region made a pilgrimage to visit him, and said, "If thou thinkest fit I will prepare a place for thee in the city that thou mayest have greater conveniences for devotion than here, and that others may be benefited by the blessing of thy prayers,[182] and may imitate thy virtuous acts." The devotee did not assent to these words. The nobles said, "To oblige the king, the proper course is for thee to come into the city for a few days and learn the nature of the place; after which, if the serenity of thy precious time suffers disturbance from the society of others, thou wilt be still free to choose." They relate that the devotee entered the city, and that they prepared for him the garden of the king's own palace, a place delightsome to the mind, and suited to tranquillise the spirit.

DISTICHS.

Like beauty's cheek, bright shone its roses red;
Its hyacinths—like fair ones' ringlets spread—
Seemed babes, which from their mother milk ne'er drew,
In winter's cold so shrinkingly they grew.

COUPLET.

And the branches—on them grew pomegranate-flowers
Like fire, suspended there, 'mid verdant bowers.

The king forthwith despatched a beautiful damsel to him.

---

[182] Sprenger's reading of this passage is far the best, or, rather, it is correct; while the reading of all others, including my own, is ungrammatical and incorrect. As the sentence begins with the second person singular, the شما *shumá* after انفاس *anfás*, and اعمال *ámál*, is a downright blunder. I saw this, but, unsupported by MSS., could not make an alteration, and am delighted to find that, on the best authority, Sprenger reads انفاست *anfásat*, and اعماست بصلاح *ba-ṣaláḥ-i ámálat*.

VERSE.

A young moon that e'en saints might lead astray,
Angel in form, a peacock in display,
When once beheld, not hermits could retain
Their holy state, nor undisturbed remain.

In like manner, after her, the king sent a slave, a youth of rare beauty and of graceful proportions.

STANZA.

*Round him, who seems cupbearer, people sink;
Of thirst they die, he gives them not to drink.*
The eyes that see him, still unsated crave,
As dropsy thirsts amid the Euphrates' wave.

The holy man began to feed on dainties and wear soft raiment, and to find gratification and enjoyment in fruits and perfumes, as well as to survey the beauty of the youth and of the damsel; and the wise have said, "The ringlets of the beautiful are the fetters of reason, and a snare to the bird of intelligence."

COUPLET.

In thy behoof, my heart, my faith, my intellect, I vow;
In truth, a subtle bird am I; the snare this day art thou.

In short, the bliss of his tranquil state began to decline; as they have said,

STANZA.

" All that exist—disciples, doctors, saints,
   The pure and eloquent alike, all fail
When once this world's base gear their minds attaints,
   As flies their legs in honey vainly trail."

At length the king felt a desire to visit him. He found the recluse altered in appearance from what he was before, with a florid complexion, and waxen fat, pillowed on a cushion of brocade, and the fairy-faced slave standing at his head, with a fan of peacock's feathers. The monarch was pleased at his felicitous state, and the conversation turned on a variety of subjects, till, at the close of it, the king said, "Of all the people in the world, I value these two sorts most—the learned and the devout." A philosophical and experienced vazir was present. He said, "O king! friendship requires that thou shouldest do good to both these two orders of men— to the wise give gold, that they may study the more; and to the devout give nothing, that they may remain devout."

COUPLET.

To the devout, nor pence nor gold divide;
If one receive it, seek another guide.

STANZA.

Kind manners, and a heart on God bestowed
　Make up the saint, without alms begged or bread
That piety bequeathes. What though no load
　Of turquoise-rings on Beauty's fingers shed
Their ray, nor from her ear the shimmering gem
　Depends; 'tis Beauty still, and needs not them.

STANZA.

O gentle darwesh! blest with mind serene,
　Thou hast no need of alms or hermit's fare.
Lady of beauteous face and graceful mien!
　Thou well the turquoise-ring and gauds canst spare.

COUPLET.

Seek I for goods which not to me belong;
Then if men call me worldly they're not wrong.[153]

Story XXXIV.

In conformity with the preceding story, an affair of

---

[153] Literally, "While I have, and seek for another's, if they do not call me hermit, perhaps they are right."

importance occurred to the king. He said, "If the termination of this matter be in accordance with my wishes, I will distribute so many dirams to holy men." When his desire was accomplished, it became incumbent on him to fulfil his vow according to the conditions. He gave a bag of dirams to one of his favourite servants, and told him to distribute them among devout personages. They say that the servant was shrewd and intelligent. He went about the whole day, and returned at night, and kissing the dirams, laid them before the king, saying, "However much I searched for the holy men I could not find them." The king replied, "What tale is this? I know that in this city there are four hundred saints." He answered, "O Lord of the earth! the devout accept them not, and he who accepts them is not devout." The king laughed and said to his courtiers, "Strong as my good intentions are towards this body of godly men, and much as I wish to express my favour towards them, I am thwarted by a proportionate enmity and rejection of them on the part of this saucy fellow, and he has reason on his side."

COUPLET.

When holy men accept of coin from thee,
Leave them, and seek some better devotee.

Story XXXV.

They asked a profoundly learned man his opinion as to pious bequests. He said, "If the allowance is received in order to tranquillize the mind, and obtain more leisure for devotion, it is lawful; but when people congregate for the sake of the endowment, it is unlawful."

COUPLET.

For sacred leisure saints receive their bread,
Not to gain food that ease is furnished.

Story XXXVI.

A darwesh arrived at a place where the master of the house was of a beneficent disposition. A number of excellent persons, who were also endowed with eloquence, attended his circle, and each one of them, as is customary with men of wit, uttered some bon-mot or pleasantry. The darwesh had traversed the desert, and was fatigued, and had eaten nothing. One of them said in jest, "Thou, too, must say something." The darwesh said, "I have not the talent and eloquence of the others, and have not read anything; be satisfied with one couplet from me." All eagerly exclaimed, "Say on." He said,

COUPLET.

"Hungry I stand, with bread so near my path,
Like one unwedded by the women's bath."

All laughed and approved his wit, and brought a table before him. The host said, "Wait a little, friend! as my servants are preparing to roast some meat, cut small." The darwesh raised his head and said,

COUPLET.

"Not on my table let this roast meat be,
Baked as I am, dry bread is roast to me."

Story XXXVII.

A disciple said to his spiritual guide, "What shall I do, for I am harassed by people through the frequency of their visits to me, and my precious moments are disturbed by their coming and going." He replied, "Lend to all who are poor, and demand a loan of all who are rich, and they will not come about thee again."

COUPLET.

If Islām's van a beggar should precede,
To China infidels would fly his greed.

Story XXXVIII.

A lawyer said to his father, "No part of those facinating speeches of the orators makes an impression on me, for this reason, that I do not see their practice correspond with their preaching."

DISTICHS.

While men to leave the world they warn,
Themselves are hoarding pelf and corn.
The sage who does but preach, will ne'er,
With all his words, man's conscience stir.
Who does no evil, truly wise is he;
Not one whose acts and doctrines disagree.

COUPLET.

The sage, whom ease and pleasure lead aside,
Is himself lost; to whom can he be guide?

The father said, "O my son! it is not proper to avert one's countenance from the instruction of good advisers solely through this unfounded notion, and to take the path of idleness, and to tax the wise with error; and, while seeking for an immaculate sage, to remain deprived of the advantages of wisdom, like that blind man who one night fell into the mire and exclaimed, "O Musalmān! shew a lamp in my path!" A bold hussey heard him and said, "Thou who canst not see a lamp, what wilt thou see with a lamp?" In like manner, the congregation of preachers[b] is like the warehouse of mercers, for there, until thou give money, thou canst not get the goods; and here, unless thou bring good intentions, thou wilt not carry off a blessing."

[b] I prefer Dr. Sprenger's reading مجلس واعظان • *majlis-i wāizān* to the old reading, مجلس وعظ • *majlis-i wāz*.

STANZA.

Heed thou well the wise man's warning,
  Though his acts his words belie;
Futile is th' objector's scorning,
  "Sleepers ope not slumber's eye."
Heed thou then well the words of warning,
  Though on a wall thou them descry.

Story XXXIX.

(IN VERSE.)

A holy man left the monastic cell, his vow
Of sojourn with recluses broke, and now
A college sought. "How differ then?" I said,
"Sages and saints, that thou the one hast fled—
The other sought?" "This his own blanket saves,"
He said, "while that the drowning rescues from the
  waves."

Story XL.

A person had fallen asleep in a state of intoxication on the highway, and the reins of self-control had escaped from his hands. A devotee passed beside him, and noticed his disgraceful condition. The young man raised his head and said, "*And when they pass by the slips and shortcomings of others, they pass by absolvingly.*"[185]

VERSE.

When thou a sinner dost behold,
Shew mercy, nor his crimes unfold.
Seest thou my faults with scornful eye?
With pity rather pass me by.

---

[185] This is a quotation from the Kur'ān, chap. xxv. v. 72. I have altered Sale's words, and, with all due deference, I must confess I think his rendering of this passage execrable.

STANZA.

Turn not, O saint! thy face from sinful me;
But rather view me with benignity.
If I act not with honour, still do thou
So act, and pass me by with courteous brow.

Story XLI.

A band of dissolute fellows came to find fault with a darwesh, and used unwarrantable language, and wounded his feelings. He carried his complaint before the chief of his order, and said, "I have undergone such and such." His chief replied, "O son! the patched road of darweshes is the garment of resignation. Every one who in this garb endures not disappointment patiently is a pretender, and it is unlawful for him to wear the robe of the darwesh.

COUPLET.

A stone makes not great rivers turbid grow:
When saints are vexed their shallowness they show.

STANZA.

Hast thou been injured? suffer it and clear
    Thyself from guilt in pardoning other's sin.
O brother! since the end of all things here
    Is into dust to moulder,[186] be thou in
Like humble mould, ere yet the change begin."

Story XLII.

(IN VERSE.)

List to my tale! In Baghdād once, dispute
Between a flag and curtain rose. Its suit
The banner, dusty and with toil oppressed,
Urged; and the curtain, angry, thus addressed:

---

[186] خاک *khāk*, signifies "dust," and خاک شدن *khāk shudan*, "to be humble." I have endeavoured to retain the equivoque.

"Myself and thou were comrades at one school;
Both now are slaves 'neath the same monarch's rule.
I in his service ne'er have rested,—still,
Whate'er the time, I journey at his will;
My foot is ever foremost in emprise;
Then why hast thou more honour in men's eyes?
With moon-faced slaves thy moments pass away;
With jasmine-scented girls thou mak'st thy stay.
I lie neglected still in servile hands,
Tossed by the winds my head, my feet in bands."
"The threshold is my couch," the curtain said,
"And ne'er, like thee, to heaven raise I my head:
He who exalts his neck with vain conceit,
Hurls himself headlong from his boasted seat."

Story XLIII.

A pious man saw an athlete who was exasperated, and infuriated, foaming at the mouth. He said, "What is the matter with this man?" Some one answered, "Such a one has abused him." "What!" said the holy man, "This contemptible fellow can lift a stone of a thousand mans'[187] weight, yet has not the power to support a word.

STANZA.

Boast not thy strength or manhood, while thy heart
Is swayed by impulse base;—if man thou art,
Or woman, matters naught;—but rather aim
All mouths to sweeten,—thus deserve the name
Of man; for manliness doth not consist
In stopping others' voices with thy fist.

STANZA.

Though one could brain an elephant, yet he
Is not a man without humanity.
In earth the source of Adam's sons began;
Art thou not humble? then thou art not man."

---

[187] A *man* varies in weight in different countries. M. Semelet fixes it 5 lb.; but in India it is, in many places, 80 lb.

Story XLIV.

They asked a person of eminence as to the character of the Brothers of Purity.[188] He replied, "The meanest of their qualities is, that they prefer the wishes of their friends to their own interests; and the wise have said, 'the brother whose aims are relative[189] to himself alone, is neither brother nor relative.'"

COUPLET.

Who goes too fast, cannot thy comrade be;
Fix not thy heart on one who loves not thee.

COUPLET.

If truth and faith sway not thy kinsman's breast,
To break off kinsmanship with him were best.

I remember that an opponent objected to the wording of this couplet, and said, "God, most glorious and most High, has, in the Glorious Book,[190] forbidden us to break the ties of blood, and has commanded us to love our relations; and what thou hast said is contrary to this." He replied, "Thou hast erred; it is in accordance with the Kur'ān. God most High has said, '*But if thy parents endeavour to prevail on thee to associate with me that concerning which thou hast no knowledge, obey them not.*'"[191]

---

[188] M. Semelet tells us, in his note on this passage, that in the third century of the Hijrah there was a college of that name, at Baghdād. There was also a monastery in Persia so called. The Sūfīs particularly affected the name, from the resemblance of صفا *safā*, and صوفي *sūfī*, and they are designated in this passage by the said title.

[189] I have used this expression in order to retain the pun on خویش *kh'ish*, "self," and خویش *kh'ish*, "relation."

[190] That is, The Kur'ān.

[191] This quotation is from the Kur'ān, ch. xxxi. v. 15. I have given Sale's version.

COUPLET.

Thou, for one friendly stranger, sacrifice
A thousand kinsmen who their God despise.

Story XLV.[192]

(IN VERSE.)

In Baghdād once, an aged man of wit
  His daughter to a cobbler gave;
The cruel fellow so the damsel bit,
  That blood began her lips to lave.
Next morning, when the father saw her plight,
  He sought his son-in-law and said,
"What mark of teeth is this? ignoble wight!
  Her lip's not leather, that thou'st fed
Upon it thus. I speak this not in jest;
  Take what is right, but cease to scoff.
When once ill habits have the soul possessed,
  Till the last day they're not left off."

Story XLVI.

A lawyer had an extremely ugly daughter, who had arrived at maturity; but, notwithstanding her dowry and a superabundance of good things, no one shewed any desire to wed her.

COUPLET.

Brocade and damask but ill grace
A bride of loathly form and face.

In short, they were compelled to unite her in the nuptial bond with a blind man. They relate that at that time there arrived a physician from Ceylon, who restored the eyes of the blind to sight. They said to the

---

[192] This story and the next seem to belong rather to Chapter V.

lawyer, "Why dost thou not get thy son-in-law cured?" He replied, "I am afraid that he should recover his sight and divorce my daughter."

HEMISTICH.

An ugly woman's spouse is better blind.

Story XLVII.

A king was regarding a company of darweshes contemptuously. One of them, acute enough to divine his feelings, said, "O king! we, in this world, are inferior to thee in military pomp, but enjoy more pleasure, and are equal with thee in death, and superior to thee in the day of resurrection.

DISTICHS.

The conqueror may in every wish succeed;
Of bread the darwesh daily stands in need;
But in that hour when both return to clay,
Naught but their winding-sheet they take away.
When man makes up his load this realm to leave,
The beggar finds less cause than kings to grieve.

The outward mark of a darwesh is a patched garment and shaven head; but his essential qualities are a living heart and mortified passions.

STANZA.

Not at strife's door sits he; when thwarted, ne'er
  Starts up to contest; all unmoved his soul.
He is no saint who from the path would stir,
  Though a huge stone should from a mountain roll.

The darwesh's course of life is spent in commemorating, and thanking, and serving, and obeying God; and in beneficence and contentment; and in the acknowledgment of one God and in reliance on Him; and in resignation and patience. Every one who is endued with these qualities is, in fact, a darwesh, though dressed in a tunic. But a babbler, who neglects prayer, and is given to sensuality, and the gratification of his appetite; who spends his days till night-fall in the pursuit of licentiousness, and passes his night till day returns in careless slumber; eats whatever is set before him, and says whatever comes uppermost; is a profligate, though he wear the habit of a darwesh.

STANZA.

O thou! whose outer robe is falsehood, pride,
    While inwardly thou art to virtue dead;
Thy curtain[193] of seven colours put aside,
    While th' inner house with mats is poorly spread."

Story XLVIII.

(IN VERSE.)

I saw some handfuls of the rose in bloom,
With bands of grass suspended from a dome.
I said, "What means this worthless grass, that it
Should in the roses' fairy circle sit?"
Then wept the grass and said, "Be still! and know
The kind their old associates ne'er forego.
Mine is no beauty, hue, or fragrance, true!
But in the garden of the Lord I grew."
        His ancient servant I,
    Reared by His bounty from the dust;
        Whate'er my quality,
    I'll in His favouring mercy trust.
        No stock of worth is mine,
    Nor fund of worship, yet He will
        A means of help divine;
    When aid is past, He'll save me still.

---

[193] It is customary in Persia to have a curtain at the portal of the house, the richness of which depends on the circumstances of the owner.

Those who have power to free,
Let their old slaves in freedom live,
Thou Glorious Majesty!
Me, too, Thy ancient slave, forgive.
Sádí! move thou to resignation's shrine,
O man of God! the path of God be thine.
Hapless is he who from this haven turns,
All doors shall spurn him who this portal spurns.

Story XLIX.

They asked a sage, "Which is better, courage or liberality?" He replied, "He who possesses liberality has no need of courage."

COUPLET.

Graved on the tomb of Bahrām Gūr we read,
"Of the strong arm the generous have no need."

STANZA.

Hátim[191] is dead; but to eternity
His lofty name will live renowned for good.
Give alms of what thou hast. The vineyard, see!
Yields more, the more the dresser prunes the wood.

[191] Abū Adi Hātim-bin-Abdu 'llāh-bin-Sādu'l Tāī, usually called Hātim Tāī, was an illustrious Arab, renowned for his generosity. He lived before Muḥammad, but his son Adi, who died at the age of 120, in the 68th year of the Hijrah, is said to have been a companion of the Prophet. Tāī is the name of a powerful Arabian tribe, to which Hātim belonged. One anecdote of Hātim's liberality is very celebrated. The Greek Emperor had sent ambassadors to him for a famous horse he possessed, whose swiftness and beauty were unrivalled, and which he valued with all an Arab's pride. When the envoys arrived, through some accident he had no food to give them; he, therefore, killed his favourite steed, and served up part of its flesh. When their hunger was satisfied, the envoys told the object of their mission, and were astounded at learning that the matchless courser had been sacrificed to shew them hospitality.

CHAPTER III.

ON THE EXCELLENCE OF CONTENTMENT.

Story I.

An African mendicant, in the street of the mercers of Aleppo, said, "O wealthy sirs! if *you* had but justice and *we* contentment, the custom of begging would be banished from the world."

STANZA.

Contentment! do thou me enrich; for those
    Who have thee not are blest with wealth in vain.
Wise Luķmān for his treasure[195] patience chose:
    Who have not patience wisdom ne'er attain.

Story II.

There were in Egypt two sons of an Amīr.[196] One studied science; the other gained wealth. The former became the most learned man of the age; and the latter king of Egypt. The rich one then looked with scornful eyes on his learned brother, and said, "I have arrived at sovereign power, and thou hast remained in thy poverty

---

[195] Ross reads گنج *ganj*, "treasure," which I much prefer to کنج *kunj*, "corner," the reading of Gladwin, Semelet, and Sprenger. Luķmān did not choose "retirement." His wisdom was φρόνησις picked up in the world, not ἐπιστήμη.

[196] Niebuhr, in his History of Arabia, tells us that the descendants of the Prophet are called Amīrs, but the general meaning of the word is "nobleman."

as at the first." He replied, "O brother! it behoves me to render thanks to God Most High, for His bounty, in that I have obtained the inheritance of the Prophets— that is to say, wisdom; and thou the inheritance of Firâun and Hāmān,[197] namely, the land of Egypt."

DISTICHS.

I am the ant which under foot men tread,
And not the hornet whose fierce sting they dread.
How, for this boon, shall I my thanks express?
That I, to injure man, am powerless.

Story III.

I have heard of a darwesh who was consumed with the flames of hunger, and who sewed rag upon rag, and consoled himself with this couplet.

COUPLET.

I'm with dry bread contented, and with tatters; for 'tis better
To bear up under sorrow, than to be another's debtor.

Some one said to him, "Why dost thou sit here? for such a one in this city has a generous mind, and displays a munificence that extends to all, and his loins are ever girded to serve the distressed, and he sits at the gate of all hearts [waiting to fulfil their wishes]. If he should become acquainted with the state of thy circumstances, he would consider it an obligation to serve a man of worth, and regard it as a precious opportunity." The darwesh

---

[197] Dr. Sprenger omits the words و هامان, *wa hāmān*, and thus gets rid of the difficulty of the name Hāmān being associated with that of Pharaoh, the only Haman we know being the favourite of Ahasuerus. However, the names occur together in the Kur'ān, chaps. xxviii. and xl., where Hāmān appears to be the vazir of Pharaoh, and therefore only of the same name as our Haman, not the same person.

replied, "Be silent! for it is better to die in indigence than to expose one's wants to another: as they have said,

STANZA.

'Better to suffer, and sew patch o'er patch,
    Than begging letters to the rich to write.
Truly it doth hell's torments fairly match,
    To mount by others to celestial light.'"

Story IV.

One of the kings of Persia sent a skilful physician to wait on Muṣṭafa[195] (on whom be peace!). He remained some years in the country of Arabia; but no one came to test his abilities, nor asked him for medicine. One day he presented himself before the Chief of the Prophets (on whom be peace!) and complained, saying, "They sent me to heal your companions, and during this long interval no one has addressed himself to me, that this slave might discharge the duty for which he was appointed." The Prophet (peace be upon him!) said, "This people have a custom of not eating anything till hunger compels them, and of withdrawing their hands from the repast while still hungry." "This," said the physician, "is the cause of their good health." He then kissed the ground respectfully and departed.

DISTICHS.

The wise will then begin their speech,
Then towards food their fingers reach,
When silence would with ills be rife,
When fasting would endanger life:
Such speech were, certes, wisdom, too,
And from such food will health accrue.

---

[195] A name of Muḥammad. *Vide* Note 179.

Story V.

A person made frequent vows of repentance and broke them again, till a venerable personage said to him, "I understand that thou hast the habit of gormandizing, and the bond of thy appetites—that is to say, thy vows of penitence—is finer than a hair; and thy appetites, as thou fosterest them, would break a chain; and a day will come when they will destroy thee."

COUPLET.

A wolf's whelp had been fostered till, one day,
Grown strong, it tore its master's life away.

Story VI.

In the annals of Ardshīr Bābakān,[199] it is related that he asked an Arabian physician how much food ought to be eaten daily. He replied, "A hundred dirhams' weight would suffice." The king replied, "What strength will this quantity give?" The physician answered, "*This quantity will carry thee; and that which is in excess of it thou must carry;*" or, "This quantity will support thee, and thou must support whatever thou addest to this."

COUPLET.

We eat to live, God's praises to repeat;
Thou art persuaded that we live to eat.

Story VII.

Two darweshes of Khurāsān, travelling together, united in companionship. One was weak, and was in the habit of breaking his fast after every two nights; and the other was strong, and made three meals a day. It happened

---

[199] This king was the first of the fourth Persian dynasty or Sassanides. He was the son of a shepherd, who married the daughter of one Bābak—hence the name. He was co-temporary with the Emperor Commodus.

that at the gate of a city they were seized, on suspicion of being spies, and were both imprisoned, and the door closed up with mud. After two weeks it was discovered that they were innocent. They opened the door, and found the strong man dead, and the weak man safe and alive. They were still in astonishment at this, when a wise man said, "The opposite of this would have been strange; for this man was a great eater, and could not support the being deprived of food, and so perished. But the other was in the habit of controlling himself; he endured, as was his wont, and was saved."

STANZA.

When to eat little is one's habit grown,
    Then, should we want, we bear it easily;
Do we indulge when plenty is our own,
    Then, when want happens, we of hardship die.

STORY VIII.

A sage forbade his son to eat much, as satiety causes sickness. The son replied, "O my father! hunger kills. Hast thou not heard what the wits have said? 'That it is better to die of repletion than to endure hunger.'" The father answered, "Observe moderation; for God Most High has said, '*Eat and drink; but do not exceed.*'"

COUPLET.

Eat not so as to cause satiety;
Nor yet so little as of want to die.

STANZA.

The sense by food is gratified; yet still
    Th' excess of it brings sickness. Did you eat
Conserve of roses in excess, 'twere ill:
    Eat late; then bread is as that conserve sweet."

STORY IX.

They said to a sick man, "What does thy heart

desire?" He replied, "Only that it may desire something." [200]

COUPLET.

For stomachs loaded or oppressed with pain,
The costliest viands are prepared in vain.

Story X.

In the city of Wāsiṭ,[201] some Ṣūfis had incurred a debt of a few dirams to a butcher. Every day he dunned them, and spoke roughly to them. The society were distressed by his reproaches, but had no remedy, save patience. A holy man among them said, "It is easier to put off the stomach with a promise of food, than the butcher with a promise of payment."

STANZA.

Better renounce the favour of the great,
  Than meet their porter's gibes at thy expense;
Rather through want of food succumb to fate,
  Than bear the butcher's dunning insolence.

Story XI.

A brave man had received a terrible wound in a war with the Tartars. Some one said to him, "Such a merchant possesses a remedy. If thou ask him, perhaps he may give thee a little." Now they say that that merchant was as notorious for his stinginess as Ḥātim Ṭāi for his liberality.

---

[200] The other translators read نَخواهد *na khwāhad*, and render thus, "Only that it may not desire anything." This, I think, destroys the point of the story. The sick man wanted food, and being asked what he would wish to eat, replied, "That his wish was, that he could fancy *any*thing."

[201] Wāsiṭ [*lit.*, "middle"] is a city lying between Kūfah and Baṣrah, on the Tigris, built A.H. 83, by Ḥajjāj bin Yūsuf.

COUPLET.

If the sun upon his table-cloth instead of dry bread lay,
In all the world none would behold again the light of day.

The warrior replied, "If I ask him for the remedy, he may give it or he may not; and if he give it, it may do me good or it may not. In every case to ask of him is deadly poison."

COUPLET.

Whoe'er to beg of sordid persons stoops,
His flesh may profit, but his spirit droops.

And the wise have said, "Were they, for example, to sell the water of life at the price of honour,[202] a wise man would not buy it; since to die honourably is better than to live disgracefully."

COUPLET.

The colocynth from friends tastes better far,
Than sweets from those whose features scowling are.

STORY XII.

One of the learned had a large family and small means. He stated his case to a great personage who entertained a favourable opinion of him. The great man was displeased with the request, and regarded with disapprobation this annoyance of begging on the part of a man of decorum.

STANZA.

Seekest thou thy friend? let not thy face be sad
   With thy misfortunes, lest thou cloud his joy:
When asking favours let thy looks be glad;
   For fortune's not to smiling brows more coy.

---

[202] There is a play on words here which cannot be preserved in English: آبِ رُو *áb rúi*, literally, "water of the face," signifies "honour," and is here made to answer to آبِ حیات *áb-i ḥaiát*, "water of life."

They relate that he increased his allowance a little, and diminished his regard for him much. After some days, when the learned man saw that the great man's wonted friendship was not continued to him, he said,

COUPLET.

"*Fie on that food which through base means you taste!
The cauldron's 'stablished, but your worth's abased.*[203]

COUPLET.

My bread increases; but my name's depressed:
Sure want is better than a base request."

Story XIII.

A darwesh was suffering from a pressing exigency. Some one said to him, "Such a one possesses incalculable wealth. If he were informed of your wants, he would probably not allow of any delay in relieving them." He replied, "I do not know him." The other answered, "I will conduct thee." He took his hand and brought him to that person's door. The darwesh beheld a man with a hanging lip, and sitting in an ill-tempered attitude: he said not a word and went back. The other said to him, "What hast thou done?" He replied, "I renounced his gift for the sake of his looks."

---

[203] There is a double equivoque in this Arabic couplet. قِدْر *ḳidr*, is "a cauldron," and قَدْر *ḳadr*, is "worth," and مُنْتَصَب *muntaṣab*, "established," signifies also inflected with نَصْب *naṣb*, this *naṣb* being the grammatical expression for *zabar*, or the short "a" vowel-sound. The قَدْر *ḳidr*, "cauldron," is said then to be مُنْتَصَب *muntaṣab*, made into قَدْر *ḳadr*, "worth;" and in the same way the قَدْر *ḳadr*, "worth," is said to be مَخْفُوض *makhfaẓ* (which, as well as "abased," signifies also *ḳasrated*, or inflected with the vowel "i") or made into قِدْر *ḳidr*, "cauldron."

STANZA.

To one of scowling face tell not thy woes,
  Lest that his evil temper should thee pain;
But if thy griefs thou shouldst at all disclose,
  Be it to one from whom thou mayst obtain,
  In his kind countenance, a ready gain.

Story XIV.

One year there befel such a drought at Alexandria that the reins of endurance escaped from the hands of men, and the gates of heaven were closed against the earth, and the complaints of the terrestrial inhabitants ascended to heaven.

STANZA.

Nor beast, nor bird, nor fish, nor ant was there,
  But to the sky arose its cry of pain.
Strange that the smoke-wreaths of the people's prayer
  Became not clouds, their streaming tear-drops rain.

In such a year, an effeminate person (be he far from my friends!), to describe whom would be indecorous, especially in the august presence of the great; yet to pass over whom altogether in a careless manner would not be right, lest some party should impute it to the inability of the speaker: wherefore, we will sum up the matter with this couplet, that a little may be a sample of much, and a handful a specimen of an ass-load.

COUPLET.

A Tartar might that wretch effeminate
Slay, and not, therefore, merit a like fate.

Such a person, a partial description of whom thou hast heard, possessed that year incalculable wealth. He gave silver and gold to the necessitous, and kept a table for travellers. A party of darweshes, who were reduced to the last extremity by the violence of their hunger, formed the intention of accepting his invitation, and came to consult with me upon the matter. I withheld my consent, and said,

STANZA.

"Lions devour not food which dogs forego,
  Of hunger though they perish in their den.
Give up thy frame to famine, want, and woe;
  But stretch not forth thy hand to baser men.
A fool a second Farīdūn may be
  In wealth; yet him you lightly should esteem.
Silk and brocade upon th' unworthy seem
Like gilding on a wall and lazuli."

STORY XV.

They said to Ḥātim Ṭāī, "Hast thou seen or heard of any one in the world more magnanimous than thyself?" He replied, "Yes! One day I had sacrificed forty camels, and had gone out with the chiefs of the Arabs to a corner of the desert; there I saw a wood-cutter, who had collected a bundle of thorns. I said, 'Why dost thou not go to Ḥātim's entertainment? for the people have assembled at his board.' He replied,

COUPLET.

'By their own efforts those who earn their bread,
  Need not by Ḥātim Ṭāī's alms be fed.'

I perceived that in magnanimity and generosity he was my superior.'"

STORY XVI.

The Prophet Mūsā[204] (on him be peace!) saw a darwesh who, to hide his nakedness, had concealed himself in the sand, and who said, "O Mūsā! pray for me, that God Most High may give me wherewith to live, for I am so

[204] Moses.

weak as to be at the point of death." Mūsa (peace be upon him!) prayed, so that God Most High granted him assistance. Some days after, when the Prophet was returning from his devotions, he saw the darwesh in custody, and surrounded by a crowd of people. He asked, "What has befallen him?" They replied, "He drank intoxicating liquor, raised a disturbance, and slew a man; now they are going to exact retaliation."

VERSE.

Had the poor cat but wings, it would erase
The sparrow's progeny from nature's face;
So, too, the feeble, could they but prevail,
Their fellow-impotents would soon assail.

Mūsa (peace be on him!) acknowledged the wisdom of the Creator, and expressed contrition for his boldness, repeating the verse, "*And if God had plenteously afforded subsistence to His creatures, they would have rebelled on the earth.*"

COUPLET.

What, proud one! plunged thee in this hapless plight?
Would that the ant ne'er had the power of flight!

VERSE.

When to a blockhead riches, rank accrue,
    His folly on his head a buffet brings.
Is not this proverb of the sages true?
    "'Twere better for the ant not to have wings."

COUPLET.

Of honey hath the Sire a plenteous store;
But the son's feverish [and must not have more].[205]

COUPLET.

That Being, who increases not thy wealth,
Better than thou, knows what is for thy health.

[205] That is, our Heavenly Father has store of blessings; but man needs chastisement rather than indulgence.

Story XVII.

I once saw an Arab amid a circle of jewellers, at Baṣrah, who was relating the following story: "Once on a time I had lost my way in the desert, and had not a particle of food left, and I had made up my mind to perish, when, suddenly, I found a purse full of pearls. Never shall I forget the gratification and delight I felt when I imagined them to be parched wheat; nor again, the bitterness and despair when I found them to be pearls."

STANZA.

In the parched desert and the drifting sands,
    What to the thirsty is or pearl or shell?
When the tired traveller foodless, powerless stands,
    No more than sherds can gold his wants expel.

Story XVIII.

An Arab in the desert, from excess of thirst, exclaimed,

VERSE.

"*O would that, ere I die,*
    I might at length one day obtain my will:
A river dashing by
    Knee-deep, while I at ease my bucket fill."

In the same way a traveller had lost his way in a vast plain, and his food and strength were exhausted, and he had some dirams in his belt. He wandered about much, but could not regain the road, and perished of fatigue. A party arrived there, and saw the dirams spread out before his face, and these words traced on the ground,

STANZA.

"Though he all yellow gold, pure gold possessed,
    His wishes still the foodless man would miss.
A turnip boiled, to the poor wretch distressed
    In deserts, than crude silver better is."

Story XIX.

I never complained of the vicissitudes of fortune, nor suffered my face to be overcast at the revolution of the heavens, except once, when my feet were bare, and I had not the means of obtaining shoes. I came to the chief mosque of Kūfah[158] in a state of much dejection, and saw there a man who had no feet. I returned thanks to God and acknowledged his mercies, and endured my want of shoes with patience, and exclaimed,

STANZA.

"Roast fowl to him that's sated will seem less
Upon the board than leaves of garden cress.
While, in the sight of helpless poverty,
Boiled turnip will a roasted pullet be."

Story XX.

A certain king, with some of his principal officers, chanced to be in a hunting-park, at a great distance from any habitation, in time of winter. Night fell; they observed the house of a peasant, and the king said, "Let us go there for the night, that we do not suffer from the cold." One of his vazīrs said, "It would not be suitable to the dignity of a king to take refuge in the hut of a miserable peasant. Let us pitch our tent here and kindle a fire." The peasant learned what had taken place. He prepared what food he had ready and took it to the king, and, after kissing the ground respectfully, said, "The lofty dignity of the king will not be lowered by thus much condescension: but these are unwilling that the rank of the peasant should be exalted." The king was pleased with his address. He transferred himself to his cottage for the night, and in the morning gave him a robe of honour and other rich presents. I have heard that the villager ran by the king's stirrup for some distance, and said,

STANZA.

"Of the king's glorious attributes, not one
    Was lost by honouring the hostelrie
Of the poor peasant, whose peaked cap the sun
    Has reached, since on his head fell, shelteringly,
The shadow of a monarch great like thee."

Story XXI.

They relate that a horrible mendicant possessed great treasures. A king said to him, "It appears that thou possessest immense wealth, and I have an emergent occasion; if thou wouldst assist me with a little of it by way of loan, when the revenue of the country comes in it shall be faithfully repaid." He replied, "It would be unworthy of the lofty dignity of Earth's Lord to defile the hand of his nobleness with the property of a beggar like me, who has scraped it up grain by grain." The king replied, "There is no occasion to be distressed on that account, for I shall give it to the Tartars—*filth to the filthy.*"

COUPLET.

Mortar, they tell us, is by no means sweet;
'Tis then to stop foul drains with it more meet.

COUPLET.

A Christian's well may not be pure, 'tis true;
'Twill do to wash the carcase of a Jew.

I have heard that he bowed not to the king's command, and began to shuffle and be insolent. The king then ordered them to take out of his clutches, by force and intimidation, the amount under discussion.

Story XXII.

DISTICHS.

When by kind means succeeds not an affair,
 Rough treatment then we must apply and force.
Whoever of himself will nothing spare,
 Others will him, too, nothing spare, of course.

Story XXII.

I met[206] with a merchant who had a hundred and fifty camels of burthen and forty slaves and servants. One night, in the island of Kîsh, he took me to his room, and did not cease the whole night from talking in a rhodomontade fashion, and saying, "I have such a correspondent in Turkistân, and such an agency in Hindûstân: and this paper is the title-deed of such a piece of ground, and for such a thing I have such a person as security." At one time he said, "I intend to go to Alexandria, as the climate is agreeable." At another, "No! for the western sea is boisterous; O Sâdî! I have one more journey before me: when that is accomplished I shall retire for the rest of my life and give up trading." I said, "What journey is that?" He replied, "I shall take Persian sulphur to China, for I have heard that it brings a prodigious price there; and thence I shall take China-ware to Greece, and Grecian brocade to India, and Indian steel to Aleppo, and mirrors of Aleppo to Yaman,[207] and striped cloth of Yaman to Persia, and after that I shall give up trading and sit at home in my shop." He continued for some time rambling in this strain until he had no power to utter more. He then said, "O Sâdî! do thou say something of what thou hast seen and heard." I replied, "Thou hast not left me a single subject to talk about."

[206] Literally, "saw"; but here one may translate it, "was in the habit of seeing."
[207] Arabia Felix.

VERSE.

Hast thou not heard what once a merchant cried,
  As in the desert from his beast he sank?
"The worldling's greedy eye is satisfied,
  Or by contentment or the grave-yard dank."

Story XXIII.

I have heard of a wealthy man who was as famous for his parsimony as Hātim Ṭāi for generosity. His outward estate was adorned with riches, but the baseness of his nature was so inherent in him that he would not have given a loaf to save a life, nor would have indulged the cat of Abū Hurairah[178] with a scrap, nor have cast a bone to the dog of the Companions of the Cave. In short, no one ever saw his mansion with the doors open, nor his table spread.

COUPLET.

No darwesh knew his viands save by smell,
Nor birds picked crumbs which from his table fell.

I have heard that he was voyaging to Egypt by the western sea with all the pride of Pharaoh, *according to the words of the Most High,* "*until his submersion arrived:*" All of a sudden an adverse wind sprang up round the vessel: as they have said,

COUPLET.

"Thy peevish mind all things must still displease.
  The ship not always finds a favouring breeze."

He raised his hands in prayer, and began to make unavailing lamentations. *God Most High has said,* "*When they embark in a ship, they pray to God.*"

COUPLET.

What will it avail the creature to stretch forth his hand
  in grief?
Raised in prayer to God in peril, but withheld from
  man's relief.[208]

STANZA.

Go, with thy silver and thy gold, provide
  Blessings to men; nor from thyself withhold
Enjoyment due; thus ever shall abide
  Thy house, its bricks of silver and of gold.[209]

They relate that he had poor relations in Egypt, who were enriched by the residue of his property, and who, at his death, rent their old garments, and cut out others of silk and stuffs of Damietta. During the same week, too, I saw one of them mounted on a fleet courser, with a fairy-faced youth running at his stirrup. I said to myself,

STANZA.

"Ah! could the dear defunct again
  Back to his kin and friends repair,
Worse than his death would be the pain
  Of restitution to his heir."

On the strength of a former acquaintance which existed between us, I pulled his sleeve and said,

COUPLET.

"Enjoy thy fortune, gentle sir! for he,
Luckless, amassed; th' enjoyment, left to thee."

---

[208] The literal translation of this impracticable couplet is—
"What avails the hand of entreaty to the needy creature.
  Who in the hour of prayer raises it to God, but at the time
    for liberality puts it under his armpit."

[209] The meaning of this is: Thou shalt obtain for thyself a heavenly dwelling, built, as it were, by the proper use of thy treasures in this world.

Story XXIV.

A strong fish fell into the net of a weak fisherman. He had not strength to secure it; the fish got the better of him, dragged the net from his hands, and escaped.

STANZA.

The slave went forth for water from the brook,
    The streamlet rose and bore the slave away.
Each time the net its prize of fishes took,
    But of the net the fish made prize to-day.

The other fishermen were vexed, and reproached him, saying, "Such a fish fell into thy net, and thou couldst not keep it!" He replied, "O brothers! what could I do? seeing that it was not my lucky day, and the fish had some days remaining."[210]

MAXIM.

A fisherman without luck cannot capture a fish in the Tigris; and unless his predestined time be come, a fish will not die on the dry land.

Story XXV.

One whose hands and feet had been cut off killed a millepede. A devout personage passed by and said, "Holy God! though it had a thousand feet, yet, when its time was come, it could not escape from one without either hands or feet."

---

[210] There is a play on the words here which cannot be well preserved in English. روزی *rúzi*, signifies "luck" as well as "days" [*i.e.* remnant of life].

DISTICHS.

When from behind speeds our last enemy,
Fate fetters us, how fleet soe'er we be.
And in that instant when comes up the foe,
'Tis vain to handle the Kaiānian bow.[211]

Story XXVI.

I saw a fat blockhead, with a gorgeous robe on his body, and an Arabian horse under him, and a turban of fine Egyptian linen on his head. Some one said, "O Sâdi! what thinkest thou of this splendid brocade on this animal who knows nothing?" I replied, "It is a villainous scrawl written in golden letters."

COUPLET.

He, among men, an ass appears to be,
Certes a very calf-like effigy.[212]

STANZA.

One cannot say this brute resembles man,
    Save by cloak, turban, outward garniture;
Go thou his goods, estates, possessions scan,
    Naught but his life is takeable, be sure.

STANZA.

Though one of birth illustrious should grow poor,
    This will his lofty station naught impair:
And though gold nails may stud his silver door,
    Think not a Jew can aught that's noble share.

---

[211] The Kaiānian is the second dynasty of Persian kings, of whom the first was Kaiḳubād or Darius the Mede. Archery is said to have reached perfection under these monarchs.

[212] There is a reference here to the Kur'ān, ch. vii. v. 148, "And the people of Moses, after his departure, took a corporeal calf, made of their ornaments, which lowed."

Story XXVII.

A thief said to a beggar, "Art thou not ashamed to hold out thy hand for the smallest particle of silver to every contemptible fellow?" He replied,

COUPLET.

"Better hold the hand for coin, though small,
Than lose, for one and half a dāng,[213] it all."

Story XXVIII.

They relate that an athlete had suffered so much from adverse fortune that he was reduced to despair, and bemoaned himself on account of his keen appetite and narrow means. He went to his father to complain, and asked his leave to set out on his travels, in order that by the strength of his arm he might succeed in grasping the skirt of his wishes.

COUPLET.

Merit and skill are weak while in the husk:
Aloes they cast on fire, and crush down musk.

The father said, "O son! put out of thy head this impracticable idea, and draw the feet of contentment under the skirt of security: as the wise have said, 'Riches are not to be gained by exertion; the best resource is to chagrin oneself less.'

COUPLET.

No one by strength of arm can fortune find:
'Tis labour lost—collyrium for the blind.

---

[213] A dāng is the sixth part of a dirham, or, according to some, the fourth part, and therefore equal to about one penny. M. Semelet remarks that this line shews that theft, in the time of Sâdi, was punished by amputation, if the thing stolen was worth one and a half dāng; I suppose, however, that this sum is used generally for any trifling value.

COUPLET.

Hast thou two hundred virtues on each hair?
With adverse fate thou still wilt badly fare.

COUPLET.

What can th' ill-starred athlete do? how thrive?
Can he, though strong, with stronger fortune strive?"

The son replied, "O father! the advantages of travel are manifold; in enlivening the mind, and acquiring advantages, and seeing wonderful things, and hearing marvels and in amusement, in passing through new countries, and in correspondence with friends, and in the acquisition of rank and courteous manners, and in the increase of wealth and profit, and as a means of obtaining companions, and making proof of different fortunes: as those who travel in the path of spirituality have said,

STANZA.

'Whilst thou art wedded to thy shop and home,
  O simpleton! a man thou ne'er wilt be;
Go blithely forth, and in the wide world roam,
  Ere thou roam'st from it to eternity.'"

The father answered, "O son! the advantage of travel in the manner thou hast mentioned is great; but it is secured to five kinds of persons. The first is the merchant, who, by the possession of riches and affluence, and active slaves, and enchanting damsels, and brave servants, enjoys all the luxuries of the world, being each day in a city, and each night at a halting-place, and each instant in an abode of pleasure.

STANZA.

In mountain-waste, or forest wild, the rich man is not strange;
  Where'er he goes his tent is pitched, and there his court is made.
But he who has not this world's gear must ever friendless range,
  Nor even in his fatherland will comfort find nor aid.

The second is the learned man, from whose sweetness of speech, and power of language, and stock of eloquence, wherever he goes, all hasten to serve him and do him honour.

STANZA.

The wise man's nature is like purest gold :
  Where'er he comes all know his value, prize his worth.
But men will, cheap as leathern money, hold
  The witless lord, save in the land that gave him birth.

The third is the beautiful person, being such that the heart[214] of persons of eminence inclines to friendship with him, and his society is regarded by them as a fortunate circumstance, and his service as a favour: as they have said: 'A little beauty is better than much wealth: a fair countenance is a salve for heart-sickness, and the key of closed doors.'

STANZA.

Let beauty travel where it will, it finds respectful greeting,
  Though its own parents, wrathfully, should drive it
    from its home.
One day, amid the Ḳur'ān's leaves, a peacock's feather meeting,
  I said, 'This place exceeds thy worth, thou dost it
    not become.'
'Peace!' it replied, 'for to each one who wears the charm of beauty,
  Go where he will, all him receive with favour as a
    duty.'

VERSE.

  When the son beauty has, and courtesy,
  Let him not care how cold his sire may be.

---

[214] M. Semelet recommends کُنَد *kunad* for کُنَند *kunand*, and Dr. Sprenger reads it; I do not, therefore, hesitate to adopt it in this translation.

He is a pearl, what if the shell be lost?
Who for a priceless[215] pearl will grudge the cost?

The fourth is he who possesses a sweet voice; who, with the throat of David, restrains the water from flowing, and arrests the bird in its flight; and, moreover, by means of this excellence, captivates the hearts of men, and spiritual persons eagerly desire his companionship.

COUPLET.

My ears attend his melody;
Who's this whose hands[216] *the lute-strings try?*

STANZA.

How winningly a soft and tender voice
   Comes to the ears of friends, whom th' early bowl
Makes blithe! in it, more than in looks, rejoice
   All hearts; these the sense gladden: that the soul.

The fifth is the artisan, who gains the means of support by the labour of his arm, so that his character is not jeoparded for bread: as the wise have said,

STANZA.

'If want from his own city should expel
   A cotton-carder, he'd not feel distress;
But if the king of Nimroz, ruined, fell
   From his high place, he'd slumber supperless.'

Qualities such as I have described are a means of consolation in travel, and a sweet cause of enjoyment; but one

---

[215] There is a very good equivoque here which cannot be repeated in English: يتيم *yatīm*, signifies "unique, precious," and also "orphan."

[216] For the حُسْنُ الْمَغَانِي *husn-u'l-magānī* in the second line, which is the common reading. Dr. Sprenger has the better (in my opinion) reading: جَسَّ الْمَغَانِي *jassa-u'l magānī*, "he handled the strings."

who has no share in all these will enter the world with vain expectations, and no one will hear his name again, or see any more trace of him.

STANZA.

He, whom t' afflict upsprings revolving fate
  Malevolent, is led by destiny
Against his will. The pigeon, who his mate
  Shall ne'er revisit, follows fate's decree
  Towards the net [in blind security]."

The son answered, "O father! how shall I act in opposition to the saying of the wise? who have pronounced that although a subsistence is allotted, yet it is on the condition of using the means of acquiring it; and though calamity is predestined, yet it is right to secure oneself against the portals by which it might have access.

STANZA.

Though, without doubt, fate will our want supply,
  Reason requires it be sought from home;
'Tis true that none will unpredestined die,
  Yet in a dragon's maw one should not come.

In my present condition I could encounter a furious elephant and contend with a devouring lion. My best course is to travel, for I am unable to endure my privations any longer.

STANZA.

Whene'er a man from home and country flies,
  All earth is his; he has no further care.
Each night the rich man to his palace hies:
  Where night descends, the poor man's home is there."

He spoke thus, and asking his father's blessing, took leave of him and set off, and at the time of his departure they heard him say,

COUPLET.

"The man of worth, whose fate is cross, will go
  Where men have never learned his name to know."

So he travelled on till he came to the brink of a stream, by the violence of which stone was dashed upon stone, and whose noise resounded to the distance of a parasang.[217]

COUPLET.

A stream so dread, not birds were safe amid its waters'
    roar;
The smallest of its waves would sweep a mill-stone from
    its shore.

There he saw a party of men who had each of them obtained a seat in a ferry-boat, for a small piece of gold, and whose baggage was ready packed. The young man's hand was closed from payment, but he loosened the tongue of compliment. In spite of all his supplication they rendered him no assistance, but said,

COUPLET.

"Thou canst not make thy strength of arm the want of
    gold supply;
And hast thou gold, thou needest not to threaten or
    defy."

The rude boatman turned from him with a laugh, and said,

COUPLET.

"Gold thou hast not; the passage o'er by force may not
    be won;
What is the strength of ten men here? bring thou the
    gold for one."

The young man was incensed at this sarcasm, and

---

[217] Chardin explains this word as سنگ فارسی *fàrs sang*, "Persian stone;" a word written by Herodotus and other Greek authors, Παρασαν/α, *parasanga:* "Il parait, par la signification du mot *Fàrs-seng*, qu'anciennement les lieues etaient marquées par de grandes et hautes pierres, tant dans l'Orient que dans l'Occident. On dit en latin, Ad primum vel secundum lapidem."

burned to revenge himself upon him. The boat had put off; he called out, "If thou wilt be content with this garment I am wearing, I will not refuse to give it." The boatman's avarice was roused; he put back the boat.

COUPLET.

The eyes of men, though sharp, are closed by avarice;
Greed will both bird and fish towards the net entice.

As soon as the young man's hand could reach the beard and collar of the boatman, he dragged him forward and knocked him down without mercy. His comrades[218] came out of the boat to help him, and meeting with the same rough treatment, turned their backs, finding it their best plan to make peace with him, and excuse him the passage-money.

DISTICHS.

Act thou forbearingly when discord's rife,
For gentleness will close the gates of strife.
When thou seest broils arise, use courtesy;
A sharp sword cuts not silk, though soft it be.
With honeyed words, good humour on thy side,
Thou, with a hair, an elephant mayst guide.

They fell at his feet, with excuses for their past conduct, and imprinted hypocritical kisses on his forehead and face, and brought him into the boat, and proceeded till they arrived at a pillar of a Grecian building which remained standing amid the waters. The boatman said, "The boat is in danger; let one of you, who is most courageous and valiant, and powerful, go to this pillar, and lay hold of the boat's hawser, that we may pass by

---

[218] Dr. Sprenger reads يارش آمدند *yārash āmadand*, M. Semelet يارش آمد *yārash āmad*. I must confess I prefer my own reading يارانش آمدند *yārānash āmadand*.

this building."[219] The young man, from the pride of valour which he felt, took no thought of his still smarting foe, and forbore to act in accordance with the saying of the wise, which they have uttered: "When thou hast wounded the heart of any one, even if thou shouldest subsequently do him a hundred favours, nevertheless deem not thyself safe from that one injury, for the shaft may have been extracted from the wound, yet the pang abide still in the heart."

COUPLET.

How truthfully to Khailtāsh, Yaktāsh[220] said;
Is thy foe hurt?—then live not free from dread.

STANZA.

Fancy not thyself safe, for thou shalt moan,
   Who hast another treated cruelly.
Against the castle-wall hurl not a stone,
   Lest from the walls a stone descend on thee.

He had no sooner twisted the hawser round his arm, and mounted the pillar, than the boatman twisted the rope from his hand, and urged on the boat. The athlete remained there helpless and astonished. For two days he endured his suffering and distress, and bore up against his hardships. On the third day sleep seized him by the collar, and plunged him in the water. After a night and a day[221] he was cast on the shore, with the breath of life

---

[219] Dr. Sprenger reads تا از عمارت عبور کنیم *tā az imārat ubūr kunīm*, which, on the whole, I prefer to the reading in my edition. M. Semelet translates, "afin que nous fassions la réparation." Gladwin renders, "that we may save the vessel"; and Ross, "till we can swing her head round," all which translations are without the vestige of a foundation in the original.

[220] Of these two Gentius says, "duo nobilissimi sunt athletæ quos celebrat thesaurus regius."

[221] شبانروز *shabānrūz*, exactly the Greek νυχθήμερον.

just remaining. He began to eat the leaves of trees, and to pull up the roots of grass, until he recovered his strength a little. He then set his face toward the woods, and went on till he arrived, thirsty and hungry, and powerless, at the brink of a well. He saw a party of persons, who had assembled round it, and who were getting a draught of water for a small payment. The young man had no coin, not even the smallest; he asked for water, they refused it; he extended the hand of violence, but succeeded not. He struck down several of them; the men made a general attack upon him, beat him unmercifully, and wounded him.

STANZA.

Gnats will an elephant o'ercome, if they
    Unite against their foe, so huge and grim.
And ants collected in one dense array,
    Though fierce the lion be, will vanquish him.

Urged by necessity, he followed a caravan, sick and wounded, and proceeded on. At night they arrived at a place which was perilous on account of robbers. He saw that a tremor pervaded the frames of the people of the caravan, and that they had made up their minds to be slain. He said, "Be not troubled, for I am one among you who will answer for fifty men, and the other braves will assist me." The men's hearts were encouraged by his vaunt, and they were glad of his company, and ministered to him food and water. The fire was blazing up in the young man's stomach, and the reins of endurance had slipped from his hands. He devoured some mouthfuls with excessive voracity, and swallowed some gulps of water, till the demon within him was appeased, and slumber overcame him, and he slept. There was, in the caravan, an old man of experience, acquainted with the world, who said, "O my friends! I am more afraid of this guard of yours than of the robbers: as they tell that an Arab had amassed a few dirhams: he could not sleep when alone in his house from dread of the Lūrīs.[222] He brought one of his friends to be with him that he might get rid of the terrors of solitude by the sight of him. The friend remained some nights in his company, but as soon as he found out where his dirhams were, he carried them off and went on his travels. The next morning they saw the Arab despoiled and lamenting. They said, 'What is the matter? has some robber carried off those dirhams of thine?' He replied, 'No! by Heaven, the guard has taken them.'

STANZA.

With a companion I ne'er felt secure
  Until I learned his inward qualities.
Wounds from a foeman's tooth are worse t' endure
  When he has shown himself in friendship's guise.

How know ye, O my friends! whether this young man, also, be not of the number of the robbers, and sent among us through stratagem, in order that, on a favourable opportunity, he may communicate with his friends? I, therefore, think it expedient to leave him asleep, and proceed on our journey." The people of the caravan approved of the old man's advice, and felt a dread of the athlete arise in their hearts. They packed up their goods, and left the young man sleeping. He did not discover this until the sun was shining on his shoulders; he then raised his head, and saw that the caravan had departed. After wandering about a long time, he could not find his way, and thirsty and hungry, he placed his face on the ground, and fixed his thoughts on destruction, and said,

---

[222] The Lūrīs are the people of Lūristān, a mountainous province of Persia, to the north-east of Khuzistān, and having Kūrdistān to the north. The inhabitants are notorious thieves.

COUPLET.

"Gone[223] are the yellow camels now: who will address me more?
The poor man has no comrade—no comrade but the poor.

COUPLET.

With the poor wanderer they will harshly deal,
Who ne'er experienced what the friendless feel."

He was uttering these words when a prince, who, in pursuit of a quarry, had got to a distance from his retinue, came and stood over him. He heard what he said; and looking on his form, saw that his external shape was comely, while his appearance betokened wretchedness. He asked him whence he was, and how he had come there? He related a portion of what had befallen him. The prince pitied him, bestowed on him a dress and gifts, and sent a confidential servant along with him to see him back to his own city. His father was glad to see him, and returned thanks for his safety. At night, he told his father what had befallen him; of the adventure of the boat, and of the injurious conduct of the boatman, and of the peasants, and of the treachery of the people of the caravan. The father said, "O son! did I not tell thee at the time of thy departure that the hands of the empty-handed, however brave they may be, are fettered, and their lion's claws broken.

COUPLET.

That needy gladiator said right well,
A grain of gold doth pounds[224] of strength excel."

The son said, "O father! undoubtedly, until thou

---

[223] The word زمم zumm, signifies "bridled," but in this place it refers to departure.

[224] Literally, "fifty mans," a weight which has been explained before.

endurest pain, thou wilt no treasure gain ; and while thou riskest not thy life, thou wilt not subdue thy foe ; and until thou scatterest abroad the seed, thou wilt not reap the harvest. Seest thou not, by a little matter of trouble which I have undergone, what an amount of treasure I have brought home; and by enduring the sting, what an abundance of honey I have obtained ?"

COUPLET.

Though more than fate supplies we ne'er can gain,
Yet must we strive that portion to obtain.

COUPLET.

From the ravening monster's[225] jaw, should the diver pause and gasp,
He'd never hold the precious pearl, the bright pearl, in his grasp.

APOPHTHEGM.

The lower mill-stone revolves not, and hence, of necessity, supports the greater burthen.

STANZA.

On what would savage lions feed ? if they
  In their deep dens abode. The hawk would win
Small sustenance did it ne'er seek its prey.
  And, like a spider's, will thy limbs grow thin,
  If thine own house alone thou huntest in.

The father said, "O son ! this time heaven has befriended thee, and thy good fortune has been thy guide, so that thy rose has come forth from the thorn, and the thorn from thy foot ; and, accordingly, one who possessed wealth, found thee out and enriched thee, and he had compassion on thee, and repaired thy broken fortunes, inquiring kindly into them ; and such an occurrence is

---

[225] Gladwin translates نهنگ *nihang*, "crocodile," but the danger to the pearl-diver would rather be from sharks.

rare, and one cannot govern one's conduct by events of rare occurrence. Beware lest thou be led by this greediness to hover a second time round this snare.

COUPLET.
The hunter does not always win the prey,
Perchance a tiger may him rend one day.

As, once a king of Persia had a very precious stone in a ring. On a certain occasion he went out with some of his favourite courtiers, to amuse himself, to the mosque near Shīrāz, called Muṣallā, and commanded that they should suspend the ring over the dome of Āzād, saying that the ring should be the property of him who could send an arrow through it. It befell that four hundred archers, who plyed their bows in his service, shot at the ring. All of them missed. But a stripling, at play, was shooting arrows at random from a monastery, when the morning breeze carried his shaft through the circle of the ring. They bestowed the ring upon him, and loaded him with gifts beyond calculation. The boy, after this, burned his bow and arrows. They asked him why he did so. He replied, 'That my first glory may remain unchanged.'

STANZA.
The sage whose bright mind mirrors truth,
May sometimes wander wide of it:
While, by mistake, the simple youth,
Will, with his shaft, the target hit."

STORY XXIX.

I have heard of a darwesh who had taken up his abode in a cave, and had closed the door before him on the world; while, in the eye of his lofty independence, kings and rich men had lost consideration.

STANZA.

Who, on himself, the door of begging opes,
   Will, to his death, in want remain.
   Quit greed, and as a monarch reign,
For proud his station who for nothing hopes.

One of the neighbouring princes signified to him that he relied on the condescension of his courteous character, that he would come and partake of his bread and salt. The Shekh consented, as to accept an invitation is enjoined by the authority of the Prophet. The next day the king went to apologize for the trouble[226] he had given him. The devotee arose and embraced the king, and treated him kindly. When the king was gone, one of the companions of the Shekh asked him, saying, "It is unusual with thee to display such tokens of regard to a king: what hidden meaning is there in this?" He replied, "Hast thou not heard that they have said,

COUPLET.

"If at another's table one has sat,
   'Tis right, in turn, to rise and on him wait."

DISTICHS.

The ear may never through one's life
Hear sound of tabor, lute, or fife:
The eye abstain from floral show:
The brain the rose's[227] scent not know:
Though pillowed not on down, the head
May on a stone find sleep instead:
And when our arms no fair one hold,
On our own breast we may them fold.
But this vile belly, base and dull,
Will never rest unless 'tis full.

---

[226] Literally, "for excusing his service (*i.e.* lack of service) to him."

[227] I omit the Narcissus, *metri causâ*.

CHAPTER IV.

ON THE ADVANTAGES OF TACITURNITY.

Story I.

I said to one of my friends, "I have chosen to abstain from speaking, for this reason, because, on the majority of occasions, it happens that in speech there is evil as well as good, and the eye of enemies notes only the evil." He replied, "O brother! he is the best enemy[228] who does not observe our good qualities."

COUPLET.

No fault's like virtue to the foeman's eye,
Who, e'en in Sâdi's[229] self, would thorns descry.

COUPLET.

Ne'er the malignant pass a good man by,
But slander him with hateful villainy.

COUPLET.

The feeble-visioned mole perchance may scorn
The sun's bright fount, that doth the world adorn.

Story II.

A merchant met with the loss of a thousand dinârs, and said to his son, "Thou must not tell any one of this

---

[228] Malice is comparatively quiet as long as the object of its hate is but an ordinary character. To be illustrious, provokes its bitterest wrath.

[229] Literally, "A rose is Sâdi, but in the eyes of enemies a thorn."

matter." The son replied, "O father! it is thy command; I will not tell; acquaint me, however, with the advantage to be derived from keeping the affair secret." The father answered, "In order that we may not have two misfortunes to encounter—first, the loss of our money; and secondly, the malignant rejoicings of our neighbours."

COUPLET.

Do not to foes thy sufferings impart,
Lest, while they seem to grieve, they joy at heart.[230]

Story III.

An intelligent young man, who possessed an ample stock of admirable accomplishments and a rare intellect, notwithstanding, uttered not a word whenever he was seated in the company of the wise. At length, his father said, "O son! why dost not thou also say somewhat of that thou knowest?" He replied, "I fear lest they should ask me something of which I am ignorant, and I should bring on myself disgrace."

STANZA.

One day a Ṣūfī (hast thou heard it told?)
  By chance was hammering nails into his shoe:
Then of his sleeve an officer caught hold,
  And said, "Come thou! and shoe my charger too!"

COUPLET.

Art silent? none can meddle with thee. When
Thou once hast spoken, thou must prove it then.

Story IV.

A learned man of high reputation had a dispute with a heretic, and did not get the better of him in argument.

---

[230] Literally, "While they repeat the deprecatory formula, There is no power or strength but in God."

He cast away his shield, and took to flight.[231] Some one said to him, "Hadst thou, notwithstanding all thy learning and address, and eminent qualities and sagacity, no argument left with which to combat an infidel?" He replied, "My knowledge is the Ḳur'ān, and the traditions of the Prophet and the doctrines of the fathers; and he believes not in these things, and will not attend to them; and in what shall I be benefited by listening to his impieties?"

COUPLET.

To those who doctrine and Ḳur'ān deny,
To answer nothing is the best reply.

Story V.

The physician Galen, on seeing a fool lay hold of the collar of a learned man and disgrace him, said, "Had this been a wise man, his dealings with a fool would not have reached this point."

DISTICHS.

The wise will not in hate or strife engage;
Nor with a simpleton contends the sage.
When fools, in savage words, their thoughts express,
The wise will soothe them by their gentleness.
Two men of judgment will not break a hair,
Thus 'twixt the headlong and the mild 'twill fare.
But should the band that parts them be a chain,
Two fools would quickly break its links in twain.

Story VI.

Saḥbān Wāil[232] has been regarded as unrivalled in eloquence, inasmuch as he could speak a whole year before an assembly without ever being guilty of repeti-

---

[231] Metaphorical expressions for giving up the dispute.
[232] Name of a celebrated Arabian poet.

tion; and should the same idea recur, he would express it in different language. And this is one of the accomplishments requisite for courtiers.

DISTICHS.

Thy speech may be attractive, just, and sweet,
Worthy to be approved by judgment nice;
But when once spoken, ne'er the same repeat,
For once to swallow sweetmeats will suffice.

Story VII.

I heard a sage say, "No one avows his ignorance but the man, who, while another is speaking, and has not yet finished, commences speaking himself."

DISTICHS.

Each several theme beginning has and end,
Therefore weave not discourse within discourse.
A man of judgment, wit, and sense, my friend!
Speaks not until thy words have had their course.

Story VIII.

Some of the servants of Sulṭān Maḥmūd asked Ḥasan Maimandī,[233] "What did the Sulṭān say to thee to-day about a certain affair?" He replied, "It will not have been concealed from you too?"[234] They answered,

---

[233] Khwājah Aḥmad-bin Ḥasan, called Maimandī, from the town of Maimand where he was born, was the vazīr of Sulṭān Maḥmūd of Ghaznī. His enemies, and particularly Altantush, the General of Maḥmūd's forces, endeavoured to ruin him with the king, but were constantly baffled through the Queen's influence. Fīrdausī, the author of the Shāh-nāmah, was introduced to the Sulṭān by Ḥasan.

[234] Dr. Sprenger reads نباشد na bāshad for my نمانَد namānad, and ظهير سرير سلطنتي و مشير تدبير مملكت ẓahīr-i sarīr-i sulṭānatī wa mushīr-i tadbīr-i mamlakat for my دستور مملكت dastūr-i mamlakat.

"Thou art the Prime Minister of the State; the Sultān does not think of telling us what he tells thee." Hasan replied, "And he does this in the confidence that I will not repeat it. Wherefore, then, do ye ask me?"

COUPLET.

Not all they know will men of prudence tell;
Nor with kings' secrets sport, and life as well.

Story IX.

I was hesitating about a bargain for a house when a Jew said to me, "I am one of the old inhabitants of this quarter. Inquire of me the intrinsic value of the house, and purchase it, for it has not a fault." I replied, "None, except that thou livest near it."

STANZA.

A house with such a neighbour as thou art
  Were worth ten silver dirhams—those, too, bad.
Yet hope we—shouldst thou from this life depart,
  A thousand for it then might well be had.

Story X.

A poet went to the chief of a band of robbers and recited a panegyric upon him. He commanded them to strip off his clothes and turn him out of the village. The dogs, too, attacked him in the rear. He wanted to take up a stone, but the ground was frozen. Unable to do anything, he said, "What a villainous set are these, who have untied their dogs and tied up the stones." The chieftain heard this from a window, and said with a laugh, "Philosopher! ask a boon of me." He replied, "If thou wilt condescend to make me a present, bestow on me my own coat."

COUPLET.

From some a man might favours hope—from thee
We hope for nothing but immunity.

HEMISTICH.

We feel thy kindness that thou lett'st us go.

The robber chief had compassion on him. He gave him back his coat, and bestowed on him a fur cloak in addition, and further presented him with some dirhams.

Story XI.

An astrologer, on entering his own house, found a man sitting with his wife. He abused and reviled him, and a disturbance arose. A sagacious person, being informed of this, said,

COUPLET.

"Canst thou tell what goes on above the sky,
And not th' interior of thy house descry?"

Story XII.

A preacher, who had a shocking voice, fancied it was very agreeable, and employed it in shouting to no purpose. *The croaking of the raven* [you would say] was in his modulations; and that that verse was intended for him, "*Verily the most detestable of sounds is the voice of an ass.*"

COUPLET.

*Preacher Abū'l-fawāris brays—from far
Persian Iṣṭakhar trembles at the jar.*[235]

The people of the town, out of respect to the office he held, put up with the infliction, and did not think it right to annoy him: till at length, a preacher of that district, who had a secret spite against him, came to see him, and said, "I have seen a dream; I hope it will turn out well." The other asked, "What hast thou seen?" The visitor

---

[235] M. Semelet thinks this couplet a quotation. He does not, however, nor does any other author that I have seen, explain who Abū'l-fawāris [*lit.*, "father of the horsemen"] is.

answered, "I beheld that thy voice was pleasant, and that people were delighted with thy discourse." The preacher reflected a little on this, and said, "What a fortunate dream it is that thou hast seen, by which thou hast acquainted me with my failings. I now understand that I have an unpleasant voice, and that people are distressed by my delivery. I vow amendment, and, in future, will never read except in a low voice."

STANZA.

I wearied of my friend's society,
  Who my bad qualities as virtues shews;
Who, in my failings, can perfection see,
  And calls my thorns the jasmine and the rose.
Give me the pert and watchful enemy,
  Who will my faults to me with zest disclose.

Story XIII.

A person was performing gratis the office of summoner to prayer in the mosque of Sanjāriyah,[236] in a voice which disgusted those who heard him. The patron of the mosque was a prince who was just and amiable. He did not wish to pain the crier, and said, "O sir! there are Mūazzins attached to this mosque to whom the office has descended from of old, each of whom has an allowance of five dināres, and I will give thee ten to go to another place." This was agreed upon, and he departed. After

---

[236] This mosque was built by Sulṭān Sanjār Saljūkī, sixth Sulṭān of the Saljūks, who was the son of Malik Shāh, and reigned over Persia and Khurāsān. He performed many exploits, and was called the second Alexander. As a mark of respect, prayers were read in his name in the mosques for a year after his decease. The Saljūks were originally Turkumāns, and entered Trans-oxiana A.H. 375. Sulṭān Sanjār succeeded his brother Muḥammad on the throne, A.H. 501.

some time he returned to the prince and said, "O my lord! thou didst me injustice in sending me from this place for ten dīnārs. In the place whence I have come they offered me twenty dīnārs to go somewhere else, and I will not accept it." The prince laughed and said, "Take care not to accept it, for they will consent to give thee even fifty dīnārs."

COUPLET.

No mattock can the clay remove from off the granite stone,
So well as thy discordant voice can make the spirit moan.

Story XIV.

A man with a harsh voice was reading the Ḳur'ān in a loud tone. A sage passed by and asked, "What is thy monthly stipend?" He replied, "Nothing." "Wherefore, then," asked the sage, "dost thou give thyself this trouble?" He replied, "I read for the sake of God." "Then," said the sage, "for God's sake! read not."

COUPLET.

If in this fashion the Ḳur'ān you read,
You'll mar the loveliness of Islām's creed.

CHAPTER V.

ON LOVE AND YOUTH.

Story I.

They asked Hasan Maimandī, "How is it that, although Sulṭān Mahmūd has so many handsome slaves, every one of whom is the wonder of the world, and the marvel of the age, he has not such a regard or affection for any one as for Ayāz,[237] who is not remarkable for beauty?" He replied, "Whatever pleases the heart appears fair to the eye."

DISTICHS.

The man for whom the Sulṭān shews esteem,
Though bad in every act, will virtuous seem.
But whom the monarch pleases to reject,
None of his retinue will e'er affect.

STANZA.

When with antipathy we eye a man,
  We see in Joseph's beauty, want of grace:
And, prepossessed, should we a demon scan,
  He'd seem a cherub with an angel's face.

Story II.

I remember that one night a dear friend of mine entered my door, and I rose from my seat with such impatience [to receive him] that I put out my lamp with my sleeve.

---

[237] Gladwin writes this name Iyaz, and I have followed him in my Vocabulary; but with Semelet, Ross, and Richardson on the other side, I feel bound to adopt the spelling given above.

VERSES.

By night a spectre came, and with its form lit up the gloom;
Methought it well would suit me for a guide throughout the
    night.[238]
" Hail!" I exclaimed, " Well art thou come! for thee is
    ample room;
I love thee, for the darkness flies before thy radiance bright."

COUPLET.

I said, astonished at my destiny,
" Whence has this happy fortune come to me?"

He sate down and began to remonstrate with me, saying, " Why, at the moment that thou sawest me, didst thou extinguish the lamp?" I replied, " I imagined that the sun had entered; and the witty have said,

STANZA.

' If one obscure the lamp with presence vile,
    Arise and him before th' assembly smite:
But, if he have sweet lips and honeyed smile,[239]
    Seize thou his sleeve, and then put out the light.' "

STORY III.

A person had not seen his friend for a long interval. At last he met him and said, " Where wert thou? for I longed after thee." He replied, " Better longing than loathing."

---

[238] These three lines are not in Ross, Gladwin or Semelet. I inserted them in my edition, and am now glad to find my judgment confirmed by Dr. Sprenger, in whose edition they are likewise to be found, with some trifling difference of reading.

[239] They would be of no use in his radiant presence, which of itself would dispel the darkness.

COUPLET.

Gay idol of my soul! late comest thou!
Not soon will I release thy garment now.

VERSE.

'Tis better that our friend we seldom see,
Than to behold him to satiety.[240]

SENTIMENT.

When a fair one comes attended by companions, she comes only to torment us; because, in that case, there must arise the jealousy and discord of rivals.

COUPLET.

Comest thou attended, then thou comest me only to distress;
Thou comest truly to make war, though peace thy looks express.

STANZA.

But for an instant should my friend prefer
To be with others, envy would me slay.
"Sádi!" he smiling cried, "Would this deter
Me this assembly's beacon? what, I say,
Imports it that in me moths quench life's ray!"

Story IV.

I remember that, in former days, I and a friend of mine were so much associated together that we were like two kernels in one almond. All at once I happened to find it requisite to take a journey. When, after some time, I returned, he began to reproach me for not sending a messenger to him during such an interval. I replied, "I was unwilling that the eyes of the messenger should be brightened by thy beauty, while I remained excluded."

---

[240] I prefer the reading بی بی to that of کم *kam* in my edition, which, however, if read, must be taken with بسر *ser*.

STANZA.

Friend of my youth! cease now me to reprove;
Thy love not steel could make me e'er repent.
That one should gaze his fill on thee does move
My envy, yet my heart would soon relent—
For seeing thee could ne'er his sight content.

Story V.

They shut up a parrot in a cage with a crow. The parrot was distressed at the ugly appearance of the other, and said, "What hateful form is this, and detested shape, and accursed face, and unpolished manners? *O crow of the desert! would that between me and thee were the space 'twixt east and west!*"

STANZA.

Should one at dawn arising thy face see,
'Twould change to twilight gloom that morning's mirth.
Such wretch as thou art should thy comrade be,
But where could such a one be found on earth!

But still more strangely the crow, too, was harassed to death by the society of the parrot, and was utterly chagrined by it. Reciting the deprecatory formula, "There is no power nor strength but in God,"[211] it complained of its fate, and, rubbing one upon the other the hands of vexation,[212] it said, "What evil fate is this, and unlucky destiny, and fickleness of fortune! It would have been commensurate with my deserts to have walked proudly along with another crow on the wall of a garden.

---

[211] This means, "There is no striving against fate." "Nisi Dominus frustra." See Kānūn-i Islām, p. 335, Gloss., 66.

[212] The only meanings given for تغابن *taghābun* in the Dictionary are, "Defrauding one another." "Neglecting, erring, straying." None of these can we apply here.

COUPLET.

'Twill for a prison to the good suffice,
To herd them with the worthless sons of vice.

What crime have I committed in punishment for which my fate has involved me in such a calamity, and imprisoned me with a conceited fool like this, at once worthless and fatuous?"

STANZA.

All would that wall with loathing fly
Which bore impressed thy effigy:
And if thy lot in Eden fell,
All others would make choice of Hell.

I have brought this example to show that, how strong soever the disgust a wise man may feel for a fool, a fool regards with a hundred times more aversion a wise man.

COUPLETS.

A pious man, 'mid dance and song, was seated with the gay;
One of Balkh's beauties saw him there, and marked the mirth decay:
"Do we, then, weary thee?" he said, "at least, uncloud thy brow;
For we, too, feel thy presence here is bitterness enow.

QUATRAIN.

This social band like roses is and lilies joined in one,
And 'mid them thou, a withered stick, upspringest all alone;
Like winter's cruel cold art thou, or like an adverse blast,—
Thou sittest there like fallen snow, ice-bound and frozen fast."

Story VI.

I had a companion with whom I had for many years travelled, and with whom I had partaken of bread and salt, and the rights of friendship were established between us without reserve. Afterwards, on account of some trifling advantage, he suffered me to be displeased, and our friendship was broken off. Yet, notwithstanding all this, there was a feeling of attachment existing on both sides; in accordance with which I heard that he one day repeated, in an assembly, these two couplets, taken from my works:—

STANZA.

"When my soul's idol to me comes with laughter arch yet kind,
She sprinkles salt upon my wound, and opes afresh the sore;
O would that I could fondly grasp her tresses unconfined!
As the skirt of the munificent is caught at by the poor."

A party of friends applauded the sentiment, not so much on account of the beauty of the verses as by reason of their own kind feeling. He, too, went beyond all of them in his eulogies, and expressed his regret for the extinction of our former intimacy, and confessed his fault. I saw that he, too, was eager for a renewal of our friendship. I sent him these verses, and effected our reconciliation.

STANZA.

Were we not plighted to fidelity?
  Yet thou wert harsh and didst thyself estrange.
When I left all and fixed my thoughts on thee,
  I knew not that so soon thou wouldest change!
Yet still, would'st thou make peace, return to me,
And then thou wilt more loved, more honoured, be.

Story VII.

A man had a beautiful wife, who died, and his wife's mother, a decrepit old woman, on account of the marriage-settlement,[213] took up her abode, and fixed herself in his house. The man was vexed to death by her propinquity, yet he did not see how to get rid of her by reason of the settlement. Some of his friends came to inquire after him, and one of them said, "How dost thou bear the loss of thy beloved one?" He replied, "The not seeing my wife is not so intolerable to me as the seeing her mother."

DISTICHS.

The tree has lost its roses, but retains
Its thorn. The treasure's gone, the snake[244] remains.
'Tis better on the lance-point fixed to see
One's eye, than to behold an enemy.
'Tis well a thousand friendships to erase
Could we thereby avoid our foeman's face.

Story VIII.

I remember that in my youth I was passing along a street when I beheld a moon-faced beauty. The season was that of the month July, when the fierce heat dried up the moisture of the mouth, and the scorching wind consumed the marrow of the bones. Through the weakness of human nature I was unable to support the power of the sun, and involuntarily took shelter under the shade of a wall, waiting to see if any one would relieve me from the pain I suffered, owing to the ardour of the sun's rays,

---

[213] As he could not pay what he had covenanted to pay, when he married, his wife's relations indemnified themselves by saddling him with the old lady, his wife's mother.

[244] It is a popular Oriental notion that treasures are guarded by serpents.

and cool my flame with water. All of a sudden, from the dark portico of a house, I beheld a bright form appear, of such beauty that the tongue of eloquence would fail in narrating her charms. She came forth as morn succeeding a dark night, or as the waters of life issuing from the gloom. She held in her hand a cup of snow-water, in which she had mixed sugar and the juice of the grape. I know not whether she had perfumed it with her own roses, or distilled into it some drops from the bloom of her countenance. In short, I took the cup from her fair hand, and drained its contents, and received new life. *" The thirst of my heart cannot be slaked with a drop of water, nor if I should drink rivers would it be lessened."*

STANZA.

Most blest that happy one whose gaze intense
    Rests on such face at each successive morn;
The drunk with wine at midnight may his sense
    Regain; but not till the last day shall dawn
    Will love's intoxication reach its bourne.

STORY IX.

Once, in the caravan of Hijāz, a darwesh accompanied us. One of the Arab chiefs had bestowed on him a hundred dīnārs, for the support of his family. All of a sudden the robbers of the tribe Khafāchah attacked the caravan, and spoiled it of everything. The merchants began to weep and lament, and pour forth unavailing complaints.

COUPLET

Thou mayest complain, or cry, Alack!
The thieves the gold will not give back.

But that darwesh, in his tattered garb, retained his composure, and his manner underwent no change. I said, "Perhaps they have not taken thy money?" He replied, "Yes! they have taken it. However, I had not such an attachment for that money[215] that I should break my heart at losing it."

COUPLET.

Thy heart from loving thing or person guard;
For to recall affection is most hard.

I said, "What thou hast uttered is à-propos of my condition; for in my youth I had formed a friendship with a young man, and entertained a sincere attachment for him to that degree that his beauty was the point of adoration of my eyes, and my intimacy with him as it were the interest on the capital of life.

STANZA.

It may be angels do not; man I trow
Ne'er did his beauty equal on this earth.
By friendship's self friends are forbidden now,
For after him his like shall ne'er find birth.

Suddenly the foot of his existence went down into the clay of death, and the smoke of separation arose from his family.[216] I watched for days at the head of his grave, and this is one of the many things which I uttered touching his loss:—

STANZA.

Death like a thorn transfixed thy foot. Ah! then,
Would that fate's cruel sword me too had slain;
Then I'd ne'er missed thee from thy fellow-men.
Thou on whose dust my head is laid—in vain!
Dust be on it! [thou ne'er shalt breathe again].

---

[215] The darwesh had only just got it as a present, and I imagine his words partly imply that he had not had time to grow fond of it.

[216] There is a play on words here which it is altogether impossible to retain in English. دُود *dūd*, "smoke," also signifies "anguish;" and the word for "family" in Persian, دودمان *dūdmān*, strongly resembles it.

STANZA.

He who, before he slept or took repose,
  Did roses and the jasmine round him fling;
Revolving time has shed his beauty's rose,
  While from his ashes now the thorns upspring.

After separation from him, I made a determination and a steadfast vow that, for the remainder of my life, I would fold up the carpet of desire and abstain from social intercourse.

STANZA.

Pleasant were the gains[217] of ocean, were there of the
    waves no fear;
Pleasant with the rose to dwell, were the thorn not lurking
    there;
Peacock-like I walked exulting in love's garden yester-
    night;
Snake-like now I writhe in anguish—she no more will
    glad my sight."

Story X.

They told to one of the Arabian kings the story of Laila and Majnūn, and of the insanity which happened to him, so that, although possessed of high qualities and perfect eloquence, he betook himself to the desert and abandoned the reins of choice. After commanding them to bring him into his presence, the king began to rebuke him, saying, "What defect hast thou seen in the nobleness of man's nature that thou hast taken up the habits of an animal, and bidden adieu to the happiness of human society?" Majnūn wept and said,

VERSE.

" *Oft have my friends reproached me for my love:*
  The day will come they'll see her and approve.

[217] That is, by traffic in ships.

STANZA.

Would that those who seek to blame me
　Could thy face, O fairest! see;
Theirs would then the loss and shame be:
　While amazed, intent on thee,
They would wound their hands while they
　Careless with the orange[248] play:

That the truth of the reality might testify to the appearance I claim for her!" The king was inspired with a desire to behold her beauty, in order to know what sort of person it was who was the cause of such mischief. He commanded, and they sought for her, and, searching through the Arab families, found her, and brought her before the king, in the court of the royal pavilion. The king surveyed her countenance, and beheld a person of a dark complexion and weak form. She appeared to him so contemptible that he thought the meanest of the servants of his ḥaram superior to her in beauty and grace. Majnūn acutely discerned his thoughts and said, "O king! it is requisite to survey the beauty of Lailā from the window of the eye of Majnūn, in order that the mystery of the spectacle may be revealed to you."

---

[248] I have amplified these lines a little. The allusion is to the story of Joseph and Zulaikhā, the wife of Potiphar. In the 12th chapter of the Ḳur'ān we read, "And certain women said publicly in the city, 'The nobleman's wife asked her servant to lie with her; he hath inflamed her breast with his love, and we perceive her to be in a manifest error.' And when she heard of this subtle behaviour she sent unto them, and prepared a banquet for them, and she gave to each of them a knife; and she said unto Joseph, 'Come forth unto them.' And when they saw him, they praised him greatly; and they cut their own hands, and said, 'This is not a mortal,'" etc.

DISTICHS.

Unmoved with pity thou me hear'st complain;
I need a comrade who can share my pain:
The livelong day I'd then my woes recite;
Wood with wood joined will ever burn more bright.

VERSE.

" *What passed within my hearing of the grove,*
  O forest leaves! did ye but learn,
Ye'd mourn with me. My friends! tell him whom love
  Has spared, I would he did but burn
  With lover's flames; he'd then my grief discern."

VERSE.

Scars may be laughed at by the sound.
  But to a fellow-sufferer reveal
Thy anguish. Of the hornet's wound
  What reck they who did never feel
Its sting? Till fortune shall bring round
  Thy woes to thee, they will but seem
  The weak illusions of a dream.
Do not my sufferings confound
  With those of others. Canst thou deem
One holding salt[249] can tell the pain of him
Who has salt rubbed upon his wounded limb?

STORY XI.

(IN VERSE.)

A gallant youth there was and fair
Pledged to a maid beyond compare;
They on the sea, as poets tell,
Together in a whirlpool fell.

---

[249] This is a favourite comparison of Oriental poets. Rubbing salt on a wound is a proverbial expression with them.

The boatman came the youth to save—
To snatch him from his watery grave:
But, 'mid those billows of despair,
He cried, " My love ! my love is there !
Save her, oh save ! " he said, and died ;
But with his parting breath he cried,
" Not from that wretch love's story hear
Who love forgets when peril's near."
Together thus these lovers died.
Be told by him who love has tried ;
For Sādī knows each whim and freak
Of love,—as well its ways can speak
As Baghdād's dwellers Arabic.
Hast thou a mistress ? her then prize,
And on all others close thine eyes.
Could Majnūn and his Laila back return,
They might love's story from this volume learn.

CHAPTER VI.

ON DECREPITUDE AND OLD AGE.

Story I.

I was engaged in a dispute with some learned men in the principal mosque of Damascus. Suddenly a young man entered the door, and said, " Is there any one among you who knows the Persian language?" They pointed to me. I said, " Is all well?"[250] He replied, "An old man, of a hundred and fifty years of age, is in the agonies of death, and says something to me in Persian, which is not intelligible to me. If thou wouldest be so kind as to trouble thyself so far as to step with me thou wilt be rewarded.[251] It may be that he wants to make his will." When I reached his pillow, he said this,

---

[250] M. Semelet translates "Cela est vrai," in which he appears to me to mistake the sense altogether. The expression خير است *khair ast*, corresponds to our " What is the matter?" but I have translated it literally. A similar expression occurs in the 2nd book of Kings, chapter v. verse 21, " He lighted down from the chariot to meet him, and said, 'Is all well?'" Of M. Semelet's MSS., one reads خبر چیست *khabar chīst*; and another, چه خدمت است *chih khidmat ast*, " What is the news?" and, " What service can I do you?"

[251] That is, by God.

STANZA.

"Methought a few short moments I would spend
   As my soul wished; alas! I gasp for air.
  At the rich board, where all life's dainties blend,
   I sate me down—partook a moment there,
    When, ah! they bade me leave the scarcely tasted
     fare."

I repeated the meaning of these words to the Damascenes in Arabic. They marvelled at his having lived so long, and yet grieving for worldly life. I said to him, "How dost thou find thyself under present circumstances?" He replied, "What shall I say?"

STANZA.

"Hast thou ne'er marked his agony,
   Out from whose jaw a tooth is wrenched?
  Then think what must his feelings be,
   Whose life, dear life, is being quenched!"

I said, "Dismiss from thy mind the idea of death, and let not thine imagination conquer thy nature; for the philosophers have said, 'Though the constitution may be vigorous, we are not to rely upon it as gifted with perpetuity, and, though a disease may be terrible, it furnishes no positive proof of a fatal termination.' If thou wilt give us leave, we will send for a physician, in order that he may use remedies for thy recovery." He replied, "Alas!

DISTICHS.

The master's bent on garnishing
His house, which, sapped, is falling in;
The skilful leech, in mute despair,
Together smites his hands as there
He marks, like broken potsherd, lie
The poor old man outstretched to die.

The old man groans in parting pain;
His wife the sandal[252] rubs in vain:
But once unpoise our nature frail,
Nor cure nor amulet avail."

Story II.

An old man, descanting about himself, said, "I had espoused a young maiden, and adorned my room with flowers, and, sitting alone with her, fastened on her my eyes and my heart. Through long nights I never slept, but passed the time in narrating witty jests and amusing stories, in order to dispel her coyness, and to make her attached to me. Among other things, I said to her one night, 'Thy lofty fate befriended thee, and the eye of thy happy destiny was open, that thou hast fallen into the arms of an old man, prudent and acquainted with the world; one who has tasted the vicissitudes of fortune, and experienced good and evil; who knows what is required in social intercourse, and performs all the conditions of friendship, and who is kind and considerate, cheerful and gentle in his language.

DISTICHS.

To win thy heart shall be my lot;
Though thou griev'st me, I'll grieve thee not.
Is sugar, parrot-like, thy food:
Be thou with my life's sweetness wooed.

Thou hast not fallen a prey to a young man, self-conceited and rude, headstrong and fickle, who each moment takes

---

[252] Preparations of sandal-wood are used by Orientals for rubbing the body, and are thought to be cooling and restorative. Thus in the *Prem Sāgar*, p. 85, l. 29, of my translation, "Thou hast removed my weariness; having met me, thou hast given to me cool sandal."

a new whim, and changes his opinion every instant, and sleeps every night in a different place, and gets a new mistress every day.

STANZA.

Young men are gay and fair to see,
But wanting in fidelity.
Who can the bulbul true suppose,
That, singing, flits from rose to rose?

But the class of old men pass their life according to the dictates of reason; not in those things which ignorant youth wishes for.

COUPLET.

A better than thyself seek out and prize;
For with one like thyself time vainly flies.'"

The old man said, "I spoke much more after this fashion, and I imagined I had got possession of her heart, and secured her affections. Suddenly she heaved a cold sigh from a heart full of melancholy, and said, 'All the words that thou hast uttered do not weigh so much in the balance of my reason as that one word which I heard from my nurse, "That to have her side pierced with an arrow was better for a young woman, than to have an old husband."' In short, it was not possible for us to agree, and a separation was decided upon. The period of probation after divorce[253] elapsed. They united her in the nuptial bands with a youth irascible and cross-looking, destitute of fortune, and on the watch for a pretext to quarrel. She had to endure harshness and violence, and to submit to annoyance and vexation, and, nevertheless,

---

[253] The period for which a woman must wait before marrying again, after her husband's death, is four months and ten days. After divorce, she must wait three menstrual periods. This is to see if she be pregnant by her former husband. *Vide* Ḳānūn-i Islām, p. 117; Ḳur'ān, ch. ii. ver. 229, 235.

she returned thanks to heaven for her blessings, saying, 'Praise be to God! that I have escaped from that excruciating torment and arrived at this blissful condition.

COUPLET.

Spite of thy passion and thy frowning brow,
I'll bear thy airs, for beautiful art thou!

STANZA.

Better with thee be tortured and consume,
   Than with another Eden's bowers possess:
More sweet from beauty's mouth the onion's fume,
   Than roses from the hand of ugliness.'"

Story III.

In the country of Diyārbakr,[254] I was the guest of an old man, who possessed great riches, and a handsome son. One night he told me that in his whole life he had never had but this one son. There was a tree, he said, in that valley to which pilgrimages were made, and whither persons resorted to pray for what they needed; and that he, too, had wept for many nights, at the foot of that tree, in prayer to God, who had bestowed on him this son. I heard his son whisper softly to his companions, "Would that I knew where that tree is, that I might pray there for my father's death!"

STANZA.

Long years, successive years have gone,
  Since thou didst visit at thy father's grave;
   What filial actions hast thou done,
That from thy son thou should'st like worship crave?

Story IV.

One day, in the pride of my youth, I had travelled hard, and at night stopped, much fatigued, at the foot

---

[254] Anciently called Mesopotamia.

of a mountain. An infirm old man, who followed the caravan, said to me, "Arise! this is not a place to slumber in." I replied, "How can I proceed, when I have not the power to stir a foot?" He rejoined, "Hast thou not heard that they have said, 'It is better to walk and rest, than to run and be oppressed?'"

STANZA.

Thou who wouldst reach the halting-place, haste not;
  Be patient! and my counsel hear aright:
Two courses may be sped by charger hot;
  The mule goes slowly, but goes day and night.

Story V.

In the circle of my acquaintance there was a sprightly and amiable youth, gay and soft-spoken, who had not a particle of melancholy in his composition, and whose mouth was never closed for laughter. An interval passed during which I did not happen to meet him. After that, I saw him when he had married a wife, and his children were growing up, and the root of his contentment was severed, and the rose of his desires withered. I asked him, "What is this state of thine?" He replied, "As soon as I had got boys I left off play."

COUPLET.

When thou art old thy pastimes put away:
Leave frolics to the young and mirthful play.

DISTICHS.

The youth's gay humour seek not from the old
The stream returns not which has onward rolled.
Not so elastic bends the yellow corn
As the young blade before the breeze of morn.

STANZA.

Youth's circling hours have passed for aye away;
  Ah me! alas that that gay time is spent!
The lion feels his strength of paw decay;
  Now, like a pard, with cheese-scraps I'm content.
An aged dame had dyed her locks of grey;
  "Granted," I said, "thy hair with silver blent
May cheat us now; yet, little mother! say,
  Canst thou make straight thy back, which time has bent?"

Story VI.

One day, in the ignorance and folly of youth, I raised my voice against my mother. Cut to the heart, she sate down in a corner and said, weeping, "Perhaps thou hast forgotten thy infancy, that thou treatest me with this rudeness?"

STANZA.

Well said that aged mother to her son
  Whose giant arm could well a tiger slay!
"Couldst thou remember days long past and gone,
  When in my arms a helpless infant lay,
And know thyself that babe, thou wouldst not now
Thus wrong me when I'm old; an athlete thou!"

Story VII.

The son of a rich miser was sick. The father's friends said to him, "The course to be adopted is to read through the Ḳur'án from beginning to end, or to offer up a sacrifice. It may be that the Most High God will grant him recovery." He reflected for a short space, and said, "It is better to read the Ḳur'án, as it is at hand: whereas the flock is at a distance." A devout person heard him, and said, "He made choice of the reading, because the Ḳur'ān is on the tip of his tongue, and the gold is in the centre of his heart."

DISTICHS.

In sooth, it is an easy task to do,
To bow the neck; but were alms needed too
'Twere hard indeed. One dinār but require,
And, like an ass, he flounders in the mire;
But for a chapter of the Ḳur'ān call,—
Ask only one, he'll gladly give thee all.

Story VIII.

They asked an old man why he did not marry. He replied, "I don't think I could fancy an old woman." They rejoined, "Espouse a young one, since thou hast substance." "Nay," he rejoined, "when I, who am old, do not like old women, how is it possible for a young woman to like me, an old man?"

CHAPTER VII.

ON THE EFFECT OF EDUCATION.

Story I.

A certain vazir had a stupid son, whom he sent to a wise man, saying, "Instruct him; perhaps he may become intelligent." The sage spent a long time in teaching him, without effect. At last he sent a person to his father, with this message, "This boy does not gain in understanding, and has driven me mad."

STANZA.

Is our first nature such that teaching can
    Affect it, soon instruction will take root:
But iron, which at first imperfect ran
    Forth from the furnace, who then can imbue it
With the capacity of polish? So
    In the seven [255] seas wouldst thou a dog make clean?
When wet, 'tis fouler than it erst has been.

Story II.

A philosopher was advising his children as follows: "Dear to me as life! acquire knowledge; for there is

---

[255] The Orientals delight in the number seven. One list of the seven seas comprises the Chinese, the Indian, the Persian, the Red Sea, the Mediterranean, the Caspian, and the Euxine.

no reliance to be placed in worldly possessions, either of land or money. You cannot take rank abroad with you; and silver and gold on a journey occasion risk, and either the thief may carry it off at one swoop, or the owner will gradually expend it: but knowledge is an ever-springing fountain, and a source of enduring wealth, and if an accomplished person ceases to be wealthy it matters not, for his knowledge is wealth existing in his mind itself. Wherever the accomplished man goes he is esteemed, and is seated in the place of honour, while the man without accomplishments has, go where he will, to pick up scraps and endure raps.

COUPLET.

'Tis hard t' obey for those who have borne rule,
Or fortune's minions in rough ways to school.

STANZA.

In Syria once commotions so arose
  That discord shook each person from his hearth.
Eftsoons the king his vazīrship bestows
  On peasants' sons, wise, though of lowly birth:
The vazīr's dullard children in their stead,
Through town and hamlet humbly beg their bread.

COUPLET.

Learn what thy father knew, if thou wouldst hold
His place. In ten days thou wilt spend his gold."

Story III.

A learned man had the education of a king's son, and used to beat him unmercifully, and scold him incessantly. The boy, unable to endure it, complained to his father, and removed his dress from his body, which was aching with blows. The father's heart was troubled, and, sending for the instructor, he said, "Thou dost not think it right to treat the children of any one of my subjects with such cruelty and harshness as thou shewest to my son. What is the reason of this?" He replied, "All persons ought to speak with reflection, and act with propriety: but this is especially requisite for kings, for whatever comes from their hand or lips, will assuredly be the common topic of conversation; while the words and actions of common people have not so much weight.

STANZA.

A hundred evil acts the poor may do,
   Their comrades of the hundred know but one;
But region after region permeates through
   One evil action by a monarch done.

Wherefore, in correcting the manners of princes, we ought to use greater strictness than in reference to others.

STANZA.

They who in youth to manners ne'er attend,
   Will in advancing years small gain acquire:
Wood, while 'tis green, thou mayst at pleasure bend;
   When dry, thou canst not change it save by fire.

COUPLET.

Surely green branches thou mayst render straight;
Th' attempt to straighten dry wood comes too late."

The king approved of the sage counsel of the master, and of the manner in which he had spoken, and bestowed on him a robe of honour and rich presents, at the same time advancing him to a higher rank.

Story IV.

I saw, in Africa, a schoolmaster of a sour countenance and harsh address, ill-natured, cruel, mulish and intemperate; such that the very sight of him dispelled the pleasure of Muslims, and whose reading of the Ḳur'ān threw a gloom over men's hearts. A multitude of fair boys and young maidens were surrendered to his cruel grasp, who neither dared to laugh, nor durst venture on conversing. Sometimes he would box the silver cheeks of the latter, and put the crystal legs of the former in the stocks. In short, I heard that people came to the knowledge of some of his disloyal acts, on which they beat him, and expelled him, and gave his school to a man of conciliating temper—a pious, good and meek person, who never uttered a word but when compelled, and never said anything which could distress any one. The children forgot the awe they had been wont to feel for their former master, when they saw that the present one possessed the qualities of an angel, and became demons to each other, and, depending on his mildness, abandoned study, and spent the chief part of their time in play, and, without finishing their copies, broke their tablets on each other's heads.

COUPLET.

When the schoolmaster gentle is and sweet,
The boys will play at leap-frog in the street.

Two weeks after, I passed by the door of the mosque, and saw there the former master, whom they had pacified and reinstated in his former office. I was sadly vexed, and uttering the deprecatory formula, "There is no power but in God," I said, "Why have they a second time made Iblis the instructor of angels?" An old man, who knew the world, heard me, and said, "Hast thou not heard that they have said:

DISTICHS.

'A monarch sent his son to school, and placed
A silver tablet round his neck, where, traced
In gold, appeared—"The fondness of thy sire
Will harm thee more than the schoolmaster's ire?"'"

Story V.

The son of a religious personage acquired incalculable riches by the bequest of his uncles. He began to indulge in licentiousness and impiety, and entered on a course of extravagance. In short, there was no sinful or criminal action that he failed to commit, nor intoxicating liquor that he abstained from drinking. At last I said to him, by way of admonition, "O my son! income is a passing current, and pleasure a revolving mill. In other words, a prodigal expenditure is safe only for one who has a permanent and settled revenue.

STANZA.

Hast thou no income—then thy wants restrain;
   For ever sing the boatmen merrily:
'If on the mountain-summits fell no rain,
   One year would make the Tigris channel dry.'

Betake thyself to a rational and moderate life, and give up thy follies; for, when thy wealth is exhausted, thou wilt have to endure hardship, and wilt suffer remorse." The youth, seduced by the delights of music and wine, was deaf to my advice, and rejected my counsel, saying, "It is opposed to the opinion of the wise to disturb, by forebodings of death, the pleasures of this transitory life.

DISTICHS.

Through fear of ill should fortune's favourites
   Make for themselves ills that are premature?
Be happy thou in whom my heart delights!
   Nor thus to-day to-morrow's pangs endure.

Much less should I do as thou sayest, I who hold the highest rank for generosity, and have made a compact to be liberal, and the fame of whose munificence is blazed abroad among all classes.

DISTICHS.

Whom mankind with the name of 'Generous' grace[26]
Must on his dirams no restriction place :
When our good fame pervades the public street,
We must no suitor with denial meet."

I saw that he did not accept my advice, and that my warm breath made no impression on his cold iron. I left off counselling him, and turned away from his society. I seated myself in the corner of security, and put in practice that saying of the sages, which they have uttered: "*Convey to them that which it behoves thee to say, and then, if they receive it not, what does it concern thee?*"

VERSE.

What though thou know'st they will not hearken, still
 Thy warning counsel give—'tis best.
Soon shalt thou see the man of headstrong will
 With his two legs by fetters pressed ;
Smiting his hands, he cries, in accents shrill,
 "To hearken to the sage is best."

After some time, what I had anticipated as to his downfall, came to pass, for he had to sew rag to rag and beg scrap by scrap. My heart was pained at his wretched state. I thought it unkind, in his then condition, to irritate and scatter salt on the wound of the poor man by reproaches ; but I said to myself,

DISTICHS.

"The profligate, in pleasure's eestacy,
 Dreads not the coming day of poverty :
Trees that in summer fruits profusely bear,
 Stand, therefore, leafless in the wintry air."

---

[26] The first and fourth lines are freely rendered. The literal translation of the first is, "Whoever has become an ensign by his liberality and bounty ;" and of the fourth, "Thou canst not close the door on any face.".

Story VI.

A king handed over his son to a teacher, and said, "This is my son; educate him as one of thine own sons." The preceptor spent some years in endeavouring to teach him without success, while his own sons were made perfect in learning and eloquence. The king took the preceptor to task, and said, "Thou hast acted contrary to thy agreement, and hast not been faithful to thy promise." He replied, "O King! education is the same, but capacities differ."

STANZA.

Silver and gold 'tis true in stones are found;
   Yet not all stones the precious metals bear :
Canopus shines to earth's most distant bound;
   But here gives leather—scented leather there.[237]

Story VII.

I have heard of an old doctor who said to a pupil, "If the minds of the children of men were as much fixed on the Giver of subsistence as they are on the subsistence itself, they would rise above the angels."

STANZA.

Thou wast by God then not forgotten when
   Thou wast a seed—thy nature in suspense ;
He gave thee soul and reason, wisdom, ken,
   Beauty and speech, reflection, judgment, sense ;
He on thy hand arrayed thy fingers ten,
   And thy arms fastened to thy shoulders. Whence
Canst thou then think, O thou most weak of men !
   He'd be unmindful of thy subsistence ?

---

[237] That is, the light of Canopus in one place causes the leather to be perfumed (a strange notion!), in another leaves it in its common state.

Story VIII.

I saw an Arab who was saying to his son, "*O my son! thou wilt be asked, in the day of resurrection, What hast thou acquired? not, From whom hast thou sprung?*"[258] or, in other words, they will demand of thee an account of thy actions, not of thy pedigree.

STANZA.

The pall suspended o'er the Kâbah's shrine
    Not from the yellow worm[259] derives its fame;
But it has dwelt some days near the Divine,
    And therefore do men venerate its name.

Story IX.

Philosophers tell us, in their writings, that scorpions are not engendered in the same way as other animals, but that they devour the entrails of their mothers, rend their bellies, and go forth to the desert; and the skins which men see in the holes of scorpions are the vestiges which are thus left. I mentioned this extraordinary circumstance to an eminent personage. He said, "My heart testifies to the truth of this legend, and it can hardly be otherwise; for since, when little, they behave thus to their mothers and fathers, they are, consequently, so pleasant and beloved when they grow old."

STANZA.

This counsel to his son a father gave:
    "Dear youth! to recollect these words be thine,—
Who for their kinsmen no affection have,
    On them the star of fortune ne'er will shine."

---

[258] This sentence, being in Arabic, is afterwards explained in Persian, which gives the appearance of tautology in English.
[259] The silk-worm.

WITTICISM.

They said to a scorpion, "Why dost thou not come abroad in winter?" He replied, "What respect is shewn to me in summer, that I should shew myself in winter also?"

Story X.

The wife of a darwesh was pregnant, and her time was completed. The darwesh, throughout his life, had never had a son. He said, "If God (may He be honoured and glorified!) gives me a son, I will bestow on my brethren all that I possess, with the exception of the garb I wear." It happened that his wife did bear a son. He made rejoicings, and, in accordance with his vow, prepared an entertainment for his friends. After some years, when I returned from travelling in Syria, I passed by the quarter where that darwesh resided, and inquired as to his circumstances. They replied, "He is in the Government prison." I asked the cause. They told me that his son had drunk intoxicating liquors, and raised an uproar, and, after shedding a man's blood, had fled the city; and that, on account of this, they had put a chain round his father's neck and heavy fetters on his feet. I exclaimed, "It was this calamitous monster whom he besought God to grant to him."

STANZA.

Wise friend! 'tis better that the fruitful bride
   In parturition should a serpent bear
Rather than sons (for thus the wise decide)—
   Sons who respond not to a father's care.

Story XI.

One year a quarrel arose among the pilgrims who were going on foot to Makkah. I also happened to be making the journey on foot. We fell upon one another tooth and nail with a vengeance, and did all that could be possibly expected from lewd fellows and combatants. I heard one who sate in a litter say to his companion, "Passing strange! the ivory[260] pawn, on completing its traverse of the chess-board, becomes a queen, that is to say, it becomes better than it was, and the foot-pilgrims to Makkah have crossed the desert and become worse!"

STANZA.

Go, tell for me the pilgrims who offend
   Their brother men, and cruel would them flay,
To them none can the pilgrim's name extend;
   The patient camel earns it more than they,
Who feeds on thorns, nor does his task gainsay.

STORY XII.

A Hindū was teaching the art of making fireworks. A sage said to him: "For thee, with thy house of reeds, this sport is out of all rule."

COUPLET.

Speak not until thou knowest speech is best,
Nor that of which the answer is unblest.

STORY XIII.

A fellow had a pain in his eyes, and went to a farrier, saying, "Give me medicine." The farrier applied to his eyes the remedies he was in the habit of using for animals, and blinded him, on which he complained to the magistrate, who pronounced that he could not recover damages; "For," said he, "if this fellow had not been an ass, he would not have consulted a farrier." The moral of the story is, that whoever commits an affair of

---

[260] There is a very good pun between عاج *áj*, "ivory," and حاج *ḥáj*, "pilgrimage to Makkah," which cannot be retained in English.

importance to an inexperienced person will smart for it, and, in addition, will be considered an imbecile by persons of intelligence.

STANZA.

The prudent man of clear intelligence
   Not to the mean will weighty things commit:
Mat-makers weave, 'tis true, yet, hast thou sense,
   Thou'lt not think weaving silk robes for them fit.

Story XIV.

A certain great man had an amiable son, who died. They asked the father what they should write on his grave-stone. He replied, "The verses of the Holy Book are too venerable and sacred to be written on such places, where they may be effaced by the weather, and the trampling of men's feet, and desecrated by dogs. If ye must write something, these two couplets will suffice:—

STANZA.

Ah me! when in the garden freshly green
   Upsprang the verdure, how my heart was gay!
Wait, friend! till spring renascent tints the scene,
   And mark young rosebuds blossom from my clay.

Story XV.

A holy man passed by a wealthy personage, and observed that he had tightly bound one of his slaves hand and foot, and was engaged in torturing him. He said, "O son! God (may He be honoured and glorified!) has placed in bondage to thee a creature like thyself, and given thee the superiority over him; thank God Most High, therefore, for His blessings, and do not allow thyself to treat him with such cruelty. Beware, lest to-morrow, in the day of resurrection, this slave be better than thee, and thou carry off disgrace.

DISTICHS.

Not over ireful with thy servant be,
Nor plague his heart, nor practise tyranny.
Thou with ten dirams didst him purchase, true!
Not thine the Power from whence his breath he drew.
Soon must thou anger, rule, and pride resign:
There is a Lord whose sway surpasses thine.
Thou'rt master of Arslān and Āghūsh [261] yet;
Beware, lest thine own Master thou forget."

It is related of the Prophet (on whom be peace!) that he said, that the bitterest of all regrets will be when they transport the good slave to paradise and convey the impious master to hell.

STANZA.

Not 'gainst the slaves that in thy service bow
   Rage thou without restraint, or madly chafe:
In the last day of reckoning wouldst thou
Mark, with shamed soul and agonised brow,
   The master fettered and the bondsman safe?

Story XVI.

In a certain year I journeyed from Balkh with some Syrians, and the road was replete with peril from robbers. A young man accompanied us as guide, skilled in the use of the buckler and the bow, trained to arms, and of prodigious strength, so that ten powerful men could not string his bow, nor the greatest athletes in the world bring his back to the ground; but he had been delicately brought up, and reared in indulgence, and had neither seen the world nor travelled. The thundering drum of the warrior had not reached his ears, nor the flash of the horseman's scymitar glittered in his eyes.

---

[261] Names of slaves, used generally to denote any bondsmen.

COUPLET.

To a stern foe ne'er captive had he been,
Nor iron rain of arrows round him seen.

It happened that I and this young man were running one after the other. Every old wall that came in the way he cast down with the strength of his arm, and tore up with the force of his wrist all the large trees that he beheld, and he boastingly exclaimed,

COUPLET.

Where is the elephant, to see the arms and shoulders of the strong?
The lion where, to feel the powers which to men of might belong?"

We were thus engaged when two Hindūs[262] lifted up their heads from behind a rock, and seemed prepared to slay us. One had a stick in his hand, and the other a sling under his arm. I said to the young man, "Why dost thou stop?"

COUPLET.

Now what thou hast of strength and courage shew;
For of himself to death comes on thy foe.

I beheld the bow and arrows drop from the hand of the young man, and a tremor pervade his frame.

COUPLET.

Not all whose forceful shaft could strike a hair,
Where warriors charge, would stand unshaken there.

---

[262] There is little doubt that Afghānistān was, at no very remote æra, peopled by Indians who were driven out by the Afghāns, and other northern tribes, and this passage seems to me a proof of it. Otherwise, whence could come these Hindūs on the road between Balkh and Syria.

We saw no remedy but to give up our clothes and arms and get free with our lives.

STANZA.

A veteran choose for deeds of high emprise
   He the fierce lion in his noose will tame;
The youth may mighty be, of giant size,
   But in the fight fear will unnerve his frame:
   War to the well-trained warrior is the same
As some nice quillet of the law is to the wise.

Story XVII.

I saw the son of a rich man seated at the head of his father's sepulchre, and engaged in a dispute with the son of a poor man, and saying, "My father's sarcophagus is of stone, and the inscription coloured with a pavement of alabaster and turquoise bricks. What resemblance has it to that of thy father? which consists of a brick or two huddled together, with a few handfuls of dust sprinkled over it." The son of the poor man heard him, and answered, "Peace! for before thy father can have moved himself under this heavy stone, my sire will have arrived in paradise. This is a saying of the Prophet: '*The death of the poor is repose.*'

COUPLET.

Doubtless the ass, on which they do impose
The lightest burthen, also easiest goes.

STANZA.

The poor man, who the agony has borne
   Of famine's pangs, treads lightly to the door
Of death. While one from blessings torn—
   From luxury and ease—will grieve the more
To lose them. This is certain. Happier he
Whom, like a captive, death from bonds sets free,
Than great men, whom it hurries to captivity."

Story XVIII.

I asked an eminent personage the meaning of this traditionary saying, "*The most malignant of thy enemies is the lust which abides within thee.*" He replied, "It is because every enemy on whom thou conferrest favours becomes a friend, save lust; whose hostility increases the more thou dost gratify it."

STANZA.

By abstinence, man might an angel be;
By surfeiting, his nature brutifies:
Whom thou obligest will succumb to thee—
Save lusts, which, sated, still rebellious rise.

Story XIX.

THE DISPUTE OF SÁDÍ WITH A PRESUMPTUOUS PRETENDER AS TO THE QUALITIES OF THE RICH AND THE POOR.

I once saw seated in an assembly a person in the garb of a darwesh—not with the character of one—engaged in pouring out a disgraceful tirade, and uttering a volume of abuse and reproachful language against the rich. His discourse, moreover, had reached this point, that the hands of poor men are tied from doing anything, while the feet of rich men's intentions are lame.

COUPLET.

The merciful are ever moneyless;
Hardhearted they who have the power to bless.

I, who have been supported by the munificence of the great, disapproved of this speech. I said, "O friend! the rich are a revenue to the poor, and storehouses for the recluse; the pilgrim's goal; the traveller's refuge; and the supporters of heavy burthens for the gratification of others. When they stretch forth their hands to their repast, their dependents and inferiors partake with them, and what is left of their bounty comes to the widowed and the old, and to their relatives and neighbours.

VERSE.

Offerings to God, bequests to furnish ease
  To the worn traveller, enfranchisement
Of slaves, alms, gifts, and sacrifices—these
  Are rich men's works. Say, when wilt thou invent
Like merits for thyself, who canst but pray,
  With twice a hundred wanderings,[263] twice a day?

If the question be as to the power of doing liberal actions and the discharge of religious duties, they are seen to be possessed in a higher degree by the rich, because they possess wealth hallowed by the usage of giving alms, pure garments, a reputation intact, and a heart free from care. And good meals greatly facilitate worship, just as clean garments have no little weight in sanctifying our devotions, for what strength is there in an empty stomach, or what liberality in an empty hand? How can the fettered feet walk, or the hungry belly bestow alms?

STANZA.

The man at night uneasy sleeps,
  Who knows not how to gain to-morrow's bread:
The ant in summer corn upheaps;
  'Tis thus in winter with abundance fed.

It is certain that leisure and poverty will not combine, and the mind of the indigent cannot be at ease. The rich man hallows the evening in prayer, and the poor man seats himself on the look-out for his supper. The former will admit of no comparison with the latter.

---

[263] That is, of mind. Ross and Gladwin translate پریشانی *parishání,* "difficulties," which is hardly the meaning. Semelet is nearer the sense with "*distractions.*" I have altered the "hundred" to "twice a hundred," to render the line more forcible.

COUPLET.

The rich man is with thoughts of God impressed :
The needy is for such thoughts too distressed.

Wherefore the worship of the former is more likely to be accepted, inasmuch as their minds are collected and attentive, not distracted and wavering; for, as they are prepared with the means of subsistence, they can betake themselves to their devotions. The Arabians say, '*God defend me from humiliating poverty, and from the neighbourhood of one I do not love!*' And tradition tells us that it was a saying of the Prophet, '*Poverty blackens the countenance in both worlds.*'" My opponent replied, "Hast thou not heard that the Prophet (on whom be peace!) said, '*Poverty is my glory*'?" I answered, "Be silent! for the allusion of the Lord of the world is to the poverty of those who are the warriors of the battle-field of resignation and who receive with submission the arrows of destiny—not to that of those who put on the patched robe of the devout, and sell the scraps bestowed on them in charity.

QUATRAIN.

O noisy drum, all emptiness within,
How without food wilt thou thy march begin!
Be manly, and from cringing cease: for this
Than thousand-beaded rosaries better is.[264]

A darwesh without spirituality will not pause until his

---

[264] I have translated the last three lines rather freely. The literal version is, "Without provisions, what plan wilt thou devise at the time of marching? Turn the face of greediness from people, if thou art a man. Do not turn in thy hand the rosary with a thousand beads." In the second line پسیچ *pasīch* clearly means "a journey," and rhymes to هیچ *hīch*; but, in Richardson's Dictionary, we find only پسیج *pasīj*, with the meanings "ready, prepared, provision for a journey."

poverty ends in infidelity, for '*Poverty borders on the denial of God.*' Moreover, without the possession of riches we cannot clothe the naked or exert ourselves in liberating the captive. Who can compare the position of such as we are with the dignity of the rich? or what resemblance is there between the hand that gives and that which receives? Dost thou not perceive that the most glorious and most high God announces, in a clear passage of the Kur'ān,²⁶⁵ regarding the blessings of the inhabitants of Paradise, that, '*To them there is an assured allowance of fruits, and they are honoured in the gardens of Paradise?*' in order that thou mayest know that he who is occupied in gaining a subsistence is excluded from the happiness of this degree of holiness, and that the kingdom of contentment is dependant²⁶⁶ on a fixed income.

COUPLET.

To those athirst the whole world seems
A spring of water—in their dreams.

Wherever thou seest one who has endured hardship and tasted the bitterness of misfortune, thou wilt find him precipitate himself with avidity into enormities without fear of the consequences or dread of punishment in a future life, inasmuch as he discriminates not between things lawful and unlawful.

STANZA.

A dog leaps up with joy when on his head
 A clod descends—he thinks a bone to spy.
So, when two men bear forth the coffined dead
 Upon their shoulders, greedy miscreants eye
The bier, and think they then a tray of meat descry.

---

²⁶⁵ Ross refers for this passage to the 28th chapter of the Kur'ān; but the only verse that is at all similar in that chapter is v. 57, "a secure asylum, to which fruits of every sort are brought, as a provision of our bounty."

²⁶⁶ *Literally,* "under the signet."

But the wealthy man is regarded with an eye of favour, and, by the possession of that which is lawful, is preserved from committing that which is unlawful. But, even supposing that I have not proved what I have adduced, nor demonstrated the truth of my arguments, I yet expect justice from thee. Hast thou ever seen the hand of a suppliant tied behind his back? or an indigent person imprisoned? or the veil of chastity rent? or the hand amputated at the wrist?[267] except by reason of poverty? Driven by necessity, brave men are taken in the act of undermining houses,[268] and are punished by having their heels bored; and it is likely that, when the passions of the poor man are roused and he has not the means of gratifying them, he will be involved in sin. And it is one among the causes of the tranquillity and content that rich men enjoy, that they each day renew their youth, and each night embrace a beauty[269] such that bright morn is ashamed[270] in her presence, and the graceful cypress, in modest acknowledgment of her superiority, finds its feet imbedded in the clay of bashfulness.

COUPLET.

Her hands in gore of hapless lovers dipped,
Her fingers with the ruddy jujube tipped.

It is impossible that, in despite of the beauty of such countenance, they should hover round that which is forbidden or engage in depravities.

---

[267] The punishment for theft.

[268] Burglars in the East effect their entrance into the houses they intend to rob by mining under the walls. This is easy enough where, as in India, the soil is light and no one is on the alert.

[269] I cannot at all agree with M. Semelet's reading of this passage, and infinitely prefer my own, by which the extreme indelicacy of the French and other editions is avoided.

[270] *Literally*, "Places its hand on its heart at her beauty."

COUPLET.

A heart that Houris charmed and made its prey,
To Yaghmā's[271] beauties when will devious stray?

COUPLET.

*Who holds the dates he loves his hands between,
Contented, pelts the clusters not, I ween.*

The majority of the necessitous stain the garment of chastity with sin, as those who are hungry steal bread.

COUPLET.

So when a ravenous cur finds meat—small care has he
If Sālih's camel or if Dajjāl's[272] ass it be.

Many decent persons have fallen into abominable wickedness through poverty, and have given their precious honour to the winds of disgrace.

COUPLET.

With hunger abstinence will scarce remain,
And want will wrest away devotion's rein."

At the moment that I uttered these words the darwesh lost his hold of the reins of endurance, and he unsheathed the sword of his tongue and let loose the steed of eloquence in the plain of shamelessness, and attacked me furiously,

---

[271] یغما *Yaghmā* is said to be a city of Turkestān, famous for its beautiful women. It also signifies "prey," whence arises an equivoque which cannot be preserved in English.

[272] صالح *Sālih*, "good, just;" the Patriarch Sālih, son of Arphaxad, who is said in the Kur'ān (ch. vii.) to have been a prophet sent to the tribe ثمود *Samūd*, who inhabited Arabia Petræa, and were descended from Aram, brother of Arphaxad. To convince them of his mission he miraculously brought a camel out of a rock, but they continued still in their unbelief, on which they were slain by the Angel Gabriel. Dajjāl is Anti-christ, who is to appear riding on an ass and to lead men astray, until killed by Mahdī, the twelfth Imām, at his coming.

saying, "Thou hast employed such exaggeration in praising them, and talked so extravagantly on the subject, that one would imagine the rich to be the antidote to the poison of poverty, or the key of the stores of Providence. They are a handful of proud, arrogant, conceited, repulsive persons, who are taken up with their wealth and their luxuries, and led away by their rank and opulence, and who can only talk insipidly and look disdainfully. They treat the learned like mendicants, and reproach the poor with their distresses. Through the pride of their wealth and the assumption of their supposed dignity, they take their seats above all others and imagine themselves better than any. They never take it into their heads to notice[273] any one, in ignorance of that saying which has been uttered by the wise, 'Whoever is inferior to others in devotion, but surpasses them in wealth, is outwardly rich but inwardly poor.'

COUPLET.

When a fool would exalt himself, for his wealth, above the wise,
Though he be an ox of ambergris,[274] him as a fool despise."

I replied, "Suffer not thyself to blame them, for they are the possessors of beneficence." He rejoined, "Thou hast

---

[273] M. Semelet thinks سر بر دارند *sar bar dārand*—the reading of Gladwin and Gentius—an error, and substitutes سر فرو دارند *sar farū dārand*. But surely the former expression may mean "they lift up the head," *i.e.*, "they notice."

[274] The Orientals think that ambergris is produced by sea-cows. M. Barbier tells us, "Ambergris is found in the sea on the coasts of India, Africa, and Brazil. It is gray striped with yellow, brownish, and white. It appears to be a concretion that, in some diseased states, is formed in whales and principally in their cæcum." It is a medicinal substance, rarely used now-a-days by the physician, but in great request among perfumers, as it increases and draws out the odour of their essences.

spoken wrongly, for they are the slaves of money. Of what use is it that they are the clouds of the month Āzar[275] and do not rain on any one; or that they are the fountains of the sun, and yet shine on none; and that they ride on the steed of power, if they will not let him go on. They will not move a step in God's service, nor bestow a diram without making you feel painfully the obligation. They amass, too, their hoards drudgingly, and protect them grudgingly; and the sages have said, 'The silver of the miser is disinterred when he is interred.'

COUPLET.

With toil and trouble one does riches gain,
Another comes and reaps them without pain."

I replied, "Thou hast gained no knowledge of the parsimony of the rich save by begging; otherwise every one who lays aside covetousness sees no difference in the liberal and the miserly. The touchstone discerns what is gold, and the beggar knows who is stingy." He said, "I speak from experience that they place their menials at their gate, and commission coarse ruffians not to admit respectable persons, and these officials of theirs lay their hands on the breasts of men of knowledge and say, 'There is nobody at home,' and, in point of fact, they speak the truth.[276]

COUPLET.

The soulless, stingy, dull, and senseless wight,
Bids thee go say, 'There's no one in,'—he's right!"

I replied, "There is an excuse for their doing this, in that they are driven to extremity by the petitions of those

---

[275] According to Gladwin, "August;" according to Richardson's Dictionary, "November."

[276] This is said as a sneer, and means that the rich are "nobodys," "persons of no worth or value."

who expect aid from them and are harassed by begging letters, and it cannot reasonably be supposed that, if the sand of the desert should become pearls, the eyes of beggars would be satisfied.

COUPLET.

> No wealth could fill the eye of avarice,
> As dew to brim a well would ne'er suffice.

Had Ḥātim Ṭā'ī, who lived in the desert, dwelt in a city, he would have been driven to desperation by the importunity of beggars, and the very clothes would have been torn off his back." The darwesh said, "I pity[277] their condition." I replied, "Not so; thou enviest their wealth." We were disputing thus and mutually opposed; when he advanced a pawn I endeavoured to repel it, and when he called out check to my king I covered it with the queen, until he had spent all the coin of his wit and discharged all the arrows of the quiver of argument.

STANZA.

> Beware, lest at that speaker's onset, who
>   Has but a borrowed and a vain tirade,
> Thou should'st thy shield fling down. Keep thyself true
>   To faith and virtue, and be not afraid
>   Of empty posts with arms above the door displayed.

At length he had not a word to say and was utterly overthrown by me. He then became outrageous and began to talk at random. It is the way with the ignorant that, when inferior to an opponent in argument, they betake themselves[278] to violence. As, when the idol-worshipper Āzur could not succeed with his son[279] in argument, he rose up to attack him, for *God most High*

---

[277] A sneer.
[278] *Literally,* "They shake the chain of enmity."
[279] Abraham.

has said, "*Of a truth if thou wilt not yield this point, then I will stone thee.*" He began to abuse me and I answered him in the same strain. He seized my collar and I his chin.

STANZA.

O'er him I tumbled, he o'er me,
A crowd with laughter us pursued,
And wondered at our colloquy
With fingers in their mouths fast glued.[280]

In short we carried our dispute before the Ḳāẓī, and agreed to abide by his just decision, so that the judge of the Musalmān might examine as to what was best, and pronounce on the points of difference between the rich and the poor.

When the Ḳāẓī beheld our faces and heard our address, he allowed his head to sink down into his vest in meditation, and, after much reflection, raised it and said, "O thou! who hast extolled the rich and thought fit to speak with severity of the poor, know that wherever there is a rose there is a thorn, and with wine is intoxication, and over a treasure is coiled a serpent, and where there are royal pearls there are also devouring monsters. So over the enjoyments of the world impends the terror of death, and between the blessings of Paradise intervenes a wall of difficulties.[281]

COUPLET.

Who would have friends, a foe's hate must sustain,
Linked are snakes, gold; thorns, flowers; joy and pain.

Seest thou not that in the garden are found together musk-willows and dry logs? so, too, among the rich are those who are thankful and unthankful, and among the poor are the patient and impatient.

---

[280] The Oriental way of denoting surprise is to bite the finger.
[281] *Vide* Ḳur'ān, ch. vii., v. 47, ed. Maracci.

COUPLET.

Could every hailstone to a pearl be turned,
Pearls in the mart like oyster shells were spurned.

The beloved of the Almighty (may He be honoured and glorified!) are the rich who have the humility of the poor, and the poor who have the magnanimity of the rich; and the prince of rich men is he who compassionates the poor, and among the poor men he is the best who depreciates the rich least. *God most High has said, ' Whosoever trusteth in God, He is sufficient for him.'* " The Ḳāẓī then turned the face of rebuke from me towards the darwesh, and said, "O thou! who hast said that the rich are absorbed in forbidden enjoyments and intoxicated with profane delights; it is true that there are a number of persons such as thou hast said, deficient in liberality and unthankful for their blessings, who gather money and hoard it, and who enjoy it but give none away. If, for example, the rain should not fall, or a deluge overwhelm the world, in the security of their own abundance they would not ask after the poor man nor fear the Most High God.

COUPLET.

What though another die of want? my bread
Fails not: to water-fowls floods cause no dread.

COUPLET.

Borne aloft in camel-litters, what, I pray, do women care
For the tired pilgrim struggling through the sand-heaps drifted there?

COUPLET.

The base who've saved their own vile wrappers cry,
'What matters though the universe should die?'

There are persons of the character I have described; but there is another numerous body who prepare a hospitable table and proclaim a liberal invitation, and whose countenances expand with affability while they in this manner pursue the path of fame and divine acceptance, and thus enjoy both this present world and a future recompense. Of these is his Majesty the King of the world, *the aided by God, the victorious and triumphant over his enemies, the holder of the reins of the human race, defender of the passes of Islām, heir to the throne of Sulaimān, the most just of the monarchs of the age, Muzaffaru'd-dīn Abū Bakr bin Sad bin Zangī (may God prolong his days and grant victory to his banners!)*

STANZA.

No sire e'er showed such kindness to his child
    As thy all-bounteous hand hath heaped on man.
Heaven on this world with favouring mercy smiled,
    And by its Providence thy reign began."

When the Kāzi had extended his discourse thus far, and had urged the steed of his rhetoric beyond the limits of our expectation, we acquiesced in the necessity of obeying his decree, overlooked what had passed, and, banishing our past differences, entered on the road of reconciliation; and, in amends for what we had mutually done, bowed our heads at each other's feet and kissed each other's head and faces. The discord ceased and our enmity terminated in peace, and our disagreement concluded with these two complets:

STANZA.

Complain not, darwesh! of vicissitude:
    Hapless if in such train of thought thou die!
And thou, rich man! while yet thou art endued
    With a kind heart and riches, gratify
Thyself and others: thus on earth make sure
Of joys; and thy reward in heaven secure.

CHAPTER VIII.

ON THE DUTIES OF SOCIETY.

Maxim I.

Riches are for the sake of making life comfortable, not life for the sake of amassing riches. I asked a wise man, "Who is fortunate and who unfortunate?" He replied, "The fortunate is he who sowed[282] and reaped; the unfortunate he who died and abandoned."

COUPLET.

Not for that worthless one a prayer afford,
Who life in hoarding spent—ne'er spent his hoard.

Maxim II.

The holy Mūsā (Peace be on him!) advised Ḳārūn,[283] saying, "*Do good unto others, as God has done good unto thee!*" He did not listen, and thou hast heard his end.

STANZA.

He who by wealth no good deeds has upstored,
 For it has marred his future destiny.
Wouldst thou derive advantage from thy hoard?
 Do good to others, as God has to thee.

---

[282] I have transposed خورد و کشت *kh'urd wa kisht*, as it is evident that "*kisht*" is put last only to rhyme with هشت *hisht*.

[283] Ḳur'ān, chap. xxviii., page 296, l. 6. Sale's Translation.

The Arabs say, "*Do good, and do not speak of it, and assuredly thy kindness will be recompensed to thee;*" that is to say, "Give and be liberal, and do not impute the obligation, and the benefit will revert to thee."

STANZA.

Where'er the tree of gracious deeds takes root,
  Its towering top and branches reach the sky:
Do not, if thou wouldst wish to taste its fruit,
  By boasting of those deeds, the axe apply.

STANZA.

Thank God that He vouchsafes to succour thee,
  And has not left thee void of grace.
Thou serv'st the king—well! do not boastful be,
  But rather thankful for thy place.

MAXIM III.

Two men have laboured fruitlessly and exerted themselves to no purpose. One is the man who has gained wealth without enjoying it; the other he who has acquired knowledge but has failed to practise it.

DISTICHS.

How much soe'er thou learn'st, 'tis all vain;
Who practise not, still ignorant remain.
A quadruped, with volumes laden, is
No whit the wiser or more sage for this:
How can the witless animal discern,
If books be piled on it? or wood to burn?

MAXIM IV.

Science is for the cultivation of religion, not for worldly enjoyments.

COUPLET.

Who makes a gain of virtue, science, lore,
Is one who garners up, then burns his store.

Maxim V.

A learned man who does not restrain his passions is like a blind man holding a torch; *he guides others but not himself.*

COUPLET.

Who life has wasted without doing aught,
His gold has squandered, and has purchased nought.

Maxim VI.

A country is adorned by wise men, and religion is perfected by the virtuous. Kings stand more in need of the counsel of the wise, than wise men do of propinquity to kings.

STANZA.

King! let my words with thee find grace;
   My book than this can nought more sage advise:
The wise alone in office place;
   Though office truly little suits the wise.

Maxim VII.

Three things lack permanency, uncombined with three other things: wealth without trading; learning without instruction;[254] and empire without a strict administration of justice.

STANZA.

By courteous speech, politeness, gentleness,
   Sometimes thou mayest direct the human will:
Anon by threats; for it oft profits less
   With sugar twice a hundred cups to fill,
Than from one colocynth its bitters to distil.

---

[254] The other translators take "controversy" to be the meaning of دراست *dirāsat*; I confess I am at a loss for authority to justify this sense. But the meaning I have given above is simple enough:—If the learned do not teach others, learning must soon come to an end.

Maxim VIII.

To shew pity to the bad is to oppress the good, and to pardon oppressors is to tyrannise over the oppressed.

COUPLET.

When thou to base men giv'st encouragement,
Thou shar'st their sins, since thou them aid hast lent.

Maxim IX.

No reliance can be placed on the friendship of princes, nor must we plume ourselves on the sweet voices of children, since that is changed by a caprice, and these by a single slumber.

COUPLET.

On the mistress of a thousand hearts, do not thy love
    bestow;
But if thou wilt, prepare eftsoons her friendship to forego.

Maxim X.

Reveal not to a friend every secret that thou possessest. How knowest thou whether at some time he may not become an enemy? Nor inflict on thy enemy every injury that is in thy power, perchance he may some day become thy friend. Tell not the secret that thou wouldest have continue hidden to any person, although he may be worthy of confidence; for no one will be so careful of thy secret as thyself.

STANZA.

Better be silent, than thy purpose tell
    To others; and enjoin them secresy.
O doh! keep back the water at the well,
    For the swoll'n stream to stop thou'lt vainly try.
In private, utter not a single word
Which thou in public wouldst regret were heard.

Maxim XI.

A weak enemy who submits and makes a shew of friendship, does so only with the intention of becoming more dangerous; and they have said, "There is no reliance to be placed in the friendship of friends; how much less in the professions of enemies!" Whosoever despises a small enemy is like him who is careless about a little fire.

STANZA.

> To-day extinguish, if thou can'st, the fire,
> Which for its victims will a world require,
> If not arrested. And ere yet his bow
> Be strung, thy arrow should transfix the foe.

Maxim XII.

Let thy words between two foes be such that if they were to become friends thou wouldest not be ashamed.

DISTICHS.

> Like fire is strife betwixt two enemies:
> The luckless mischief-maker wood supplies.
> Struck with confusion and ashamed is he,
> If e'er the two belligerents agree.
> Can we in this aught rational discern—
> To light a fire which will ourselves first burn?

STANZA.

> In talk with friends speak soft and low,
>   Lest thy bloodthirsty foeman thee should hear:
> A wall may front thee—true! but dost thou know
>   If there be not behind a listening ear?

Maxim XIII.

Whoever comes to an agreement with the enemies of his friends, does so with the intention of injuring the latter.

COUPLET.

> Eschew that friend, if thou art wise,
> Who consorts with thy enemies.

Maxim XIV.

When, in transacting business, thou art in doubt, make choice of that side from which the least injury will result.

COUPLET.

Reply not roughly to smooth language, nor
Contend with him who knocks at peace's door.

Maxim XV.

As long as a matter can be compassed by money, it is not right to imperil life. The Arabs say, "*The sword is the last resource.*"

COUPLET.

When thou hast failed in every known resource,
Then to the sword 'tis right to have recourse.

Maxim XVI.

Compassionate not the weakness of a foe, for were he to become powerful he would have no pity on thee.[285]

COUPLET.

Twist not thy moustaches boastful, nor with pride thy
    weak foe scan :
Every bone contains some marrow, every garment cloaks
    a man.

APOPHTHEGM.

He who slays a bad man, rids mankind of annoyance from him, and the man himself from an increase of punishment [which his future misdeeds would have merited] from God (may He be honoured and glorified!).[286]

---

[285] These maxims are a very good index of Oriental feeling; and all who know the East will admit that they are most religiously observed.

[286] An unlucky maxim for a criminal. So, in taking off his head, you are in fact consulting not only the public weal, but the welfare of the criminal himself.

STANZA.

Pity is commendable—that we own;
   Yet on the tyrant's wound no ointment place.
He that has mercy to a serpent shown,
   Has acted cruelly to Adam's race.

Maxim XVII.

To act in accordance with an enemy's advice is foolish, but it is permissible to hear it, in order to do the opposite, for that will be exactly the right course.

DISTICHS.

Beware of what thy foeman bids thee do,
   Lest on thy knees thou smite thy hands, and grieve.
Straight as a dart may be the road—'tis true—
   He points to; yet 'twere better it to leave.

Maxim XVIII.

Anger that has no limit causes terror, and unseasonable kindness does away with respect. Be not so severe as to cause disgust, nor so lenient as to make people presume.

DISTICHS.

Sternness and gentleness are best combined:
The leech both salves and scarifies, you find.
The sage is not too rigorous, nor yet
Too mild, lest men their awe of him forget:
He seeks not for himself too high a place;
Nor will himself too suddenly abase.

DISTICHS.

Once to his sire a shepherd said, "O Sage!
Teach me one maxim worthy of thy age."
"Use gentleness," he said, "yet not so much,
That the wolf be emboldened thee to clutch."

Maxim XIX.

Two persons are the foes of a state and of religion; a king without clemency, and a religious man without learning.

COUPLET.

Ne'er to that king may states allegiance own,
Who bows not humbly at th' Almighty's throne.

MAXIM XX.

A king ought not to indulge his resentment against his enemies to such an extent as to shake the confidence of his friends; for the fire of wrath falls first on the wrathful man himself, and after, its flame may or may not reach the enemy.

DISTICHS.

It suits not Adam's children, earthly-born,
T' indulge in pride, ferocity, and scorn.
When I behold in thee such heat and ire,
I cannot think thee sprung from earth, but fire.

STANZA.

In Bailkān[287] once a devotee I saw,
  "From folly purge me by thy words," I said.
"Go!" he replied, "thou who art skilled in law,
  Be as earth humble, or what thou hast read
  Might in the earth as well be buried."

MAXIM[288] XXI.

The wicked man is overtaken in the grasp of an enemy from whose torturing clutches he can never escape, go where he will.

COUPLET.

Though bad men seek in heaven to flee from ill,
E'en there their vices will pursue them still.

---

[287] A city in Armenia Major, near the ports of the Caspian Sea.
[288] This is headed مطایبه *muṭāyabah,* "pleasantry," as the next is پند *pand,* "advice," as others are ملاطفه *mulāṭafah,* "facetiæ," and تنبیه *tambīh,* "admonition;" but, as it is difficult to see how these differ from حکمت *ḥikmat,* and from one another, I have rendered them all "Maxim."

Maxim XXII.

When thou seest discord arise among the forces of the enemy, take courage; and when they are united [289] beware then of rout.

STANZA.

Go! with thy friends sit free from care,
    If thou thy foes shouldst see with discord rent.
But if thou mark'st agreement there,
Go string thy bow, thyself prepare,
    And pile thy missiles on the battlement.

Maxim XXIII.

When an enemy has tried every expedient in vain, he will pretend friendship,[290] and then, by this pretext, execute designs which no enemy could have effected.

Maxim XXIV.

Crush the serpent's head with the hand of an enemy, which must result in one of two good things. If the latter be successful, thou hast killed a snake; and if the former, thou hast freed thyself from an enemy.

COUPLET.

Though thy foe be feeble, be not in the battle void of care;
He will dash the lion's brains out when he's driven to despair.

Maxim XXV.

When thou knowest tidings that will pain the heart of any one, be silent, so that another may be the first to convey them.

---

[289] There is a play on words here, which I have not been able to preserve in English. جمع شدن *jamá shudan* signifies "to be collected, united," and also, "to be of good cheer."

[290] *Literally,* "Agitate the chain of friendship."

####### COUPLET.

> O nightingale! spring's tidings breathe,
> Ill rumours to the owls bequeath.

Maxim XXVI.

Do not acquaint a king with the treason of any one, unless when thou art assured that the disclosure will meet with his full approval, else thou art but labouring for thy own destruction.

####### COUPLET.

> Then, only then, to speak intend
> When speaking can effect thy end.

Maxim XXVII.

He who gives advice to a conceited man is himself in need of counsel.

Maxim XXVIII.

Be not caught by the artifice of a foe, nor purchase pride of a flatterer; for the one has set the snare of hypocrisy, and the other has opened the mouth of greediness. The fool is puffed up with flattery, like a corpse whose inflated heels appear plump.

####### STANZA.

> Heed not the flatterer's fulsome talk,
>   He from thee hopes some trifle to obtain;
> Thou wilt, shouldst thou his wishes baulk,
>   Two hundred times as much of censure gain.

Maxim XXIX.

Until some one points out to an orator his defects, his discourse will never be amended.

####### COUPLET.

> To vaunt of one's own speaking is not meet,
> At fools' approval and one's own conceit.

Maxim XXX.

Every one thinks his own judgment perfect, and his own son beautiful.

VERSE.

A Jew and Musalmān once so contended
  That laughter seized me as their contest grew.
The true believer thus his cause defended:
  "Is this bond false, then may I die a Jew!"
The Jew replied: "By Moses' books I vow that
  'Tis true, or else a Musalmān am I!"
So from earth's face were Wisdom's self to fly,
Not one could be amongst us found t' allow that
  He judgment lacked, or himself stultify.

Maxim XXXI.

Ten men can eat at one board, but two dogs cannot satisfy themselves at one carcase. The greedy man continues to hunger, though a world supply his wants; and the contented man is satisfied with a crust.

COUPLET.

A single loaf the stomach will supply;
But not earth's richest gifts the greedy eye.

DISTICHS.

When my sire's age had reached its latest day,
He gave me this advice, and passed away:—
"Lust is a fire;—from it thyself keep well;
Nor kindle 'gainst thyself the flames of Hell.
Thou hast not patience to endure that flame, I trow;
With patience, as with water, quench it now."

Maxim XXXII.

Whosoever does no good when he has the ability to do it, in the time of inability to aid others will himself suffer distress.

COUPLET.

Ill-starred, indeed, is he who injures men :
Is fortune adverse, he is friendless then.

Maxim XXXIII.

Life hangs on a single breath; and the world of existence is between two non-existences. Those who barter religion for the world are asses; they sell Joseph and get what in return? *Did I not covenant with you, O sons of Adam! that ye should not serve Satan? for verily he is your avowed enemy.*

COUPLET.

With thy friend thou faith hast broken at the bidding
    of thy foe:
See with whom thou'st joined alliance, and from whom
    thou'st sought to go.

Maxim XXXIV.

Satan prevails not against the righteous; nor a king against the poor.

DISTICHS.

Lend not to him who prayer neglects, though he
Gasping with want and inanition be;
For he who renders not to God His due,
What will he care for that he owes to you?

STANZA.

I've heard that they so temper Eastern clay [291]
    That they in forty years one cup prepare:
Hundreds are made in Baghdād in a day,
    And hence the lowness of the price they bear.

---

[291] The other translators render خاکِ مشرق *khāk-i mashrik*, "in the land of the East," "dans le pays d'Orient," etc.; but surely the translation I have given is at least as defensible.

VERSE.

The young bird from its egg comes forth and meets at
 once its fate,
While infant man is destitute of reason and of sense :
Too soon matured the first arrives at nothing high or great;
 The second with slow steps attains a proud pre-eminence.
Crystal is everywhere beheld, and hence contemned its
 state;
 But since the ruby's rarely found, its worth's the
  consequence.

MAXIM XXXV.

Affairs succeed by patience; and he that is hasty falleth headlong.

DISTICHS.

I've in the desert with these eyes beheld
The hurrying pilgrim to the slow-stepped yield :
The rapid courser in the rear remains,
While the slow camel still its step maintains.

MAXIM XXXVI.

There is no better ornament for the ignorant than silence, and did he but know this he would not be ignorant.

STANZA.

Hast thou not perfect excellence, 'tis best
 To keep thy tongue in silence, for 'tis this
Which shames a man ; as lightness does attest
 The nut is empty, nor of value is.

STANZA.

Once, in these words, a fool rebuked an ass,—
 " Go, thou who all thy life hast lived in vain ! "
A sage said to him, " Blockhead ! why dost pass
 Thy time in this ? Gibes will be all thy gain.
To learn of thee a brute no power has :
 Learn thou of brutes in silence to remain."

DISTICHS.

Whoe'er his answer does not ponder, will,
In most affairs, be found to answer ill;
Thy speech embellish with man's sense and wit,
Or learn in silence like a brute to sit.

Maxim XXXVII.

Whoever disputes with a man more wise than himself, to make people think him wise, will be thought ignorant.

COUPLET.

When one more wise than thou begins to speak,
Do not, tho' skilful, to oppose him seek.

Maxim XXXVIII.

Whoso sits with bad men will not see aught good.

DISTICHS.

With demons did an angel take his seat,
He'd learn but terror, treason, and deceit:
Thou from the bad wilt nothing learn but ill;
The wolf will ne'er the furrier's office fill.

Maxim XXXIX.

Divulge not the secret faults of men; for at the same time that thou disgracest them thou wilt destroy thy own credit.

Maxim XL.

He that has acquired learning and not practised what he has learnt, is like a man who ploughs but sows no seed.

Maxim XLI.

Worship cannot be performed by the body without the mind, and a shell without a kernel will not do for merchandise.

Maxim XLII.

Not every one who is ready at wrangling is correct in his dealings.

COUPLET.

Forms enow beneath the mantle wear the outward signs of grace;
But if thou shouldst them unwimple, thou wouldst find a grandam's face.

Maxim XLIII.

If every night was a night of power,[292] the Night of Power would lose its value.

COUPLET.

Were each stone such ruby as is found in Badakhshānyan earth,
How would then the ruby differ from the pebble in its worth?

Maxim XLIV.

Not every one whose outward form is graceful possesses the graces of the mind; for action depends on the heart, not on the exterior.

---

[292] Gladwin seems to me to destroy the pith of this sentence by rendering شب قدر *shab-i kadr*, "many of such nights;" to say nothing of making a singular noun plural. Chapter xcvii. of the Ḳur'ān is as follows: "Verily, we sent down the Ḳur'ān in the night of Al Ḳadr. And what shall make thee understand how excellent the night of Al Ḳadr is? The night of Al Ḳadr is better than a thousand months. Therein do the angels descend, and the spirit Gabriel also, by the permission of their Lord, with his decrees concerning every matter. It is peace until the rising of the morn." The Moslem doctors are not agreed when to fix this night; but most think it one of the last nights of Ramazān, and the seventh reckoned backwards, whence it will fall between the 23rd and 24th days of that month.

STANZA.

From a man's qualities a day's enough
  To make us of his learning's limit sure.
Plume not thyself as though the hidden stuff
  Thou of his heart hast reached; nor be secure,
For not e'en long revolving years can tell
The foul things which in man unnoticed dwell.

MAXIM XLV.

He who joins battle with the great sheds his own blood.

STANZA.

Say'st thou, "Behold! how great I am!"
  The squint-eyed even thus of one makes two;
Who play at butting with a ram
  Will quick enough a broken forehead rue.

MAXIM XLVI.

It is not the part of wise men to grapple with a lion, or strike the fist against a sword.

COUPLET.

Not in contention with the furious stand,
And near the mighty humbly clasp thy hand.[293]

MAXIM XLVII.

A weak man, who has the fool-hardiness to contend with a strong one, assists his adversary in destroying himself.

STANZA.

He who was nursed in soft repose
  Cannot with warriors to the battle go;
Vain with his weakly arm to close,
  And struggle with an iron-wristed foe.

---

[293] *Literally,* "Put thy hand under thy armpit;" *i.e.* "Put thyself in a peaceful attitude."

Maxim XLVIII.

Whoso will not listen to advice aims at hearing himself reproached.

COUPLET.

He who will not to friends' advice attend,
Must not complain when they him reprehend.

Maxim XLIX.

Persons devoid of virtue cannot endure the sight of the virtuous; just as market-curs, when they see dogs of the chase, bark at them, but dare not approach them.

Maxim L.

When a base fellow cannot vie with another in merit, he will attack him with malicious slander.

COUPLET.

Weak envy absent virtue slanders,—Why?
Since it is dumb, perforce, when it is by.

Maxim LI.

But for the tyranny of hunger no bird would fall into the snare—nay, the fowler himself would not set the snare.

COUPLET.

The belly binds the hands, the feet unnerves;
He heeds not heaven who his belly serves.

Maxim LII.

Wise men eat late; devout men but half satisfy their appetites; and hermits take only enough to support life; the young eat till the dishes are removed, and the old till they sweat; but the Ḳalandars[291] stuff till they have no room in their stomachs to breathe, and not a morsel is left on the table for any one.

[291] A sort of faḳīr.

COUPLET.

The glutton for two nights no sleep can get;
The first from surfeit, the next from regret.²⁹⁵

MAXIM LIII.

To consult with women is ruin, and to be liberal to the mischievous is a crime.

COUPLET.

To sharp-toothed tigers kind to be
To harmless flocks is tyranny.²⁹⁶

MAXIM LIV.

Whoso slays not his enemy when he is in his power is his own enemy.

COUPLET.

When a stone is in the hand; on a stone the serpent's pate;
He is not a man of sense who to strike should hesitate.

There are, however, persons who think the opposite of this advisable, and have said, "It is better to pause in the execution of prisoners, inasmuch as the option [of slaying or pardoning them] is retained. Whereas, if a prisoner

---

²⁹⁵ *Literally*, "One who is a captive in the bonds of the belly." Gladwin translates the دل تنگی *dil tangī*, in the second line, "want." M. Semelet, more literally, "inquiétude de cœur." I suppose it to be "regret," for having eaten the supplies for the next day. Dr. Sprenger reads معدهٔ خالی *mi'dah-i khālī*, for معدهٔ سنگی *mi'dah-i sangī*, which I cannot approve.

²⁹⁶ As the couplet in my edition occurs, and has been already translated under Maxim VIII., I prefer rendering Dr. Sprenger's and M. Semelet's reading, which is as follows:—

ترحّم بر پلنگِ تیز دندان
ستمگاري بود بر گوسفندان

and which occurs in my edition after the next couplet.

be put to death without deliberation, it is probable that the best course will be let slip, since the step is irremediable."

COUPLETS.

'Tis very easy one alive to slay;
Not so to give back life thou tak'st away:
Reason demands that archers patience show,
For shafts once shot return not to the bow.

MAXIM LV.

The sage who engages in controversy with ignorant people must not expect to be treated with honour; and if a fool should overpower a philosopher by his loquacity, it is not to be wondered at, for a common stone will break a jewel.

COUPLET.

What marvel is it if his spirits droop?
A nightingale—and with him crows to coop!

COUPLETS.

What if a vagabond on merit rail?
Let not the spirits of the worthy fail:
A common stone may break a golden cup:
Its value goes not down, the stone's not up.

MAXIM LVI.

If in a company of dissolute fellows the discourse of a wise man is not received with attention, be not astonished; for the sound of the lute is drowned by that of the drum, and the perfume of ambergris is overpowered by the fœtor of garlic.

VERSE.

Proud has the loud-voiced wittol grown,
That impudence the wise has overthrown;
Know'st thou not Ḥijāz' strains too low-toned are
To mingle with the brazen drum of war.

If a jewel fall into the mire it remains as precious as

before: and though dust should ascend to heaven, its former worthlessness will not be altered. A capacity without education is pitiable, and education without capacity is thrown away. Ashes, though akin to what is exalted, inasmuch as fire is essentially noble, yet, not possessing any intrinsic worth, are no better than dirt; and the value of sugar is not derived from the cane, but from its own inherent qualities. Musk is that which of itself yields a sweet smell, not that which the perfumer says is musk.[297] The wise man is like the tray of the druggist—silent, but evincing its own merits; and the ignorant man resembles the drum of the warrior—loud-voiced, and empty, and bragging vainly.

VERSE.

A learned man, as sages state,
Among the dull illiterate,
Is like a beauty 'mid the blind,
Or Ḳur'ān to the impious mind.
In Canaan's land, when sin prevailed,
The Prophet's birth no fruit entailed.
If innate worth is in thee born,
[Thy origin deserves not scorn,]
The rose aye blossoms on the thorn;
[The worthless may engender worth,]
And Āzur gave to Abraham birth.

MAXIM LVII.

It is not right to estrange in a moment a friend whom it takes a lifetime to secure.

TRIPLET.

'Tis years before the pebble can put on
The ruby's nature.—Wilt thou on a stone
In one short moment mar what time has done?

---

[297] He may call that which is adulterated or counterfeit "musk."

Maxim LVIII.

Reason is a captive in the hands of the passions, as a weak man in the hands of an artful woman.

COUPLET.

Shut on that house the door of sweet content,
Where woman can aloud her passions vent.

Maxim LIX.

Purpose without power is mere weakness and deception; and power without purpose is fatuity and insanity.

COUPLET.

Have judgment, counsel, sense, and then bear rule;
Wealth, empire, are self-murder [298] to the fool.

Maxim LX.

The liberal man, who enjoys and bestows, is better than the devotee, who fasts and lays by. Whoso abandons lust in order to gain acceptance with the world has fallen from venial desires into those which are unpardonable.

COUPLET.

Hermits, who are not so through piety,
Darken a glass and then attempt to see.

COUPLET.

Little to little added much will grow:
The barn's store, grain by grain, is gathered so.

Many littles make a mickle, many drops a flood.

Maxim LXI.

It is not right for a learned man to pass over leniently

---

[298] I prefer Gladwin's and Gentius' renderings of this passage to those of Semelet and Ross. Literally, the sense of the second line is, "For the territories and wealth of the ignorant are the weapons of warfare against himself."

the foolish impertinencies of the vulgar, for this is detrimental to both parties: the awe which the former ought to inspire is diminished, and the folly of the latter augmented.

COUPLET.

Art thou with fools too courteous and too free,
Their pride and folly will augmented be.

Maxim LXII.

Wickedness, by whomsoever committed, is odious: but most of all in men of learning; for learning is the weapon with which Satan is combated; and when a man is made captive with arms in his hand, his shame is more excessive.

COUPLET.

Better an ignorant and wretched state
Than to be learned and yet profligate;
That from the path his blindness did beguile;
This saw, and in a pitfall slipped the while.

Maxim LXIII.

People forget the name of him whose bread they have not tasted during his lifetime. Joseph the just (Peace be on him!), during the famine in Egypt, would not eat so as to satisfy his appetite, that he might not forget the hungry. It is the poor widow that relishes the grapes, not the owner of the vineyard.[299]

COUPLETS.

He who in pleasure and abundance lives,
What knows he of the pang that hunger gives?
He can affliction best appreciate,
Who has himself experienced the same state.

[299] That is, We estimate blessings when we are deprived of them, and value highly what is beyond our reach.

STANZA.

O thou! who rid'st a mettled courser, see
   How toils, 'mid mire, the poor thorn-loaded ass!
From poor men's houses, let no fire for thee
   Be brought. The wreaths which from their chimney
      pass,
Are sighs wrung from their hearts by destiny.[300]

Maxim LXIV.

Inquire not of the distressed darwesh in his destitution and time of want, "How art thou?" save on the condition that thou puttest ointment on his wound and settest money before him.

STANZA.

   The ass has fallen with its burthen—well!
      Thou mark'st it—then be pitiful, nor tread
   It down; but if thou askest how it fell,
   [Let not thy help to this be limited],
   But bravely strive to drag it forth instead.[301]

Maxim LXV.

Two things are impossible: to obtain more food than what Providence destines for us; and to die before the time known to God.

STANZA.

   Fate is not altered by a thousand sighs:
      Complain or render thanks—arrive it will:
   The angel at whose bidding winds arise
      Cares little for the widow's lamp, if still
   It burns, or by the storm extinguished dies.

---

[300] That is, do not wring from the poor the smallest trifle. The comparison between smoke and a sigh has occurred twice before. It is a simile in which Orientals delight, inept as it appears to us.

[301] *Literally,* "Gird up thy loins and, like brave men, lay hold of the ass's tail."

Maxim LXVI.

O thou! who seekest subsistence, sit down, that thou mayest be fed; and thou who desirest to die! go not [in pursuit of death]; for thou canst not preserve thy life [beyond the destined term].

STANZA.

Wouldst thou by toil or not thy wants supply,
   The Glorious and High God will give thee food.
Nor, mortal! canst thou unpredestined die,
Didst thou in maw of ravenous tigers lie,
   Or savage lions thirsting for thy blood.

Maxim LXVII.

It is impossible to lay hands on that which is not predestined for us, and that which is predestined will reach us wherever we are.

TRIPLET.

Hast thou not heard with what excess of pain
Sikandar sought the shades? nor yet could gain
Life's water, which he strove thus to attain.

Maxim LXVIII.

A fisherman cannot catch fish in the Tigris without the aid of destiny; nor can a fish perish on dry land unless fated to do so.

COUPLET.

Poor greedy wretch! where'er he drags himself,
Death him pursues, while he's pursuing pelf.

Maxim LXIX.

A wicked rich man is a gilded clod, and a pious darwesh is a beauty soiled with earth. The latter is the tattered garment of Moses patched together, and the former is the ulcer of Pharaoh[302] covered with jewels. The sufferings of the good have a joyful aspect, while the prosperity of the wicked looks downward.

STANZA.

Tell those to whom rank, wealth are given,
  Who care not for the sons of pain;
That in the bright abodes of Heaven
  They neither wealth nor rank will gain.

Maxim LXX.

The envious man begrudgeth God's blessings, and is the foe of the innocent.

STANZA.

A wretched crack-brained fellow once I saw,
  Who slandered one of lofty dignity;
I said, "Good sir! I grant thee that a flaw
  May in thy fortunes be observed,—but why
Impute it to the man who lives more happily?

SECOND STANZA.

Oh! on the envious man invoke no curse,
  For of himself, poor wretch! accursed is he;
On him no hatred can inflict aught worse
  Than his self-fed, self-torturing enmity.

Maxim LXXI.

A student without the inclination to learn is a lover without money; and a pilgrim without spirituality is a

---

[302] Ross translates ريش, *rīsh*, in this passage, "embroidered mantle," a strange freedom. M. Semelet renders it "la barbe," which is downright nonsense. Gladwin seems to me to have expressed the right meaning. One of the seven plagues was a boil and blain breaking out on the Egyptians.

bird without wings; and a devotee without learning[303] is a house without a door.

Maxim LXXII.

The intent of revealing the Ḳur'ān was, to give men the means of learning good morality, not that they should employ themselves in the mere recitation of the text. The man who is devout but illiterate, is one who performs his journey though it be on foot; while the man who is learned but negligent, is a sleeping rider. A sinner who lifts up his hand [in prayer] is better than a devotee who lifts up his head [in pride].

COUPLET.

Better the kind and courteous man of arms
Than lawyer who his fellow-creatures harms.

Maxim LXXIII.

A learned man without practice is a bee without honey.

COUPLET.

Go, tell the hornet—fierce, ungentle thing,
We want no honey: but at least don't sting!

Maxim LXXIV.

A man without courage is a woman,[304] and a devotee with covetous desires is a robber.

---

[303] ‘ilm, here, is "learning" rather than "knowledge," as Gladwin renders it. The devotee may have knowledge of spiritual things; but, not having learning, he may be unable to teach others, and thus resemble a house well furnished and spacious, but inaccessible.

[304] There is an equivoque in the Persian which cannot be preserved in English. zan is "a woman," rah-zan "a robber." Gladwin translates muruwat, in my opinion, incorrectly.

STANZA.

Thou! who t'appease the crowd and win repute
   Hast made the robe of outward actions white;
Know, to resign the world doth better suit
   The pious, and to be regardless quite
Whether the sleeve be long or short to sight.

Maxim LXXV.

Two sorts of persons cannot cease to feel regret at heart, nor can they extricate the foot of remorse from the mire: one is the merchant, whose vessel has been wrecked; and the other, the heir who has become the associate of Ḳalandars. In accordance with this they have said: "Though the robe bestowed by the Sulṭān is precious, people's own clothes are more regarded; and though the tray of dishes at the table of the great is full of delicacies, yet the scraps of one's own wallet are better relished."

COUPLET.

Than the mayor's kid and loaf more dainty far
Are our poor herbs—self-earned—and vinegar.

Maxim LXXVI.

It is contrary to right reason, and a violation of the precepts of the wise, to take medicine about which we are in doubt; and to travel by a road we do not know, save in the company of a caravan.

Maxim LXXVII.

They asked the Imām and spiritual guide—Muhammad bin Muhammad Ghizālī—(may the mercy of God be upon him!) by what means he had attained such a degree of learning. He replied, "In this way: I was not ashamed to ask whatever I did not know."

STANZA.

Hope thou with reason for good health, when thou
    Dost to the skilful leech thy pulse present;
Ask what thou know'st not—with the stigma, now,
    (If shame there be) of asking be content;
And thus in learning grow pre-eminent.

Maxim LXXVIII.

Whenever thou art certain of being informed of a thing, be not precipitate in inquiry; for this will lessen thy credit and respectability.

VERSE.

When Lukmān marked how wax-like iron grew,
    Moulded in David's hands; though wondrous, he
Forbore to ask his secret; for he knew
    He of himself would learn the mystery.

Maxim LXXIX.

It is one of the essentials of society that thou either play the part of host thyself, or act so as to conciliate the host.[305]

STANZA.

Let thy story aye befit
    The hearer's taste, wouldst thou that he approve;[306]
They who would with Majnūn sit,
    Must still of Laila talk—still talk of love.

---

[305] Gladwin translates, "Amongst the qualifications for society, it is necessary either that you attend to the concerns of your household, or else devote yourself to religion." This is, no doubt, the implied meaning. Life is compared to an entertainment, where, if you choose the part of host, you must entertain religious men; or, if you would be a guest, be a religious man yourself, and so please the Great Host, that is, God.

[306] I should wish to read, in the second line of this stanza, اگر خواهی *agar khwāhi*, instead of اگر دانی *agar dāni*, which appears to me to be nonsense. If a man knew that another was well disposed to him, he might presume, on that, to say unpalatable things; but if he wished to ingratiate himself, he would choose a pleasing subject.

Maxim LXXX.

Whoso associates with the wicked will be accused of following their ways, though their principles may have made no impression upon him; just as if a person were in the habit of frequenting taverns, he would not be supposed to go there for prayer, but to drink intoxicating liquors.

DISTICHS.

> Thyself thou'lt surely stigmatise,
> In choosing for thy friends th' unwise.
> I asked a sage for one sound rule;
> He said, "Consort not with a fool,
> For this of wise men fools will make,
> And even fools deteriorate."

Maxim LXXXI.

So tractable is the camel that, as is well known, if a child took hold of its bridle and led it a hundred parasangs, it would not withdraw its neck from obeying him: but if they came to a dangerous road which might cause its destruction, and the child, through ignorance, wished to go that way, it would wrest the reins from his grasp, and would not after that obey him: for, in the time when rough dealing is required, kindness is blameable; and they have said: "An enemy will not become friendly by being treated with kindness; but, on the contrary, his avarice will be increased."

STANZA.

> Thou to the courteous humble be, as dust;
>   But rough to those with whom thou hast a feud;[307]
> A soft file will not cleanse deep-seated rust:
>   Then use not gentle language with the rude.

---

[307] I have translated this line freely. Literally, it is, "If he oppose thee, fill his two eyes with mud."

Maxim LXXXII.

Whoever interrupts the conversation of others to display the extent of his wisdom, will assuredly discover the depth of his folly: and the wise have said:

STANZA.

"Until they him interrogate,
    The prudent man will aye continue mute;
For though his words might be sedate,
    Men would to folly the display impute."

Maxim LXXXIII.

I had once a sore under my robe. My religious superior (on whom be the mercy of God!) every day asked me, "How art thou?" and he did not inquire, "On what part is thy wound?" forbearing, because it is not right to mention every member: and the wise have said: "Whoever does not weigh his words, will receive an answer that will vex him."

STANZA.

Until thou knowest that a speech is sooth,
    Thou shouldest not unclose thy lips to speak:
Better to be confined for speaking truth
    Than, by false speaking, thy release to seek.

Maxim LXXXIV.

The uttering of a falsehood is like a violent blow; for, even should the wound be healed, the scar will remain. Thus, when the brothers of Joseph (peace be on him!) had acquired the character of telling untruths, their words were not believed, even when they said that which was true. God Most High has said, "*But your passions have suggested this to you.*"[308]

---

[308] *Vide* Sale's Kur'ān. II. 85. Jacob is speaking.

STANZA.

When 'tis one's habit aye the truth to say,
    A slip is pardoned readily;
But should one be renowned the other way,
    Even in his truth we error see.

Maxim LXXXV.

The most glorious of created things, in outward form, is man; and the most vile of living things, is a dog; yet, by the unanimous consent of the wise, a grateful dog is better than an ungrateful man.

STANZA.

The scrap thou on a dog bestowest, it—
    Though pelted oft—will yet remember still;
But though thro' life the base thou benefit,
    They for the merest trifle would thee kill.

Maxim LXXXVI.

The sensual ne'er can eminence attain;
And those who have not merit should not reign.

DISTICHS.

Spare not the glutton ox, for know that he
Who much devours will also slothful be:
If thou must needs be fatted like the ox,
Then like the ass submit to people's knocks.

Maxim LXXXVII.

It is said, in the Gospel,[309] "O son of Adam! if I give thee wealth, thou wilt occupy thyself with riches and

---

[309] This is probably a quotation from some spurious Gospel. Ross refers to Proverbs. chap. xxx. ver. 7, 8, 9. "Two things have I required of thee; deny me them not before I die: Remove far from me vanity and lies: give me neither poverty nor riches; feed me with food convenient for me: Lest I be full and deny thee, and say, Who is the Lord? or lest I be poor, and steal, and take the name of my God in vain."

neglect me; and, if I make thee poor, then thou wilt cower down in distress. Wherefore, in what state wilt thou find the happiness of praising me? or when wilt thou hasten to serve me?"

STANZA.

With riches now thou art too proud, elate;
  Or sinkest down too low beneath the rod:
Since this in joy and sorrow is thy state,
  When wilt thou turn from selfishness to God?

Maxim LXXXVIII.

The will of Him who has no like brings down one man from a royal throne, and preserves another in the belly of a fish.

COUPLET.

He who parts not from Thy praises will enjoy tranquillity,
Though—as was the Prophet Jonas—in the fish-maw he
    should be.

Maxim LXXXIX.

When God draws the sword of His wrath, prophets and saints draw back their heads [in fear of the stroke], and if He smile graciously with His eyes, He raises the bad to an equality with the good.

STANZA.

If in judgment He should, wrathful, words severe of
    anger say,
  What pardon e'en for saints were there?
Pray Him, therefore, from His mercy's face the veil to
    take away,
  And free e'en sinners from despair.

Maxim XC.

Whoso learns not from this world's lesson to take the right way, will be overtaken by the punishments of the next. *God Most High has said,* " *And we will cause them* to taste the lesser punishment of this world, besides the more grievous punishment of the next; peradventure they will repent."[310]

COUPLET.

The great admonish first—observant be!
Lest, if thou heed not words, they shackle thee.

Those endued with a happy disposition are warned by the anecdotes and precedents of former generations, so as not to become themselves a warning to those who follow them.

STANZA.

No bird will settle on the grain,
 That sees another bird already snared;
Take warning then from others' pain,
 Or else to point a moral be prepared.

MAXIM XCI.

How can one, the ear of whose choice has been made heavy, hear? and how can he, who is drawn by the noose of happy destiny, decline to proceed.[311]

STANZA.

The dark night of the friends of Heaven
 Shines with the brilliant light of day;
Not to man's might is this rich blessing given,
 It comes from God—no other way.

QUATRAIN.

To whom, save Thee, shall I complain? Thou only
 Rulest; and no arm equals thine in might;
Guided by Thee, none are e'er lost or lonely;
 Whom Thou forsakest, none can guide aright.

---

[310] *Vide* Kur'ān, chap. xxxii. ver. 22; Sale's Translation. p. 311.

[311] This seems to be the doctrine of Predestination. Ross and Gladwin both omit to translate the word ارادت *irādat*, and the latter omits also سعادت *saādat*.

Maxim XCII.

A beggar whose end is blest is better than a king who dies miserably.

COUPLET.

Better feel sorrow ere we gladness know,
Than to be happy and then suffer woe.

Maxim XCIII.

The sky supplies the earth with showers, while the earth renders back dust. *Every vessel allows that to permeate through it which it contains.*[312]

COUPLET.

My temper seems unpleasing in thy eyes;
Change not for that thy better qualities.

God Most High sees [our sins], but casts a veil over them; and our neighbour blazes abroad [our offences], though he sees them not.

COUPLET.

Save us, good Lord! could men in secret see,
None were from others' interference free!

Maxim XCIV.

Gold is procured from the vein by digging the mine, and from the miser's clutches by digging out his mind.[313]

STANZA.

Base men enjoy not, and to lonely haunts
  Slink sullen, and they say, "On hope to feed
Is better than to gratify one's wants."
  One day thou'lt see the victim of his greed
A corse,—his foes exulting and his money freed.[314]

---

[312] In other words, "That which exudes from a vessel is of the same nature as its contents." Our proverb is, "You cannot make a silk purse out of a sow's ear."

[313] جان کندن *jan kandan*, means, literally, "to dig out the soul," and is generally applied to the agonies of death.

[314] That is, from his clutches.

Maxim XCV.

Whoso shews no compassion to the weak will suffer from the violence of the strong.

DISTICHS.

Not every arm that is of might possessed,
Can crush the poor or ruin the distressed:
Grieve not the feeble, lest in turn thou, too,
Th' oppressor's power and injustice rue.

Maxim XCVI.

The prudent man, when he beholds contention arising, steps aside; and when he sees that peace prevails, casts anchor there: for, in the one case, safety lies in withdrawing, and, in the other, he is assured of tranquillity.

Maxim XCVII.

The gamester wants three sixes, but three aces turn up.

COUPLET.

Far better is the pasture than the plain [315]
But the horse guides not for himself the rein.

Maxim XCVIII.

A darwesh said in his prayers, "O God! have mercy on the wicked, for Thou hast already had mercy on the good, in that Thou hast created them good!"

Maxim XCIX.

The first person who introduced distinctions of dress, and the habit of wearing rings on the finger, was Jamshíd.[316] They asked him, Why he had conferred all these ornaments on the left arm, while the right was the more excellent? He replied, "The right arm is completely adorned in being the right."

---

[315] مَیْدان *maidán*, "plain," is used for the "parade-ground," "place of exercise," "battle-field."

[316] An ancient king of Persia, being the fourth monarch of the first or Píshdádyan dynasty. He built Istakhar or Persepolis, and was dethroned by Zaḥḥák.

STANZA.

Said Farīdūn to China's men of art,
　"Round my pavilion's walls embroider this,—
'If thou art wise, to bad men good impart;
　The good enough of honour have and bliss.'"

MAXIM C.

They asked an eminent personage why, when the right hand was so superior to the left, men were in the habit of placing the signet-ring on the left hand? He rejoined, "Knowest thou not that merit is always neglected?"

COUPLET.

He from whom fate, subsistence, fortunes spring,
Now makes a man of merit, now a king.

MAXIM CI.

He may advise kings safely who has neither fear for his head nor cupidity.

DISTICHS.

Whether thou money at his feet dost spread,
Who truly worships God; or o'er his head
Wavest the Indian scymitar; no dread
Has he of mortal man: in this
True faith consists,—this orthodoxy is,

MAXIM CII.

A king is for the coercion of oppressors, and the superintendent of police to repress murder, and the judge for hearing complaints against thieves. Two parties, whose aim is justice only, never refer matters to the judge.

STANZA.

Art thou assured that thou must justice do—
　Then better do it gently, without strife.
Who pay not taxes willingly, will rue
The law's exactions, and the misproud crew
　Of insolent officials. Stubbornness is rife
With a twin evil—shame and damage too.

Maxim CIII.

All men's teeth are blunted by sour things except the judge's, whose edge is taken off by sweets.

COUPLET.

The judge five cucumbers as a bribe will take,
And grant ten beds of melons for their sake.

Maxim CIV.

What can an old prostitute do but vow not to sin any more? or a superintendent of police discharged from office, except promise not to cease from injustice?

COUPLET.

He leads the hermit's life, who chooses it
In youth; for age cannot its corner quit.

Maxim CV.

They asked a philosopher, Why, when God Most High had created so many famous fruitful trees, the cypress alone was called free, which bore no fruit? and what was the meaning of this? He replied, "Every tree has its appointed time and season, so that, during the said season, it flourishes; and when that is past, it droops. But the cypress is not exposed to either of these vicissitudes, and is at all times fresh and green; and this is the condition of the free."

STANZA.

Place not thy heart on transitory things.
   Long shall the Tigris on by Baghdād flow,
When all the glory of the Caliph kings
Has passed away. Be, if thou canst be so,
Like the date, generous. Canst thou nought bestow
   From lack of means; at least resolve to be,
   Like the green cypress, fetterless and free.

Maxim CVI.

Two persons die remorseful; he who possessed and enjoyed not, and he who knew but did not practise.

STANZA.

A miser may have merit; yet none see
  His face, but strive his actions to abuse:
While twice a hundred failings there may be,
  In those who do a liberal conduct use;
    Yet will their generosity those faults excuse.

CONCLUSION OF THE BOOK.

The book of the Gulistān is ended by the assistance of God. Throughout the work I have forborne to borrow ornaments from the verses of preceding poets, as is customary with authors.

COUPLET.

Better patch up one's own old garment, than
Borrow the raiment of another man.

For the most part, Sādi's discourse is commingled with pleasantry and cheerful wit; and this furnishes a pretext to the shortsighted for saying that it is not the part of wise men to rack the brain with absurdities, or expend the midnight oil unprofitably. It is, however, not concealed from the clear minds of the really enlightened, for whom this discourse is intended, that the pearls of salutary counsel are strung on the thread of my diction, and the bitter medicine of advice mixed up in it with the honey of mirthful humour; lest the mind of the reader should be disgusted, and he should thus remain excluded from the beneficial acceptance of my words.

DISTICHS.

I have fulfilled my mission, and have given
  Wholesome advice: my life's endeavour this.
What though men hear not. Messengers of Heaven
  Can but discharge their duty: and it is
  To tell their message—point the way to bliss.

Reader! for him who wrote this book, ask grace;
And let the scribe, too, in thy prayers find place:
Next for thyself whate'er thou wishest pray;
Lastly, a blessing for the owner say.
By aid of the all-gracious king,
This work here to an end we bring.

TRÜBNER'S ORIENTAL SERIES.

"A knowledge of the commonplace, at least, of Oriental literature, philosophy, and religion is as necessary to the general reader of the present day as an acquaintance with the Latin and Greek classics was a generation or so ago. Immense strides have been made within the present century in these branches of learning; Sanskrit has been brought within the range of accurate philology, and its invaluable ancient literature thoroughly investigated; the language and sacred books of the Zoroastrians have been laid bare; Egyptian, Assyrian, and other records of the remote past have been deciphered, and a group of scholars speak of still more recondite Accadian and Hittite monuments; but the results of all the scholarship that has been devoted to these subjects have been almost inaccessible to the public because they were contained for the most part in learned or expensive works, or scattered throughout the numbers of scientific periodicals. Messrs. TRÜBNER & Co., in a spirit of enterprise which does them infinite credit, have determined to supply the constantly-increasing want, and to give in a popular, or, at least, a comprehensive form, all this mass of knowledge to the world."—*Times.*

New Edition in preparation,

Post 8vo, with Map,

THE INDIAN EMPIRE: ITS HISTORY, PEOPLE, AND PRODUCTS.

Being a revised form of the article "India," in the "Imperial Gazetteer," remodelled into chapters, brought up to date, and incorporating the general results of the Census of 1881.

By the Hon. W. W. HUNTER, C.S.I., C.I.E., LL.D.,

Member of the Viceroy's Legislative Council,

Director-General of Statistics to the Government of India.

"The article 'India,' in Volume IV., is the touchstone of the work, and proves clearly enough the sterling metal of which it is wrought. It represents the essence of the 100 volumes which contain the results of the statistical survey conducted by Dr. Hunter throughout each of the 240 districts of India. It is, moreover, the only attempt that has ever been made to show how the Indian people have been built up, and the evidence from the original materials has been for the first time sifted and examined by the light of the local research in which the author was for so long engaged."—*Times.*

THE FOLLOWING WORKS HAVE ALREADY APPEARED:—

Third Edition, post 8vo, cloth, pp. xvi.—428, price 16s.

ESSAYS ON THE SACRED LANGUAGE, WRITINGS, AND RELIGION OF THE PARSIS.

BY MARTIN HAUG, PH.D.,

Late of the Universities of Tübingen, Göttingen, and Bonn; Superintendent of Sanskrit Studies, and Professor of Sanskrit in the Poona College.

EDITED AND ENLARGED BY DR. E. W. WEST.

To which is added a Biographical Memoir of the late Dr. HAUG by Prof. E. P. EVANS.

I. History of the Researches into the Sacred Writings and Religion of the Parsis, from the Earliest Times down to the Present.
II. Languages of the Parsi Scriptures.
III. The Zend-Avesta, or the Scripture of the Parsis.
IV. The Zoroastrian Religion, as to its Origin and Development.

"'Essays on the Sacred Language, Writings, and Religion of the Parsis,' by the late Dr. Martin Haug, edited by Dr. E. W. West. The author intended, on his return from India, to expand the materials contained in this work into a comprehensive account of the Zoroastrian religion, but the design was frustrated by his untimely death. We have, however, in a concise and readable form, a history of the researches into the sacred writings and religion of the Parsis from the earliest times down to the present—a dissertation on the languages of the Parsi Scriptures, a translation of the Zend-Avesta, or the Scripture of the Parsis, and a dissertation on the Zoroastrian religion, with especial reference to its origin and development."—*Times*.

Post 8vo, cloth, pp. viii.—176, price 7s. 6d.

TEXTS FROM THE BUDDHIST CANON
COMMONLY KNOWN AS "DHAMMAPADA."
With Accompanying Narratives.

Translated from the Chinese by S. BEAL, B.A., Professor of Chinese, University College, London.

The Dhammapada, as hitherto known by the Pāli Text Edition, as edited by Fausböll, by Max Müller's English, and Albrecht Weber's German translations, consists only of twenty-six chapters or sections, whilst the Chinese version, or rather recension, as now translated by Mr. Beal, consists of thirty-nine sections. The students of Pāli who possess Fausböll's text, or either of the above named translations, will therefore needs want Mr. Beal's English rendering of the Chinese version; the thirteen above-named additional sections not being accessible to them in any other form; for, even if they understand Chinese, the Chinese original would be unobtainable by them.

"Mr. Beal's rendering of the Chinese translation is a most valuable aid to the critical study of the work. It contains authentic texts gathered from ancient canonical books, and generally connected with some incident in the history of Buddha. Their great interest, however, consists in the light which they throw upon everyday life in India at the remote period at which they were written, and upon the method of teaching adopted by the founder of the religion. The method employed was principally parable, and the simplicity of the tales and the excellence of the morals inculcated, as well as the strange hold which they have retained upon the minds of millions of people, make them a very remarkable study."—*Times*.

"Mr. Beal, by making it accessible in an English dress, has added to the great services he has already rendered to the comparative study of religious history."—*Academy*.

"Valuable as exhibiting the doctrine of the Buddhists in its purest, least adulterated form, it brings the modern reader face to face with that simple creed and rule of conduct which won its way over the minds of myriads, and which is now nominally professed by 145 millions, who have overlaid its austere simplicity with innumerable ceremonies, forgotten its maxims, perverted its teaching, and so inverted its leading principle that a religion whose founder denied a God, now worships that founder as a god himself." —*Scotsman*.

Second Edition, post 8vo, cloth, pp. xxiv.—360, price 10s. 6d.

THE HISTORY OF INDIAN LITERATURE.

By ALBRECHT WEBER.

Translated from the Second German Edition by JOHN MANN, M.A., and THÉODOR ZACHARIAE, Ph.D., with the sanction of the Author.

Dr. BUHLER, Inspector of Schools in India, writes:—"When I was Professor of Oriental Languages in Elphinstone College, I frequently felt the want of such a work to which I could refer the students."

Professor COWELL, of Cambridge, writes:—"It will be especially useful to the students in our Indian colleges and universities. I used to long for such a book when I was teaching in Calcutta. Hindu students are intensely interested in the history of Sanskrit literature, and this volume will supply them with all they want on the subject."

Professor WHITNEY, Yale College, Newhaven, Conn., U.S.A., writes:—"I was one of the class to whom the work was originally given in the form of academic lectures. At their first appearance they were by far the most learned and able treatment of their subject; and with their recent additions they still maintain decidedly the same rank."

"Is perhaps the most comprehensive and lucid survey of Sanskrit literature extant. The essays contained in the volume were originally delivered as academic lectures, and at the time of their first publication were acknowledged to be by far the most learned and able treatment of the subject. They have now been brought up to date by the addition of all the most important results of recent research."—*Times.*

Post 8vo, cloth, pp. xii.—198, accompanied by Two Language Maps, price 12s.

A SKETCH OF THE MODERN LANGUAGES OF THE EAST INDIES.

By ROBERT N. CUST.

The Author has attempted to fill up a vacuum, the inconvenience of which pressed itself on his notice. Much had been written about the languages of the East Indies, but the extent of our present knowledge had not even been brought to a focus. It occurred to him that it might be of use to others to publish in an arranged form the notes which he had collected for his own edification.

"Supplies a deficiency which has long been felt."—*Times.*

"The book before us is then a valuable contribution to philological science. It passes under review a vast number of languages, and it gives, or professes to give, in every case the sum and substance of the opinions and judgments of the best-informed writers."—*Saturday Review.*

Second Corrected Edition, post 8vo, pp. xii.—116, cloth, price 5s.

THE BIRTH OF THE WAR-GOD.

A Poem. By KALIDASA.

Translated from the Sanskrit into English Verse by RALPH T. H. GRIFFITH, M.A.

"A very spirited rendering of the *Kumarasambhava*, which was first published twenty-six years ago, and which we are glad to see made once more accessible."—*Times.*

"Mr. Griffith's very spirited rendering is well known to most who are at all interested in Indian literature, or enjoy the tenderness of feeling and rich creative imagination of its author."—*Indian Antiquary.*

"We are very glad to welcome a second edition of Professor Griffith's admirable translation. Few translations deserve a second edition better."—*Athenæum.*

Post 8vo, pp. 432, cloth, price 16s.

A CLASSICAL DICTIONARY OF HINDU MYTHOLOGY AND RELIGION, GEOGRAPHY, HISTORY, AND LITERATURE.

By JOHN DOWSON, M.R.A.S.,
Late Professor of Hindustani, Staff College.

"This not only forms an indispensable book of reference to students of Indian literature, but is also of great general interest, as it gives in a concise and easily accessible form all that need be known about the personages of Hindu mythology whose names are so familiar, but of whom so little is known outside the limited circle of *savants*."—*Times*.

"It is no slight gain when such subjects are treated fairly and fully in a moderate space; and we need only add that the few wants which we may hope to see supplied in new editions detract but little from the general excellence of Mr. Dowson's work."—*Saturday Review*.

Post 8vo, with View of Mecca, pp. cxii.—172, cloth, price 9s.

SELECTIONS FROM THE KORAN.

By EDWARD WILLIAM LANE,
Translator of "The Thousand and One Nights;" &c., &c.
A New Edition, Revised and Enlarged, with an Introduction by
STANLEY LANE POOLE.

". . . Has been long esteemed in this country as the compilation of one of the greatest Arabic scholars of the time, the late Mr. Lane, the well-known translator of the 'Arabian Nights.' . . . The present editor has enhanced the value of his relative's work by divesting the text of a great deal of extraneous matter introduced by way of comment, and prefixing an introduction."—*Times*.

"Mr. Poole is both a generous and a learned biographer. . . . Mr. Poole tells us the facts . . . so far as it is possible for industry and criticism to ascertain them, and for literary skill to present them in a condensed and readable form."—*Englishman, Calcutta*.

Post 8vo, pp. vi.—368, cloth, price 14s.

MODERN INDIA AND THE INDIANS,

BEING A SERIES OF IMPRESSIONS, NOTES, AND ESSAYS.

By MONIER WILLIAMS, D.C.L.,
Hon. LL.D. of the University of Calcutta, Hon. Member of the Bombay Asiatic Society, Boden Professor of Sanskrit in the University of Oxford.

Third Edition, revised and augmented by considerable Additions, with Illustrations and a Map.

"In this volume we have the thoughtful impressions of a thoughtful man on some of the most important questions connected with our Indian Empire. . . . An enlightened observant man, travelling among an enlightened observant people, Professor Monier Williams has brought before the public in a pleasant form more of the manners and customs of the Queen's Indian subjects than we ever remember to have seen in any one work. He not only deserves the thanks of every Englishman for this able contribution to the study of Modern India—a subject with which we should be specially familiar—but he deserves the thanks of every Indian, Parsee or Hindu, Buddhist and Moslem, for his clear exposition of their manners, their creeds, and their necessities."—*Times*.

Post 8vo, pp. xliv.—376, cloth, price 14s.

METRICAL TRANSLATIONS FROM SANSKRIT WRITERS.

With an Introduction, many Prose Versions, and Parallel Passages from Classical Authors.

By J. MUIR, C.I.E., D.C.L., LL.D., Ph.D.

". . . An accessible introduction to Hindu poetry."—*Times*.

". . . A volume which may be taken as a fair illustration alike of the religious and moral sentiments and of the legendary lore of the best Sanskrit writers."—*Edinburgh Daily Review*.

Second Edition, post 8vo, pp. xxvi.—244, cloth, price 10s. 6d.

THE GULISTAN;

Or, ROSE GARDEN OF SHEKH MUSHLIU'D-DIN SADI OF SHIRAZ.

Translated for the First Time into Prose and Verse, with an Introductory Preface, and a Life of the Author, from the Atish Kadah,

By EDWARD B. EASTWICK, C.B., M.A., F.R.S., M.R.A.S.

"It is a very fair rendering of the original."—*Times.*

"The new edition has long been desired, and will be welcomed by all who take any interest in Oriental poetry. The *Gulistan* is a typical Persian verse-book of the highest order. Mr. Eastwick's rhymed translation . . . has long established itself in a secure position as the best version of Sadi's finest work."—*Academy.*

"It is both faithfully and gracefully executed."—*Tablet.*

In Two Volumes, post 8vo, pp. viii.—408 and viii.—348, cloth, price 28s.

MISCELLANEOUS ESSAYS RELATING TO INDIAN SUBJECTS.

By BRIAN HOUGHTON HODGSON, Esq., F.R.S.,

Late of the Bengal Civil Service; Corresponding Member of the Institute; Chevalier of the Legion of Honour; late British Minister at the Court of Nepál, &c., &c.

CONTENTS OF VOL. I.

SECTION I.—On the Koceh, Bódo, and Dhimál Tribes.—Part I. Vocabulary—Part II. Grammar.—Part III. Their Origin, Location, Numbers, Creed, Customs, Character, and Condition, with a General Description of the Climate they dwell in.—Appendix.

SECTION II.—On Himalayan Ethnology.—I. Comparative Vocabulary of the Languages of the Broken Tribes of Nepál.—II. Vocabulary of the Dialects of the Kiranti Language.—III. Grammatical Analysis of the Vayu Language. The Vayu Grammar.—IV. Analysis of the Báhing Dialect of the Kiranti Language. The Báhing Grammar.—V. On the Vayu or Hayu Tribe of the Central Himáláya.—VI. On the Kiranti Tribe of the Central Himáláya.

CONTENTS OF VOL. II.

SECTION III.—On the Aborigines of North-Eastern India. Comparative Vocabulary of the Tibetan, Bódo, and Gáro Tongues.

SECTION IV.—Aborigines of the North-Eastern Frontier.

SECTION V.—Aborigines of the Eastern Frontier.

SECTION VI.—The Indo-Chinese Borderers, and their connection with the Himalayans and Tibetans. Comparative Vocabulary of Indo-Chinese Borderers in Arakan. Comparative Vocabulary of Indo-Chinese Borderers in Tenasserim.

SECTION VII.—The Mongolian Affinities of the Caucasians.—Comparison and Analysis of Caucasian and Mongolian Words.

SECTION VIII.—Physical Type of Tibetans.

SECTION IX.—The Aborigines of Central India.—Comparative Vocabulary of the Aboriginal Languages of Central India.—Aborigines of the Eastern Ghats.—Vocabulary of some of the Dialects of the Hill and Wandering Tribes in the Northern Sircars.—Aborigines of the Nilgiris, with Remarks on their Affinities.—Supplement to the Nilgirian Vocabularies.—The Aborigines of Southern India and Ceylon.

SECTION X.—Route of Nepalese Mission to Pekin, with Remarks on the Water-Shed and Plateau of Tibet.

SECTION XI.—Route from Káthmándú, the Capital of Nepál, to Darjeeling in Sikim.—Memorandum relative to the Seven Cosis of Nepál.

SECTION XII.—Some Accounts of the Systems of Law and Police as recognised in the State of Nepál.

SECTION XIII.—The Native Method of making the Paper denominated Hindustan Nepalese.

SECTION XIV.—Pre-eminence of the Vernaculars; or, the Anglicists Answered; Being Letters on the Education of the People of India.

"For the study of the less-known races of India Mr. Brian Hodgson's 'Miscellaneous Essays' will be found very valuable both to the philologist and the ethnologist."—*Times.*

Third Edition, Two Vols., post 8vo, pp. viii.—268 and viii.—326, cloth, price 21s.

THE LIFE OR LEGEND OF GAUDAMA,

THE BUDDHA OF THE BURMESE. With Annotations.

The Ways to Neibban, and Notice on the Phongyies or Burmese Monks.

BY THE RIGHT REV. P. BIGANDET,

Bishop of Ramatha, Vicar-Apostolic of Ava and Pegu.

"The work is furnished with copious notes, which not only illustrate the subject-matter, but form a perfect encyclopædia of Buddhist lore."—*Times.*

"A work which will furnish European students of Buddhism with a most valuable help in the prosecution of their investigations."—*Edinburgh Daily Review.*

"Bishop Bigandet's invaluable work."—*Indian Antiquary.*

"Viewed in this light, its importance is sufficient to place students of the subject under a deep obligation to its author."—*Calcutta Review.*

"This work is one of the greatest authorities upon Buddhism."—*Dublin Review.*

Post 8vo, pp. xxiv.—420, cloth, price 18s.

CHINESE BUDDHISM.

A VOLUME OF SKETCHES, HISTORICAL AND CRITICAL.

BY J. EDKINS, D.D.

Author of "China's Place in Philology," "Religion in China," &c., &c.

"It contains a vast deal of important information on the subject, such as is only to be gained by long-continued study on the spot."—*Athenæum.*

"Upon the whole, we know of no work comparable to it for the extent of its original research, and the simplicity with which this complicated system of philosophy, religion, literature, and ritual is set forth."—*British Quarterly Review.*

"The whole volume is replete with learning. . . . It deserves most careful study from all interested in the history of the religions of the world, and expressly of those who are concerned in the propagation of Christianity. Dr. Edkins notices in terms of just condemnation the exaggerated praise bestowed upon Buddhism by recent English writers."—*Record.*

Post 8vo, pp. 496, cloth, price 18s.

LINGUISTIC AND ORIENTAL ESSAYS.

WRITTEN FROM THE YEAR 1846 TO 1878.

BY ROBERT NEEDHAM CUST,

Late Member of Her Majesty's Indian Civil Service; Hon. Secretary to the Royal Asiatic Society;

and Author of "The Modern Languages of the East Indies."

"We know none who has described Indian life, especially the life of the natives, with so much learning, sympathy, and literary talent."—*Academy.*

"They seem to us to be full of suggestive and original remarks."—*St. James's Gazette.*

"His book contains a vast amount of information. The result of thirty-five years of inquiry, reflection, and speculation, and that on subjects as full of fascination as of food for thought."—*Tablet.*

"Exhibit such a thorough acquaintance with the history and antiquities of India as to entitle him to speak as one having authority."—*Edinburgh Daily Review.*

"The author speaks with the authority of personal experience. . . . It is this constant association with the country and the people which gives such a vividness to many of the pages."—*Athenæum.*

Post 8vo, pp. civ.—348, cloth, price 18s.

BUDDHIST BIRTH STORIES; or, Jataka Tales.

The Oldest Collection of Folk-lore Extant:

BEING THE JATAKATTHAVANNANA,

For the first time Edited in the original Pâli.

BY V. FAUSBÖLL;

And Translated by T. W. RHYS DAVIDS.

Translation. Volume I.

"These are tales supposed to have been told by the Buddha of what he had seen and heard in his previous births. They are probably the nearest representatives of the original Aryan stories from which sprang the folk-lore of Europe as well as India. The introduction contains a most interesting disquisition on the migrations of these fables, tracing their reappearance in the various groups of folk-lore legends. Among other old friends, we meet with a version of the Judgment of Solomon."—*Times.*

"It is now some years since Mr. Rhys Davids asserted his right to be heard on this subject by his able article on Buddhism in the new edition of the 'Encyclopædia Britannica.'"—*Leeds Mercury.*

"All who are interested in Buddhist literature ought to feel deeply indebted to Mr. Rhys Davids. His well-established reputation as a Pali scholar is a sufficient guarantee for the fidelity of his version, and the style of his translations is deserving of high praise."—*Academy.*

"No more competent expositor of Buddhism could be found than Mr. Rhys Davids. In the Jâtaka book we have, then, a priceless record of the earliest imaginative literature of our race; and . . . it presents to us a nearly complete picture of the social life and customs and popular beliefs of the common people of Aryan tribes, closely related to ourselves, just as they were passing through the first stages of civilisation."—*St. James's Gazette.*

Post 8vo, pp. xxviii.—362, cloth, price 14s.

A TALMUDIC MISCELLANY;

OR, A THOUSAND AND ONE EXTRACTS FROM THE TALMUD, THE MIDRASHIM, AND THE KABBALAH.

Compiled and Translated by PAUL ISAAC HERSHON,

Author of "Genesis According to the Talmud," &c.

With Notes and Copious Indexes.

"To obtain in so concise and handy a form as this volume a general idea of the Talmud is a boon to Christians at least."—*Times.*

"Its peculiar and popular character will make it attractive to general readers. Mr. Hershon is a very competent scholar. . . . Contains samples of the good, bad, and indifferent, and especially extracts that throw light upon the Scriptures."—*British Quarterly Review.*

"Will convey to English readers a more complete and truthful notion of the Talmud than any other work that has yet appeared."—*Daily News.*

"Without overlooking in the slightest the several attractions of the previous volumes of the 'Oriental Series,' we have no hesitation in saying that this surpasses them all in interest."—*Edinburgh Daily Review.*

"Mr. Hershon has . . . thus given English readers what is, we believe, a fair set of specimens which they can test for themselves."—*The Record.*

"This book is by far the best fitted in the present state of knowledge to enable the general reader to gain a fair and unbiassed conception of the multifarious contents of the wonderful miscellany which can only be truly understood—so Jewish pride asserts—by the life-long devotion of scholars of the Chosen People."—*Inquirer.*

"The value and importance of this volume consist in the fact that scarcely a single extract is given in its pages but throws some light, direct or refracted, upon those Scriptures which are the common heritage of Jew and Christian alike."—*John Bull.*

"It is a capital specimen of Hebrew scholarship; a monument of learned, loving, light-giving labour."—*Jewish Herald.*

TRÜBNER'S ORIENTAL SERIES.

Post 8vo, pp. xii.—228, cloth, price 7s. 6d.

THE CLASSICAL POETRY OF THE JAPANESE.

By BASIL HALL CHAMBERLAIN,

Author of "Yeigo Heñkaku Shirañ."

"A very curious volume. The author has manifestly devoted much labour to the task of studying the poetical literature of the Japanese, and rendering characteristic specimens into English verse."—*Daily News.*

"Mr. Chamberlain's volume is, so far as we are aware, the first attempt which has been made to interpret the literature of the Japanese to the Western world. It is to the classical poetry of Old Japan that we must turn for indigenous Japanese thought, and in the volume before us we have a selection from that poetry rendered into graceful English verse."—*Tablet.*

"It is undoubtedly one of the best translations of lyric literature which has appeared during the close of the last year."—*Celestial Empire.*

"Mr. Chamberlain set himself a difficult task when he undertook to reproduce Japanese poetry in an English form. But he has evidently laboured *con amore*, and his efforts are successful to a degree."—*London and China Express.*

Post 8vo, pp. xii.—164, cloth, price 10s. 6d.

THE HISTORY OF ESARHADDON (Son of Sennacherib),

KING OF ASSYRIA, B.C. 681–668.

Translated from the Cuneiform Inscriptions upon Cylinders and Tablets in the British Museum Collection; together with a Grammatical Analysis of each Word, Explanations of the Ideographs by Extracts from the Bi-Lingual Syllabaries, and List of Eponyms, &c.

By ERNEST A. BUDGE, B.A., M.R.A.S.,

Assyrian Exhibitioner, Christ's College, Cambridge.

"Students of scriptural archæology will also appreciate the 'History of Esarhaddon.'"—*Times.*

"There is much to attract the scholar in this volume. It does not pretend to popularise studies which are yet in their infancy. Its primary object is to translate, but it does not assume to be more than tentative, and it offers both to the professed Assyriologist and to the ordinary non-Assyriological Semitic scholar the means of controlling its results."—*Academy.*

"Mr. Budge's book is, of course, mainly addressed to Assyrian scholars and students. They are not, it is to be feared, a very numerous class. But the more thanks are due to him on that account for the way in which he has acquitted himself in his laborious task."—*Tablet.*

Post 8vo, pp. 448, cloth, price 21s.

THE MESNEVI

(Usually known as THE MESNEVIYI SHERIF, or HOLY MESNEVI)

OF

MEVLANA (OUR LORD) JELALU 'D-DIN MUHAMMED ER-RUMI.

Book the First.

Together with some Account of the Life and Acts of the Author,
of his Ancestors, and of his Descendants.

Illustrated by a Selection of Characteristic Anecdotes, as Collected
by their Historian,

MEVLANA SHEMSU-'D-DIN AHMED, EL EFLAKI, EL 'ARIFI.

Translated, and the Poetry Versified, in English,

By JAMES W. REDHOUSE, M.R.A.S., &c.

"A complete treasury of occult Oriental lore."—*Saturday Review.*

"This book will be a very valuable help to the reader ignorant of Persia, who is desirous of obtaining an insight into a very important department of the literature extant in that language."—*Tablet.*

Post 8vo, pp. xvi.—280, cloth, price 6s.

EASTERN PROVERBS AND EMBLEMS
ILLUSTRATING OLD TRUTHS.

By Rev. J. LONG,

Member of the Bengal Asiatic Society, F.R.G.S.

"We regard the book as valuable, and wish for it a wide circulation and attentive reading."—*Record.*
"Altogether, it is quite a feast of good things."—*Globe.*
"It is full of interesting matter."—*Antiquary.*

Post 8vo, pp. viii.—270, cloth, price 7s. 6d.

INDIAN POETRY;

Containing a New Edition of the "Indian Song of Songs," from the Sanscrit of the "Gita Govinda" of Jayadeva; Two Books from "The Iliad of India" (Mahabharata), "Proverbial Wisdom" from the Shlokas of the Hitopadesa, and other Oriental Poems.

By EDWIN ARNOLD, C.S.I., Author of "The Light of Asia."

"In this new volume of Messrs. Trübner's Oriental Series, Mr. Edwin Arnold does good service by illustrating, through the medium of his musical English melodies, the power of Indian poetry to stir European emotions. The 'Indian Song of Songs' is not unknown to scholars. Mr. Arnold will have introduced it among popular English poems. Nothing could be more graceful and delicate than the shades by which Krishna is portrayed in the gradual process of being weaned by the love of

'Beautiful Radha, jasmine-bosomed Radha,'

from the allurements of the forest nymphs, in whom the five senses are typified."—*Times.*
"No other English poet has ever thrown his genius and his art so thoroughly into the work of translating Eastern ideas as Mr. Arnold has done in his splendid paraphrases of language contained in those mighty epics."—*Daily Telegraph.*
"The poem abounds with imagery of Eastern luxuriousness and sensuousness; the air seems laden with the spicy odours of the tropics, and the verse has a richness and a melody sufficient to captivate the senses of the dullest."—*Standard.*
"The translator, while producing a very enjoyable poem, has adhered with tolerable fidelity to the original text."—*Overland Mail.*
"We certainly wish Mr. Arnold success in his attempt 'to popularise Indian classics,' that being, as his preface tells us, the goal towards which he bends his efforts."—*Allen's Indian Mail.*

Post 8vo, pp. xvi.—296, cloth, price 10s. 6d.

THE MIND OF MENCIUS;
OR, POLITICAL ECONOMY FOUNDED UPON MORAL PHILOSOPHY.

A SYSTEMATIC DIGEST OF THE DOCTRINES OF THE CHINESE PHILOSOPHER MENCIUS.

Translated from the Original Text and Classified, with Comments and Explanations,

By the Rev. ERNST FABER, Rhenish Mission Society.

Translated from the German, with Additional Notes,

By the Rev. A. B. HUTCHINSON, C.M.S., Church Mission, Hong Kong.

"Mr. Faber is already well known in the field of Chinese studies by his digest of the doctrines of Confucius. The value of this work will be perceived when it is remembered that at no time since relations commenced between China and the West has the former been so powerful—we had almost said aggressive—as now. For those who will give it careful study, Mr. Faber's work is one of the most valuable of the excellent series to which it belongs."—*Nature.*

Post 8vo, pp. vi.—208, cloth, price 8s. 6d.

THE BHAGAVAD-GÎTÂ.

Translated, with Introduction and Notes
BY JOHN DAVIES, M.A. (Cantab.)

"Let us add that his translation of the Bhagavad Gîtâ is, as we judge, the best that has as yet appeared in English, and that his Philological Notes are of quite peculiar value."—*Dublin Review.*

Post 8vo, pp. 96, cloth, price 5s.

THE QUATRAINS OF OMAR KHAYYAM.

Translated by E. H. WHINFIELD, M.A.,
Barrister-at-Law, late H.M. Bengal Civil Service.

Post 8vo, pp. xxxii.—336, cloth, price 10s. 6d.

THE QUATRAINS OF OMAR KHAYYAM.

The Persian Text, with an English Verse Translation.
By E. H. WHINFIELD, late of the Bengal Civil Service.

"Mr. Whinfield has executed a difficult task with considerable success, and his version contains much that will be new to those who only know Mr. Fitzgerald's delightful selection." *Academy.*

"There are several editions of the Quatrains, varying greatly in their readings. Mr. Whinfield has used three of these for his excellent translation. The most prominent features in the Quatrains are their profound agnosticism, combined with a fatalism based more on philosophic than religious grounds, their Epicureanism and the spirit of universal tolerance and charity which animates them."—*Calcutta Review.*

Post 8vo, pp. xxiv.—268, cloth, price 9s.

THE PHILOSOPHY OF THE UPANISHADS AND ANCIENT INDIAN METAPHYSICS.

As exhibited in a series of Articles contributed to the *Calcutta Review.*
By ARCHIBALD EDWARD GOUGH, M.A., Lincoln College, Oxford;
Principal of the Calcutta Madrasa.

"For practical purposes this is perhaps the most important of the works that have thus far appeared in 'Trübner's Oriental Series.' . . . We cannot doubt that for all who may take it up the work must be one of profound interest."—*Saturday Review.*

In Two Volumes. Vol. I., post 8vo, pp. xxiv.—230, cloth, price 7s. 6d.

A COMPARATIVE HISTORY OF THE EGYPTIAN AND MESOPOTAMIAN RELIGIONS.

By DR. C. P. TIELE.
Vol. I. HISTORY OF THE EGYPTIAN RELIGION.
Translated from the Dutch with the Assistance of the Author.
By JAMES BALLINGAL.

"It places in the hands of the English readers a history of Egyptian Religion which is very complete, which is based on the best materials, and which has been illustrated by the latest results of research. In this volume there is a great deal of information, as well as independent investigation, for the trustworthiness of which Dr. Tiele's name is in itself a guarantee; and the description of the successive religions under the Old Kingdom, the Middle Kingdom, and the New Kingdom, is given in a manner which is scholarly and minute."—*Scotsman.*

Post 8vo, pp. xii.—302, cloth, price 8s. 6d.

YUSUF AND ZULAIKHA.

A POEM BY JAMI.

Translated from the Persian into English Verse.

BY RALPH T. H. GRIFFITH.

"Mr. Griffith, who has done already good service as translator into verse from the Sanskrit, has done further good work in this translation from the Persian, and he has evidently shown not a little skill in his rendering the quaint and very oriental style of his author into our more prosaic, less figurative, language. . . . The work, besides its intrinsic merits, is of importance as being one of the most popular and famous poems of Persia, and that which is read in all the independent native schools of India where Persian is taught."—*Scotsman.*

Post 8vo, pp. viii.—266, cloth, price 9s.

LINGUISTIC ESSAYS.

BY CARL ABEL.

"All these essays of Dr. Abel's are so thoughtful, so full of happy illustrations, and so admirably put together, that we hardly know to which we should specially turn to select for our readers a sample of his workmanship."—*Tablet.*

"An entirely novel method of dealing with philosophical questions and impart a real human interest to the otherwise dry technicalities of the science."—*Standard.*

"Dr. Abel is an opponent from whom it is pleasant to differ, for he writes with enthusiasm and temper, and his mastery over the English language fits him to be a champion of unpopular doctrines."—*Athenæum.*

"Dr. Abel writes very good English, and much of his book will prove entertaining to the general reader. It may give some useful hints, and suggest some subjects for profitable investigation, even to philologists."—*Nation (New York).*

Post 8vo, pp. ix.—281, cloth, price 10s. 6d.

THE SARVA-DARSANA-SAMGRAHA;

OR, REVIEW OF THE DIFFERENT SYSTEMS OF HINDU PHILOSOPHY.

BY MADHAVA ACHARYA.

Translated by E. B COWELL, M.A., Professor of Sanskrit in the University of Cambridge, and A. E. GOUGH, M.A., Professor of Philosophy in the Presidency College, Calcutta.

This work is an interesting specimen of Hindu critical ability. The author successively passes in review the sixteen philosophical systems current in the fourteenth century in the South of India; and he gives what appears to him to be their most important tenets.

"The translation is trustworthy throughout. A protracted sojourn in India, where there is a living tradition, has familiarised the translators with Indian thought."—*Athenæum.*

Post 8vo, pp. lxv.—368, cloth, price 14s.

TIBETAN TALES DERIVED FROM INDIAN SOURCES.

Translated from the Tibetan of the KAH-GYUR.

BY F. ANTON VON SCHIEFNER.

Done into English from the German, with an Introduction,

BY W. R. S. RALSTON, M.A.

"Mr. Ralston, whose name is so familiar to all lovers of Russian folk-lore, has supplied some interesting Western analogies and parallels, drawn, for the most part, from Slavonic sources, to the Eastern folk-tales, culled from the Kahgyur, one of the divisions of the Tibetan sacred books."—*Academy.*

"The translation . . . could scarcely have fallen into better hands. An Introduction . . . gives the leading facts in the lives of those scholars who have given their attention to gaining a knowledge of the Tibetan literature and language."—*Calcutta Review.*

"Ought to interest all who care for the East, for amusing stories, or for comparative folk-lore."—*Pall Mall Gazette.*

Post 8vo, pp. xvi.—224, cloth, price 9s.

UDÂNAVARGA.

A COLLECTION OF VERSES FROM THE BUDDHIST CANON.

Compiled by DHARMATRÂTA.

BEING THE NORTHERN BUDDHIST VERSION OF DHAMMAPADA.

Translated from the Tibetan of Bkah-hgyur, with Notes, and
Extracts from the Commentary of Pradjnavarman,

By W. WOODVILLE ROCKHILL.

"Mr. Rockhill's present work is the first from which assistance will be gained for a more accurate understanding of the Pali text; it is, in fact, as yet the only term of comparison available to us. The 'Udânavarga,' the Thibetan version, was originally discovered by the late M. Schiefner, who published the Tibetan text, and had intended adding a translation, an intention frustrated by his death, but which has been carried out by Mr. Rockhill. . . . Mr. Rockhill may be congratulated for having well accomplished a difficult task."—*Saturday Review.*

In Two Volumes, post 8vo, pp. xxiv.—566, cloth, accompanied by a
Language Map, price 25s.

A SKETCH OF THE MODERN LANGUAGES OF AFRICA.

By ROBERT NEEDHAM CUST,

Barrister-at-Law, and late of Her Majesty's Indian Civil Service.

"Any one at all interested in African languages cannot do better than get Mr. Cust's book. It is encyclopædic in its scope, and the reader gets a start clear away in any particular language, and is left free to add to the initial sum of knowledge there collected."—*Natal Mercury.*

"Mr. Cust has contrived to produce a work of value to linguistic students."—*Natal.*

Post 8vo, pp. xii.—312, with Maps and Plan, cloth, price 14s.

A HISTORY OF BURMA.

Including Burma Proper, Pegu, Taungu, Tenasserim, and Arakan. From the Earliest Time to the End of the First War with British India.

By LIEUT.-GEN. SIR ARTHUR P. PHAYRE, G.C.M.G., K.C.S.I., and C.B.,
Membre Correspondant de la Société Académique Indo-Chinoise
de France.

"Sir Arthur Phayre's contribution to Trübner's Oriental Series supplies a recognised want, and its appearance has been looked forward to for many years. . . . General Phayre deserves great credit for the patience and industry which has resulted in this History of Burma."—*Saturday Review.*

Third Edition. Post 8vo, pp. 276, cloth, price 7s. 6d.

RELIGION IN CHINA.

By JOSEPH EDKINS, D.D., PEKING.

Containing a Brief Account of the Three Religions of the Chinese, with Observations on the Prospects of Christian Conversion amongst that People.

"Dr. Edkins has been most careful in noting the varied and often complex phases of opinion, so as to give an account of considerable value of the subject."—*Scotsman.*

"As a missionary, it has been part of Dr. Edkins' duty to study the existing religions in China, and his long residence in the country has enabled him to acquire an intimate knowledge of them as they at present exist."—*Saturday Review.*

"Dr. Edkins' valuable work, of which this is a second and revised edition, has, from the time that it was published, been the standard authority upon the subject of which it treats."—*Nonconformist.*

"Dr. Edkins . . . may now be fairly regarded as among the first authorities on Chinese religion and language."—*British Quarterly Review.*

Third Edition. Post 8vo, pp. xv.-250, cloth, price 7s. 6d.

OUTLINES OF THE HISTORY OF RELIGION TO THE SPREAD OF THE UNIVERSAL RELIGIONS.

BY C. P. TIELE,
Doctor of Theology, Professor of the History of Religions in the University of Leyden.
Translated from the Dutch by J. ESTLIN CARPENTER, M.A.

"Few books of its size contain the result of so much wide thinking, able and laborious study, or enable the reader to gain a better bird's-eye view of the latest results of investigations into the religious history of nations. As Professor Tiele modestly says, 'In this little book are outlines—pencil sketches, I might say—nothing more.' But there are some men whose sketches from a thumb-nail are of far more worth than an enormous canvas covered with the crude painting of others, and it is easy to see that these pages, full of information, these sentences, cut and perhaps also dry, short and clear, condense the fruits of long and thorough research."—*Scotsman.*

Post 8vo, pp. x.-274, cloth, price 9s.

THE LIFE OF THE BUDDHA AND THE EARLY HISTORY OF HIS ORDER.

Derived from Tibetan Works in the Bkah-hgyur and Bstan-hgyur.
Followed by notices on the Early History of Tibet and Khoten.
Translated by W. W. ROCKHILL, Second Secretary U.S. Legation in China.

"The volume bears testimony to the diligence and fulness with which the author has consulted and tested the ancient documents bearing upon his remarkable subject."—*Times.*

"Will be appreciated by those who devote themselves to those Buddhist studies which have of late years taken in these Western regions so remarkable a development. Its matter possesses a special interest as being derived from ancient Tibetan works, some portions of which, here analysed and translated, have not yet attracted the attention of scholars. The volume is rich in ancient stories bearing upon the world's renovation and the origin of castes, as recorded in these venerable authorities."—*Daily News.*

Third Edition. Post 8vo, pp. viii.-464, cloth, price 16s.

THE SANKHYA APHORISMS OF KAPILA,

With Illustrative Extracts from the Commentaries.
Translated by J. R. BALLANTYNE, LL.D., late Principal of the Benares College.
Edited by FITZEDWARD HALL.

"The work displays a vast expenditure of labour and scholarship, for which students of Hindoo philosophy have every reason to be grateful to Dr. Hall and the publishers."—*Calcutta Review.*

In Two Volumes, post 8vo, pp. cviii.-242, and viii.-370, cloth, price 24s.
Dedicated by permission to H.R.H. the Prince of Wales.

BUDDHIST RECORDS OF THE WESTERN WORLD,

Translated from the Chinese of Hiuen Tsiang (A.D. 629).
BY SAMUEL BEAL, B.A.,
(Trin. Coll., Camb.); R.N. (Retired Chaplain and N.I.); Professor of Chinese, University College, London; Rector of Wark, Northumberland, &c.

An eminent Indian authority writes respecting this work:—"Nothing more can be done in elucidating the History of India until Mr. Beal's translation of the 'Si-yu-ki' appears."

"It is a strange freak of historical preservation that the best account of the condition of India at that ancient period has come down to us in the books of travel written by the Chinese pilgrims, of whom Hwen Thsang is the best known."—*Times.*

"We are compelled at this stage to close our brief and inadequate notice of a book for easy access to which Orientalists will be deeply grateful to the able translator."—*Literary World.*

Post 8vo, pp. xlviii.-398, cloth, price 12s.
THE ORDINANCES OF MANU.
Translated from the Sanskrit, with an Introduction.
By the late A. C. BURNELL, Ph.D., C.I.E.
Completed and Edited by E. W. HOPKINS, Ph.D.,
of Columbia College, N.Y.

"This work is full of interest; while for the student of sociology and the science of religion it is full of importance. It is a great boon to get so notable a work in so accessible a form, admirably edited, and competently translated."—*Scotsman.*

"Few men were more competent than Burnell to give us a really good translation of this well-known law book, first rendered into English by Sir William Jones. Burnell was not only an independent Sanskrit scholar, but an experienced lawyer, and he joined to these two important qualifications the rare faculty of being able to express his thoughts in clear and trenchant English. . . . We ought to feel very grateful to Dr. Hopkins for having given us all that could be published of the translation left by Burnell."—F. MAX MÜLLER in the *Academy.*

Post 8vo, pp. xii.-234, cloth, price 9s.
THE LIFE AND WORKS OF ALEXANDER CSOMA DE KOROS,
Between 1819 and 1842. With a Short Notice of all his Published and Unpublished Works and Essays. From Original and for most part Unpublished Documents.
By THEODORE DUKA, M.D., F.R.C.S. (Eng.), Surgeon-Major
H.M.'s Bengal Medical Service, Retired, &c.

"Not too soon have Messrs. Trübner added to their valuable Oriental Series a history of the life and works of one of the most gifted and devoted of Oriental students, Alexander Csoma de Koros. It is forty-three years since his death, and though an account of his career was demanded soon after his decease, it has only now appeared in the important memoir of his compatriot, Dr. Duka."—*Bookseller.*

In Two Volumes, post 8vo, pp.   and   , cloth, price   .
MISCELLANEOUS ESSAYS
ON SUBJECTS CONNECTED WITH THE
MALAY PENINSULA AND THE INDIAN ARCHIPELAGO.
Reprinted from "Dalrymple's Oriental Repertory," "Asiatick Researches," and the "Journal of the Asiatic Society of Bengal."

Post 8vo, pp. xii.-72, cloth, price 5s.
THE SATAKAS OF BHARTRIHARI.
Translated from the Sanskrit
By the REV. B. HALE WORTHAM, M.R.A.S.,
Rector of Eggesford, North Devon.

Bhartrihari is believed to have lived in the first or second century A.D. He was a celebrated poet and grammarian, and is best known by his three "Satakas, or Centuries of Verses:" 1. "The Sringara Sataka." 2. "The Niti Sataka." 3. "Vairagya Sataka."

LONDON: TRÜBNER & CO., 57 AND 59 LUDGATE HILL.

TRÜBNER'S Oriental & Linguistic Publications.

A CATALOGUE

OF

BOOKS, PERIODICALS, AND SERIALS,

ON THE

History, Languages, Religions, Antiquities, Literature, and Geography of the East,

AND KINDRED SUBJECTS.

PUBLISHED BY

TRÜBNER & CO.

LONDON:
TRÜBNER & CO., 57 AND 59, LUDGATE HILL.
1888.

MISCELLANEOUS ESSAYS RELATING TO INDIAN SUBJECTS. By B. H. HODGSON, F.R.S., late of the Be.C.S., etc. 2 vols. pp. viii.-408, and viii. 348. 1880. 28s.

THE LIFE OR LEGEND OF GAUDAMA, the Buddha of the Burmese. With Annotations, The Ways to Neibban, and Notice on the Phongyies or Burmese Monks. By the Right Rev. P. BIGANDET, Bishop of Ramatha. Third Edition. 2 vols. pp. xx. and 268, and viii. and 326. 1880. 21s.

THE GULISTAN; or, Rose Garden of Shekh Mushliu'd-din Sadi of Shiraz. Translated for the first time into Prose and Verse, with a Preface and a Life of the Author, from the Atish Kadah, by E. B. EASTWICK, F.R.S. M.R.A.S., etc. Second Edition, pp. xxvi. and 244. 1880. 10s. 6d.

CHINESE BUDDHISM. A Volume of Sketches, Historical and Critical. By J. EDKINS, D.D., pp. xxvi. and 454. 1880. 18s.

THE HISTORY OF ESARHADDON (SON OF SENNACHERIB) KING OF ASSYRIA, B.C. 681-668. Translated from the Cuneiform Inscriptions in the British Museum. The Original Texts, a Grammatical Analysis of each Word, Explanations of the Ideographs, and list of Eponyms, etc. By E. A. BUDGE, B.A., etc. pp. xii. and 164. 1880. 10s. 6d.

A TALMUDIC MISCELLANY; or, One Thousand and One Extracts from the Talmud, the Midrashim, and the Kabbalah. Compiled and Translated by P. J. Hershon. With a Preface by the Rev. F. W. FARRAR, D.D., Canon of Westminster. With Notes and Copious Indexes. pp. xxviii. and 362. 1880. 14s.

BUDDHIST BIRTH STORIES; or, Jātaka Tales. The oldest collection of Folk-lore extant: being the Jātakatthavannanā, for the first time edited in the original Pali, by V. FAUSBÖLL, and translated by T. W. Rhys Davids. Translation. Vol. I. pp. cxvi. and 348. 1880. 18s.

THE CLASSICAL POETRY OF THE JAPANESE. By BASIL CHAMBERLAIN, Author of "Yeigio Henkaku, Ichiran." pp. xii. and 228. 1880. 7s. 6d.

LINGUISTIC AND ORIENTAL ESSAYS. Written from 1846 to 1887. By R. CUST. pp. 496. 1880. 10s. 6d. Second Series, pp. 562, with 6 Maps. 1887. 21s.

THE MESNEVI. (Usually known as the Mesnevīyi Sherif, or Holy Mesnevī) of Mevlānā (our Lord) Jelālu'd-Din Muhammed er-Rūmī. Book I. With a Life of the Author. Illustrated by a Selection of Characteristic Anecdotes, by Mevlānā Shemsu'd-Din Ahmed el Eflākī, el 'Ārifī. Translated and the Poetry Versified in English, by J. W. REDHOUSE, M.R.A.S. pp. xv. and 135, v. and 290. 1881. 21s.

EASTERN PROVERBS AND EMBLEMS, Illustrating Old Truths. By the Rev. J. LONG, M.R.A.S., F.R.G.S. pp. xvi. and 280. 1881. 6s.

INDIAN POETRY. Containing "The Indian Song of Songs," from the Sanskrit of the "Gīta Govinda" of Jayadeva; Two Books from "the Iliad of India" (Mahabharata); and other Oriental Poems. Fourth Edition. By Sir EDWIN ARNOLD, M.A., K.C.I.E., etc. pp. viii. and 270. 1886. 7s. 6d.

HINDU PHILOSOPHY. The Sankhya Karika of Iswara Krishna. An Exposition of the System of Kapila. With an Appendix on the Nyaya and Vaiseshika Systems. By J. DAVIES, M.A. pp. viii. and 152. 1881. 6s.

THE RELIGIONS OF INDIA. By A. BARTH. Authorised Translation by Rev. J. WOOD. pp. 356. 1881. 16s.

A MANUAL OF HINDU PANTHEISM. The Vedantasara. Translated with Copious Annotations, by Major G. A. JACOB, B.S.C. With Preface by E. B. COWELL, M.A., Prof. of Sanskrit in Cambridge University. pp. x. and 129. 1881. 6s.

THE QUATRAINS OF OMAR KHAYYÁM. Translated by E. H. WHINFIELD,
M.A., late of H.M. Bengal Civil Service. pp. 96. 1881. 5s.

THE QUATRAINS OF OMAR KHAYYÁM. Persian Text, and English Verse
Translation by E. H. WHINFIELD, M.A., late Be.C.S. pp. 368. 1883.
10s. 6d.

THE MIND OF MENCIUS; or, Political Economy founded upon Moral
Philosophy. A Systematic Digest of the Doctrine of the Chinese Philosopher
Mencius. Translated from the Original Text, and Classified with Comments
and Explanations by the Rev. Ernst FABER, Rhenish Mission Society.
Translated from the German with Additional Notes, by the Rev. A. B.
HUTCHINSON, C.M.S., Hong-Kong. pp. xvi. and 294. 1881. 10s. 6d.

TSUNI-||GOAM, THE SUPREME BEING OF THE KHOI-KHOI. By THEO-
PHILUS HAHN, Ph.D., Custodian of the Grey Collection, Cape Town, etc. pp.
xii. and 154. 1881. 7s. 6d.

YUSEF AND ZULAIKHA. A Poem by Jámi. Translated from the Persian
into English Verse. By R. T. H. GRIFFITH. pp. xiv. and 304. 1882. 8s. 6d.

THE INDIAN EMPIRE: its History, People, and Products. By Sir W. W.
HUNTER, K.C.I.E., LL.D. Second Edition. pp. 780. With Map. 1886. 21s.

A COMPREHENSIVE COMMENTARY TO THE QURAN: comprising Sale's
Translation and Preliminary Discourse, with Additional Notes and Emendations.
With a complete Index to the Text, Preliminary Discourse, and Notes. By Rev.
E. M. WHERRY, M.A., Lodiana. Vol. I. pp. xii. and 392. 1882. 12s. 6d.
Vol. II. pp. xii.-408. 1884. 12s. 6d. Vol. III. pp. viii.-416. 1885.
12s. 6d. Vol. IV. pp. xiii.-340. 1886. 10s. 6d.

COMPARATIVE HISTORY OF THE EGYPTIAN AND MESOPOTAMIAN RELIGIONS.
By C. P. Tiele. Egypt, Babel-Assur, Yemen, Harran, Phœnicia, Israel.
Vol. I. History of the Egyptian Religion. Translated from the Dutch, with the
co-operation of the Author, by JAMES BALLINGAL. pp. xxiv.-230, 1882. 7s. 6d.

THE SARVA-DARSANA-SAMGRAHA; or Review of the different Systems of
Hindu Philosophy. By Madhava Acharya. Translated by E. B. COWELL,
M.A., Cambridge; and A. E. GOUGH, M.A., Calcutta. pp. xii.-282. 1882. 10s. 6d.

TIBETAN TALES, Derived from Indian Sources. Translated from the
Tibetan of the Kah-Gyur. By F. ANTON VON SCHIEFNER. Done into English
from the German, with an Introduction, by W. R. S. RALSTON, M.A. pp.
lxvi.-368. 1882. 14s.

LINGUISTIC ESSAYS. By CARL ABEL, Ph.Dr. pp. viii.-266. 1882. 9s.
CONTENTS.—Language as the Expression of National Modes of Thought—The Conception of
Love in some Ancient and Modern Languages—The English Verbs of Command—The discrimi-
nation of Synonyms—Philological Method—The Connection between Dictionary and Grammar
—The Possibility of a Common Literary Language for the Slave Nations—Coptic Intensification
—The Origin of Language—The Order and Position of Words in the Latin Sentence.

HINDŪ PHILOSOPHY. The Bhagavad Gítá or the Sacred Lay. A
Sanskrit Philosophical Poem. Translated, with Notes, by JOHN DAVIES, M.A.
(Cantab.), M.R.A.S. pp. vi.-208. 1882. 8s. 6d.

THE PHILOSOPHY OF THE UPANISHADS and Ancient Indian Metaphysics.
By A. E. GOUGH, M.A. Calcutta. Pp. xxiv.-268. 1882. 9s.

UDANAVARGA: A Collection of Verses from the Buddhist Canon. Compiled by DHARMATRATA. The Northern Buddhist Version of Dhammapada.
Translated from the Tibetan of Bkah hgyur. Notes and Extracts from the Commentary of Pradjnavarman, by W. W. ROCKHILL. Pp. xvi.-224. 1883. 9s.

A HISTORY OF BURMA. Including Burma Proper, Pegu, Taungu, Tenasserim, and Arakan. From the Earliest Time to the End of the First War with British India. By Lieut.-General Sir A. P. PHAYRE, G.C.M.G., K.C.S.I., &c. pp. xii. and 312, with Maps and Plan. 1883. 14s.

A SKETCH OF THE MODERN LANGUAGES OF AFRICA. By R. N. CUST. Accompanied by a Language Map. By E. G. RAVENSTEIN. Two Vols. pp. xvi.-288, viii.-278, with Thirty-one Autotype Portraits. 1883. 18s.

OUTLINES OF THE HISTORY OF RELIGION TO THE SPREAD OF THE UNIVERSAL RELIGIONS. By Prof C. P. TIELE. Translated from the Dutch by J. E. CARPENTER, M.A., with the Author's assistance. Third Edition, pp. xx. and 250. 1884. 7s. 6d.

RELIGION IN CHINA; containing a brief Account of the Three Religions of the Chinese; with Observations on the Prospects of Christian Conversion amongst that People. By JOSEPH EDKINS, D.D., Peking. Third Edition, pp. xvi. and 260. 1884. 7s. 6d.

THE LIFE OF THE BUDDHA AND THE EARLY HISTORY OF HIS ORDER. From Tibetan Works in the Bkah-hgyur and Bstan-hgyur. With notices on the Early History of Tibet and Khoten. Translated by W. W. ROCKHILL, Second Secretary U.S. Legation in China. pp. 284. 1884. 9s.

BUDDHIST RECORDS OF THE WESTERN WORLD. Translated from the Chinese of Hiuen Tsiang (A.D. 629) by S. BEAL. Dedicated by permission to H.R.H. the Prince of Wales. 2 vols. pp. 250 and 378. 1884. 24s.

THE SANKHYA APHORISMS OF KAPILA. With Illustrative Extracts from the Commentaries. Translated by J. R. BALLANTYNE, LL.D., late Principal of Benares College. Edited by F. HALL. Third Edition. pp. 472. 1884. 16s.

THE ORDINANCES OF MANU. Translated from the Sanskrit, with Introduction by the late A. C. BURNELL, Ph.D., C.I.E. Completed and Edited by E. W. HOPKINS, Ph.D., Columbia College, New York. pp. 446. 1884. 12s.

LIFE AND WORKS OF ALEXANDER CSOMA DE KÖRÖS between 1819 and 1842. With a Short Notice of all his Published and Unpublished Works and Essays. From Original and for the most part Unpublished Documents. By T. DUKA, M.D., F.R.C.S. (Eng.), Surgeon-Major H.M.'s Bengal Medical Service, Retired, etc. pp. xii.-234. 1885. 9s.

LEAVES FROM MY CHINESE SCRAP-BOOK. By F. H. BALFOUR, Author of "Waifs and Strays from the Far East," etc. pp. 216. 1887. 7s. 6d.

ANCIENT PROVERBS AND MAXIMS FROM BURMESE SOURCES; or, the Niti Literature of Burma. By J. GRAY, Author of "Elements of Pali Grammar," etc. pp. 192. 1886. 6s.

MASNAVI I MA'NAVI: the Spiritual Couplets of Mauláná Jalálu-'d-Dín Muhammad i Rúmí. Translated and abridged by E. H. WHINFIELD, M.A. pp. xxxii. and 330. 1887. 7s. 6d.

THE SATAKAS OF BHARTRIHARI. Translated from the Sanskrit by the Rev. B. HALE WORTHAM, B.A., M.R.A.S. pp. xii.-72. 1886. 5s.

MÁNAVA-DHARMA-CÁSTRA: the Code of Manu. Original Sanskrit Text with Critical Notes. By J. JOLLY, Ph.D., Professor of Sanskrit in the University of Wurzburg; late Tagore Professor of Law in the University of Calcutta. pp. viii. and 346. 1887. 10s. 6d.

MISCELLANEOUS PAPERS RELATING TO INDO-CHINA. Reprinted for the Straits Branch of the Royal Asiatic Society, from Dalrymple's "Oriental Repertory," and the "Asiatic Researches" and "Journal" of the Asiatic Society of Bengal. pp. xii.-318, vi.-112. 1887. 21s.

MISCELLANEOUS PAPERS RELATING TO INDO-CHINA AND THE INDIAN ARCHIPELAGO. Reprinted for the Straits Branch of the R. Asiatic Society, from the "Journals" of the R. Asiatic, Bengal Asiatic, and R. Geographical Societies; the "Transactions" and "Journal" of the Asiatic Society of Batavia, and the "Malayan Miscellanies." Second series. 2 vols. pp. viii. and 307, and 313. With Five Plates and a Map. 1887. £1 5s.

FOLK TALES OF KASHMIR. By the Rev. J. HINTON KNOWLES, F.R.G.S., M.R.A.S., etc. (C.M.S.) Missionary to the Kashmiris. Pp. xii.-510. 1888. 16s.

SERIALS AND PERIODICALS.

Asiatic Society of Great Britain and Ireland.—JOURNAL OF THE ROYAL ASIATIC SOCIETY OF GREAT BRITAIN AND IRELAND, from the Commencement to 1863. First Series, complete in 20 Vols. 8vo., with many Plates, Price £10; or, in Single Numbers, as follows:—Nos. 1 to 14, 6s. each; No. 15, 2 Parts, 4s. each; No. 16, 2 Parts, 4s. each; No. 17, 2 Parts, 4s. each; No. 18, 6s. These 18 Numbers form Vols. I. to IX.—Vol. X., Part 1, o.p.; Part 2, 5s.; Part 3, 5s.—Vol. XI., Part 1, 6s.; Part 2 not published.—Vol. XII., 2 Parts, 6s. each.—Vol. XIII., 2 Parts, 6s. each.—Vol. XIV., Part 1. 5s.; Part 2 not published.—Vol. XV., Part 1, 6s.; Part 2, with 3 Maps, £2 2s.—Vol. XVI., 2 Parts, 6s. each.—Vol. XVII., 2 Parts, 6s. each.—Vol. XVIII., 2 Parts, 6s. each.—Vol. XIX., Parts 1 to 4, 16s.—Vol. XX., Parts 1 and 2, 4s. each. Part 3, 7s. 6d.

Asiatic Society.—JOURNAL OF THE ROYAL ASIATIC SOCIETY OF GREAT BRITAIN AND IRELAND. *New Series.* Vol. I. In Two Parts. pp. iv. and 490, sewed. 1864-5. 16s.

CONTENTS.—I. Vajra-chhediká, the "Kin Kong King," or Diamond Sûtra. Translated from the Chinese by the Rev. S. Beal.—II. The Páramitá-hridaya Sútra, or, in Chinese, "Mo ho-pô-ye-po-lo-mih-to-sin-king," i.e. "The Great Páramitá Heart Sûtra." Translated from the Chinese by the Rev. S. Beal.—III. On the Preservation of National Literature in the East. By Col. F. J. Goldsmid.—IV. On the Agricultural, Commercial, Financial, and Military Statistics of Ceylon. By E. R. Power.—V. Contributions to a Knowledge of the Vedic Theogony and Mythology. By J. Muir, D.C.L.—VI. A Tabular List of Original Works and Translations, published by the late Dutch Government of Ceylon at their Printing Press at Colombo. Compiled by Mr. M. P. J. Ondaatje.—VII. Assyrian and Hebrew Chronology compared, with a view of showing the extent to which the Hebrew Chronology of Ussher must be modified, in conformity with the Assyrian Canon. By J. W. Bosanquet.—VIII. On the existing Dictionaries of the Malay Language. By Dr. H. N. van der Tuuk.—IX. Bilingual Readings: Cuneiform and Phœnician. Notes on some Tablets in the British Museum, containing Bilingual Legends (Assyrian and Phœnician). By Major-Gen. Sir H. Rawlinson, K.C.B.—X. Translations of Three Copper-plate Inscriptions of the Fourth Century A.D., and Notices of the Châlukya and Gurjjara Dynasties. By Prof. J. Dowson, Staff College, Sandhurst.—XI. Yama and the Doctrine of a Future Life, according to the Rig-, Yajur-, and Atharva-Vedas. By J. Muir, D.C.L.—XII. On the Jyotisha Observation of the Place of the Colures, and the Date derivable from it. By W. D. Whitney, Prof. of Sanskrit, Yale College, U.S.A.—Note on the preceding Article. By Sir E. Colebrooke, Bart., M.P.—XIII. Progress of the Vedic Religion towards Abstract Conceptions of the Deity. By J. Muir, D.C.L.—XIV. Brief Notes on the Age and Authenticity of the Work of Aryabhata, Varâhamihira, Brahmagupta, Bhattotpala, and Bhâ-skarâchârya. By Dr. Bhâu Dájí.—XV. Outlines of a Grammar of the Malagasy Language. By H. N. Van der Tuuk.—XVI. On the Identity of Xandrames and Krananda. By E. Thomas, Esq.

Vol. II. In Two Parts. pp. 522, sewed. 1866-7. 16s.

CONTENTS.—I. Contributions to a Knowledge of Vedic Theogony and Mythology. No. 2. By J. Muir.—II. Miscellaneous Hymns from the Rig- and Atharva-Vedas. By J. Muir.—III. Five hundred questions on the Social Condition of the Natives of Bengal. By the Rev. J. Long.—IV. Short account of the Malay Manuscripts belonging to the Royal Asiatic Society. By

Dr. H. N. van der Tuuk.—V. Translation of the Amitâbha Sûtra from the Chinese. By the Rev. S. Beal.—VI. The initial coinage of Bengal. By E. Thomas.—VII. Specimens of an Assyrian Dictionary. By E. Norris.—VIII. On the Relations of the Priests to the other classes of Indian Society in the Vedic age. By J. Muir.—IX. On the Interpretation of the Veda. By the same.— X. An attempt to Translate from the Chinese a work known as the Confessional Services of the great compassionate Kwan Yin, possessing 1000 hands and 1000 eyes. By the Rev. S. Beal.— XI. The Hymns of the Gaupâyanas and the Legend of King Asamâti. By Prof. Max Müller. —XII. Specimen Chapters of an Assyrian Grammar. By the Rev. E. Hincks, D.D.

Vol. III. In Two Parts. pp. 516, sewed. With Photograph. 1868. 22s.

CONTENTS.—I. Contributions towards a Glossary of the Assyrian Language. By H. F. Talbot. —II. Remarks on the Indo-Chinese Alphabets. By Dr. A. Bastian.—III. The poetry of Mohamed Rabadan, Arragonese. By the Hon. H. E. J. Stanley.—IV. Catalogue of the Oriental Manuscripts in the Library of King's College, Cambridge. By E. H. Palmer, B.A.—V. Description of the Amravati Tope in Guntur. By J. Fergusson, F.R.S.—VI. Remarks on Prof. Brockhaus' edition of the Kathâsarit-sâgara, Lambaka IX. XVIII. By Dr. H. Kern, Prof. of Sanskrit, University of Leyden.—VII. The source of Colebrooke's Essay "On the Duties of a Faithful Hindu Widow." By Fitzedward Hall, D.C.L. Supplement: Further detail of proofs that Colebrooke's Essay, "On the Duties of a Faithful Hindu Widow," was not indebted to the Vivâdabhangârnava. By F. Hall.—VIII. The Sixth Hymn of the First Book of the Rig Veda. By Prof. Max Müller.—IX. Sassanian Inscriptions. By E. Thomas.—X. Account of an Embassy from Morocco to Spain in 1690 and 1691. By the Hon. H. E. J. Stanley.—XI. The Poetry of Mohamed Rabadan, of Arragon. By the same.—XII. Materials for the History of India for the Six Hundred Years of Mohammadan rule, previous to the Foundation of the British Indian Empire. By Major W. Nassau Lees, LL.D.—XIII. A Few Words concerning the Hill people inhabiting the Forests of the Cochin State. By Capt. G. E. Fryer, M.S.C.—XIV. Notes on the Bhojpurí Dialect of Hindí, spoken in Western Behar. By J. Beames, B.C.S.

Vol. IV. In Two Parts. pp. 521, sewed. 1869-70. 16s.

CONTENTS.—I. Contribution towards a Glossary of the Assyrian Language. By H. F. Talbot. Part II.—II. On Indian Chronology. By J. Fergusson, F.R.S.—III. The Poetry of Mohamed Rabadan of Arragon. By the Hon. H. E. J. Stanley.—IV. On the Magar Language of Nepal. By J. Beames, B.C.S.—V. Contributions to the Knowledge of Parsee Literature. By E. Sachau, Ph.D.—VI. Illustrations of the Lamaist System in Tibet, drawn from Chinese Sources. By W. F. Mayers, of H.B.M. Consular Service, China.—VII. Khuddaka Pátha, a Páli Text, with a Translation and Notes. By R. C. Childers, late Ceylon C.S.—VIII. An Endeavour to elucidate Rashiduddin's Geographical Notices of India. By Col. H. Yule, C.B.—IX. Sassanian Inscriptions explained by the Pahlavi of the Pársís. By E. W. West.—X. Some Account of the Senbyú Pagoda at Mengún, near the Burmese Capital, in a Memorandum by Capt. E. H. Sladen, Political Agent at Mandalé; with Remarks on the Subject by Col. H. Yule, C.B.—XI. The Brhat-Sanhitá; or, Complete System of Natural Astrology of Varâha-Mihira. Translated from Sanskrit into English by Dr. H. Kern.—XII. The Mohammedan Law of Evidence, and its influence on the Administration of Justice in India. By N. B. E. Baillie.—XIII. The Mohammedan Law of Evidence in connection with the Administration of Justice to Foreigners. By the same.—XIV. A Translation of a Bactrian Pálí Inscription. By Prof. J. Dowson.—XV. Indo-Parthian Coins. By E. Thomas.

Vol. V. In Two Parts. pp. 463, sewed. With 10 full-page and folding Plates. 1871-2. 18s. 6d.

CONTENTS.—1. Two Játakas. The original Páli Text, with an English Translation. By V. Fausböll.—II. On an Ancient Buddhist Inscription at Keu-yung kwan, in North China. By A. Wylie.—III. The Brhat Sanhitá; or, Complete System of Natural Astrology of Varâha-Mihira Translated from Sanskrit into English by Dr. H. Kern.—IV. The Pongol Festival in Southern India. By C. E. Gover.—V. The Poetry of Mohamed Rabadan, of Arragon. By the Right Hon. Lord Stanley of Alderley.—VI. Essay on the Creed and Customs of the Jangams. By C. P. Brown.—VII. On Malabar, Coromandel, Quilon, etc. By C. P. Brown.—VIII. On the Treatment of the Nexus in the Neo-Aryan Languages of India. By J. Beames, B.C.S.—IX. Some Remarks on the Great Tope at Sánchi. By the Rev. S. Beal.—X. Ancient Inscriptions from Mathura. Translated by Prof. J. Dowson.—Note to the Mathura Inscriptions. By Major-Gen. A. Cunningham.—XI. Specimen of a Translation of the Adi Granth. By Dr. E. Trumpp.—XII. Notes on Dhammapada, with Special Reference to the Question of Nirvana. By R. C. Childers, late Ceylon C.S.—XIII. The Brhat-Sanhitá; or, Complete System of Natural Astrology of Varâhamihira. Translated from Sanskrit into English by Dr. H. Kern.—XIV. On the Origin of the Buddhist Arthakathâs. By the Mudliar L. Comrilla Vijasinha, Government Interpreter to the Ratnapura Court, Ceylon. With Introduction by R. C. Childers, late Ceylon C.S.—XV. The Poetry of Mohamed Rabadan, of Arragon. By the Right Hon. Lord Stanley of Alderley.— XVI. Proverbia Communia Syriaca. By Capt. R. F. Burton. XVII. Notes on an Ancient Indian Vase, with an Account of the Engraving thereupon. By C. Horne, late B.C.S.—XVIII. The Bhar Tribe. By the Rev. M. A. Sherring, LL.D., Benares. Communicated by C. Horne, late B.C.S. XIX. Of Jehad in Mohammedan Law, and its application to British India. By N. B. E. Baillie.—XX. Comments on Recent Pehlvi Decipherments. With an Incidental Sketch of the Derivation of Aryan Alphabets. And Contributions to the Early History and Geography of Tabaristán. Illustrated by Coins. By E. Thomas, F.R.S.

Vol. VI., Part I, pp. 212, sewed, with two plates and a map. 1872. 8s.

CONTENTS.—The Ishmaelites, and the Arabic Tribes who Conquered their Country. By A. Sprenger.—A Brief Account of Four Arabic Works on the History and Geography of Arabia. By Captain S. B. Miles.—On the Methods of Disposing of the Dead at Llassa, Thibet, etc. By Charles Horne, late B.C.S. The Brhat-Sanhitâ; or, Complete System of Natural Astrology of Varâha-mihira, Translated from Sanskrit into English by Dr. H. Kern.—Notes on Hwen Thsang's Account of the Principalities of Tokhâristân, in which some Previous Geographical Identifications are Reconsidered. By Colonel Yule, C.B.—The Campaign of Ælius Gallus in Arabia. By A. Sprenger.—An Account of Jerusalem, Translated for the late Sir H. M. Elliot from the Persian Text of Nâsir ibn Khusrû's Safanámah by the late Major A. R. Fuller.—The Poetry of Mohamed Rabadan, of Arragon. By the Right Hon. Lord Stanley of Alderley.

Vol. VI., Part II., pp. 213 to 400 and lxxxiv., sewed. Illustrated with a Map, Plates, and Woodcuts. 1873. 8s.

CONTENTS.—On Hionen-Thsang's Journey from Patna to Ballabhi. By James Fergusson, D.C.L., F.R.S.—Northern Buddhism. [Note from Colonel H. Yule, addressed to the Secretary.]—Hwen Thsang's Account of the Principalities of Tokhâristân, etc. By Colonel H. Yule, C.B.—The Brhat-Sanhitâ; or, Complete System of Natural Astrology of Varâha-mihira. Translated from Sanskrit into English by Dr. H. Kern.—The Initial Coinage of Bengal, under the Early Muhammadan Conquerors. Part II. Embracing the preliminary period between A.H. 614-634 (A.D. 1217-1236-7). By Edward Thomas, F.R.S.—The Legend of Dipañkara Buddha. Translated from the Chinese (and intended to illustrate Plates XXIX. and L., 'Tree and Serpent Worship'). By S. Beal.—Note on Art. IX., antè pp. 213-274. on Hiouen-Thsang's Journey from Patna to Ballabhi. By James Fergusson D.C.L., F.R.S.—Contributions towards a Glossary of the Assyrian Language. By H. F. Talbot.

Vol. VII., Part I., pp. 170 and 24, sewed. With a plate. 1874. 8s.

CONTENTS.—The Upasampadá-Kammavácá, being the Buddhist Manual of the Form and Manner of Ordering of Priests and Deacons. The Páli Text, with a Translation and Notes. By J. F. Dickson, B.A.—Notes on the Megalithic Monuments of the Coimbatore District, Madras. By M. J. Walhouse, late M.C.S.—Notes on the Sinhalese Language. No. 1. On the Formation of the Plural of Neuter Nouns. By R. C. Childers, late Ceylon C.S.—The Pali Text of the Mahâparinibbâna Sutta and Commentary, with a Translation. By R. C. Childers, late Ceylon C.S.—The Brhat-Sanhitâ; or, Complete System of Natural Astrology of Varâha-mihira. Translated from Sanskrit into English by Dr. H. Kern.—Note on the Valley of Choombi. By Dr. A. Campbell, late Superintendent of Darjeeling.—The Name of the Twelfth Imâm on the Coinage of Egypt. By H. Sauvaire and Stanley Lane Poole.—Three Inscriptions of Parâkrama Bâhu the Great from Pulastipura, Ceylon (date circa 1180 A.D.). By T. W. Rhys Davids.—Of the Kharáj or Muhammadan Land Tax; its Application to British India, and Effect on the Tenure of Land. By N. B. E. Baillie.—Appendix: A Specimen of a Syriac Version of the Kalilah wa-Dimnah, with an English Translation. By W. Wright.

Vol. VII., Part II., pp. 191 to 394, sewed. With seven plates and a map. 1875. 8s.

CONTENTS.—Sigiri, the Lion Rock, near Pulastipura, Ceylon; and the Thirty-ninth Chapter of the Mahâvamsa. By T. W. Rhys Davids.—The Northern Frontagers of China. Part I. The Origines of the Mongols. By H. H. Howorth.—Inedited Arabic Coins. By Stanley Lane Poole.—Note on the Dinârs of the Abbasside Dynasty. By Edward Thomas Rogers.—The Northern Frontagers of China. Part II. The Origines of the Manchus. By H. H. Howorth.—Notes on the Old Mongolian Capital of Shangtu. By S. W. Bushell, B.Sc., M.D.—Oriental Proverbs in their Relations to Folklore, History, Sociology; with Suggestions for their Collection, Interpretation, Publication. By the Rev. J. Long.—Two Old Simhalese Inscriptions. The Sahasa Malla Inscription, date 1200 A.D., and the Ruwanwæli Dagaba Inscription, date 1191 A.D. Text, Translation, and Notes. By T. W. Rhys Davids.—Notes on a Bactrian Pali Inscription and the Samvat Era. By Prof. J. Dowson.—Note on a Jade Drinking Vessel of the Emperor Jahângîr. By Edward Thomas, F.R.S.

Vol. VIII., Part I., pp. 156, sewed, with three plates and a plan. 1876. 8s.

CONTENTS.—Catalogue of Buddhist Sanskrit MSS. in the Possession of the R.A.S. (Hodgson Collection). By Prof. E. B. Cowell and J. Eggeling.—On the Ruins of Sigiri in Ceylon. By T. H. Blakesley, Ceylon.—The Pâtimokkha, being the Buddhist Office of the Confession of Priests. The Pali Text, with a Translation and Notes. By J. F. Dickson, M.A., Ceylon C.S.—Notes on the Sinhalese Language. No. 2. Proofs of the Sanskritic Origin of Sinhalese. By R. C. Childers, late of the Ceylon Civil Service.

Vol. VIII., Part II., pp. 157-308, sewed. 1876. 8s.

CONTENTS.—An Account of the Island of Bali By R. Friederich.—The Pali Text of the Mahâparinibbâna Sutta and Commentary, with a Translation. By R C. Childers, late Ceylon C.S.—The Northern Frontagers of China. Part III. The Kara Khitai. By H. H. Howorth.—Inedited Arabic Coins. II. By S. L. Poole.—On the Form of Government under the Native Sovereigns of Ceylon. By A. de Silva Ekanâyaka, Mudaliyar, Ceylon.

Vol. IX., Part I., pp. 156, sewed, with a plate. 1877. 8s.

CONTENTS.—Bactrian Coins and Indian Dates. By E. Thomas, F.R.S.—The Tenses of the Assyrian Verb. By the Rev. A. H. Sayce, M.A.—An Account of the Island of Bali. By R. Friederich (continued from Vol. VIII. N.S. p. 218).—On Ruins in Makran. By Major Mockler.—Inedited Arabic Coins. III. By Stanley Lane Poole.—Further Note on a Bactrian Pali Inscription and the Samvat Era. By Prof. J. Dowson.—Notes on Persian Belûchistan. From the Persian of Mirza Mehdy Khân. By A. H. Schindler.

Vol IX., Part II., pp. 292, sewed, with three plates. 1877. 10s. 6d.

CONTENTS.—The Early Faith of Asoka. By E. Thomas, F.R.S.—The Northern Frontagers of China. Part II. The Manchus (Supplementary Notice). Part IV. The Kin or Golden Tatars. By H. H. Howorth.—On a Treatise on Weights and Measures by Eliyá, Archbishop of Nisibin. By M. H. Sauvaire.—On Imperial and other Titles. By Sir T. E. Colebrooke, Bart., M.P.—Affinities of the Dialects of the Chepang and Kusundah Tribes of Nipál with those of the Hill Tribes of Arracan. By Capt. C. J. F. Forbes F.R.G.S., M.A.S. Bengal, etc.—Notes on Some Antiquities found in a Mound near Damghan. By A. H. Schindler.

Vol. X., Part I., pp. 156, sewed, with two plates and a map. 1878. 8s.

CONTENTS.—On the Non-Aryan Languages of India. By E. L. Brandreth.—A Dialogue on the Vedantic Conception of Brahma. By Pramadá Dása Mittra, late Offg. Prof. of Anglo-Sanskrit, Gov. College, Benares.—An Account of the Island of Bali. By R. Friederich (continued from Vol. IX. N.S. p. 120).—Unpublished Glass Weights and Measures. By E. T. Rogers.—China via Tibet. By S. C. Boulger.—Notes and Recollections on Tea Cultivation in Kumaon and Garhwál. By J. H. Batten, late B.C.S.

Vol. X., Part II., pp. 146, sewed. 1878. 6s.

CONTENTS.—Note on Pliny's Geography of the East Coast of Arabia. By Major-Gen. S. B. Miles, B.S.C. The Maldive Islands; with a Vocabulary taken from François Pyrard de Laval, 1602–1607. By A. Gray, late Ceylon C.S.—On Tibeto-Burman Languages. By Capt. C. J. F. S. Forbes, Burmese C.S. Commission.—Burmese Transliteration. By H. L. St. Barbe, Resident at Mandelay.—On the Connexion of the Môns of Pegu with the Koles of Central India. By Capt. C. J. F. S. Forbes, Burmese C.C.—Studies on the Comparative Grammar of the Semitic Languages, with Special Reference to Assyrian. By P. Haupt. The Oldest Semitic Verb-Form.—Arab Metrology. II. El-Djabarty. By M. H. Sauvaire.—The Migrations and Early History of the White Huns; principally from Chinese Sources. By T. W. Kingsmill.

Vol. X., Part III., pp. 204, sewed. 1878. 8s.

CONTENTS.—On the Hill Canton of Sálár,—the most Easterly Settlement of the Turk Race. By Robert B. Shaw.—Geological Notes on the River Indus By Griffin W. Vyse, Executive Engineer P.W.D. Panjab.—Educational Literature for Japanese Women. By B. H. Chamberlain.—On the Natural Phenomenon Known in the East by the Names Sub-hi-Kâzib, etc., etc. By J. W. Redhouse.—On a Chinese Version of the Sáukhya Kárikâ, etc., found among the Buddhist Books comprising the Tripitaka and two other works. By the Rev. S. Beal.—The Rock-cut Phrygian Inscriptions at Doganlu. By E. Thomas, F.R.S.—Index.

Vol. XI., Part I., pp. 128, sewed, with seven illustrations. 1879. 5s.

CONTENTS.—On the Position of Women in the East in the Olden Time. By E. Thomas, F.R.S.—Notice of Scholars who have Contributed to our Knowledge of the Languages of British India during the last Thirty Years. By R. N. Cust.—Ancient Arabic Poetry: its Genuineness and Authenticity. By Sir W. Muir, K.C.S.I.—Note on Manrique's Mission and the Catholics in the time of Sháh Jahán. By H. G. Keene.—On Sandhi in Pali. By the late R. C. Childers.—On Arabic Amulets and Mottoes. By E. T. Rogers.

Vol. XI., Part II., pp. 256, sewed, with map and plate. 1879. 7s. 6d.

CONTENTS.—On the Identification of Places on the Makran Coast mentioned by Arrian, Ptolemy, and Marcian. By Major E. Mockler.—On the Proper Names of the Mohammadans. By Sir T. E. Colebrooke, Bart., M.P.—Principles of Composition in Chinese, as deduced from the Written Characters. By the Rev. Dr. Legge. On the Identification of the Portrait of Chosroes II. among the Paintings in the Caves at Ajanta. By James Fergusson, Vice-President.—A Specimen of the Zoongee (or Zurngee) Dialect of a Tribe of Nagas, bordering on the Valley of Assam, between the Dikho and Desoi Rivers, embracing over Forty Villages. By the Rev. Mr. Clark.

Vol. XI, Part III. pp. 104, cxxiv, 16, sewed. 1879. 8s.

CONTENTS.—The Gaurian compared with the Romance Languages. Part I. By E. L. Brandreth.—Dialects of Colloquial Arabic. By E. T. Rogers.—A Comparative Study of the Japanese and Korean Languages. By W. G. Aston.—Index.

Vol. XII. Part I. pp. 152, sewed, with Table. 1880. 5s.

CONTENTS.—On "The Most Comely Names," i.e. the Laudatory Epithets, or the Titles of Praise bestowed on God in the Qur'ân or by Muslim Writers. By J. W. Redhouse.—Notes on a newly-discovered Clay Cylinder of Cyrus the Great. By Major-Gen. Sir H. C. Rawlinson, K.C.B.—Note on Hiouen-Thsang's Dhanakacheka. By Robert Sewell, M.C.S.—Remarks by Mr. Fergusson on Mr. Sewell's Paper.—A Treatise on Weights and Measures. By Eliyá, Archbishop of Nisibin. By H. Sauvaire. (Supplement to Vol. IX., pp. 291-313)—On the Age of the Ajantá Caves. By Rájendralála Mitra, C.I.E.—Notes on Babu Rájendralá Mitra's Paper on the Age of the Caves at Ajantá. By J. Fergusson, F.R.S.

Vol. XII. Part II. pp. 182, sewed, with map and plate. 1880. 6s.

CONTENTS.—On Sanskrit Texts Discovered in Japan. By Prof. Max Müller.—Extracts from Report on the Islands and Antiquities of Bahrein. By Capt. Durand. Followed by Notes by Major-Gen. Sir H. C. Rawlinson, K.C.B.—Notes on the Locality and Population of the Tribes dwelling between the Brahmaputra and Ningthi Rivers. By the late G. H. Damant, Political Officer Nāga Hills.—On the Saka, Samvat, and Gupta Eras. A Supplement to his Paper on Indian Chronology. By J. Fergusson, D.C.L.—The Megha-Sûtra. By C. Bendall.—Historical and Archæological Notes on a Journey in South-Western Persia, 1877-1878. By A. Houtum-Schindler.—Identification of the "False Dawn" of the Muslims with the "Zodiacal Light" of Europeans. By J. W. Redhouse.

Vol. XII. Part III. pp. 100, sewed. 1880. 4s.

CONTENTS.—The Gaurian compared with the Romance Languages. Part II. By E. L. Brandreth.—The Uzbeg Epos. By Arminius Vambéry.—On the Separate Edicts at Dhauli and Jaugada. By Prof. Kern.—Grammatical sketch of the Kakhyen Language. By Rev. J. N. Cushing.—Notes on the Libyan Languages, in a Letter addressed to R. N. Cust, Esq., by Prof. F. W. Newman.

Vol. XII. Part IV. pp. 152, with 3 plates. 1880. 8s.

CONTENTS.—The Early History of Tibet, from Chinese Sources. By S. W. Bushell, M.D.—Notes on some Inedited Coins from a Collection made in Persia during the Years 1877-79. By Guy Le Strange, M.R.A.S.—Buddhist Nirvāna and the Noble Eightfold Path. By Oscar Frankfurter, Ph.D.—Index.—Annual Report, 1880.

Vol. XIII. Part I. pp. 120, sewed. 1881. 5s.

CONTENTS.—Indian Theistic Reformers. By Prof. Monier Williams, C.I.E.—Notes on the Kawi Language and Literature. By Dr. H. N. Van der Tuuk.—The Invention of the Indian Alphabet. By John Dowson. The Nirvana of the Northern Buddhists. By the Rev. J. Edkins, D.D.—An Account of the Malay "Chiri," a Sanskrit Formula. By W. E. Maxwell.

Vol. XIII. Part II. pp. 170, with Map and 2 Plates. 1881. 8s.

CONTENTS.—The Northern Frontagers of China. Part V. The Khitai or Khitans. By H. H. Howorth.—On the Identification of Nagarahara, with reference to the Travels of Hiouen-Thsang. By W. Simpson.—Hindu Law at Madras. By J. H. Nelson, M.C.S.—On the Proper Names of the Mohammedans. By Sir T. E. Colebrooke, Bart., M.P.—Supplement to the Paper on Indian Theistic Reformers, published in the January Number of this Journal. By Prof. Monier Williams, C.I.E.

Vol. XIII. Part III. pp. 178, with plate. 1881. 7s. 6d.

CONTENTS.—The Avâr Language. By C. Graham.—Caucasian Nationalities. By M. A. Morrison.—Translation of the Markandeya Purana. Books VII., VIII. By the Rev. B. H. Wortham.—Lettre à M. Stanley Lane Poole sur quelques monnaies orientales rares ou inédites de la Collection de M. Ch. de l'Eclu-e. Par H. Sauvaire.—Aryan Mythology in Malay Traditions. By W. E. Maxwell, Colonial Civil Service.—The Koi, a Southern Tribe of the Gond. By the Rev. J. Cain, Missionary.—On the Duty which Mohammedans in British India owe, on the Principles of their own Law, to the Government of the Country. By N. B. E. Baillie.—The L-Poem of the Arabs, by Shanfara. Re-arranged and translated by J. W. Redhouse, M.R.A.S.

Vol. XIII. Part IV. pp. 130, cxxxvi. 16, with 3 plates. 1881. 10s. 6d.

CONTENTS.—The Andaman Islands and the Andamanese. By M. V. Portman.—Notes on Marco Polo's Itinerary in Southern Persia. By A. Houtum-Schindler.—Two Malay Myths: The Princess of the Foam, and the Raja of Bamboo. By W. E. Maxwell.—The Epoch of the Guptas. By E. Thomas, F.R.S.—Two Chinese-Buddhist Inscriptions found at Buddha Gaya. By the Rev. S. Beal. With 2 Plates.—A Sanskrit Ode addressed to the Congress of Orientalists at Berlin. By Rama Dasa Sena, the Zemindar of Berhampore: with a Translation by S. Krishnavarma—Supplement to a paper, "On the Duty which Mahommedans in British India owe, on the Principles of their own Law, to the Government of the Country." By N. B. E. Baillie.—Index.

Vol. XIV. Part I. pp. 124, with 4 plates. 1882. 5s.

CONTENTS.—The Apology of Al Kindy: An Essay on its Age and Authorship. By Sir W Muir, K.C.S.I.—The Poet Pampa. By L. Rice.—On a Coin of Shams ud Dunya wa ud Din Mahmūd Snah. By C. J. Rodgers, Amritsar.—Note on Pl xxviii. fig. 1. of Mr. Fergusson's "Tree and Serpent Worship," 2nd Edition. By S. Beal, Prof of Chinese, London University.—On the present state of Mongolian Researches. By Prof. B. Julg, in a Letter to R. N. Cust.—A Sculptured Tope on an Old Stone at Dras, Ladak. By W. Simpson. F.R.G.S —Sanskrit Ode addressed to the Fifth International Congress of Orientalists assembled at Berlin, September, 1881. By the Lady Pandit Rama-bai, of Silchar, Kachar, Assam; with a Translation by Prof. Monier Williams, C.I.E.—The Intercourse of China with Eastern Turkestan and the Adjacent Countries in the Second Century B.C. By T. W. Kingsmill.—Suggestions on the Formation of the Semitic Tenses. A Comparative and Critical Study. By G. Bertin.—On a Lolo MS. written on Satin. By M. T. de La Couperie.

Vol. XIV. Part II. pp. 164, with three plates. 1882. 7s. 6d.

CONTENTS.—On Tartar and Turk. By S. W. KOELLE, Ph.D.—Notice of Scholars who have Contributed to our Knowledge of the Languages of Africa. By R. N. Cust.—Grammatical Sketch of the Hausa Language. By the Rev. J. F. Schön, F.R.G.S.,—Buddhist Saint Worship. By A. Lillie.—Gleanings from the Arabic. By H. W. Freeland, M.A.—Al Kahirah and its Gates. By H. C. Kay, M.A.—How the Mahâbhârata begins. By Edwin Arnold, C.S.I.—Arab Metrology, IV. Ed-Dahaby. By M. H. Sauvaire.

Vol. XIV. Part III. pp. 208, with 8 plates. 1882. 8s.

CONTENTS.—The Vaishnava Religion, with special reference to the Sikshâ-patrî of the Modern Sect called Svâmi-Nârâyana. By Monier Williams, C.I.E., D.C.L.—Further Notes on the Apology of Al-Kindy. By Sir W. Muir, K.C.S.I., D.C.L., LL.D.—The Buddhist Caves of Afghanistan. By W. Simpson.—The Identification of the Sculptured Tope at Sanchi. By W. Simpson.—On the Genealogy of Modern Numerals. By Sir E. C. Bayley, K.C.S.I., C.I.E.—The Cuneiform Inscriptions of Van, deciphered and translated, by A. H. Sayce.

Vol. XIV. Part IV. pp. 330, clii. 1882. 14s.

CONTENTS.—The Cuneiform Inscriptions of Van, deciphered and translated, by A. H. Sayce.—Sanskrit Text of the Mkshâ-Patrî of the Svâmi-Nârayana Sect. Edited and Translated by Prof. M. Williams, C.I.E.—The Successors of the Siljuks in Asia Minor. By S. L. Poole.—The Oldest Book of the Chinese (The Yh-King) and its Authors. By T. de la Couperie.

Vol. XV. Part I. pp. 134, with 2 plates. 1883. 6s.

CONTENTS.—The Genealogy of Modern Numerals. Part II. Simplification of the Ancient Indian Numeration. By Sir E. C. Bayley, C.I.E.—Parthian and Indo-Sassanian Coins. By E. Thomas, F.R.S.—Early Historical Relations between Phrygia and Cappadocia. By W. M. Ramsay.

Vol. XV. Part II. pp. 158, with 6 tables. 1883. 5s.

CONTENTS.—The Tattva-muktavali of Gauda-pûrnânandachakravartin. Edited and Translated by Professor E. B. Cowell.—Two Modern Sanskrit slokas. Communicated by Prof. E. B. Cowell.—Malagasy Place-Names. By the Rev. James Sibree, jun.—The Namakkâra, with Translation and Commentary. By H. L. St. Barbe.—Chinese Laws and Customs. By Christopher Gardner.—The Oldest Book of the Chinese (the Yh-King) and its Authors (continued). By Terrien de LaCouperie.—Gleanings from the Arabic. By H. W. Freeland.

Vol. XV. Part III. pp. 62-cxl. 1883. 6s.

CONTENTS.—Early Kannada Authors. By Lewis Rice.—On Two Questions of Japanese Archæology. By B. H. Chamberlain, M.R.A.S.—Two Sites named by Hiouen-Thsang in the 10th Book of the Si-yu-ki. By the Rev. S. Beal.—Two Early Sources of Mongol History. By H. H. Howorth, F.S.A.—Proceedings of Sixtieth Anniversary of the Society, held May 21, 1883.

Vol. XV. Part IV. pp. 140-iv.-20, with plate. 1883. 5s.

CONTENTS.—The Rivers of the Vedas, and How the Aryans Entered India. By Edward Thomas, F.R.S.—Suggestions on the Voice-Formation of the Semitic Verb. By G. Bertin, M.R.A.S.—The Buddhism of Ceylon. By Arthur Lillie, M.R.A.S.—The Northern Frontagers of China. Part VI. Hia or Tangut. By H. H. Howorth, F.S.A.—Index.—List of Members.

Vol. XVI. Part I. pp. 138, with 2 plates. 1884. 7s.

CONTENTS.—The Story of Devasmitâ. Translated from the Kathâ Sarit Sâgara, Tarânga 13, Sloka 54, by the Rev. B. Hale Wortham.—Pujāhs in the Sutlej Valley, Himalayas. By William Simpson, F.R.G.S.—On some New Discoveries in Southern India. By R. Sewell, Madras C.S.—On the Importance to Great Britain of the Study of Arabic. By Habib A. Salmoné.—Grammatical Note on the Gwamba Language in South Africa. By P. Berthoud, Missionary of the Canton de Vaud, Switzerland, stationed at Valdézia, Spelonken, Transvaal. (Prepared at the request of R. N. Cust.)—Dialect of Tribes of the Hindu Khush, from Colonel Biddulph's Work on the subject (corrected). Grammatical Note on the Simnûnî Dialect of the Persian Language. By the Rev. J. Bassett, American Missionary, Tabriz. (Communicated by R. N. Cust.)

Vol. XVI. Part II. pp. 184, with 1 plate. 9s.

CONTENTS.—Etymology of the Turkish Numerals. By S. W. Koelle, Ph.D., late Missionary of the Church Missionary Soc., Constantinople.—Grammatical Note and Vocabulary of the Kon-kû, a Kolarian Tribe in Central India. (Communicated by R. N. Cust.) The Pariah Caste in Travancore. By S. Mateer.—Some Bihārī Folk-Songs. By G. A. Grierson, B.C.S., Offg. Magistrate, Patna. Some further Gleanings from the Si-yu-ki. By the Rev. S. Beal.—On the Sites of Brahmanâbâd and Mansûrah in Sindh; with notices of others of less note in their Vicinity. By Maj.-Gen. M. R. Haig.—Antar and the Slave Daji. A Bedoueen Legend. By St. C. Baddeley.—The Languages of the Early Inhabitants of Mesopotamia. By G. Pinches.

Vol. XVI. Part III. pp. 74.—clx. 10s. 6d.

CONTENTS.—On the Origin of the Indian Alphabet. By R. N. Cust.—The Yi king of the Chinese as a Book of Divination and Philosophy. By Rev. Dr. Edkins.—On the Arrangement of the Hymns of the Rig-veda. By F. Pincott.—Proceedings of the Sixty-first Anniversary Meeting of the Society, May 19. 1884.

Vol. XVI. Part IV. pp. 134. 8s.

CONTENTS.—S'uka-sandesah. A Sanskrit Poem, by Lakshmi-dāsa. With Preface and Notes in English by H. H. Rama Varma, the Maharaja of Travancore, G.C.S.I.—The Chinese Book of the Odes, for English Readers. By C. F. R. Allen.—Note sur les Mots Sanscrits composés avec पति.

Par J. van den Gheyn, S.J.—Some Remarks on the Life and Labours of Csoma de Körös, delivered on the occasion when his Tibetan Books and MSS. were exhibited before the R.A.S. June 16, 1884. By Surgeon-Major T. Duka, M.D., late of the Bengal Army.—Arab Metrology. V. Ez-Zahrâwy. Translated and Annotated by M. H. Sauvaire, de l'Académie de Marseille.

Vol. XVII., Part I., pp. 144, with 5 plates. 1885. 10s. 6d.

CONTENTS.—Story of Shiuten Dôji. From a Japanese "Makimono" in Six "Ken," or Rolls. By F. V. Dickins.—The Bearing of the study of the Bantu Languages of South Africa on the Aryan Family of Languages. By the Rev. F. W. Kolbe.—Notes on Assyrian and Akkadian Pronouns. By G. Bertin.—Buddhist Remains near Sambhur, in Western Rajputana, India. By Surgeon-Major T. H. Hendley.—Gleanings from the Arabic. By H. W. Freeland.—Dialects of Tribes of Hindu Khush, from Colonel Biddulph's Work on the Subject. II. Shina (Gilgit Dialect). III. Khowar (Chitral Valley).

Vol. XVII., Part II., pp. 194, with 1 map. 1885. 9s.

CONTENTS.—Languages of the Caucasus. By R. N. Cust.—The Study of the South Indian Vernaculars. By G. U. Pope, D.D.—The Pallavas. By the Rev. T. Foulkes.—Translation of Books 91–93 of the Márkandeya Purána. By the Rev. B. H. Wortham.—Notes on Prof. E. B. Tylor's "Arabian Matriarchate," propounded by him as President of the Anthropological Section, British Association, Montreal, 1884. By J. W. Redhouse, LL.D.—The Northern Frontagers of China. Part VII. The Shato Turks. By H. H. Howorth.

Vol. XVII., Part III., pp. 344, with 2 plates. 1885. 10s. 6d.

CONTENTS.—Age of the Avesta. By Prof. de Harlez.—Chinese Game of Chess. By H. F. W. Holt.—Customs and Superstitions connected with the Cultivation of Rice in the Southern Province of Ceylon. By C. H. J. le Mesurier.—Vernacular Literature and Folk-Lore of the Panjab. By T. H. Thornton, C.S.I.—Beginnings of Writing in and around Tibet. By T. de Lacouperie.—Index. Proceedings of the Sixty-second Anniversary Meeting of the Society held on the 18th of May, 1885. List of Members.

Vol. XVIII., Part I., pp. 128, with 2 plates. 1886. 5s.

CONTENTS.—Ancient Navigation in the Indian Ocean. By the Rev. J. Edkins, D.D., Peking.—La Calle and the Country of Khomair, with a Note on North African Marbles; being the Report of a recent Tour addressed to H.M. Secretary of State. By Consul-General R. L. Playfair.—Bushmen and their Language. By G. Bertin.—Inscriptions at Cairo and the Burju-z Zafar. By Henry C. Kay.—Gleanings from the Arabic: Lament of Maisun, the Bedouin wife of Muawiya. By H. W. Freeland, M.A.—Discovery of Caves on the Murghab. By Capt. De Laessoë and the Hon. M. G. Talbot, R.E. With Notes by W. Simpson.—The Alchemist: A Persian Play. Translated by Guy Le Strange.

Vol. XVIII., Part II., pp. 196. 1886. 10s. 6d.

CONTENTS.—On Buddhism in its Relation to Brahmanism. By Sir M. Monier-Williams, K.C.I.E.—The Stories of Jimutavahana, and of Harisarman. Translated by Rev. B. Hale Wortham.—Geographical Distribution of the Modern Torki Languages. By M. A. Morrison. With a Note, Table of Authorities, and a Language Map.—A Modern Contributor to Persian Literature Riza Kuli Khan and his Works. By Sidney Churchill. —Some Bhoj'puri Folk Songs. Edited and Translated by G. A. Grierson.—Observations on the various Texts and Translations of the so-called "Song of Meysun"; an Inquiry into Meysun's Claim to its Authorship; and an Appendix on Arabic Transliteration and Pronunciation. By J. W. Redhouse.

Vol. XVIII., Part III., pp. 314, with 10 plates. 1886. 10s. 6d.

CONTENTS.—Rock-Cut Caves and Statues of Bamian. By Capt. the Hon. M. G. Talbot, R.E. With Notes hereon, and on Sketches of Capt. P. J. Maitland, by W. Simpson.—Sumerian Language and its Affinities. By Prof. Dr. Fritz Hommel, Munich.—Early Buddhist Symbolism. By R. Sewell.—Pre-Akkadian Semites. By G. Bertin.—Arrangement of the Hymns of the Adi Granth. By F. Pincott. Annual Report.

Vol. XVIII., Part IV., pp. 112, with 11 plates. 1886. 7s. 6d.
 CONTENTS.—Ancient Sculptures in China. By R. K. Douglas.—Mosque of Sultan Nasir Mohammed Ebn Kalaoun in the Citadel of Cairo. By Major C. M. Watson, R.E.—Languages of Melanesia. By Prof. G. von der Gabelentz.—Notes on the History of the Banu 'Okayl. By H. C. Kay.—Foreign Words in the Hebrew Text of the Old Testament. By the Rev. S. Leathes, D.D.

Vol. XIX., Part I., pp. 192, with 3 plates. 1887. 10s.
 CONTENTS.—Story of the Old Bamboo Hewer: A Japanese Romance of the Tenth Century. Translated with Notes, etc., by F. V. Dickins.—Brahui Grammar, after the German of the late Dr. Trumpp. By Dr. T. Duka.—Some useful Hindi Books. By G. A. Grierson.—Original Vocabularies of Five West Caucasian Languages, compiled by Mr. Peacock.—Arī. A Version in Chinese, by the Marquis Tseng, of a Poem written in English and Italian by H. W. Freeland.

Vol. XIX., Part II., pp. 160, with 3 plates. 1887. 10s.
 CONTENTS.—Narrative of Fâ-hien. By the Rev. S. Beal.—Priority of Labial Letters illustrated in Chinese Phonetics. By the Rev. J. Edkins.—Education in Egypt. By H. Cunynghame.—The Tri-Ratna. By F. Pincott.—Description of the Noble Sanctuary at Jerusalem in 1470 A.D. By Kamâl (or Shams) ad Dîn as Suyuti. Extracts re-translated by Guy le Strange.

Vol. XIX., Part III., pp. 218, with 5 plates. 1887. 10s.
 CONTENTS.—Life and Labours of A. Wylie, Agent of B. and F. Bible Society in China. By H. Cordier.—Modern Languages of Oceania, With Language Map. By Dr. R. N. Cust.—Ibnu Batuta in Sindh. By Major-General Haig.—Formosa Notes on MSS., Races and Languages. By Prof. T. de Lacouperie, Including a Note on Nine Formosan MSS. by E. Baber.—Revenues of the Moghul Empire. By H G. Keene.—Annual Report for 1886.

Vol. XIX., Part IV., pp. 202, with 1 plate. 1887. 10s.
 CONTENTS.—The Miryeks or Stone-men of Corea. By Prof. T. de Lacouperie (Plate).—Pre-Sanskrit Element in Ancient Tamil Literature. By E. S. W. Senathi Raja.—Were Zenobia and Zebba'u Identical? By J. W. Redhouse.—First Mandala of the Rig-Veda. By F. Pincott.—Origin and Development of the Cuneiform Syllabary. By G. Bertin.—Babylonian Chronicle. By T. G. Pinches.—Index—List of Members.

Vol. XX., Part I., pp. 164, with 3 plates. 1888. 10s.
 CONTENTS.—Cuneiform Inscriptions of Van. By the Rev. Prof. A. H. Sayce, M.A.—Some Suggestions of Origin in Indian Architecture. By W. Simpson.—The Chaghatai Mughals. By E. E. Oliver.—Sachau's Alberuni. By Major-Gen. Sir F. J. Goldsmid, C.B., K.C.S.I.

Asiatic Society.—TRANSACTIONS OF THE ROYAL ASIATIC SOCIETY OF GREAT BRITAIN AND IRELAND. Complete in 3 vols. 4to., 80 Plates of Facsimiles, etc., cloth. London, 1827 to 1835. Published at £9 5s.; reduced to £5 5s.
 The above contains contributions by Professor Wilson, G. C. Haughton, Davis, Morrison, Colebrooke, Humboldt, Dorn, Grotefend, and other eminent Oriental scholars.

Asiatic Society of Bengal.—JOURNAL. 8vo. 8 numbers per annum. 4s. each number. PROCEEDINGS. Published Monthly. 1s. each number.

Asiatic Society of Bengal.—JOURNAL. A Complete Set from the beginning in 1832 to the end of 1878, being Vols. 1 to 47. Proceedings, from the commencement in 1865 to 1878. A set quite complete. Calcutta, 1832 to 1878. Extremely scarce. £100.

Asiatic Society of Bengal.—CENTENARY REVIEW of the, from 1784 to 1883. Part I. History of the Society. By RAJENDRALALA MITRA, LL.D., C.I.E. Part II. Archæology, History, Literature, etc. By Dr. A. F. R. HOERNLE. Part III. Natural Science, etc. By BABOO P. N. BOSE. Part I. contains an Alphabetical Index to the Papers and Contributions to the "Asiatick Researches," and the "Journal and Proceedings of the Asiatic Society of Bengal," from the commencement up to 1883. Part II. contains a Classified Subject Index of the Society's Publications during the same period, under the heads of (1) Antiquities; (2) Coins, Weights, Measures, etc.; (3) History; (4) Language and Literature; (5) Religion, Manners and Customs.

Part III. contains a similar Index, classified under the heads of (1) Mathematical and Physical Science; (2) Geology; (3) Zoology; (4) Botany; (5) Geography; (6) Ethnology; (7) Chemistry. Royal 8vo. pp. 216—ciii.; 109, xcvi. 20, cloth. 1885. 10s.

Asiatic Society, Royal.—Bombay Branch.—JOURNAL. Nos. 1 to 35 in 8vo. with many plates. A complete set. Extremely scarce. Bombay, 1844-78. £13 10s.

Asiatic Society Royal.—Bombay Branch.—JOURNAL. Nos. 1 to 45. 5s. to 10s. 6d. each number. Several Numbers are out of print.

Asiatic Society, Royal.—Ceylon Branch (Colombo.)—JOURNAL. Part for 1845. 8vo. pp. 120, sewed. Price 7s. 6d.

CONTENTS:—On Buddhism. No. 1. By the Rev. D. J. Gogerly.—Translated Ceylonese Literature. By W. Knighton.—The Elements of the Voice in reference to the Roman and Singalese Alphabets. By the Rev. J. C. Macvicar.—Crime in Ceylon. By the Hon. J. Stark.—Ancient Coins. By S. C. Chitty.—Collection of Statistical Information in Ceylon. By John Capper.—On Buddhism. No 2. By the Rev. D. J. Gogerly.

1846. 8vo. pp. 176, sewed. Price 7s. 6d.

CONTENTS:—On Buddhism. By Rev. D. J. Gogerly.—Sixth Chapter of the Tiruvathavur Purana, translated with Notes. By S. C. Chitty.—The Discourse on the Minor Results of Conduct, or the Discourse Addressed to Subha. By Rev. D. J. Gogerly.—On the State of Crime in Ceylon. By Hon J. Stark.—Language and Literature of the Singalese. By Rev. S. Hardy.—Education Establishment of the Dutch in Ceylon. By Rev. J. D. Palm.—Account of the Dutch Church in Ceylon. By Rev. J. D. Palm.—Some Experiments in Electro-Agriculture. By J. Capper.—Singalo Wada, translated by Rev. D. J. Gogerly.—Colouring Matter Discovered in the husk of the Cocoa Nut. By Dr. R. Gygax.

1847-48. 8vo. pp. 221, sewed. Price 7s. 6d.

CONTENTS:—The Mineralogy of Ceylon. By Dr. R. Gygax.—The Dutch Church in Ceylon. By Rev. J. D. Palm.—On the History of Jaffna, from the Earliest Period to the Dutch Conquest. By S. C. Chitty.—The Rise and Fall of the Calany Ganga, from 1843 to 1846. By J. Capper.—The Discourse respecting Ratapala. Translated by Rev. D. J. Gogerly.—The Manufacture of Salt in the Chilaw and Putlam Districts. By A. O. Brodie.—A Royal Grant engraved on a Copper Plate. Translated, with Notes. By Rev. D. J. Gogerly.—Ancient and Modern Coins of Ceylon. By Hon. Mr. J. Stark.—Notes on the Climate and Salubrity of Putlam. By A. O. Brodie.—Revenue and Expenditure of the Dutch Government in Ceylon, during the last years of their Administration. By J. Capper.—On Buddhism. By Rev. D. J. Gogerly.

1853-55. Part I. 8vo. pp. 56, sewed. Price 7s. 6d. (or the 3 parts £1).

CONTENTS:—Buddhism; Chariya Pitaka. By Rev. D. J. Gogerly.—Laws of the Buddhist Priesthood. By Rev. D. J. Gogerly.—Statistical Account of the Districts of Chilaw Korle, Seven Korles. By A. O. Brodie.—Catalogue of Ceylon Birds. By E. F. Kelaart, and and Putlam, N.W.P. By A. O. Brodie.—Rock Inscription at Gooroo Godde Wihare, in the Magool. By E. L. Layard.

1853-55. Part II. 8vo. pp. 102, with extra plates, sewed. Price 7s. 6d.

CONTENTS:—Catalogue of Ceylon Birds. By E. F. Kelaart and E. L. Layard.—Forms of Salutations and Address known among the Singalese. By Hon. J. Stark.—Rock Inscriptions. By A. O. Brodie.—On the Veddhas of Bintenne. By Rev. J. Gillings.—Rock Inscription at Piramanenkandel. By S. C. Chitty.—Analysis of the Great Historical Poem of the Moors, entitled Surah. By S. C. Chitty.

1853-55. Part III. 8vo. pp. 150, sewed. Price 7s. 6d.

CONTENTS:—Analysis of the Great Historical Poem of the Moors, entitled Surah. By S. C. Chitty.—Description of New or little known Species of Reptiles found in Ceylon. By E. F. Kelaart.—Laws of the Buddhist Priesthood. By the Rev. D. J. Gogerly.—Ceylon Ornithology. By E. F. Kelaart.—Account of the Rodiyas, with a Specimen of their Language. By S. C. Chitty.—Rock Inscriptions in the North-Western Province. By A. O. Brodie.

1865-6. 8vo. pp. xi. and 184. Price 7s. 6d.

CONTENTS:—On Demonology and Witchcraft in Ceylon. By D. de Silva Gooneratne Modliar.—First Discourse Delivered by Buddha. By Rev. D. J. Gogerly. Pootoor Well—The Air Breathing Fish of Ceylon. By Barcroft Boake, B.A.—On the Origin of the Sinhalese Language. By J. D'Alwis.—Remarks on the Poisonous Properties of the Calotropis Gigantea, etc. By W. C. Ondaatjie.—On the Crocodiles of Ceylon. By Barcroft Boake.—Native Medicinal Oils.

1867-70. Part I. 8vo. pp. 150. Price 10s.

Contents:—On the Origin of the Sinhalese Language. By James De Alwis.—A Lecture on Buddhism. By the Rev. D. J. Gogerly.—Description of two Birds new to the recorded Fauna of Ceylon. By H. Nevill.—Description of a New Genus and Five New Species of Marine Univalves from the Southern Province, Ceylon. By G. Nevill.—A Brief Notice of Robert Knox and his Companions in Captivity in Kandy for the space of Twenty Years, discovered among the Dutch Records preserved in the Colonial Secretary's Office, Colombo. By J. R. Blake.

1867-70. Part II. 8vo. pp. xl. and 45. Price 7s. 6d.

Contents:—Summary of the Contents of the First Book in the Buddhist Canon, called the Párájika Book.—By the Rev. S. Coles.—Párájika Book—No. 1.—Párájika Book—No. 2.

1871-72. 8vo. pp. 66 and xxxiv. Price 7s. 6d.

Contents:—Extracts from a Memoir left by the Dutch Governor, Thomas Van Rhee, to his successor, Governor Gerris de Heer, 1697. Translated from the Dutch Records preserved in the Colonial Secretariat at Colombo. By R. A. van Cuylenberg, Government Record Keeper.—The Food Statistics of Ceylon. By J. Capper.—Specimens of Sinhalese Proverbs. By L. de Zoysa, Mudaliyar, Chief Translator of Government.—Ceylon Reptiles: being a preliminary Catalogue of the Reptiles found in, or supposed to be in Ceylon, compiled from various authorities. By W. Ferguson.—On an Inscription at Dondra. No. 2. By T. W. Rhys Davids, Esq.

1873. Part I. 8vo. pp. 79. Price 7s. 6d.

Contents:—On Oath and Ordeal. By Bertram Fulke Hartshorne.—Notes on Prinochilus Vincens. By W. V. Legge.—The Sports and Games of the Singhalese. By Leopold Ludovici.—On Miracles. By J. De Alwis.—On the Occurrence of Scolopax Rusticola and Gallinago Scolopacina in Ceylon. By W. V. Legge.—Transcript and Translation of an Ancient Copper-plate Sannas. By Mudliyar Louis de Zoysa, Chief Translator to Government.

1874. Part I. 8vo. pp. 94. Price 7s. 6d.

Contents:—Description of a supposed New Genus of Ceylon. Batrachians. By W. Ferguson.—Notes on the Identity of Piyadasi and Asoka. By Mudaliyar Louis de Zoysa.—The Island Distribution of the Birds in the Society's Museum. By W. V. Legge.—Brand Marks on Cattle. By J. De Alwis.—Notes on the Occurrence of a rare Eagle new to Ceylon; and other interesting or rare birds. By S. Bligh.—Extracts from the Records of the Dutch Government in Ceylon. By R. van Cuylenberg.—Stature of Gotama Buddha. By J. De Alwis.

1879. 8vo. pp. 58. Price 5s.

Contents.—Notes on Ancient Sinhalese Inscriptions.—On the Preparation and Mounting of Insects for the Binocular Microscope.—Notes on Neophron Pucnopterus (Savigny) from Nuwara Eliya.—On the Climate of Dimbula.—Note on the supposed cause of the existence of Patanas or Grass Lands of the Mountain Zone of Ceylon.

1880. Part I. 8vo. pp. 90. Price 5s.

Contents.—Text and Translation of the Inscription of Mahinde III. at Mihintale.—Glossary.—A Paper on the Vedic and Buddhistic Polities.—Customs and Ceremonies connected with the Paddi Cultivation—Gramineae, or Grasses Indigenous to or Growing in Ceylon.

1880. Part II. 8vo. pp. 48. Price 5s.

Contents.—Gramineae, or Grasses Indigenous to or Growing in Ceylon.—Translation of two Jatakas.—On the supposed Origin of Tamana, Nuwara, Tambapanni and Taprobane.—The Rocks and Minerals of Ceylon.

1881. Vol. VII. Part I. (No. 23.) 8vo. pp. 56. Price 5s.

Contents.—Hindu Astronomy; as compared with the European Science. By S. Mervin.—Sculptures at Horana. By J. G. Smither.—Gold. By A. C. Dixon.—Specimens of Sinhalese Proverbs. By L. De Zoysa.—Ceylon Bee Culture By S. Jayatilaka.—A Short Account of the Principal Religious Ceremonies observed by the Kandyans of Ceylon. By C. J. R. Le Mesurier.—Valentyn's Account of Adam's Peak. By A. Spence Moss.

1881. Vol. VII. Part II. (No. 24.) 8vo. pp. 162. Price 5s.

Contents.—The Ancient Emporium of Kalah, etc., with Notes on Fa-Hian's Account of Ceylon. By H. Nevill.—The Sinhalese Observance of the Kaláwa. By L. Nell.—Note on the Origin of the Veddás, with Specimens of their Songs and Charms. By L. de Zoysa.—A Hónlyam Image. By L. Nell.—Note on the Mirá Kantiri Festival of the Muhammadans. By A. T. Shams-ud-dín.—Tericulture in Ceylon. By J. L. Vanderstraaten.—Sinhalese Omens. By S. Jayatilaka.

1882. Extra Number. 8vo. pp. 60. Price 5s.

Contents.—Ibn Batuta in the Maldives and Ceylon. Translated from the French of M. M. Defremery and Sanguinetti. By A. Gray.

Asiatic Society (Royal).—North China Branch of.—Journal.—Old Series, 4 numbers, and New Series, Parts 1 to 12. The following numbers are sold separately: Old Series—No. II. May, 1859, pp. 145 to 256. No. III. December, 1859, pp. 112. 7s. 6d. each. Vol. II. No. 1, Sept., 1860, pp. 128. 7s. 6d. New Series—No. 1. Dec., 1864, pp. 174. 7s. 6d. No. II.

Dec., 1865, pp. 187, with maps. 7s. 6d. No. III. Dec., 1866, pp. 121. 9s. No. IV. Dec., 1867, pp 266. 10s. 6d. No. VI. for 1869 and 1870, pp. 216. 7s. 6d. No. VII. (1871-2) pp. 270. 10s. No. VIII. pp. 200. 10s. 6d. No. IX. pp. 254. 10s. 6d. No. X. pp. 336 and 279. £1 1s. No. XI. (1877) pp. 200. 10s. 6d. No. XII. (1878) pp. 337, with maps. £1 1s. No. XIII. (1879) pp. 138, with plates. 10s. 6d. No. XIV. (1879) pp. 80, with plates, 4s. No. XV. (1880) pp. 390, with plates, 15s. Vol. XVI. (1881) pp. 248. 12s. 6d. Vol. XVII. (1882) pp. 246 with plates. 12s. 6d. Vol. XVIII. (1883) pp. 228, with 2 plates.

Asiatic Society (Royal).—China Branch of the,—Journal. — 8vo. sewed. Vol. XIX. Part I. (1884) pp. 125. Vol. XX. (1885) pp. 322, with plate. Vol. XXI. (1886) pp. 370, with plate.

Asiatic Society of Japan.—TRANSACTIONS. Vol. I. From 30th October, 1872, to 9th October, 1873. 8vo. pp. 110, with plates. 1874. Vol. II. 1873. 8vo. pp. 249. 1874. Vol. III. Part I. 1874. Vol. III. Part II. 1875. Vol. IV. 1875. Vol. V. Part I. 1876. Vol. V. Part II. (A Summary of the Japanese Penal Codes. By J. H. Longford.) Vol. VI. Part I. pp. 190. Vol. VI. Part II. 1878. Vol. VI. Part II. 1878. 7s. 6d. each Part.—Vol. VII. Part I. (Milne's Journey across Europe and Asia.) 5s.—Vol. VII. Part II. March, 1879. 5s.—Vol. VII. Part III. June. 1879. 7s. 6d. Vol. VII. Part IV. Nov., 1879. 10s. 6d. Vol. VIII. Part I. Feb., 1880. 7s. 6d. Vol. VIII. Part II. May, 1880. 7s. 6d. Vol. VIII. Part. III. Oc., 1880. 10s. 6d. Vol. VIII. Part IV. Dec., 1880. 5s. Vol. IX. Part I. Feb., 1881. 7s. 6d. Vol. IX. Part II. Aug., 1881. 7s. 6d. Vol. IX. Part III. Dec., 1881. 5s. Vol. X. Part I. May, 1882. 10s. Vol. X. Part II. Oct., 1882. 7s. 6d. Vol. X Supplement, 1883. £1. Vol. XI. Part I. April, 1883. 7s. 6d. Vol. XI. Part II. Sep., 1883. 7s. 6d. Vol. XII. Part I. Nov., 1883. 5s. Vol. XII. Part II. May, 1884. 5s.

Asiatic Society, Royal.—Straits Branch.—JOURNAL. No. 1. 8vo. pp. pp. 130, sewed, 3 Maps and Plate. July, 1878. Price 9s.

CONTENTS.—Inaugural Address of the President. By the Ven. Archdeacon Hose, M.A.—Distribution of Minerals in Sarawak. By A. Hart Everett.—Breeding Pearls. By N. B. Dennys, Ph.D.—Dialects of the Melanesian Tribes of the Malay Peninsula. By M. de Mikluho-Maclay.—Malay Spelling in English. Report of Government Committee (reprinted).—Geography of the Malay Peninsula. Part I. By A. M. Skinner.—Chinese Secret Societies. Part I. By W. A. Pickering.—Malay Proverbs. Part. I. By W. E. Maxwell.—The Snake-eating Hamadryad. By N. B. Dennys, Ph.D.—Gutta Percha. Py H. I. Murton.—Miscellaneous Notices.

No. 2. 8vo. pp. 130, 2 Plates, sewed. December, 1878. Price 9s.

CONTENTS: - The Song of the Dyak Head-feast. By Rev. J. Perham.—Malay Proverbs. Part II. By E. W. Maxwell.—A Malay Nautch. By F. A. Swettenham.—Pidgin English. By N. B. Dennys, Ph.D.—The Founding of Singapore. By Sir T. S Raffles.—Notes on Two Perak Manuscripts. By W. E. Maxwell.—The Metalliferous Formation of the Peninsula. By D. D. Daly.—Suggestions regarding a new Malay Dictionary. By the Hon. C. J. Irving.—Ethnological Excursions in the Malay Peninsula. By N. von Mikluho-Maclay.—Miscellaneous Notices.

No. 3. 8vo. pp. iv. and 146, sewed. July, 1879. Price 9s.

CONTENTS:—Chinese Secret Societies, by W. A. Pickering.—Malay Proverbs, Part III, by W. E. Maxwell.—Notes on Gutta Percha, by F. W. Burbidge, W. H. Treacher H. J. Murton.—The Maritime Code of the Malays, reprinted from a translation by Sir S. Raffles.—A Trip to Gunong Bumut, by D. F. A. Hervey.—Caves at Sungei Batu in Selangor, by D. D. Daly.—Geography of Aching, translated from the German by Dr. Beiber.—Account of a Naturalist's Visit to Selangor, by A. J. Hornady.—Miscellaneous Notices: Geographical Notes, Routes from Selangor to Pahang, Mr. Deane's Survey Report, A Tiger's Wake, Breeding Pearls, The Maritime Code, and Sir F. Raffles' Meteorological Returns.

No. 4. 8vo. pp. xxv. and 65, sewed. December, 1879. Price 9s.

CONTENTS.—List of Members.—Proceedings, General Meeting.—Annual Meeting.—Council's Annual Report for 1879.—Treasurer's Report for 1879.—President's Address.—Reception of Professor Nordenskjold.—The Marine Code. By Sir S. Raffles.—About Kinta. By H. W. C. Leech.—About Shin and Bernam. By H. W. Leech.—The Aboriginal Tribes of Perak. By W. E. Maxwell.—The Vernacular Press in the Straits. By E. W. Birch.—On the Guliga of Borneo. By A. H. Everett.—On the name "Sumatra."—A Correction.

No. 5. 8vo. pp. 160, sewed. July, 1879. Price 9s.

CONTENTS.—Selesilah (Book of the Descent) of the Rajas of Bruni. By H. Low.—Notes to Ditto.—History of the Sultans of Bruni.—List of the Mahomedan Sovereigns of Bruni.—Historic Tablet—Acheh. By G. P. Tolson.—From Perak to Shin and down the Shin and Bernam Rivers. By F. A. Swettenham.—A Contribution to Malayan Bibliography. By N. B. Dennys.—Comparative Vocabulary of some of the Wild Tribes inhabiting the Malayan Peninsula, Borneo, etc.—The Tiger in Borneo. By A. H. Everett.

No. 6. 8vo. pp. 133, with 7 Photographic Plates, sewed. December, 1880. Price 9s.

CONTENTS.—Some Account of the Independent Native States of the Malay Peninsula, Part I. By F. A. Swettenham.—The Ruins of Boro Burdur in Java. By the Ven. Archdeacon G. F. Hose. A Contribution to Malayan Bibliography. By N. B. Dennys.—Report on the Exploration of the Caves of Borneo. By A. H. Everett.—Introductory Remarks. By J. Evans.—Notes on the Report.—Notes on the Collection of Bones. By G. Bush.—A Sea-Dyak Tradition of the Deluge and Subsequent Events. By the Rev. J. Perham.—The Comparative Vocabulary.

No. 7. 8vo. pp. xvi. and 92. With a Map, sewed. June, 1881. Price 9s.

CONTENTS.—Some account of the Mining Districts of Lower Perak. By J. Errington de la Croix.—Folklore of the Malays. By W. E. Maxwell.—Notes on the Rainfall of Singapore. By J. J. L. Wheatley.—Journal of a Voyage through the Straits of Malacca on an Expedition to the Molucca Islands. By Captain W. C. Lennon.

No. 8. 8vo. pp. 56. With a Map, sewed. December, 1881. Price 9s.

CONTENTS.—The Endau and its Tributaries. By D. F. A. Hervey.—Itinerary from Singapore to the Source of the Sembrong and up the Madek.—Petara, or Sea Dyak Gods. By the Rev. J. Perham.—Klouwang and its Caves, West Coast of Atchin. Translated by D. F. A. Hervey.—Miscellaneous Notes: Varieties of "Getah" and "Rotan."—The "Ipoh" Tree, Perak.—Comparative Vocabulary.

No. 9. 8vo. pp. xxii. and 172. With three Col. Plates, sd. June, 1882. Price 12s.

CONTENTS.—Journey on Foot to the Patani Frontier in 1876. By W. E. Maxwell.—Probable Origin of the Hill Tribes of Formosa. By John Dodd.—History of Perak from Native Sources. By W. E. Maxwell.—Malayan Ornithology. By Captain H. R. Kelham.—On the Transliteration of Malay in the Roman Character. By W. E. Maxwell.—Kota Glanggi, Pahang. By W. Cameron. Natural History Notes. By N. B. Dennys.—Statement of Haji of the Madek Ali.—Pantang Kapur of the Madek Jakun.—Stone from Batu Pahat.—Rainfall at Lankat, Sumatra.

No. 10. 8vo. pp. xv. and 117, sewed. December, 1882. Price 9s.

CONTENTS.—Journal of a Trip from Sarawak to Meri. By N. Denison.—The Mentra Traditions. By the Hon. D. F. A. Hervey.—Probable Origin of the Hill Tribes of Formosa. By J. Dodd.—Sea Dyak Religion. By the Rev. J. Perham.—The Dutch in Perak. By W. E. Maxwell.—Outline History of the British Connection with Malaya. By the Hon. A. M. Skinner.—Extracts from Journals of the Societé de Geographie of Paris.—Memorandum on Malay Transliteration.—The Chiri.—Register of Rainfall.

No. 11. 8vo. pp. 170. With a Map, sewed. June, 1883. Price 9s.

CONTENTS.—Malayan Ornithology. By Captain H. R. Kelham.—Malay Proverbs. By the Hon. W. E. Maxwell.—The Pigmies. Translated by J. Errington de la Croix.—On the Patani. By W. Cameron.—Latah. By H. A. O'Brien.—The Java System. By the Hon. A. M. Skinner.—Batu Kodok. Prigi Acheh.—Dutch Occupation of the Dindings, etc.

No. 12. 8vo. pp. xx. and 288, sewed. December, 1883. Price 9s.

CONTENTS.—Malayan Ornithology. By Captain H. R. Kelham.—Gutta-producing Trees. By L. Wray.—Shamanism in Perak. By the Hon. W. E. Maxwell.—Changes in Malayan Dialects. By A. M. Ferguson.—Straits Meteorology. By the Hon. A. M. Skinner.—Occasional Notes. By the Hon. W. E. Maxwell.

No. 13. 8vo. pp. xx. and 116, sewed. June, 1884. Price 9s.

CONTENTS.—The Pigmies. Translated by J. Errington de la Croix.—Valentyn's Description of Malacca.—By Hon. D. F. A. Hervey.—The Stream Tin Deposit of Perak. By the Rev. J. E. Tenison-Woods.—Rembau. By the Hon. D. F. A. Hervey.—The Tawaran and Putatan Rivers. By S. Elphinstone Dalrymple.—Miscellaneous Notes.

No. 14. 8vo. pp. 176, sewed. December, 1884. Price 9s.

CONTENTS.—Journey to the Summit of Gunong Bubu. By the Rev. J. E. Tenison-Woods, F.G.S., F.L.S., etc.—Sea Dyak Religion. By the Rev. J. Perham.—The History of Perak from Native Sources. By the Hon. W. E. Maxwell.—British North Borneo. By E. P. Gueritz.—Jelebu.—By H. A. O'Brien.

No. 15. 8vo. 172. sewed. June, 1885. Price 9s.

Contents.—Journal kept during a Journey across the Malay Peninsula (with Maps). By F. A. Swettenham.—The Object and Results of a Dutch Expedition into the Interior of Sumatra in the years 1877, 1878, and 1879. Translated from the French, by R. N. Bland.—Further Notes on the Rainfall of Singapore. By J. J. L. Wheatley. - A Glimpse at the Manners and Customs of the Hill Tribes of North Formosa. By J. Dodd.—Genealogy of the Royal Family of Brunei. Translated from the Malay by W. H. Treacher.—French Land Decree in Cambodia. Translated from the French by the Hon. W. E. Maxwell, C.M.G.—Malay Language and Literature. By Dr. Reinhold Rost.—A Missionary's Journey through Laos from Bangkok to Ubon. By the Rev. N. J. Couvreur, Singapore.—Valentyn's Account of Malacca. Translated from the Dutch.

No. 16. 8vo, pp. 220, sewed. December, 1885. Price 9s.

Contents.—Plan for a Volunteer Force in the Muda Districts, Province Wellesley. By the late J. R. Logan.—A Description of the Chinese Lottery known as "Hua-Hoey." By C. W. S. Kynnersley.—On the Roots in the Malay Language. From the Dutch of J. Pijnappel.—Klierg's War Raid to the Skies; a Dyak Myth. By the Rev. J. Perham.—Valentyn's Account of Malacca. Translated from the Dutch (continued from Journal, No. 15).—On Mines and Miners in Kinta, Perak. By A. Hole, Inspector of Mines, Kinta.

No. 17. 8vo. pp. 160-84, sewed. June, 1886. Price 9s.

Contents.—Biography of Siam. By E. M. Satow.—Sri Rama; a Fairy Tale told by a Malay Rhapsodist. By W. E. Maxwell.—History of Malacca from Portuguese Sources. Contributed by E. Koch.—Occasional Notes.

No. 18. 8vo. pp. xx. and 376, sewed. December, 1886. Price 9s.

Contents.—Biography of Siam. By E. M. Satow.—English, Sulu, and Malay Vocabulary. By T. H. Haynes.—Raja Donan, a Malay Fairy Tale told by a Malay Rhapsodist. By W. E. Maxwell.—The Survey Question in Cochin China. By M. Camouilly.—Notes on Economic Plants, Straits Settlements, by N. Cautley.—Index to Journal of the Indian Archipelago. By N. B. Dennys.

American Oriental Society.—JOURNAL OF THE AMERICAN ORIENTAL SOCIETY. Vols. I. to X. and Vol. XII. (all published). 8vo. Boston and New Haven, 1849 to 1881. A complete set. Very rare. £14.

Volumes 2 to 5 and 8 to 10 and 12 may be had separately at £1 1s. each.

Antananarivo Annual and Madagascar Magazine.—A Record of Information on the Topography and Natural Productions of Madagascar, and the Customs, Traditions, Language and Religious Beliefs of its People. Edited by the Rev. J. Sibree, F.R.G.S., and Rev. R. Baron, F.L.S. Demy 8vo. pp. iv. and 132, with plate, paper. 2s. 6d.

Anthropological Society of London, MEMOIRS READ BEFORE THE, 1863-1866. 8vo. pp. 542, cloth. 21s. Vol. II. 8vo., pp. x. 464, cloth. 21s.

Anthropological Institute of Great Britain and Ireland (The Journal of the). Published Quarterly. 8vo. sewed.

Biblical Archæology, Society of.—TRANSACTIONS OF THE. 8vo. Vol. I. Part. I., 12s. 6d. Vol. I., Part II., 12s. 6d. (this part cannot be sold separately, or otherwise than with the complete sets). Vols. II. and III., 2 parts, 10s. 6d. each. Vol. IV., 2 parts, 12s. 6d. each. Vol. V., Part. I., 15s. ; Part. II., 12s. 6d. Vol. VI, 2 parts, 12s. 6d. each. Vol. VII. Part I. 10s. 6d. Parts II. and III. 12s. 6d. each. Vol. VIII., 3 parts, 12s. 6d. each. Vol. IX. Part I. 12s. 6d.
PROCEEDINGS. Vol. 1. Session 1878-79. 2s. 6d. Vol. II. 2s. 6d. Vols. III., IV., and V. 5s. each. Vols. VI., VII., and VIII. (1885-6). 6s. each.

Bibliotheca Indica. A Collection of Oriental Works published by the Asiatic Society of Bengal. Old Series. Fasc. 1 to 261. New Series. Fasc. 1 to 607. (Special List of Contents and prices to be had on application.)

Browning Society's Papers.—Demy 8vo. wrappers. 1881-84. Part I., pp. 116. 10s. Bibliography of Robert Browning from 1833-81. Part II. pp. 142. 10s. Part III., pp. 168. 10s. Part IV., pp. 148. 10s. Part V., pp. 104. 10s. 1885-86. Part VII., pp. 168. 10s. Part VIII., pp. 176. 10s.

Browning.—Bibliography of Robert Browning from 1833-81. Compiled by F. J. FURNIVALL. Demy 8vo. pp. 170, wrapper. Third Edition. Enlarged. 1883. 12s.

Browning's Poem's (Illustrations to).—4to. boards. Parts I. and II. 10s. each.

Calcutta Review (THE).—Published Quarterly. Price 6s. per annum.

Calcutta Review.—A COMPLETE SET FROM THE COMMENCEMENT IN 1844 to 1882. Vols 1. to 75, or Numbers 1 to 140. A fine clean copy. Calcutta, 1844-82. Index to the first fifty volumes of the Calcutta Review, 2 parts. (Calcutta, 1873). Nos. 39 and 40 have never been published. £66. Complete sets are of great rarity.

Calcutta Review (Selections from the).—Crown 8vo. sewed. Nos. 1. to 45. 5s. each.

Cambridge Philological Society (Transactions of the).—Vol. I. From 1872 to 1880. 8vo. pp. xvi. and 420, wrapper. 1881. 15s.

CONTENTS—Preface.—The Work of a Philological Society. J. P. Postgate.—Transactions of the Cambridge Philological Society from 1872 to 1879.—Transactions for 1879-1880.—Reviews.—Appendix.

Vol. II. for 1881 and 1882. 8vo. pp. viii.-286, wrapper, 1883. 12s.
Vol. III. Part I. 1886. 3s. 6d.

Cambridge Philological Society (Proceedings of the).—Parts I and II. 1882. 1s. 6d.; III. 1s.; IV.-VI. 2s. 6d.; VII. and VIII. 2s. IX. 1s.; X. and XI. 1s. 6d.; XII. 1s. 6d.; XIII.-XV. 2s. 6d.

China Review; or, Notes and Queries on the Far East. Published bi-monthly. 4to. Subscription £1 10s. per volume.

Chinese Recorder and Missionary Journal.—Shanghai. Subscription per volume (of 6 parts) 15s.

A complete set from the beginning. Vols. 1 to 10. 8vo. Foochow and Shanghai, 1861-1879. £9.

Containing important contributions on Chinese Philology, Mythology, and Geography, by Edkins, Giles, Bretschneider, Scarborough, etc. The earlier volumes are out of print.

Chrysanthemum (The).—A Monthly Magazine for Japan and the Far East. Vol. I. and II., complete. Bound £1 1s. Subscription £1 per volume.

Geographical Society of Bombay.—JOURNAL AND TRANSACTIONS. A complete set. 19 vols. 8vo. Numerous Plates and Maps, some coloured. Bombay, 1844-70. £10 10s.

An important Periodical, containing grammatical sketches of several languages and dialects, as well as the most valuable contributions on the Natural Sciences of India. Since 1871 the above is amalgamated with the 'Journal of the Bombay Branch of the Royal Asiatic Society.'

Indian Antiquary (The).—A Journal of Oriental Research in Archæology, History, Literature, Languages, Philosophy, Religion, Folklore, etc. Edited by J. F. FLEET, C.I.E., M.R.A.S., etc., and CAPT. R. C. TEMPLE, F.R.G.S., M.R.A.S., etc. 4to. Published 12 numbers per annum. Subscription £1 16s. A complete set. Vols. 1 to 11. £28 10s. (The earlier volumes are out of print.)

Indian Archipelago and Eastern Asia, Journal of the.—Edited by J. R. LOGAN, of Pinang. 9 vols. Singapore, 1847-55. New Series. Vols. I. to IV. Part 1, (all published), 1856-59. A complete set in 13 vols. 8vo. with many plates. £30.

Vol. I. of the New Series consists of 2 parts; Vol. II. of 4 parts; Vol. III. of No. 1 (never completed), and of Vol. IV. also only one number was published. A few copies remain of several volumes that may be had separately.

Indian Notes and Queries. A Monthly Periodical devoted to the Systematic Collection of Authentic Notes and Scraps of Information regarding the Country and the People. Edited by Captain R. C. TEMPLE, etc. 4to. Subscription per annum. 16s.

Japan, Transactions of the Seismological Society of, Vol. I. Parts i. and ii. April-June, 1880. 10s. 6d. Vol. II. July-December, 1880. 5s. Vol. III. January-December, 1881. 10s. 6d. Vol. IV. January-June. 1882. 9s.

Literature, **Royal Society of.**—See under "Royal."

Madras Journal of Literature and Science.—Published by the Committee of the Madras Literary Society and Auxiliary Royal Asiatic Society, and edited by MORRIS, COLE, and BROWN. A complete set of the Three Series (being Vols. I. to XVI, First Series; Vols. XVII. to XXII. Second Series: Vol. XXIII. Third Series, 2 Numbers, no more published). A fine copy, uniformly bound in 23 vols. With numerous plates, half calf. Madras, 1834-66. £42.

Equally scarce and important. On all South-Indian topics, especially those relating to Natural History and Science, Public Works and Industry, this Periodical is an unrivalled authority.

Madras Journal of Literature and Science. 1878. (I. Volume of the Fourth Series.) Edited by Gustav Oppert, Ph.D. 8vo. pp. vi. and 234, and xlvii. with 2 plates. 1879. 10s. 6d. Contents.—I. On the Classification of Languages. By Dr. G. OPPERT.—II. On the Ganga Kings. By LEWIS RICE. 1879. pp. 318. 10s. 6d. 1880. pp. vi. and 232. 10s. 1881. pp. vi. and 338. 10s.

Orientalist (The).—A Monthly Journal of Oriental Literature, Arts, Folk-lore, etc. Edited by W. GOONETELLIKE. Annual Subscription, 12s.

Pandit (The).—A Monthly Journal of the Benares College, devoted to Sanskrit Literature. Old Series. 10 vols. 1866-1876. New Series, vols. 1 to 9. 1876-1887. £1 4s. per volume.

Panjab Notes and Queries, now **Indian Notes and Queries,** which see above.

Peking Gazette.—Translations of the Peking Gazette for 1872 to 1885. 8vo. cloth. 10s. 6d. each.

Philological Society (Transactions of The). A Complete Set, including the Proceedings of the Philological Society for the years 1842-1853. 6 vols. The Philological Society's Transactions, 1854 to 1876. 15 vols. The Philological Society's Extra Volumes. 9 vols. In all 30 vols. 8vo. £19 13s. 6d.

Proceedings (The) of the Philological Society 1842-1853. 6 vols. 8vo. £3.

Transactions of the Philological Society, 1854-1876. 15 vols. 8vo. £10 16s.

*** The Volumes for 1867, 1868-9, 1870-2, and 1873-4, are only to be had in complete sets, as above.

Separate Volumes.

For 1854: containing papers by Rev. J. W. Blakesley, Rev. T. O. Cockayne, Rev. J. Davies, Dr. J. W. Donaldson, Dr. Theod. Goldstücker, Prof. T. Hewitt Key, J. M. Kemble, Dr. R. G. Latham, J. M. Ludlow, Hensleigh Wedgwood, etc. 8vo. cl. £1 1s.

For 1855: with papers by Dr. Carl Abel, Dr. W. Bleek, Rev. Jno. Davies, Miss A. Gurney, Jas. Kennedy, Prof. T. H. Key, Dr. R. G. Latham, Henry Malden, W. Ridley, Thos. Watts, Hensleigh Wedgwood, etc. In 4 parts. 8vo. £1 1s.

*** Kamilaroi Language of Australia, by W. Ridley; and False Etymologies, by H. Wedgwood, separately. 1s.

For 1856-7: with papers by Prof. Aufrecht, Herbert Coleridge, Lewis Kr. Daa,
M. de Haan, W. C. Jourdain, James Kennedy, Prof. Key, Dr. G. Latham, J. M.
Ludlow, Rev. J. J. S. Perowne, Hensleigh Wedgwood, R. F. Weymouth, Jos.
Yates, etc. 7 parts. 8vo. (The Papers relating to the Society's Dictionary
are omitted.) £1 1s. each volume.

For 1858: including the volume of Early English Poems, Lives of the Saints,
edited from MSS. by F. J. Furnivall; and papers by Ern. Adams, Prof.
Aufrecht, Herbert Coleridge, Rev. Francis Crawford, M. de Haan Hettema,
Dr. R. G. Latham, Dr. Lottner, etc. 8vo. cl. 12s.

For 1859: with papers by Dr. E. Adams, Prof. Aufrecht, Herb. Coleridge, F. J.
Furnivall, Prof. T. H. Key, Dr. C. Lottner, Prof. De Morgan, F. Pulszky,
Hensleigh Wedgwood, etc. 8vo. cl. 12s.

For 1860-1: including The Play of the Sacrament; and Pascon agau Arluth, the
Passion of our Lord, in Cornish and English, both from MSS., edited by Dr.
W. Stokes; and papers by Dr. E. Adams, T. F. Barham, Rev. D. Coleridge,
H. Coleridge, Sir J. F. Davis, D. P. Fry, Prof. T. H. Key, Dr. C. Lottner,
Bishop Thirlwall, H. Wedgwood, R. F. Weymouth, etc. 8vo. cl. 12s.

For 1862-3: with papers by C. B. Cayley, D. P. Fry, Prof. Key, H. Malden,
Rich. Morris, F. W. Newman, Robert Peacock, Hensleigh Wedgwood, R. F.
Weymouth, etc. 8vo. cl. 12s.

For 1864: containing 1. Manning's (Jas.) Inquiry into the Character and Origin
of the Possessive Augment in English, etc.; 2. Newman's (Francis W.) Text of
the Iguvine Inscriptions, with Interlinear Latin Translation; 3. Barnes's (Dr.
W.) Grammar and Glossary of the Dorset Dialect; 4. Gwreans An Bys—The
Creation: a Cornish Mystery, Cornish and English, with Notes by Whitley
Stokes, etc. 8vo. cl. 12s.

*** Separately: Manning's Inquiry, 3s.—Newman's Iguvine Inscription, 3s.—
Stokes's Gwreans An Bys, 8s.

For 1865: including Wheatley's (H. B.) Dictionary of Reduplicated Words in the
English Language; and papers by Prof. Aufrecht, Ed. Brock, C. B. Cayley,
Rev. A. J. Church, Prof. T. H. Key, Rev. E. H. Knowles, Prof. H. Malden,
Hon. G. P. Marsh, John Rhys, Guthbrand Vigfusson, Hensleigh Wedgwood, H.
B. Wheatley, etc. 8vo. cl. 12s.

For 1866: including 1. Gregor's (Rev. Walter) Banffshire Dialect, with Glossary
of Words omitted by Jamieson; 2. Edmondston's (T.) Glossary of the Shetland
Dialect; and papers by Prof. Cassal, C. B. Cayley, Danby P. Fry, Prof. T. H
Key, Guthbrand Vigfusson, Hensleigh Wedgwood, etc. 8vo. cl. 12s.

*** The Volumes for 1867, 1868-9, 1870-2, and 1873-4, are out of print.
Besides contributions in the shape of valuable and interesting papers, the volume for
1867 also includes: 1. Peacock's (Rob. B.) Glossary of the Hundred of Lonsdale;
and 2. Ellis (A. J.) On Palaeotype representing Spoken Sounds; and on the
Diphthong "Oy." The volume for 1868-9—1. Ellis's (A. J.) Only English
Proclamation of Henry III. in Oct. 1258; to which are added "The Cuckoo's Song"
and "The Prisoner's Prayer," Lyrics of the XIII. Century, with Glossary; and 2.
Stokes's (Whitley) Cornish Glossary. That for 1870-2—1. Murray's (Jas. A. H.)
Dialect of the Southern Counties of Scotland, with a linguistical map. That for
1873-4 Sweet's (H.) History of English Sounds.

For 1875-6: containing Annual Addresses (Rev. R. Morris President), Fourth
and Fifth. Sources of Aryan Mythology by E. L. Brandreth; C. B. Cayley on
Italian Diminutives; Changes made by four young Children in Pronouncing
English Words, by Jas. M. Menzies; Manx Language, by H. Jenner; Dialect
of West Somerset, by F. T. Elworthy; English Metre, by Prof. J. B. Mayor;
Words, Logic, and Grammar, by H. Sweet; The Russian Language and its
Dialects, by W. R. Morfill; Relics of the Cornish Language in Mount's Bay,
by H. Jenner. Dialects and Prehistoric Forms of Old English. By Henry

Sweet; The Dialects of Monmouthshire, Herefordshire, Worcestershire, Gloucestershire, Berkshire, Oxfordshire, South Warwickshire, South Northamptonshire, Buckinghamshire, Hertfordshire, Middlesex, and Surrey, with a New Classification of the English Dialects. By Prince L. L. Bonaparte (Two Maps), Index, etc. Part I., 6s.; Part II., 6s.; Part III., 2s.

For 1877-8-9; containing the President's (H. Sweet) Sixth, Seventh, and (Dr. J. A. H. Murray) Eighth Annual Addresses. Accadian Phonology. by Prof. A. H. Sayce; *Here* and *There* in Chaucer, by **Dr. R. Weymouth**; Grammar of the Dialect of West Somerset. by **F. T. Elworthy**; English Metre, by Prof. J. B. Mayor; Malagasy Language, by the Rev. W. E. Cousins; Anglo-Cymric Score, by **A. J. Ellis, F R.S**; Sounds and Forms of Spoken Swedish, by Henry Sweet; Russian Pronunciation, by Henry Sweet. Index, etc. Part I., 3s.; Part II., 7s. Part III. 8s.

For 1880-81: containing Some Phonetic Laws in Persian, by Prof. Charles Rieu, Ph.D., Portuguese Simple Sounds, compared with those of Spanish, French, English, etc., by H.I.H. Prince L. L. Bonaparte; The Middle Voice in Virgil's Æneid, Book VI., by B. Dawson, B.A.; Difficulty in Russian Grammar, by C. B. Cayley; The Polabes, by W. R. Mortill, M.A.; The Makua Language, by Rev. C. Maples, M.A.; Distribution of English Place Names, by W. R. Browne, M.A.; *Dare*, "To Give"; and †-*Dere* "To Put," by Prof. Postgate, M.A.; Differences between the Speech ov Edinboro' and London, by T. B. Sprague, M.A.; Ninth Annual Address of President (Dr. J. A. H. Murray) and Reports; Sound-Notation, by H. Sweet, M.A.; On Gender, by E. L. Brandreth; Tenth Annual Address of President (A. J. Ellis, B.A.) and Reports; Distribution of Place-Names in the Scottish Lowlands, by W. R. Browne, M.A.; Some Latin and Greek Etymologies, and the change of L to D in Latin, by J. P. Postgate, M.A.; Proceedings, etc.; The N of AN, etc., in the Authorized and Revised Versions of the Bible. By B. Dawson, B.A.; Notes on Translations of the New Testament. By B. Dawson, B A.; Simple Sounds of all the Living Slavonic Languages compared with those of the Principal Neo-Latin and Germano Scandinavian Tongues By H.I.H. Prince L.-L. Bonaparte; The Romonsch or Rhætian Languages in the Grisons and Tirol. By R. Martineau, M.A.—A Rough List of English Words found in Anglo-French, especially during the Thirteenth and Fourteenth Centuries; with numerous References. By Rev. W. W. Skeat, M.A.; The Oxford MS. of the only English Proclamation of Henry III., 18 October, 1258. By Rev. W. W. Skeat, M.A.; and Errata in A. J. Ellis's copy of the only English Proclamation of Henry III., in Phil. Trans. 1869. Index; List of Members. Part I. 12s. Part II. 8s. Part III. 7s.

For 1882-3-4: 1. Eleventh Annual Address (A. J. Ellis, B.A.); Obituary of Dr. J. Muir and Mr. H. Nicol. Work of the Society. Reports. Some Latin Etymologies. By Prof. Postgate, M.A. Initial Mutations in the Living Celtic, Basque, Sardinian, and Italian Dialects. By H. I. H. Prince L.-L. Bonaparte. Spoken Portuguese. By H. Sweet, M.A. The Bosworth-Toller Anglo-Saxon Dictionary. By J. Platt, jun. The Etymology of "Surround." By Rev. Prof. Skeat. Old English Verbs in -*egan* and their Subsequent History By Dr. J. A. H. Murray. Words connected with the Vine in Latin and the Neo-Latin Dialects. By H. I. H. Prince L.-L. Bonaparte. Names of European Reptiles in the Living Neo-Latin Languages. By H. I. H. Prince L.-L. Bonaparte. Monthly Abstracts. English Borrowed Words in Colloquial Welsh. By T. Powell. Oscan Inscription Discovered at Capua in 1876. By G. A. Schrumpf. On πέλωρ, πέλωρος, πελώριος. By R. F. Weymouth. Portuguese Vowels, according to Mr. R G. Vianna, Mr. H. Sweet and Myself. By H.I.H. Prince L.-L. Bonaparte. Spoken North Welsh. By Henry Sweet. Italian and Uralic Possessive Suffixes Compared. By H.I.H. Prince L.-L. Bonaparte. Albanian in

Terra d'Otranto. By H.I.H. Prince L.-L.-Bonaparte. Thirteenth Annual Address of President (J. A. H. Murray). Simple Tenses in Modern Basque and Old Basque, etc. By H.I.H. Prince L.-L. Bonaparte. Index. Monthly Abstracts. List of Members. Part I. 10s. Part II. 10s. Part III. 15s.

For 1885–7: English Etymology. By Rev. Prof. Skeat. Critical Etymologies. By H. Wedgwood. Pâli Miscellanies: Notes and Queries on Pâli. By Dr. R. Morris. On the Revised Version of the New Testament. By B. Dawson. Titin: A Study of Child Language. By Sr. D. A. Machado-y-Alvarez, of Seville. Notes on English Etymology, and on Words of Brazilian and Peruvian Origin. By Rev. Prof. Skeat. Celtic Declension. By W. Stokes. Neo-Celtic Verb Substantive. By W. Stokes. Influence of Analogy as explaining certain Examples of Unoriginal L and R. By Dr. F. Stock. Sound-Changes in Melanesian Languages. By Rev. R. H. Codrington. Notes on English Etymology. By Rev. Prof. Skeat. Notes on the Revised Version of the Old Testament. By B. Dawson. Monthly Abstracts. List of Members. Fourteenth Annual Address of President (Rev. Prof. Skeat). Obituary: Mr. Bradshaw, Mr. Walter Raleigh Browne, Prof. Cassal, Archbishop Trench, Dr. Stock. Report by the President on the Work of the Philological Society. The President on Ghost Words. W. R. Morfill on Slavonic Philology (April 1884 to 1886). J. Boxwell on Sontali. Prof. Thurneysen on Celtic Philology. Prof. de Lacouperie on the Languages of China before the Chinese. The Breton Glosses at Orleans. By W. Stokes. Remarks on the Oxford Edition of the Battle of Ventry. By S. H. O'Grady. On the Derivations of "Cad, Luther, Ted." By. H. Wedgwood, M.A. The Origin of the Augment. By Rev. A. H. Sayce, M.A. On the Place of Sanskrit in the Development of Aryan Speech in India. By J. Boxwell, B.C.S. The Primitive Home of the Aryans. By Rev. Prof. Sayce, M.A. Notes on English Etymology. By Rev. Prof. Skeat, LL.D. Index. Monthly Abstracts. List of Members. Part I. 10s. Part II. 15s.

The Society's Extra Volumes.

Early English Volume, 1862–64, containing: 1. Liber Cure Cocorum, A.D. c. 1440. — 2. Hampole's (Richard Rolle) Pricke of Conscience, A.D. c. 1340. — 3. The Castell off Love, A.D. c. 1320. 8vo. cloth. 1865. £1.

Or separately: Liber Cure Cocorum, Edited by Rich. Morris, 3s.; Hampole's (Rolle) Pricke of Conscience, edited by Rich. Morris, 12s.; and The Castell off Love, edited by Dr. R. F. Weymouth, 6s.

Dan Michel's Ayenbite of Inwyt, or Remorse of Conscience, in the Kentish Dialect, A.D. 1340. From the Autograph MS. in Brit. Mus. Edited with Introduction, Marginal Interpretations, and Glossarial Index, by Richard Morris. 8vo. cloth. 1866. 12s.

Levins's (Peter, A.D. 1570) Manipulus Vocabulorum: a Rhyming Dictionary of the English Language. With an Alphabetical Index by H. B. Wheatley. 8vo. cloth. 1867. 16s.

Skeat's (Rev. W. W.) Moeso-Gothic Glossary, with an Introduction, an Outline of Moeso-Gothic Grammar, and a List of Anglo-Saxon and old and modern English Words etymologically connected with Moeso-Gothic. 1868. 8vo. cl. 9s.

Ellis (A. J.) on Early English Pronunciation, with especial Reference to Shakspere and Chaucer; containing an Investigation of the Correspondence of Writing with Speech in England from the Anglo-Saxon Period to the Present Day, etc. 4 parts. 8vo. 1869–75. £2.

Mediæval Greek Texts: A Collection of the Earliest Compositions in Vulgar Greek, prior to A.D. 1500. With Prolegomena and Critical Notes by W. Wagner. Part I. Seven Poems, three of which appear for the first time. 1870. 8vo. 10s. 6d.

Poona Sarvajanik Sabha, Journal of the. Edited by S. H. CHIPLONKAR. Published quarterly. 3s. each number.

Royal Society of Literature of the United Kingdom (Transactions of The). First Series, 6 Parts in 3 Vols., 4to., Plates; 1827-39. Second Series, 13 Vols. or 38 Parts. 8vo., Plates; 1843-86. A complete set, as far as published, £11 10s. Very scarce. The first series of this important series of contributions of many of the most eminent men of the day has long been out of print and is very scarce. Of the Second Series, Vol. I.–IV., each containing three parts, are quite out of print, and can only be had in the complete series, noticed above. Three Numbers, price 4s. 6d. each, form a volume. The price of the volume complete, bound in cloth, is 13s. 6d.

Separate Publications.

I. FASTI MONASTICI AEVI SAXONICI: or an Alphabetical List of the Heads of Religious Houses in England previous to the Norman Conquest, to which is prefixed a Chronological Catalogue of Contemporary Foundations. By WALTER DE GRAY BIRCH. Royal 8vo. cloth. 1872. 7s. 6d.

II. LI CHANTARI DI LANCELLOTTO; a Troubadour's Poem of the XIV. Cent. Edited from a MS. in the possession of the Royal Society of Literature, by WALTER DE GRAY BIRCH. Royal 8vo. cloth. 1874. 7s.

III. INQUISITIO COMITATUS CANTABRIGIENSIS, nunc primum, e Manuscripto unico in Bibliothecâ Cottoniensi asservato, typis mandata; subjicitur Inquisitio Eliensis; curâ N. E. S. A. Hamilton. Royal 4to. With map and 3 facsimiles. 1876. £2 2s.

IV. A COMMONPLACE BOOK OF JOHN MILTON. Reproduced by the antotype process from the original MS. in the possession of Sir Fred. U. Graham, Bart., of Netherby Hall. With an Introduction by A. J. Horwood. Sq. folio. Only one hundred copies printed. 1876. £2 2s.

V. CHRONICON ADÆ DE USK, A.D. 1377-1404. Edited, with a Translation and Notes, by ED. MAUNDE THOMPSON. Royal 8vo. 1876. 10s. 6d.

Syro-Egyptian Society.—Original Papers read before the Syro-Egyptian Society of London. Volume I. Part 1. 8vo. sewed, 2 plates and a map, pp. 144. 3s. 6d.

Temple.—THE LEGENDS OF THE PANJAB. By Captain R. C. TEMPLE, Bengal Staff Corps, F.G.S., etc. Crown 8vo. Vol. I. (Nos. 1 to 12), cloth, £1 10s. Vol. II. (No. 13 to 24), cloth, £1 10s. Vol. III. in course of publication. Subscription in Nos. 24s.

Trübner's American, European and Oriental Literary Record.—A Register of the most important works published in North and South America, in India, China, Europe, and the British Colonies; with occasional Notes on German, Dutch, Danish, French, etc., books. 4to. In Monthly Numbers. Subscription 5s. per annum, or 6d. per number. A complete set, Nos. 1 to 142. London, 1865 to 1879. £12 12s.

Yorkshire Notes and Queries.—With the Yorkshire Genealogist, Yorkshire Bibliographer, and Yorkshire Folk-lore Journal. Edited by J. HORSFALL TURNER, Idel, Bradford. Eighty pages, with Illustrations. Distinct pagination of each subject. Published Quarterly, demy 8vo. Price 1s. 6d. each or 5s. per annum, if paid in advance.

Archæology, Ethnography, Geography, History, Law, Literature, Numismatics, and Travels.

Abel.—Slavic and Latin. Ilchester Lectures on Comparative Lexicography. Delivered at the Taylor Institution, Oxford. By Carl Abel, Ph.D. Post 8vo. pp. viii.-124, cloth. 1883. 5s.

Abel.—Linguistic Essays. See Trübner's Oriental Series, p. 5.

Alberuni's India. See "Sachau," page 38.

Ali.—The Proposed Political, Legal and Social Reforms in the Ottoman Empire and other Mohammedan States. By Moulaví Cherágh Ali, H.H. the Nizam's Civil Service. Demy 8vo. cloth, pp. liv.-184. 1883. 8s.

Arnold.—Indian Idylls. From the Sanskrit of the Mahâbhârata. By Sir Edwin Arnold, M.A., K.C.I.E., &c. Post 8vo. cloth, pp. xii.-282. 1883. 7s. 6d.

Arnold.—Indian Poetry. See "Trübner's Oriental Series," page 4.

Arnold.—Pearls of the Faith. See page 41.

Arnold.—India Revisited. By Sir Edwin Arnold, M.A., K.C.I.E., etc., Author of the "Light of Asia," etc. With Thirty-two Full-page Illustrations from Photographs selected by the Author. Crown 8vo. pp. 324, cloth. 1886. 7s. 6d.

Arnold.—The Song Celestial. See page 96.

Arnold.—The Secret of Death. See page 96.

Arnold.—Lotus and Jewel. Containing "In an Indian Temple," "A Casket of Gems," "A Queen's Revenge." With other Poems. By Sir E. Arnold, M.A., K.C.I.E, etc. Crown 8vo. pp. vi. and 264. 1887. 7s. 6d.

Baddeley.—Lotus Leaves. By St. Clair Baddeley. Fcap. folio, pp. xii. and 118, half-vellum. 1887. 8s. 6d.

Baden-Powell.—A Manual of Jurisprudence for Forest Officers. By B. H. Baden-Powell, B.C.S. 8vo. half-bound, pp. xxii-554. 1882. 12s.

Baden-Powell.—A Manual of the Land Revenue Systems and Land Tenures of British India. By B. H. Baden-Powell, B.C.S. Crown 8vo. half-bound, pp. xii.-788. 1882. 12s.

Badley.—Indian Missionary Record and Memorial Volume. By the Rev. B. H. Badley, of the American Methodist Mission. New Edition. 8vo. cloth. [*In Preparation.*]

Balfour.—Waifs and Strays from the Far East. See p. 59.

Balfour.—The Divine Classic of Nan-Hua. See page 59.

Balfour.—Taoist Texts. See page 41.

Ballantyne.—Sankhya Aphorisms of Kapila. See p. 6.

Beal.—See pages 6, 41 and 42.

Bellew.—From the Indus to the Tigris: Journey through Balochistan, Afghanistan, Khorassan, and Iran, in 1872; with a Synoptical Grammar and Vocabulary of the Brahoe Language, and a Record of Meteorological Observations and Altitudes on the March. By H. W. Bellew, C.S.I., Surgeon B.S.C. Demy 8vo. pp. viii.-496, cloth. 1874. 10s. 6d.

Bellew.—Kashmir and Kashgar. A Narrative of the Journey of the Embassy to Kashgar in 1873-74. By H. W. Bellew, C.S.I. Demy 8vo. cloth, pp. xxxii. and 420. 1875. 16s. 6d.

Bellew.—THE RACES OF AFGHANISTAN. Being a Brief Account of the Principal Nations inhabiting that Country. By Surgeon-Major H. W. BELLEW, C.S.I., late on Special Political Duty at Kabul. Crown 8vo. pp. 124, cloth. 1880. 7s. 6d.

Beveridge.—THE DISTRICT OF BAKARGANJ; its History and Statistics. By H. BEVERIDGE, B.C.S. 8vo. cloth, pp. xx. and 460. 1876. 21s.

Bhandarkar.—EARLY HISTORY OF THE DEKKAN, DOWN TO THE MAHOMEDAN CONQUEST. By R. G. BHANDARKAR, M.A., Prof. of Oriental Languages, Dekkan College. 8vo. pp. vi.-122, wrappers. 1885. 5s.

Bibliotheca Orientalis: or, a Complete List of Books published in France, Germany, England, and the Colonies, on the History, Religions, Literature, etc., of the East. Edited by C. FRIEDERICI. Part I., 1876, sewed, pp. 86, 2s. 6d. Part II., 1877, pp. 100, 3s. 6d. Part III., 1878, 3s. 6d. Part IV., 1879, 3s. 6d. Part V., 1880. 3s.

Biddulph.—TRIBES OF THE HINDOO KOOSH. By Major J. BIDDULPH, B.S.C., Political Officer at Gilgit. 8vo. pp. 340, cloth. 1880. 15s.

Blades.—AN ACCOUNT OF THE GERMAN MORALITY PLAY, ENTITLED DEPOSITIO CORNUTI TYPOGRAPHICI, as Performed in the 17th and 18th Centuries. With a Rhythmical Translation of the German Version of 1648. By W. BLADES, Typographer. To which is added a Literal Reprint of the Unique Original Version, written in Plaet Deutsch, by PAUL DE WISE, and printed in 1621. Small 4to. pp. xii.-144, with facsimile Illustrations, in an appropriate binding. 1885. 7s. 6d.

Bleek.—REYNARD THE FOX IN SOUTH AFRICA; or, Hottentot Fables and Tales. See page 51.

Blochmann.—SCHOOL GEOGRAPHY OF INDIA AND BRITISH BURMAH. By H. BLOCHMANN, M.A. 12mo. wrapper, pp. vi. and 100. 2s. 6d.

Bombay Code, The.—The Unrepealed Bombay Regulations, Acts of the Supreme Council, relating to Bombay, and Acts of the Governor of Bombay in Council. With Chronological Table. Royal 8vo. pp. xxiv.-774, cloth 1880. £1 1s.

Bombay Presidency.—GAZETTEER OF THE. Demy 8vo. half-bound, Vol. II., 14s. Vols. III.-VII., 8s. each; Vol. VIII., 9s.; X., XI., XII., XIV., XVI., 8s. each; Vols. XXI., XXII., XXIII., 9s. each.

Bretschneider.—NOTES ON CHINESE MEDIÆVAL TRAVELLERS TO THE WEST. By E. BRETSCHNEIDER, M.D. Demy 8vo. sd., pp. 130. 5s.

Bretschneider.—ON THE KNOWLEDGE POSSESSED BY THE ANCIENT CHINESE OF THE ARABS AND ARABIAN COLONIES, and other Western Countries mentioned in Chinese Books. By E. BRETSCHNEIDER, M.D., Physician to the Russian Legation at Peking. 8vo. pp. 28, sewed. 1871. 1s.

Bretschneider.—NOTICES OF THE MEDIÆVAL GEOGRAPHY AND HISTORY OF CENTRAL AND WESTERN ASIA. Drawn from Chinese and Mongol Writings, and Compared with the Observations of Western Authors in the Middle Ages. By E. BRETSCHNEIDER, M.D. 8vo. sewed, pp. 233, with two Maps. 1876. 12s. 6d.

Bretschneider.—ARCHÆOLOGICAL AND HISTORICAL RESEARCHES ON PEKING AND ITS ENVIRONS. By E. BRETSCHNEIDER, M.D., Physician to the Russian Legation at Peking. Imp. 8vo. sewed, pp. 64, with 4 Maps. 1876. 5s.

Bretschneider.—BOTANICON SINICUM. Notes on Chinese Botany, from Native and Western Sources. By E. BRETSCHNEIDER, M.D. Crown 8vo. pp. 228, wrapper. 1882. 10s. 6d.

Bretschneider—INTERCOURSE OF THE CHINESE WITH WESTERN COUNTRIES IN THE MIDDLE AGES, AND ON KINDRED SUBJECTS. By E. BRETSCHNEIDER, M.D. *(In the Press.)*

Brown.—THE ICELANDIC DISCOVERERS OF AMERICA; OR, HONOUR TO WHOM HONOUR IS DUE. By MARIE A. BROWN. Crown 8vo. pp. viii. and 214, cloth. With Eight Plates. 1887. 7s. 6d.

Budge.—ASSYRIAN TEXTS. See p. 56.

Budge.—HISTORY OF ESARHADDON. See Trübner's Oriental Series, p. 4.

Bühler.—ELEVEN LAND-GRANTS OF THE CHAULUKYAS OF AṆHILVÂḌ. A Contribution to the History of Gujarât. By G. BÜHLER. 16mo. sewed, pp. 126, with Facsimile. 3s. 6d.

Burgess.—ARCHÆOLOGICAL SURVEY OF WESTERN INDIA. By James Burgess, LL.D., etc., etc. Royal 4to. half bound. Vol. 1. Report of the First Season's Operations in the Belgâm and Kaladgi Districts. 1874. With 56 photographs and lith. plates, pp. viii. and 45. 1875. £2 2s. Vol. 2. Report of the Second Season's Operations. The Antiquities of Kâthiâwâd and Kachh. 1874–5. With Map, Inscriptions, Photographs, etc., pp. x. and 242. 1876. £3 3s. Vol. 3. Report of the Third Season's Operations. 1875–76. The Antiquities in the Bidar and Aurangabad District. pp. viii. and 138. With 66 photographic and lithographic plates. 1878. £2 2s. Vols. 4. and 5. Reports on the Buddhist Cave Temples, the Elura Cave Temples, the Brahmanical and Jaina Caves in Western India; containing Views, Plans, Sections, and Elevations of Façades of Cave Temples; Drawings of Architectural and Mythological Sculptures; Facsimiles of Inscriptions, etc.; Translation of Inscriptions, etc., pp. x.-140 and viii.-90, half morocco, gilt tops with 165 Plates and Woodcuts. 1883. £6 6s.

Burgess.—ARCHÆOLOGICAL SURVEY OF SOUTHERN INDIA. Vol. I. The Buddhist Stupas of Amaravati and Jaggayyapeta in the Krishna District, Madras Presidency, Surveyed in 1882. By JAMES BURGESS, LL.D., C.I.E., etc., Director-General of the Survey. With Translations of the Asoka Inscriptions at Jaugada and Dhauli by GEORGE BÜHLER, LL.D., C.I.E., etc., Prof. of Sanskrit in the University of Vienna. Containing Sixty-nine Collotype and other Plates of Buddhist Sculpture and Architecture, etc., in South-Eastern India; Facsimiles of Inscriptions, etc.; and Thirty-two Woodcuts. Super-royal 4to. pp. x. and 131, half-morocco. 1887. £4 4s.

Burgess.—THE ROCK TEMPLES OF ELURA OR VERUL. A Handbook for Visitors. By J. BURGESS. 8vo. 3s. 6d., or with Twelve Photographs, 9s. 6d.

Burgess.—THE ROCK TEMPLES OF ELEPHANTA Described and Illustrated with Plans and Drawings. By J. BURGESS. 8vo. cloth, pp. 80, with drawings, price 6s.; or with Thirteen Photographs, price £1.

Burne.—SHROPSHIRE FOLK-LORE. A Sheaf of Gleanings. Edited by C. S. BURNE, from the Collections of G. F. JACKSON. With Map of Cheshire. Demy 8vo. pp. xvi.-664, cloth. 1886. 25s.

Burnell.—ELEMENTS OF SOUTH INDIAN PALÆOGRAPHY. From the Fourth to the Seventeenth Century A.D. By A. C. BURNELL. Second Enlarged Edition, 35 Plates and Map. 4to. pp. xiv. and 148. 1878. £2 12s. 6d.

Byrne.—GENERAL PRINCIPLES OF THE STRUCTURE OF LANGUAGE. By JAMES BYRNE, M.A., Dean of Clonfert; Ex-Fellow of Trinity College, Dublin. 2 vols. demy 8vo. pp. xxx. and 504, xviii. and 396, cloth. 1885. 36s.

Byrne.—ORIGIN OF THE GREEK, LATIN AND GOTHIC ROOTS. By JAMES BYRNE, M.A., Dean of Clonfert, etc. Demy 8vo. pp. viii. and 360, cl. 1888. 18s.

Carletti.—HISTORY OF THE CONQUEST OF TUNIS. Translated by J. T. CARLETTI. Crown 8vo. cloth, pp. 40. 1883. 2s. 6d.

Cesnola.—THE HISTORY, TREASURES, AND ANTIQUITIES OF SALAMIS, IN THE ISLAND OF CYPRUS. By A. P. DI CESNOLA, F.S.A. With an Introduction by S. BIRCH, D.C.L. With over 700 Illustrations and Map of Ancient Cyprus. Royal 8vo. pp. xlviii.-325, cloth, 1882. £1 11s. 6d.

Chamberlain.—JAPANESE POETRY. See page 4.

Chattopadhyaya.—THE YATRAS; or the Popular Dramas of Bengal. Post 8vo. pp. 50, wrapper. 1882. 2s.

Clarke.—THE ENGLISH STATIONS IN THE HILL REGIONS OF INDIA: their Value and Importance, with some Statistics of their Produce and Trade. By HYDE CLARKE, V.P.S.S. Post 8vo. paper, pp. 48. 1881. 1s

Colebrooke.—THE LIFE AND MISCELLANEOUS ESSAYS OF HENRY THOMAS COLEBROOKE. In 3 vols. Demy 8vo. cloth. 1873. Vol. I. The Biography by his Son, Sir T. E. COLEBROOKE, Bart., M.P. With Portrait and Map. pp. xii. and 492. 14s. Vols. II. and III. The Essays. A New Edition, with Notes by E. B. COWELL, Professor of Sanskrit in the University of Cambridge. pp. xvi.-544, and x.-520. 28s.

Conway.—VERNER'S LAW IN ITALY. An Essay in the History of the Indo-European Sibilants. By R. S. CONWAY, Gonville and Caius College, Cambridge; Classical Scholar in the University of Cambridge; Exhibitioner in Latin in the University of London. With a Dialect Map of Italy by E. HEAWOOD, B.A., F.R.G.S. Demy 8vo. pp. vi. and 120, cloth. 1887. 5s.

Crawford.—RECOLLECTIONS OF TRAVELS IN NEW ZEALAND AND AUSTRALIA. By J. C. CRAWFORD, F.G.S., Resident Magistrate, Wellington, etc., etc. With Maps and Illustrations. 8vo. cloth, pp. xvi. and 468. 1880. 18s.

Cunningham.—CORPUS INSCRIPTIONUM INDICARUM. Vol. I. Inscriptions of Asoka. Prepared by ALEXANDER CUNNINGHAM, C.S.I., etc. 4to. cloth, pp. xiv. 142 and vi., with 31 plates. 1879. 42s.

Cunningham.—THE STUPA OF BHARHUT. A Buddhist Monument, ornamented with numerous Sculptures illustrative of Buddhist Legend and History in the third century B.C. By ALEXANDER CUNNINGHAM, C.S.I., C.I.E., Director-General Archæological Survey of India, etc. Royal 4to. cloth, gilt, pp. viii. and 144, with 51 Photographs and Lithographic Plates. 1879. £3 3s.

Cunningham.—THE ANCIENT GEOGRAPHY OF INDIA. I. The Buddhist Period, including the Campaigns of Alexander, and the Travels of Hwen-Thsang. By ALEXANDER CUNNINGHAM, Major-General, Royal Engineers (Bengal Retired). With thirteen Maps. 8vo. pp. xx. 590, cloth. 1870. 28s.

Cunningham.—ARCHÆOLOGICAL SURVEY OF INDIA. Reports, made during the years 1862-1882. By A. CUNNINGHAM, C.S.I., Major-General, etc. With Maps and Plates. Vols. I to 13. 8vo. cloth. 10s. and 12s. each.

Cust.—PICTURES OF INDIAN LIFE. Sketched with the Pen from 1852 to 1881. By R. N. CUST, late of H.M. Indian Civil Service, and Hon. Sec. to the Royal Asiatic Society. Crown 8vo. cloth, pp. x. and 346. 1881. 7s. 6d.

Cust.—INDIAN LANGUAGES. See "Trübner's Oriental Series," page 3.

Cust.—AFRICAN LANGUAGES. See "Trübner's Oriental Series," page 6.

Cust.—LINGUISTIC AND ORIENTAL ESSAYS. See "Trübner's Oriental Series," page 4.

Cust.—LANGUAGE: AS ILLUSTRATED BY BIBLE TRANSLATION. By R. N. CUST, LL.D. Demy 8vo. pp. 86, wrapper. 1886. 1s.

Dahl.—NATIONAL SONGS, BALLADS AND SKETCHES by the most Celebrated Scandinavian Authors. Translated by J. A. DAHL, Professor of the English Language. Square crown 8vo. pp. 128, cloth. 1887. 2s. 6d.

Dalton.—DESCRIPTIVE ETHNOLOGY OF BENGAL. By Col. E. T. DALTON, C.S.I., B.S.C., etc. Illustrated by Lithograph Portraits copied from Photographs. 38 Lithograph Plates. 4to. half-calf, pp. 340. £6 6s.

Da Cunha.—NOTES ON THE HISTORY AND ANTIQUITIES OF CHAUL AND BASSEIN. By J GERSON DA CUNHA, M.R.C.S. and L.M. Eng., etc. 8vo. cloth, pp. xvi. and 262. With 17 photographs, 9 plates and a map. £1 5s.

Da Cunha.—CONTRIBUTIONS TO THE STUDY OF INDO-PORTUGUESE NUMISMATICS. By J. G. DA CUNHA, M.R.C.S., etc. Crown 8vo. stitched in wrapper. Fasc. I. to IV., each 2s. 6d.

Das.—THE INDIAN RYOT, LAND TAX, PERMANENT SETTLEMENT, AND THE FAMINE. Chiefly compiled by ABHAY CHARAN DAS. Post 8vo. cloth, pp. iv.-662. 1881. 12s.

Davids.—COINS, ETC., OF CEYLON. See "Numismata Orientala," Vol. I. Part VI.

Dennys.—CHINA AND JAPAN. A Guide to the Open Ports, together with Pekin, Yeddo, Hong Kong, and Macao; a Guide Book and Vade Mecum for Travellers. etc. By W. F. MAYERS, H.M.'s Consular Service; N. B. DENNYS, late H.M.'s Consular Service; and C. KING, Lieut R.M.A. Edited by N. B. DENNYS. 8vo. pp. 600, 56 Maps and Plans, cloth. £2 2s.

Dowson.—DICTIONARY of Hindu Mythology, etc. See "Trübner's Oriental Series," page 3.

Edmundson—MILTON AND VONDEL. A Curiosity of Literature. By G. EDMUNDSON, M.A. Crown 8vo. pp. vi.-224, cloth. 1885. 6s.

Egerton.—AN ILLUSTRATED HANDBOOK OF INDIAN ARMS; being a Classified and Descriptive Catalogue of the Arms exhibited at the India Museum; with an Introductory Sketch of the Military History of India. By the Hon. W. EGERTON, M.A., M.P. 4to. sewed, pp. viii. and 162. 1880. 2s. 6d.

Elliot.—MEMOIRS ON THE HISTORY, FOLKLORE, AND DISTRIBUTION OF THE RACES OF THE NORTH WESTERN PROVINCES OF INDIA. By the late Sir H. M. ELLIOT, K.C.B. Edited, etc., by JOHN BEAMES, B.C.S., etc. In 2 vols. demy 8vo., pp. xx., 370, and 396, cloth. With two Plates, and four coloured Maps. 1869. 36s.

Elliot.—COINS OF SOUTHERN INDIA. See "Numismata Orientalia." Vol. III. Part II. page 36.

Elliot.—THE HISTORY OF INDIA, as told by its own Historians. The Muhammadan Period. Edited from the Posthumous Papers of the late Sir H. M. ELLIOT, K.C.B., by Prof. J. DOWSON. 8 vols. 8vo. cloth. 1867-1877. Sets. £8 8s. ; or separately, Vol. I. pp xxxii. and 542. £2 2s.—Vol. II. pp. x. and 580. 18s.—Vol. III. pp. xii and 627. 24s.—Vol. IV pp. x. and 563. 21s.—Vol. V. pp. xii. and 576. 21s.—Vol. VI. pp. viii. and 574. 21s.—Vol. VII. pp. viii. and 574. 21s.—Vol. VIII. pp. xxxii., 444, and lxviii. 24s.

Farley.—EGYPT, CYPRUS, AND ASIATIC TURKEY. By J. L. FARLEY, Author of "The Resources of Turkey," etc. Demy 8vo. cl., pp. xvi.-270. 1878. 10s. 6d.

Featherman.—THE SOCIAL HISTORY OF THE RACES OF MANKIND. By A. FEATHERMAN. Demy 8vo. cloth. The Aramaeans. pp. xvii. and 664. 1881. £1 1s. The Nigritians. pp. 826. 1885. 31s. 6d. Papuo and Malayo-Melanesians. pp. 526. 1885. 25s. Oceano-Melanesians. pp. 452. 1887. 25s.

Ferguson.—SUMMARY OF INFORMATION REGARDING CEYLON: Its Natural Features, Climate, Population, Religion, Industries, Agriculture, Government, Laws, Objects of Interest, etc., in 1887, the Queen's "Jubilee Year." Compiled by A. M. and J. FERGUSON, Editors of the *Ceylon Observer*, *Tropical Agriculturist*, etc., etc. Post 8vo. iv.-26. wrapper. 1887. 2s.

Fergusson and Burgess.—THE CAVE TEMPLES OF INDIA. By JAMES FERGUSSON, D.C.L., F.R.S., and JAMES BURGESS, F.R.G.S. Imp. 8vo. half bound, pp. xx. and 536, with 98 Plates. £2 2s.

Fergusson.—ARCHÆOLOGY IN INDIA. With especial reference to the Works of Babu Rajendralala Mitra. By J. FERGUSSON, C.I.E. 8vo. pp. 116, with Illustrations, sewed. 1884. 5s.

Forchhammer. — AN ESSAY ON THE SOURCES AND DEVELOPMENT OF BURMESE LAW. From the Era of the First Introduction of the Indian Law to the Time of the British Occupation of Pegu. By Dr. E. FORCHHAMMER, Ph.D., Professor of Pali at the Government High School, Rangoon. Imperial 8vo. pp. vi.-110, cloth. 1885. 10s. 6d.

Fornander.—AN ACCOUNT OF THE POLYNESIAN RACE: Its Origin and Migration, and the Ancient History of the Hawaiian People to the Times of Kamehameha I. By A. FORNANDER, Circuit Judge of the Island of Maui, H.I. Post 8vo. cloth. Vol. I., pp. xvi. and 248. 1877. 7s. 6d. Vol. II., pp. viii. and 400. 1880. 10s. 6d. Vol. III., pp. xii.-292. 1885. 9s.

Forsyth.—REPORT OF A MISSION TO YARKUND IN 1873, under Command of SIR T. D. FORSYTH, K.C.S.I., C.B., Bengal Civil Service, with Historical and Geographical Information regarding the Possessions of the Ameer of Yarkund. With 45 Photographs, 4 Lithographic Plates, and a large Folding Map of Eastern Turkestan. 4to. cloth, pp. iv. and 573. £5 5s.

Gardner.—PARTHIAN COINAGE. See "Numismata Orientalia." Vol. I. Part V.

Garrett.—A CLASSICAL DICTIONARY OF INDIA, illustrative of the Mythology, Philosophy, Literature, Antiquities, Arts, Manners, Customs, etc., of the Hindus. By JOHN GARRETT. 8vo. pp. x. and 798. cloth. 28s.

Garrett.—SUPPLEMENT TO THE ABOVE CLASSICAL DICTIONARY OF INDIA. By J. GARRETT, Dir. of Public Instruction, Mysore. 8vo. cloth, pp. 160. 7s. 6d.

Garrett.—MORNING HOURS IN INDIA. Practical Hints on Household Management, the Care and Training of Children, etc. By ELIZABETH GARRETT. Crown 8vo. pp. x.-124, cloth. 1887. 3s. 6d.

Gazetteer of the Central Provinces of India. Edited by CHARLES GRANT, Secretary to the Chief Commissioner of the Central Provinces. Second Edition. With a very large folding Map of the Central Provinces of India. Demy 8vo. pp. clvii. and 582, cloth. 1870. £1 4s.

Geiger.—CONTRIBUTIONS TO THE HISTORY OF THE DEVELOPMENT OF THE HUMAN RACE. Lectures and Dissertations by L. GEIGER. Translated from the German by D. Asher, Ph.D. Post 8vo cloth pp. x. and 156. 1880. 6s.

Goldstücker.—ON THE DEFICIENCIES IN THE PRESENT ADMINISTRATION OF HINDU LAW; being a paper read at the Meeting of the East India Association on the 8th June, 1870. By THEODOR GOLDSTÜCKER, Professor of Sanskrit in University College, London, &c. Demy 8vo. pp. 56, sewed. 1s. 6d.

Gover.—THE FOLK-SONGS OF SOUTHERN INDIA. By CHARLES E. GOVER. 8vo. pp. xxiii. and 299, cloth. 1872. 10s. 6d.

Grierson.—BIHAR PEASANT LIFE; being a Discursive Catalogue of the Surroundings of the People of that Province, with many Illustrations from Photographs taken by the Author. Prepared under Orders of the Government of Bengal. By GEORGE A. GRIERSON, B.C.S. Royal 8vo. pp. xxviii.-580, half-bound. 15s.

Griffin.—THE RAJAS OF THE PUNJAB. History of the Principal States in the Punjab, and their Political Relations with the British Government. By LEPEL H. GRIFFIN, B.C.S.; Under Sec. to Gov. of the Punjab, Author of "The Punjab Chiefs," etc. Second edition. Royal 8vo., pp. xiv. and 630. 1873. 21s.

Griffis.—COREA; WITHOUT AND WITHIN. Chapters on Corean History, Manners and Religion. With Hendrick Hamel's Narrative of Captivity and Travels in Corea, Annotated. By W. E. GRIFFIS. Crown 8vo. pp. 316, with Map and Illustrations, cloth. 1885. 6s.

Griffis.—THE MIKADO'S EMPIRE. Book I. History of Japan from 660 B.C. to 1872 A.D. Book II. Personal Experiences, Observations, and Studies in Japan, 1870–74. By W. E. GRIFFIS. Illustrated. Second Edition. 8vo. pp. 626, cloth. 1883. £1.

Growse.—MATHURA: A District Memoir. By F. S. GROWSE, B.C.S., C.I.E. Second Revised Edition. Illustrated. 4to. boards, pp. xxiv. and 520. 1880. 42s.

Hahn.—Tsuni||Goam. See Trübner's Oriental Series, page 5.

Head.—COINAGE OF LYDIA AND PERSIA. See "Numismata Orientalia." Vol. I. Part III.

Heaton.—AUSTRALIAN DICTIONARY OF DATES AND MEN OF THE TIME. Containing the History of Australasia, from 1542 to May, 1879. By J. H. HEATON. Royal 8vo. cloth pp. iv.–554. 1879. 15s.

Hebrew Literature Society. See page 82.

Hilmy.—THE LITERATURE OF EGYPT AND THE SOUDAN. From the Earliest Times to the Year 1885, inclusive. A Bibliography. Comprising Printed Books; Periodical Writings and Papers of Learned Societies; Maps and Charts; Ancient Papyri; Manuscripts, Drawings, etc. By H.H. PRINCE IBRAHIM-HILMY. Dedicated to H.H. the Khedive Ismail. Vol. I. (A-L), demy 4to. pp. viii.–398, cloth. 1886. £1 11s. 6d.

Hindoo Mythology Popularly Treated.—An Epitomised Description of the various Heathen Deities illustrated on the Silver Swami Tea Service presented, as a Memento of his visit to India, to H.R.H. the Prince of Wales, K.G., by His Highness the Gaekwar of Baroda. Small 4to. pp. 42, limp cloth. 1875. 3s. 6d.

Hodgson.—ESSAYS ON THE LANGUAGES, LITERATURE, AND RELIGION OF NEPAL AND TIBET; with Papers on their Geography, Ethnology, and Commerce. By B. H. HODGSON, late British Minister at Nepál. Royal 8vo. cloth, pp. 288. 1874. 14s.

Hodgson.—ESSAYS ON INDIAN SUBJECTS. See "Trübner's Oriental Series," p. 4.

Hunter.—THE IMPERIAL GAZETTEER OF INDIA. By Sir WILLIAM WILSON HUNTER, K.C.S.I., C.I.E., LL.D., late Director-General of Statistics to the Government of India. Published by Command of the Secretary of State for India. 14 vols. 8vo. half morocco. 1887. £3 3s.

"A great work has been unostentatiously carried on for the last twelve years in India, the importance of which it is impossible to exaggerate. This is nothing less than a complete statistical survey of the entire British Empire in Hindostan. . . . We have said enough to show that the 'Imperial Gazetteer' is no mere dry collection of statistics; it is a treasury from which the politician and economist may draw countless stores of valuable information, and into which the general reader can dip with the certainty of always finding something both to interest and instruct him."—*Times.*

Hunter.—A STATISTICAL ACCOUNT OF BENGAL. By Sir W. W. HUNTER, K.C.S.I., LL.D., etc. Director-Gen. of Statistics to the Government of India.

VOL.
I. 24 Parganás and Sundarbans.
II. Nadiyá and Jessor.
III. Midnapur, Húgli and Hourah.
IV. Bardwán, Birbhúm and Bánkurá.
V. Dacca, Bákarganj, Farídpur and Maimansinh.
VI. Chittagong Hill Tracts, Chittagong, Noákháli, Tipperah, and Hill Tipperah State.
VII. Meldah, Rangpur and Dinájpur.
VIII. Rájsháhí and Bográ.
IX. Murshidábád and Pábná.

VOL.
X. Dárjíling, Jalpáiguri and Kuch Behar
XI. Patná and Sáran. [State.
XII. Gayá and Sháhábád
XIII. Tirhut and Chaupáran.
XIV. Bhágalpur and Sontál Parganás.
XV. Mongḥyr and Purniah.
XVI. Hazáribágh and Lohárdagá.
XVII. Singbhúm, Chutiá Nágpur Tributary States and Mánbhúm.
XVIII. Cuttack and Balasor.
XIX. Puri, and Orissa Tributary States.
XX. Fisheries, Botany, and General Index

Published by command of the Government of India. In 20 Vols. 8vo. half-morocco. £5.

Hunter.—A STATISTICAL ACCOUNT OF ASSAM. By Sir W. W. HUNTER, K.C.S.I., LL.D., etc. 2 vols. 8vo. half-morocco, pp. 420 and 490, with Two Maps. 1879. 10s.

Hunter.—FAMINE ASPECTS OF BENGAL DISTRICTS. A System of Famine Warnings. By Sir W. W. HUNTER, K.C.S.I., LL.D., etc. Crown 8vo. cloth, pp. 216. 1874. 7s. 6d.

Hunter.—THE INDIAN MUSALMANS. By Sir W. W. HUNTER, K.C.S.I. LL.D., etc. Third Edition. 8vo. cloth. pp. 219. 1876. 10s. 6d.

Hunter.—A BRIEF HISTORY OF THE INDIAN PEOPLE. By Sir W. W. Hunter, K.C.S.I., LL.D., etc. Crown 8vo. pp. 222 with map, cloth. 1884. 3s. 6d.

Hunter.—Indian Empire. See Trübner's Oriental Series, page 5.

Hunter.—AN ACCOUNT OF THE BRITISH SETTLEMENT OF ADEN in Arabia. Compiled by Captain F. M. HUNTER, Assistant Political Resident, Aden. Demy 8vo. half-morocco, pp. xii.-232. 1877. 7s. 6d.

India.—FINANCE AND REVENUE ACCOUNTS OF THE GOVERNMENT OF, for 1882-83. Fcp. 8vo. pp. viii.-220, boards. 1884. 2s. 6d.

Jacobs.—THE JEWISH QUESTION. 1875-1884. A Bibliographical Hand-list. Compiled by JOSEPH JACOBS, B.A., late Scholar of St. John's College, Cambridge. Fcap. 8vo. pp. xii.-96, wrapper. 2s.

Japan.—MAP OF NIPPON (Japan): Compiled from Native Maps, and the Notes of recent Travellers. By R. H. BRUNTON, F.R.G.S., 1880. In 4 sheets, 21s.; roller, varnished, £1 11s. 6d.; Folded, in case, £1 5s. 6d.

Juvenalis Satiræ.—With a Literal English Prose Translation and Notes. By J. D. LEWIS, M.A. Second, Revised, and considerably Enlarged Edition. 2 Vols. post 8vo. pp. xii.-230, and 400, cloth. 1882. 12s.

Kaegi.—THE RIG VEDA: the Oldest Literature of the Indians. By ADOLPH KAEGI, Professor in the University of Zürich. 8vo. pp. viii.-198, cloth. 1886. 7s. 6d.

Kerrison.—A COMMON-PLACE BOOK OF THE FIFTEENTH CENTURY. Containing a Religious Play and Poetry, Legal Forms, and Local Accounts. Printed from the Original MS. at Brome Hall, Suffolk. By Lady CAROLINE KERRISON. Edited, with Notes, by LUCY TOULMIN SMITH. Demy 8vo. with Two Facsimiles, pp. viii.-176, parchment. 1886. 7s. 6d.

Kitts.—A COMPENDIUM OF THE CASTES AND TRIBES FOUND IN INDIA. Compiled from the (1881) Census Reports for the Various Provinces (excluding Burmah) and Native States of the Empire. By E. J. KITTS, B.C.S. Fcap. folio, pp. xii. 90, boards. 1886. 5s.

Knowles.—A Dictionary of Kashmiri Proverbs and Sayings. Explained and Illustrated from the Rich and Interesting Folk-lore of the Valley. By the Rev. J. Hinton Knowles, F.R.G.S., etc. (C.M.S.), Missionary to the Kashmiris. Crown 8vo. pp. viii.-263, cloth. 1885. 8s.

Leitner.—Sinin-I-Islam. Being a Sketch of the History and Literature of Muhammadanism and their place in Universal History. *For the use of Maulvis.* By G. W. Leitner. Part I. The Early History of Arabia to the fall of the Abassides. 8vo. sewed. *Lahore.* 6s.

Leitner.—History of Indigenous Education in the Panjab since Annexation, and in 1882. By G. W. Leitner, LL.D., late on special duty with the Education Commission appointed by the Government of India. Fcap. folio, pp. 588, paper boards. 1883. £5.

Leland.—Fusang; or, the Discovery of America by Chinese Buddhist Priests in the Fifth Century. By Charles G. Leland. Crown 8vo. cloth, pp. xix. and 212. 1875. 7s. 6d.

Leland.—The Gypsies. See page 69.

Leonowens.—Life and Travel in India. Being Recollections of a Journey before the Days of Railroads. By Anna H. Leonowens. 8vo. pp. 326, Illustrated, cloth. 1885. 10s. 6d.

Linde.—Tea in India. A Sketch, Index, and Register of the Tea Industry in India, with a Map of all the Tea Districts, etc. By F. Linde, Surveyor. Folio, wrapper, pp. xxii.-30, map mounted and in cloth boards. 1879. 63s.

Long.—Eastern Proverbs and Emblems. See page 4.

Lowell.—Chosön: the Land of the Morning Calm. A Sketch of Korea. By Percival Lowell. Super-royal 8vo. pp. x.-412, cloth. 1886. 24s.

McCrindle.—The Commerce and Navigation of the Erythræan Sea. Being a Translation of the Periplus Maris Erythraei, by an Anonymous Writer, and of Arrian's Account of the Voyage of Nearkhos, from the Mouth of the Indus to the Head of the Persian Gulf. With Introduction, Commentary, Notes, and Index. Post 8vo. cloth, pp. iv. and 238. 1879. 7s. 6d.

McCrindle.—Ancient India as Described by Megasthenes and Arrian. A Translation of Fragments of the Indika of Megasthenês collected by Dr. Schwanbeck, and of the First Part of the Indika of Arrian. By J. W. McCrindle, M.A., Principal of Gov. College, Patna. With Introduction, Notes, and Map of Ancient India. Post 8vo. cloth, pp. xii.-224. 1877. 7s. 6d.

McCrindle.—Ancient India as described by Ktêsias, the Knidian, a translation of the abridgment of his "Indica," by Photios, and fragments of that work preserved in other writers. By J. W. McCrindle, M.A. With Introduction, Notes, and Index. 8vo. cloth, pp. viii.—104. 1882. 6s.

McCrindle—Ancient India as Described by Ptolemy. A Translation of the Chapters which describe India and Central and Eastern Asia in the Treatise on Geography written by Klaudios Ptolemaios, the Celebrated Astronomer; with Introduction, Commentary, Map of India according to Ptolemy, and a very Copious Index. By J. W. McCrindle, M.A. Demy 8vo. pp. xii.-373, cloth. 1885. 7s. 6d.

MacKenzie.—The History of the Relations of the Government with the Hill Tribes of the North-East Frontier of Bengal. By A. MacKenzie, B.C.S., Sec. to the Gov. Bengal. Royal. 8vo. pp. xviii.-586, cloth, with Map. 1884. 16s.

Madden.—COINS OF THE JEWS. See "Numismata Orientalia," Vol. II.

Man.—ON THE ABORIGINAL INHABITANTS OF THE ANDAMAN ISLANDS. By E. H. MAN, Assistant Superintendent Andaman and Nicobar Islands, F.R.G.S., M.R.A.S., etc. With Report of Researches into the Language of the South Andaman Islands, by A. J. ELLIS, F.R.S., F.S.A. Reprinted from "The Journal of the Anthropological Institute of Great Britain and Ireland." Demy 8vo. pp. xxviii.-298, with Map and Eight Plates, cloth. 1885. 10s. 6d.

Mariette.—Monuments of Upper Egypt. See page 65.

Markham.—THE NARRATIVES OF THE MISSION OF GEORGE BOGLE, B.C.S., to the Teshu Lama, and of the Journey of T. Manning to Lhasa. Edited, with Notes, Introduction, and lives of Bogle and Manning. by C. R. MARKHAM, C.B. Second Edition. 8vo. Maps and Illus., pp. clxi. 314, cl. 1879. 21s.

Marsden's Numismata Orientalia. New International Edition. *See* under NUMISMATA ORIENTALIA.

Marsden.—NUMISMATA ORIENTALIA ILLUSTRATA. The Plates of the Oriental Coins, Ancient and Modern, of the Collection of the late W. Marsden. Engraved from Drawings made under his Directions. 4to. 57 Plates, cl. 31s. 6d.

Martin.—THE CHINESE: THEIR EDUCATION, PHILOSOPHY, AND LETTERS. By W. A. P. MARTIN, D.D., LL.D., President of the Tungwen College, Pekin. 8vo. pp. 320, cloth. 1881. 7s. 6d.

Mason.—BURMA: Its People and Productions; or, Notes on the Fauna, Flora, and Minerals of Tenasserim, Pegu and Burma. By the Rev. F. MASON, D.D. Vol. I. Geology, Mineralogy, and Zoology. Vol. II. Botany. Rewritten by W. THEOBALD, late Deputy-Sup. Geological Survey of India. 2 vols. Royal 8vo. pp. xxvi. and 560; xvi. and 781 and xxxvi. cloth. 1864. £3.

Matthews.—ETHNOLOGY AND PHILOLOGY OF THE HIDATSA INDIANS. By WASHINGTON MATTHEWS, Assistant Surgeon, U.S. Army. *Contents:*—Ethnography, Philology, Grammar, Dictionary, and English-Hidatsa Vocabulary. 8vo. cloth. £1 11s. 6d.

Mayers.—China and Japan. See DENNYS.

Mayers.—THE CHINESE GOVERNMENT. A Manual of Chinese Titles, categorically arranged and explained, with an Appendix. By W. F. MAYERS. Second Edition, with Additions by G. M. H. PLAYFAIR. Roy. 8vo. cloth, pp. lxx.-158. 1886. 15s.

Metcalfe.—THE ENGLISHMAN AND THE SCANDINAVIAN; or, a Comparison of Anglo-Saxon and Old Norse Literature. By FREDERICK METCALFE, M.A., Author of "The Oxonian in Iceland, etc. Post 8vo. cloth, pp. 512. 1880. 18s.

Milton and Vondel.—See EDMUNDSON.

Mitra.—THE ANTIQUITIES OF ORISSA. By RAJENDRALALA MITRA. Published under Orders of the Government of India. Folio, cloth. Vol. I. pp. 180. With a Map and 36 Plates. 1875. £6 6s. Vol. II. pp. vi. and 178. 1880. £4 4s.

Mitra.—BUDDHA GAYA; the Hermitage of Sákya Muni. By RAJENDRALALA MITRA, LL.D., C.I.E. 4to. cloth, pp. xvi. and 258, with 51 plates. 1878. £3.

Mitra.—THE SANSKRIT BUDDHIST LITERATURE OF NEPAL. By RAJENDRALALA MITRA, LL.D., C.I.E. 8vo. cloth, pp. xlviii.-340. 1882. 12s. 6d.

Moor.—THE HINDU PANTHEON. By EDWARD MOOR, F.R.S. A new edition, with additional Plates. Condensed and Annotated by the Rev. W. O. SIMPSON. 8vo. cloth, pp. xiii. and 401, with 62 Plates. 1864. £3.

Morris.—A DESCRIPTIVE AND HISTORICAL ACCOUNT OF THE GODAVERY DISTRICT in the Presidency of Madras. By H. MORRIS, formerly M.C.S. 8vo. cloth, with map, pp. xii. and 390. 1878. 12s.

Müller.—ANCIENT INSCRIPTIONS IN CEYLON. By Dr. EDWARD MÜLLER. 2 Vols. Text, crown 8vo., pp. 220, cloth and plates, oblong folio, cloth. 1883. 21s.

Munro.—MAJOR-GENERAL SIR T. MUNRO, Bart., K.C.B., Governor of Madras. Selections from his Minutes and other Official Writings. Edited, with an Introductory Memoir and Notes, by Sir A. J. ARBUTHNOT, K.C.S.I., C.I.E. New Edition. Demy 8vo. pp. cxliv.-625, with Map, cloth. 1887. £1 1s.

North.—NORTH'S PLUTARCH, FOUR CHAPTERS OF; Containing the Lives of Caius Marcius, Coriolanus, Julius Cæsar, Marcus Antonius, and Marcus Brutus, as Sources to Shakespeare's Tragedies; Coriolanus, Julius Cæsar, and Antony and Cleopatra; and partly to Hamlet and Timon of Athens. Photo-lithographed in the size of the Edition of 1595. With Preface, Notes comparing the Text of the Editions of 1579, 1595, 1603, and 1612; and Reference Notes to the Text of the Tragedies of Shakespeare. Edited by Prof. F. A. LEO, Ph.D., Member of the Directory of the German Shakespeare Society; and Lecturer at the Academy of Modern Philology at Berlin. Folio, pp. 22, 130 of facsimiles, half-morocco. Library Edition (limited to 250 copies), £1 11s. 6d.; Amateur Edition (50 copies on a superior large hand-made paper), £3 3s.

Notes, ROUGH, OF JOURNEYS made in the years 1868–1873, in Syria, India, Kashmir, Japan, Mongolia, Siberia, United States, Sandwich Islands, Australasia, etc. Demy 8vo. pp. 624, cloth. 1875. 14s.

Numismata Orientalia.—THE INTERNATIONAL NUMISMATA ORIENTALIA. Edited by EDWARD THOMAS, F.R.S., etc. Vol. I. Illustrated with 20 Plates and a Map. Royal 4to. cloth. 1878. £3 13s. 6d.

Also in 6 Parts sold separately, royal 4to., wrappers, viz.:—

Part I.—Ancient Indian Weights. By E. THOMAS, F.R.S., etc. Pp. 84, with Plate and Map of the India of Manu. 9s. 6d. II.—Coins of the Urtuki Turkumans. By S. L. POOLE. Pp 44, with 6 Plates. 9s. III. The Coinage of Lydia and Persia, from the Earliest Times to the Fall of the Dynasty of the Achæmenidæ. By B. V. HEAD, Assistant-Keeper of Coins, British Museum. Pp. viii. and 56, with three Autotype Plates. 10s. 6d. IV. The Coins of the Tuluni Dynasty. By E. T. ROGERS. Pp. iv. and 22, and 1 Plate. 5s. V. The Parthian Coinage. By P. GARDNER, M.A. Pp. iv. and 65, with 8 Autotype Plates. 18s. VI. The Ancient Coins and Measures of Ceylon. With a Discussion of the Ceylon Date of the Buddha's Death. By T. W. RHYS DAVIDS, late Ceylon C. S. Pp. 60, with Plate. 10s.

Numismata Orientalia.—Vol. II. COINS OF THE JEWS. History of the Jewish Coinage in the Old and New Testaments. By F. W. MADDEN, M.R.A.S., Member of the Numismatic Society of London, etc. With 279 woodcuts and a plate of alphabets. Royal 4to. sewed, pp. xii. and 330. 1881. £2.
Or as a separate volume, cloth, £2 2s.

Numismata Orientalia.—Vol III. Part I. THE COINS OF ARAKAN, OF PEGU, AND OF BURMA. By Lieut.-General Sir ARTHUR PHAYRE, C.B., K.C.S.I., G.C.M.G., late Commissioner of British Burma. Royal 4to., pp. viii. and 48, with 5 Autotype Illustrations, sewed. 1882. 8s. 6d. Also contains the Indian Balhara and the Arabian Intercourse with India in the Ninth and following centuries. By EDWARD THOMAS, F.R.S. Vol. III. Part II. The Coins of Southern India. By Sir W. ELLIOT. Royal 4to. pp. viii.-168, with Map and 4 Plates. 1886. 25s.

Nutt.—A SKETCH OF SAMARITAN HISTORY, DOGMA, AND LITERATURE. An Introduction to " Fragments of a Samaritan Targum." By J. W. NUTT, M.A., &c., &c. Demy 8vo. pp. 180, cloth. 1874. 5s.

Olcott.—A Buddhist Catechism, according to the Canon of the Southern Church. By Col. H. S. Olcott, 24mo. pp. 32, wrapper. 1881. 1s.

Oppert.—ON THE ANCIENT COMMERCE OF INDIA: A Lecture. By Dr. G. OPPERT. 8vo. paper, 50 pp. 1879. 1s.

Oppert.—CONTRIBUTIONS TO THE HISTORY OF SOUTHERN INDIA. Part I. INSCRIPTIONS. By Dr. G. OPPERT. 8vo. paper, pp. vi. and 74, with a Plate. 1882. 4s.

Orientalia Antiqua; OR DOCUMENTS AND RESEARCHES RELATING TO THE HISTORY OF THE WRITINGS, LANGUAGES, AND ARTS OF THE EAST. Edited by TERRIEN DE LA COUPERIE, M.R.A.S., etc., etc. Fcap. 4to. pp. 96, with 14 Plates, wrapper. Part I. 5s.

Oxley.—EGYPT: and the Wonders of the Land of the Pharaohs. By W. OXLEY. Illustrated by a New Version of the Bhagavat-Gita, an Episode of the Mahabharat, one of the Epic Poems of Ancient India. Crown 8vo. pp. viii -328, cloth. 1884. 7s. 6d.

Palmer.—EGYPTIAN CHRONICLES, with a harmony of Sacred and Egyptian Chronology, and an Appendix on Babylonian and Assyrian Antiquities. By WILLIAM PALMER, M.A., late Fellow of Magdalen College, Oxford. 2 vols. 8vo. cloth, pp. lxxiv. and 428, and viii. and 636. 1861. 12s.

Patell.—COWASJEE PATELL'S CHRONOLOGY, containing corresponding Dates of the different Eras used by Christians, Jews, Greeks, Hindús, Mohamedans, Parsees, Chinese, Japanese, etc. By COWASJEE SORABJEE PATELL. 4to. pp. viii. and 184, cloth. 50s.

Pathya-Vakya, or Niti-Sastra. Moral Maxims from the Writings of Oriental Philosophers. Paraphrased, and Translated into English by A. D. A. WIJAYASINHA. Foolscap 8vo. sewed, pp. viii. and 54. 1881. 8s.

Paton.—A HISTORY OF THE EGYPTIAN REVOLUTION, from the Period of the Mamelukes to the Death of Mohammed Ali; from Arab and European Memoirs, Oral Tradition, and Local Research. By A. A. Paton. Second Edition. 2 vols. demy 8vo. cloth, pp. xii. and 395, viii. and 446. 1870. 7s. 6d.

Phillips.—KOPAL-KUNDALA. A Tale of Bengali Life. Translated from the Bengali of Bunkim Chandra Chatterjee by H. A. D. PHILIPS, Bengal C.S. Crown 8vo. pp. 240, cloth. 1885. 6s.

Pfoundes.—Fu So Mimi Bukuro.—A BUDGET OF JAPANESE NOTES. By CAPT. PFOUNDES, of Yokohama. 8vo. sewed, pp. 184. 7s. 6d.

Phayre.—COINS OF ARAKAN, ETC. See "Numismata Orientalia," Vol. III. Part I.

Piry.—LE SAINT EDIT. LITTERATURE CHINOISE. See page 63.

Playfair.—THE CITIES AND TOWNS OF CHINA. A Geographical Dictionary by G. M. H. PLAYFAIR, of Her Majesty's Consular Service in China. 8vo. cloth, pp. 506. 1879. 25s.

Poole.—COINS OF THE URTUKI TURKUMÁNS. See "Numismata Orientalia," Vol. I. Part II.

Poole.—A SCHEME OF MOHAMMADAN DYNASTIES DURING THE KHALIFATE. By S. L. POOLE, B.A. Oxon., M.R.A.S., Author of "Selections from the Koran," etc. 8vo. sewed, pp. 8, with a plate. 1880. 2s.

Poole.—An Index to Periodical Literature. By W. F. Poole, LL.D., Librarian of the Chicago Public Library. Third Edition, brought down to January, 1882. Royal 8vo. pp. xxviii. and 1442, cloth. 1883. £3 13s. 6d.

Ralston.—Tibetan Tales. See Trübner's Oriental Series, page 5.

Ram Raz.—Essay on the Architecture of the Hindus. By Ram Raz, Native Judge and Magistrate of Bangalore. With 48 plates. 4to. pp. xiv. and 64, sewed. London, 1834. £2 2s.

Rapson.—The Struggle between England and France for Supremacy in India. (The "Le Bas" Prize Essay for 1886.) By E. J. Rapson, B.A. Crown 8vo. pp. viii. and 120, cloth. 1887. 4s. 6d.

Ravenstein.—The Russians on the Amur; its Discovery, Conquest, and Colonization, with a Description of the Country, its Inhabitants, Productions, and Commercial Capabilities, and Personal Accounts of Russian Travellers. By E. G. Ravenstein, F.R.G.S. With 4 tinted Lithographs and 3 Maps. 8vo. cloth, pp. 500. 1861. 15s.

Raverty.—Notes on Afghanistan and Part of Baluchistan, Geographical, Ethnographical, and Historical. By Major H. G. Raverty, Bombay N. I. (Retired). Fcap. folio, wrapper. Sections I. and II. pp. 98. 1880. 2s. Section III. pp. vi. and 218. 1881. 5s. Section IV. pp. x-136. 1883. 3s.

Rice.—Mysore Inscriptions. Translated for the Government by Lewis Rice. 8vo. pp. vii. 336, and xxx. With a Frontispiece and Map. Bangalore, 1879. £1 10s.

Rockhill.—Life of the Buddha. See page 6.

Roe and Fryer.—Travels in India in the Seventeenth Century. By Sir Thomas Roe and Dr. John Fryer. 8vo. cloth, pp. 474. 1873. 7s. 6d.

Rogers.—Coins of the Tuluni Dynasty. See "Numismata Orientalia," Vol. I. Part IV.

Routledge.—English Rule and Native Opinion in India. From Notes taken in the years 1870-74. By James Routledge. Post 8vo. cloth, pp. 344. 1878. 10s. 6d.

Rowbotham.—A History of Music. By John Frederick Rowbotham, late Scholar of Balliol College, Oxford. 3 vols. demy 8vo. pp. xx. and 342, cloth. Vol. I. 1885. Vol. II. 1886. Vol. III. 1887. Each Volume, 18s.

Roy.—The Lyrics of Ind.—By Dejendra Lala Roy, M.A. &c., Author of "The Aryan Melodies." Crown 8vo. pp. viii.—79, cloth. 1887. 2s. 6d.

Sachau.—Alberuni's India. An Account of the Religion, Philosophy, Literature, Chronology, Astronomy, Customs, Laws, and Astrology of India, about A.D. 1030. Edited in the Arabic Original by Dr. Edward Sachau, Professor in the Royal University of Berlin. With an Index of the Sanskrit Words. 4to. pp. xli. and 374, cloth. 1887. £3 3s.

Sangermano.—A Description of the Burmese Empire. Compiled chiefly from Native Documents, by the Rev. Father Sangermano, and translated from his MS. by W. Tandy, D.D., Member of the Roman Sub-Committee of the Oriental Translation Fund. Royal 8vo. pp. x.—228, cloth. 1885. 8s.

Sástri.—Folklore in Southern India. By Pandit S. M. Natésa Sástri, Government Archaeological Survey. In Two Parts, crown 8vo. pp. 136 wrapper. 1886. 3s.

Schiefner.—Tibetan Tales. See Trübner's Oriental Series, page 5.

Schlagintweit.—Glossary of Geographical Terms from India and Tibet, with Native Transcription and Transliteration. By Hermann de Schlagintweit. With an Atlas in imperial folio, of Maps, Panoramas, and Views. Royal 4to., pp. xxiv. and 293. 1863. £4.

Sewell.—Report on the Amaravati Tope, and Excavations on its Site in 1877. By R. Sewell, M.C.S. Royal 4to. 4 plates, pp. 70, boards. 1880. 3s.

Sewell.—Archæological Survey of Southern India. Lists of the Antiquarian Remains in the Presidency of Madras. Compiled under the Orders of Government, by R. Sewell, M.C.S. Vol. I. 4to. pp. 400, cloth. 1882. 20s.

Sherring.—Hindu Tribes and Castes as represented in Benares. By the Rev. M. A. Sherring. With Illustrations. 4to. Cloth. Vol. I. pp. xxiv. and 408. 1872. *Now* £6 6s. Vol. II. pp. lxviii. and 376. 1879. £2 8s. Vol. III. pp. xii. and 336. 1881. £1 12s.

Sherring—The Sacred City of the Hindus. An Account of Benares in Ancient and Modern Times. By the Rev. M. A. Sherring, M.A., LL.D.; and Prefaced with an Introduction by Fitzedward Hall, Esq., D.C.L. 8vo. cloth, pp. xxxvi. and 388, with numerous full-page illustrations. 1868. 21s.

Sibree.—The Great African Island. Chapters on Madagascar. Researches in the Physical Geography, Geology, Natural History and Botany, and in the Customs, Language, Superstitions, Folk-Lore and Religious Belief, and Practices of the Different Tribes, Illustrations of Scripture and Early Church History, from Native Statists and Missionary Experience. By the Rev. Jas. Sibree, jun., F.R.G.S., of the London Missionary Society, etc. Demy 8vo. cloth, with Maps and Illustrations. pp. xii. and 372. 1880. 10s. 6d.

Steel and Temple. — Wide-Awake Stories. A Collection of Tales told by Little Children between Sunset and Sunrise in the Punjab and Kashmir. By F. A. Steel and R. C. Temple. Crown 8vo. pp. xii.—446, cloth. 1884. 9s.

Strangford.—Original Letters and Papers of the late Viscount Strangford, upon Philological and Kindred Subjects. Edited by Viscountess Strangford. Post 8vo. cloth, pp. xxii. and 284. 1878. 12s. 6d.

Thomas.—Ancient Indian Weights. See Numismata Orientalia," Vol. I. Part I.

Thomas.—Comments on Recent Pehlvi Decipherments. See page 92.

Thomas.—Sassanian Coins. Communicated to the Numismatic Society of London. By E. Thomas, F.R.S. Two parts. With 3 Plates and a Woodcut. 12mo. sewed, pp. 43. 5s.

Thomas.—The Indian Balhará, and the Arabian Intercourse with India in the ninth and following centuries. By Edward Thomas. See Numismata Orientalia, Vol. III. Part I. page 30.

Thomas.—Records of the Gupta Dynasty. Illustrated by Inscriptions, Written History, Local Tradition and Coins. To which is added a Chapter on the Arabs in Sind. By Edward Thomas, F.R.S. Folio, with a Plate, handsomely bound in cloth, pp. iv. and 64. 1876. Price 14s.

Thomas.—The Chronicles of the Pathán Kings of Dehli. Illustrated by Coins, Inscriptions, and other Antiquarian Remains. By Edward Thomas, F.R.S. With numerous Copperplates and Woodcuts. Demy 8vo. cloth, pp. xxiv. and 467. 1871. £1 8s.

Thomas.—The Revenue Resources of the Mughal Empire in India, from A.D. 1593 to A.D. 1707. A Supplement to "The Chronicles of the Pathán Kings of Delhi." By E. Thomas, F.R.S. 8vo. pp. 60, cloth. 3s. 6d.

Thorburn.—BANNÚ; or, Our Afghán Frontier. By S. S. THORBURN, Settlement Officer, Bannú District. 8vo. cloth, pp. x. and 480. 1876. 18s.

Vaughan. — THE MANNERS AND CUSTOMS OF THE CHINESE OF THE STRAITS SETTLEMENTS. By J. D. VAUGHAN, Advocate and Solicitor, Supreme Court, Straits Settlements. 8vo, pp. iv.-120, boards. 1879. 7s. 6d.

Watson.—INDEX TO THE NATIVE AND SCIENTIFIC NAMES OF INDIAN AND OTHER EASTERN ECONOMIC PLANTS AND PRODUCTS, By J. F. WATSON, M.A., M.D., etc. Imperial 8vo., cloth, pp. 650. 1868. £1 11s. 6d.

Wedgwood.—CONTESTED ETYMOLOGIES in the Dictionary of the Rev. W. W. Skeat. By HENSLEIGH WEDGWOOD. Crown 8vo. cloth, pp. viii.-194. 1882. 5s.

West and Buhler.—A DIGEST OF THE HINDU LAW of Inheritance, Partition, Adoption; Embodying the Replies of the Sastris in the Courts of the Bombay Presidency. With Introductions and Notes by the Hon. Justice RAYMOND WEST and J. G. BÜHLER, C.I.E. Third Edition. 8vo. pp. xc.-1450, wrapper. 1884. 36s.

Wheeler.—THE HISTORY OF INDIA FROM THE EARLIEST AGES. By J. TALBOYS WHEELER, Assistant Secretary to the Government of India in the Foreign Department, etc. etc. Demy 8vo. cl. 1867-1881.
    Vol. I. The Vedic Period and the Maha Bharata. pp. lxxv. and 576. Out of Print. Vol. II., The Ramayana and the Brahmanic Period. pp. lxxxviii. and 680, with two Maps. 21s. Vol. III. Hindu, Buddhist, Brahmanical Revival. pp. 484, with two maps. 18s. Vol. IV. Part I. Mussulman Rule. pp. xxxii. and 320. 14s. Vol. IV. Part II. Moghul Empire—Aurangzeb. pp. xxviii. and 280. 12s.

Wheeler.—EARLY RECORDS OF BRITISH INDIA. A History of the English Settlement in India, as told in the Government Records, the works of old travellers and other contemporary Documents, from the earliest period down to the rise of British Power in India. By J. TALBOYS WHEELER. Royal 8vo. cloth, pp. xxxii. and 392. 1878. 15s.

Williams.—MODERN INDIA AND THE INDIANS. See Trübner's Oriental Series, p. 3.

Wilson.—PANJAB CUSTOMARY LAW. Vol. IV. GENERAL CODE OF TRIBAL CUSTOM IN THE SIRSA DISTRICT OF THE PUNJAB. Drawn up by J. WILSON, Settlement Officer. Imperial 8vo. pp. viii. and 194, cloth. 1886. 7s.

Wirgman.—A SKETCH BOOK OF JAPAN. By C. WIRGMAN. Containing 39 Humorous Sketches on the Manners and Customs of the Japanese, with accompanying Explanations. Royal 8vo. oblong, bound in Japanese gilt cloth. 1885. 15s.

Wise.—COMMENTARY ON THE HINDU SYSTEM OF MEDICINE. By T. A. WISE, M.D., Bengal Medical Service. 8vo., pp. xx. and 432, cloth. 7s. 6d.

Wise.—REVIEW OF THE HISTORY OF MEDICINE. By THOMAS A. WISE, M.D. 2 vols. 8vo. cloth. Vol. I., pp. xcviii. and 397; Vol. II., pp. 574. 10s.

Worsaae.—THE PRE-HISTORY OF THE NORTH, BASED ON CONTEMPORARY MEMORIALS. By the late CHAMBERLAIN J. J. A. WORSAAE, Dr. Phil., Hon. F.S.A., F.S.A. Scot., M.R.I.A., &c., &c. Translated, with a brief Memoir of the Author, by H. F. MORLAND SIMPSON, M.A. Crown 8vo. pp. xxx. and 206, cloth, with Map and Illustrations. 1886. 6s.

Wright.—THE CELT, THE ROMAN, AND THE SAXON; a History of the Early Inhabitants of Britain down to the Conversion of the Anglo-Saxons to Christianity. Illustrated by the Ancient Remains brought to light by Recent Research. By THOMAS WRIGHT, M.A., F.S.A., &c., &c. Corrected and Enlarged Edition. Crown 8vo. pp. xiv. and 562, with nearly 300 Engravings, cloth. 1885. 9s.

THE RELIGIONS OF THE EAST.

Adi Granth (The); OR, THE HOLY SCRIPTURES OF THE SIKHS, translated from the original Gurmukhī, with Introductory Essays, by Dr. ERNEST TRUMPP, Prof. Oriental Languages, Munich. Roy. 8vo. cl. pp. 866. £2 12s. 6d.

Alabaster.—THE WHEEL OF THE LAW: Buddhism illustrated from Siamese Sources by the Modern Buddhist, a Life of Buddha, and an account of the Phrabat. By HENRY ALABASTER, Interpreter of H.M. Consulate-General in Siam. Demy 8vo. pp. lviii. and 324, cloth. 1871. 14s.

Amberley.—AN ANALYSIS OF RELIGIOUS BELIEF. By VISCOUNT AMBERLEY. 2 vols. 8vo. cl., pp. xvi. 496 and 512. 1876. 30s.

Apastambíya Dharma Sutram.—APHORISMS OF THE SACRED LAWS OF THE HINDUS, by Apastamba. Edited, with a Translation and Notes, by G. Bühler. 2 parts. 8vo. cloth, 1868-71. £1 4s. 6d.

Arnold.—THE LIGHT OF ASIA; or, The Great Renunciation (Mahâbhinishkramana). Being the Life and Teaching of Gautama, Prince of India, and Founder of Buddhism (as told by an Indian Buddhist). By Sir EDWIN ARNOLD, M.A., K.C.I.E., etc. Cheap Edition. Crown 8vo. parchment, pp. xvi. and 238. 1887. 3s. 6d. Library Edition, post 8vo. cloth. 7s. 6d. Illustrated Edition. 4to. pp. xx.-196, cloth. 1884. 21s.

Arnold.—INDIAN POETRY. See "Trübner's Oriental Series," page 4.

Arnold.—PEARLS OF THE FAITH; or, Islam's Rosary. Being the Ninety-nine Beautiful Names of Allah (Asmâ-el-'Husnâ), with Comments in Verse from various Oriental sources as made by an Indian Mussulman. By Sir E. ARNOLD, M.A., K.C.I.E., etc. Fourth Ed. Cr. 8vo. cl., pp. xvi.-320. 1887. 7s. 6d.

Balfour.—TAOIST TEXTS; Ethical, Political, and Speculative. By F. H. BALFOUR. Imp. 8vo. pp. vi. 118, cloth. [1884.] 10s. 6d.

Ballantyne.—The Sankhya Aphorisms of Kapila. See p. 6.

Banerjea.—THE ARIAN WITNESS, or the Testimony of Arian Scriptures in corroboration of Biblical History and the Rudiments of Christian Doctrine. Including Dissertations on the Original Home and Early Adventures of Indo-Arians. By the Rev. K. M. BANERJEA. 8vo. sewed, pp. xviii. and 236. 8s. 6d.

Barth.—RELIGIONS OF INDIA. See "Trübner's Oriental Series," page 4.

Beal.—A CATENA OF BUDDHIST SCRIPTURES FROM THE CHINESE. By S. BEAL, B.A. 8vo. cloth, pp. xiv. and 436. 1871. 15s.

Beal.—THE ROMANTIC LEGEND OF SÁKHYA BUDDHA. From the Chinese-Sanscrit by the Rev. S. BEAL. Crown 8vo. cloth, pp. 400. 1875. 12s.

Beal.—THE DHAMMAPADA. See "Trübner's Oriental Series," page 3.

Beal.—Abstract of Four Lectures on Buddhist Literature in China. Delivered at University College, London. By Samuel Beal. Demy 8vo. cloth, pp. 208. 1882. 10s. 6d.

Beal.—Buddhist Records of the Western World. See "Trübner's Oriental Series," p. 6.

Bigandet.—Gaudama, the Buddha of the Burmese. See "Trübner's Oriental Series," page 4.

Brockie.—Indian Philosophy. Introductory Paper. By William Brockie. 8vo. pp. 26, sewed. 1872. 6d.

Brown.—The Dervishes; or, Oriental Spiritualism. By John P. Brown, Sec. and Dragoman of Legation of U.S.A. Constantinople. With twenty-four Illustrations. 8vo. cloth, pp. viii. and 415. 14s.

Burnell.—The Ordinances of Manu. See "Trübner's Oriental Series." page 6.

Callaway.—The Religious System of the Amazulu. See page 51.

Chalmers.—The Origin of the Chinese; an Attempt to Trace the connection of the Chinese with Western Nations in their Religion, Superstitions Arts, Language, and Traditions. By John Chalmers, A.M. Foolscap 8vo. cloth, pp. 78. 5s.

Chatterji.—The Bhagavad Gitâ; or The Lord's Lay.—With Commentary and Notes, as well as references to the Christian Scriptures. Translated from the Sanskrit for the benefit of those in search of Spiritual Light. By Mohini M. Chatterji, M.A. Royal 8vo. pp. ix. and 283, cloth. 1887. 10s. 6d.

Clarke.—Ten Great Religions: an Essay in Comparative Theology. By James Freeman Clarke. 8vo. cloth, pp. x. and 528. 1871. 10s. 6d.

Clarke.—Ten Great Religions. Part II. A Comparison of All Religions. By J. F. Clarke. Demy 8vo., pp. xxviii.-414, cloth. 1883. 10s. 6d.

Clarke.—Serpent and Siva Worship, and Mythology in Central America, Africa and Asia. By Hyde Clarke, Esq. 8vo. sewed. 1s.

Conway.—The Sacred Anthology. A Book of Ethnical Scriptures. Collected and edited by M. D. Conway. 5th edition. Demy 8vo. cloth, pp. xvi. and 480. 1876. 12s.

Coomára Swamy.—The Dathávansa; or, the History of the Tooth-Relic of Gotama Buddha. Pali Text, and English Translation, with Notes. By Sir M. Coomára Swámy, Mudeliár. Demy 8vo. pp. 174, cloth. 1874. 10s. 6d. Translation only, with Notes. pp. 100. 6s.

Coomára Swamy.—Sutta Nipáta; or, the Dialogues and Discourses of Gotama Buddha. Translated from the Pali, with Introduction and Notes. By Sir M. Coomára Swamy. Cr. 8vo. cloth, pp. xxxvi. and 160. 1874. 6s.

Coran.—Extracts from the Coran in the Original, with English Rendering. Compiled by Sir William Muir, K.C.S.I., LL.D., Author of the "Life of Mahomet." Second Edition. Crown 8vo. pp. 72, cloth. 1885. 2s. 6d.

Cowell.—The Sarva Darsana Samgraha. See "Trübner's Oriental Series." p. 5.

Cunningham.—The Bhilsa Topes; or, Buddhist Monuments of Central India; comprising a brief Historical Sketch of the Rise, Progress, and Decline of Buddhism; with an Account of the Opening and Examination of the various Groups of Topes around Bhilsa. By Brev.-Major A. Cunningham. Illustrated. 8vo. cloth, 33 Plates, pp. xxxvi. 370. 1854. £2 2s.

Da Cunha.—Memoir on the History of the Tooth-Relic of Ceylon; with an Essay on the Life and System of Gautama Buddha. By J. Gerson da Cunha. 8vo. cloth, pp. xiv. and 70. With 4 photographs and cuts. 7s. 6d.

Davids.—Buddhist Birth Stories. See "Trübner's Oriental Series," page 4.

Davies.—Hindu Philosophy. See "Trübner's Oriental Series," page 5.

Dowson.—Dictionary of Hindu Mythology, etc. See "Trübner's Oriental Series," page 3.

Dickson.—The Pâtimokkha, being the Buddhist Office of the Confession of Priests. The Pali Text, with a Translation, and Notes, by J. F. Dickson, M.A. 8vo. sd., pp. 69. 2s.

Edkins.—Chinese Buddhism. See "Trübner's Oriental Series," page 4.

Edkins.—Religion in China. See "Trübner's Oriental Series," p. 6.

Eitel.—Handbook for the Student of Chinese Buddhism. By the Rev. E. J. Eitel, L. M. S. Crown 8vo. cloth, pp. viii. and 224. 1870. 18s.

Eitel.—Buddhism: its Historical, Theoretical, and Popular Aspects. In Three Lectures. By Rev. E. J. Eitel, M.A. Ph.D. Third Revised Edition. Demy 8vo. pp. x—146, limp cloth. 1885. 6s.

Examination (Candid) of Theism.—By Physicus. Post 8vo. cloth, pp. xviii. and 198. 1878. 7s. 6d.

Faber.—A Systematical Digest of the Doctrines of Confucius, according to the Analects, Great Learning, and Doctrine of the Mean. with an Introduction on the Authorities upon Confucius and Confucianism. By Ernst Faber, Rhenish Missionary. Translated from the German by P. G. von Möllendorff. 8vo. sewed, pp. viii. and 131. 1875. 12s. 6d.

Faber.—Introduction to the Science of Chinese Religion. A Critique of Max Müller and other Authors. By the Rev. E. Faber, Rhenish Missionary in Canton. Crown 8vo. stitched in wrapper, pp. xii. and 154. 1880. 7s. 6d.

Faber.—The Mind of Mencius. See "Trübner's Oriental Series," p. 5.

Giles.—Record of the Buddhist Kingdoms. Translated from the Chinese by H. A. Giles, of H.M. Consular Service. 8vo. sewed, pp. x.-129. 5s.

Gough.—The Philosophy of the Upanishads. See "Trübner's Oriental Series," p. 5.

Gubernatis.—Zoological Mythology; or, the Legends of Animals. By Angelo de Gubernatis, Professor of Sanskrit and Comparative Literature in the Instituto di Studii Superiori e di Perfezionamento at Florence, etc. In 2 vols. 8vo. pp. xxvi. and 432, vii. and 442. 28s.

Gulshan I Raz: The Mystic Rose Garden of Sa'd ud din Mahmud Shabistari. The Persian Text, with an English Translation and Notes, chiefly from the Commentary of Muhammed Bin Yahya Lahiji. By E. H. Whinfield, M.A., late of H.M.B.C.S. 4to. cloth, pp. xvi. 94 and 60. 1880. 10s. 6d.

Gulshan I Raz: The Dialogue of the. Crown 8vo. pp. iv.-64, cloth. 1887. 3s.

Hardy.—Christianity and Buddhism Compared. By the late Rev. R. Spence Hardy, Hon. Member Royal Asiatic Society. 8vo. sd. pp. 138. 6s.

Haug.—The Parsis. See "Trübner's Oriental Series," p. 3.

Haug.—THE AITAREYA BRAHMANAM OF THE RIG VEDA: containing the Earliest Speculations of the Brahmans on the meaning of the Sacrificial Prayers and on the Origin, Performance, and Sense of the Rites of the Vedic Religion. Sanskrit Text Edited, Translated, and Explained by MARTIN HAUG, Ph.D. Superintendent of Sanskrit Studies in the Poona College, etc. 2 Vols. Crown 8vo pp. 312, and 544, cloth. 1863. £2 2s.

Hawken.—UPA-SASTRA: Comments, Linguistic and Doctrinal, on Sacred and Mythic Literature. By J. D. HAWKEN. 8vo. cloth, pp.viii. -288. 7s. 6d.

Hershon.—TALMUDIC MISCELLANY. See "Trübner's Oriental Series," page 4.

Hodgson.—ESSAYS RELATING TO INDIAN SUBJECTS. See "Trübner's Oriental Series," p. 4.

Inman.—ANCIENT PAGAN AND MODERN CHRISTIAN SYMBOLISM EXPOSED AND EXPLAINED. By THOMAS INMAN, M.D. Second Edition. With Illustrations. Demy 8vo. cloth, pp. xl. and 148. 1874. 7s. 6d.

Johnson.—ORIENTAL RELIGIONS and thei Relation to Universal Religion. By SAMUEL JOHNSON. I. India. 2 Volumes, post 8vo. pp. 108 and 402, cloth. 21s. II. Persia. Demy 8vo. pp. xliv.-784, cloth. 1885. 18s.

Journal of the Ceylon Branch of the Royal Asiatic Society.—For Papers on Buddhism contained in it, see page 15.

Kistner.—BUDDHA AND HIS DOCTRINES. A Bibliographical Essay. By OTTO KISTNER. Imperial 8vo., pp. iv. and 32, sewed. 2s. 6d.

Koran.—Arabic text. Lithographed in Oudh. Foolscap 8vo. pp. 502, sewed. Lucknow, A.H. 1295 (1877). 9s.

Koran.—See also under "Coran."

Lane.—THE KORAN. See "Trübner's Oriental Series," p. 3.

Legge.—CONFUCIANISM IN RELATION TO CHRISTIANITY. See page 62.

Legge.—THE LIFE AND TEACHINGS OF CONFUCIUS. With Explanatory Notes. By JAMES LEGGE, D.D. Sixth Edition. Crown 8vo. cloth, pp. vi. and 338. 1887. 10s. 6d.

Legge.—THE LIFE AND WORKS OF MENCIUS. With Essays and Notes. By JAMES LEGGE. Crown 8vo. cloth, pp. 402. 1875. 12s.

Legge.—THE SHE KING; or, The Book of Ancient Poetry. Translated in English Verse, with Essays and Notes. By JAMES LEGGE, D.D., LL.D., etc., etc. Pp. vi. and 432, cloth. 1876. 12s.

Legge.—CHINESE CLASSICS. See page 62.

Leigh.—THE RELIGION OF THE WORLD. By H. STONE LEIGH. 12mo. pp. xii, 66, cloth. 1869. 2s. 6d.

M'Clatchie.—CONFUCIAN COSMOGONY. A Translation (with the Chinese Text opposite) of Section 49 (Treatise on Cosmogony) of the "Complete Works" of the Philosopher Choo-Foo-Tze. With Explanatory Notes by the Rev. TH. M'CLATCHIE, M.A. Small 4to. pp. xviii. and 162. 1874. 12s. 6d.

Mitra.—BUDDHA GAYA, the Hermitage of Sákya Muni. By RAJENDRALALA MITRA, LL.D., C.I.E. 4to. cloth, pp. xvi. and 258, with 51 Plates. 1878. £3.

Muhammed.—THE LIFE OF MUHAMMED. Based on Muhammed Ibn Ishak. By Abd El Malik Ibn Hisham. Edited by Dr. FERDINAND WÜSTENFELD. The Arabic Text. 8vo. pp. 1026, sewed. 21s. Introduction, Notes, and Index in German. 8vo. pp. lxxii. and 266, sewed. 7s. 6d.

The text based on the Manuscripts of the Berlin, Leipsic, Gotha and Leyden Libraries, has been carefully revised by the learned editor, and printed with the utmost exactness.

Muir.—TRANSLATIONS FROM THE SANSKRIT. See "Trübner's Oriental Series," p. 3.

Muir.—ORIGINAL SANSKRIT TEXTS.—See page 102.

Muir.—EXTRACTS FROM THE CORAN. See Coran, page 42.

Müller.—THE SACRED HYMNS OF THE BRAHMINS, as preserved to us in the oldest collection of religious poetry, the Rig-Veda-Sanhita, translated and explained. By F. MAX MÜLLER, M.A., Oxford. Volume I. Hymns to the Maruts or the Storm Gods. 8vo. pp clii. and 264. 1869. 12s. 6d.

Müller.—THE HYMNS OF THE RIG VEDA IN THE SAMHITA AND PADA TEXTS. Reprinted from the Editio Princeps by F. MAX MÜLLER, M.A. Second Edition. With the two texts on parallel pages. 2 vols., 8vo. pp. 800-828, stitched in wrapper. 1877. £1 12s.

Müller.—LECTURE ON BUDDHIST NIHILISM. By F. MAX MÜLLER, M.A. Delivered before the Association of German Philologists at Kiel, 28th September, 1869. (Translated from the German.) Sewed. 1869. 1s.

Newman.—HEBREW THEISM. By F. W. NEWMAN. Royal 8vo. stiff wrappers, pp. viii. and 172. 1874. 4s. 6d.

Piry.—LE SAINT EDIT, ÉTUDE DE LITTERATURE CHINOISE. Préparée par A. THÉOPHILE PIRY, du Service des Douanes Maritimes de Chine. 4to. pp. xx. and 320, cloth. 1879. 21s.

Priaulx.—QUÆSTIONES MOSAICÆ; or, the first part of the Book of Genesis compared with the remains of ancient religions. By OSMOND DE BEAUVOIR PRIAULX. 8vo. pp. viii. and 548, cloth. 12s.

Redhouse.—THE MESNEVI. See "Trübner's Oriental Series," p. 4.

Rig-Veda Sanhita.—A COLLECTION OF ANCIENT HINDU HYMNS. Constituting the First to the Eighth Ashtaka, or Books of the Rig-veda; the oldest authority for the religious and social institutions of the Hindus. Translated from the Original Sanskrit by the late H. H. WILSON, M.A. 2nd Ed., with a Postscript by Dr. F. HALL. 8vo. cloth, Vol. I. pp. lii. and 348. 21s. Vol. II. pp. xxx. and 346. 1854. 21s. Vol. III. pp. xxiv. and 525. 1857. 21s. Vol. IV. Edited by E. B. COWELL, M.A. pp. 214. 1866. 14s.

A few copies of Vols. II. and III. still left. [*Vols. V. and VI. in the Press.*]

Rig-Veda Sanhita.—See MÜLLER.

Rockhill.—LIFE OF THE BUDDHA. See "Trübner's Oriental Series," p. 6.

Sacred Books (The) OF THE EAST. Translated by various Oriental Scholars, and Edited by F. Max Muller. All 8vo. cloth. 1879-1888.

First Series.

Vol. I. The Upanishads. Translated by F. Max Müller. Part I. The Khândogya-Upanishad; the Talavakâra-Upanishad; the Aitareya-Aranyaka; the Kaushitaki-Brâhmana-Upanishad and the Vâgasaneyi-Samhitâ-Upanishad. 10s. 6d.

Vol. II. The Sacred Laws of the Âryas, as taught in the Schools of Âpastamba, Gautama, Vâsishtha, and Baudhâyana. Translated by Georg Bühler. Part I. Apastamba and Gautama. 10s. 6d.

Vol. III. The Sacred Books of China. The Texts of Confucianism. Translated by James Legge. Part I. The Shû King. The Religious Portions of the Shih King. The Hsiâo King. 12s. 6d.

Vol. IV. The Zend-Avesta. Part I. The Vendîdâd. Translated by James Darmesteter. 10s. 6d.

Vol. V. Pahlavi Texts. Part I. The Bundahis, Bahman Yast, and Shâyast-la-Shâyast. Translated by E. W. West. 12s. 6d.

Vol. VI. The Qur'ân. Part I. Translated by E. H. Palmer. 10s. 6d.

Vol. VII. The Institutes of Vishnu. Translated by Julius Jolly. 10s. 6d.

Vol. VIII. The Bhagavadgîtâ with other extracts from the Mahâbhârata. Translated by Kashinath Trunbak Telang. 10s. 6d.

Vol. IX. The Qur'ân. Part II. Translated by E. H. Palmer. 10s. 6d.

Vol. X. The Suttanipâta, etc. Translated by V. Fausböll. 10s. 6d.

Vol. XI. The Mahâparinibbâna Sutta; the Tevigga Sutta; the Mahâsudassana Sutta; the Dhamma-Kakkappavattana Sutta. Translated by T. W. Rhys Davids. 10s. 6d.

Vol. XII. The Satapatha-Brâhmana. Translated by Prof. Eggeling. Vol. I. 12s. 6d.

Vol. XIII. The Pâtimokkha. Translated by T. W. Rhys Davids. The Mahavagga. Part I. Translated by Dr. H. Oldenberg. 10s. 6d.

Vol. XIV. The Sacred Laws of the Aryans, as taught in the Schools of Vâsishtha and Baudhâyana. Translated by Prof. Georg Bühler. 10s. 6d.

Vol. XV. The Upanishads. Part II. Translated by F. Max Müller. 10s. 6d.

Vol. XVI. The Yi King. Translated by James Legge. 10s. 6d.

Vol. XVII. The Mahâvagga. Part II. Translated by T. W. Rhys Davids, and Dr. H. Oldenberg. 10s. 6d.

Vol. XVIII. The Dâdistân-i Dinîk and Mainyô-i Khard. Pahlavi Texts. Part II. Translated by E. W. West. 12s. 6d.

Vol. XIX. The Fo-sho-hing-tsan-king. Translated by Samuel Beal. 10s. 6d.

Vol. XX. The Vâyu-Purâna. Translated by Prof. Bhandarkar, of Elphinstone College, Bombay. 10s. 6d.

Vol. XXI. The Saddharma-pundarîka. Translated by Prof. Kern. 12s. 6d.

Vol. XXII. The Akârânga-Sûtra. Translated by Prof. Jacobi. 10s. 6d.

Vol. XXIII. The Zend-Avesta. Part II. The Sirôzahs, Yasts, and Nyayis. Translated by J. Darmesteter. 10s. 6d.

Vol. XXIV. Pahlavi Texts. Part III. Dinâ-î Mainôg-î Khirad, Sikand-gûmânîk, and Sad Dar. Translated by E. W. West. 10s. 6d.

Second Series.

Vol. XXV. Manu. Translated by G. Bühler. 21s.

Vol. XXVI. The Satapatha-Brâhmana. Part II. Translated by J. Eggeling. 12s. 6d.

Vols. XXVII. and XXVIII. The Sacred Books of China. The Texts of Confucianism. Translated by J. Legge. Parts III. and IV. The Lî-kî, or Collection of Treatises on the Rule of Propriety, or Ceremonial Usages. 12s. 6d. each.

Vols. XXIX. and XXX. The Grihya-sûtras. Rules of Vedic Domestic Ceremonies. Translated by Hermann Oldenberg. Part I. (Vol. XXIX.) 12s. 6d. Part II. (Vol. XXX.) [*In the Press.*]

Vol. XXXI. The Zend-Avesta. Part III. The Yasna, Visparad, Âfrînagân, Gâhs, and Miscellaneous Fragments. Translated by L. H. Mills. 12s. 6d.

In the Press.

Vol. XXXII. Vedic Hymns. Translated by F. Max Müller.
Vol. XXXIII. Nârada, and some Minor Law-books. Translated by Julius Jolly.
Vol. XXXIV. The Vedânta-Sûtras, with Saṇkara's Commentary. Translated by G. Thibaut.

The Second Series will consist of Twenty-four Volumes in all.

Schlagintweit.—BUDDHISM IN TIBET. Illustrated by Literary Documents and Objects of Religions Worship. With an Account of the Buddhist Systems preceding it in India. By EMIL SCHLAGINTWEIT, LL.D. With a Folio Atlas of 20 Plates, and 20 Tables of Native Prints in the Text. Royal 8vo., pp. xxiv. and 404. £2 2s.

Sell.—THE FAITH OF ISLAM. By the Rev. E. SELL, Fellow of the University of Madras. Demy 8vo. cloth, pp. xiv. and 270. 1880. 6s. 6d.

Sell.—IHN-I-TAJWID; or, Art of Reading the Quran. By the Rev. E. SELL, B.D. 8vo., pp. 48, wrappers. 1882. 2s. 6d.

Sherring.—THE HINDOO PILGRIMS. By the Rev. M. A. SHERRING, Fcap. 8vo. cloth, pp. vi. and 125. 5s.

Singh—SAKHEE BOOK; or, the Description of Gooroo Gobind Singh's Religion and Doctrines. translated from Gooroo Mukhi into Hindi, and afterwards into English. By Sirdar Attar Singh, Chief of Bhadour. With the Author's photograph. 8vo. pp. xviii. and 205. Benares. 1873. 15s.

Sinnett.—THE OCCULT WORLD. By A. P. SINNETT, President of the Simla Eclectic Theosophical Society. Fourth Edition. Fcap. 8vo., pp. xiv. and 140, cloth. 1884. 3s. 6d.

Syed Ahmad.—A SERIES OF ESSAYS ON THE LIFE OF MOHAMMED, and Subjects subsidiary thereto. By SYED AHMAD KHAN BAHADOR, C.S.I. 8vo. pp. 532, with 4 Genealogical Tables, 2 Maps, and Coloured Plate. £1 10s.

Tiele—OUTLINES OF THE HISTORY OF RELIGION. See "Trübner's Oriental Series," page 6.

Tiele.—History of Egyptian Religion. See "Trübner's Oriental Series," page 5.

Vishnu-Purana (The); a System of Hindu Mythology and Tradition Translated from the Sanskrit, with Notes derived chiefly from other Purânas. By the late H. H. WILSON, M.A., Boden Prof. of Sanskrit in the University of Oxford, etc. Edited by FITZEDWARD HALL. 6 vols. 8vo. cloth. Vol. I. pp. cxl. and 200; Vol. II. pp. 343; Vol. III., pp. 348; Vol IV. pp. 346; Vol. V. Part I. pp. 392. 10s. 6d. each. Vol. V., Part 2, Index, compiled by F. Hall. pp. 268. 12s.

Wake.—THE EVOLUTION OF MORALITY. A History of the Development of Moral Culture. By C. S. WAKE. Two vols. 8vo. pp. 522 and 486, cloth. 1878. 21s.

Wherry.—Commentary on the Quran. See page 5.

Wilson.—ESSAYS AND LECTURES CHIEFLY ON THE RELIGION OF THE HINDUS. By the late H. H. WILSON, M.A., F.R.S., etc. Collected and edited by Dr. REINHOLD ROST. 2 vols. pp. 414 and 422, cloth. 21s.

COMPARATIVE PHILOLOGY.

POLYGLOTS.

Beames.—OUTLINES OF INDIAN PHILOLOGY. With a Map, showing the Distribution of the Indian Languages. By JOHN BEAMES. Second enlarged and revised edition. Crown 8vo. cloth, pp. viii. and 96. 1868. 5s.

Beames.—A COMPARATIVE GRAMMAR OF THE MODERN ARYAN LANGUAGES OF INDIA (to wit), Hindi, Panjabi, Sindhi, Gujarati, Marathi, Uriya, and Bengali. By JOHN BEAMES, Bengal C.S., M.R.A.S., &c. 8vo. cloth. Vol. I. On Sounds. pp. xvi. and 360. 1872. 16s. Vol. II. The Noun and the Pronoun. pp. xii. and 348. 1875. 16s. Vol III. The Verb. pp. xii. and 316. 1879. 16s.

Bellows.—ENGLISH OUTLINE VOCABULARY, for the use of Students of the Chinese, Japanese, and other Languages. Arranged by JOHN BELLOWS. With Notes on the writing of Chinese with Roman Letters. by Professor SUMMERS, King's College, London. Crown 8vo., pp. 6 and 368, cloth. 1867. 6s.

Bellows.—OUTLINE DICTIONARY, FOR THE USE OF MISSIONARIES, Explorers, and Students of Language. By F. MAX MÜLLER, M.A., Oxford. With Introduction on the proper use of the English Alphabet in transcribing Foreign Languages. Vocabulary compiled by J. BELLOWS. Crown 8vo. pp. 400, limp morocco. 1867. 7s. 6d.

Caldwell.—A COMPARATIVE GRAMMAR OF THE DRAVIDIAN, OR SOUTH-INDIAN FAMILY OF LANGUAGES. By the Rev. R. CALDWELL, LL.D. Second, enlarged, Edition. Demy 8vo. pp. 806, cloth. 1875. 28s.

Calligaris.—LE COMPAGNON DE TOUS, OU DICTIONNAIRE POLYGLOTTE. Par le Colonel LOUIS CALLIGARIS, Grand Officier, etc. (French—Latin—Italian—Spanish—Portuguese—German—English—Modern Greek—Arabic—Turkish.) 2 vols. 4to., pp. 1157 and 746. Turin. £4 4s.

Campbell.—SPECIMENS OF THE LANGUAGES OF INDIA, including Tribes of Bengal, the Central Provinces, and the Eastern Frontier. By Sir G. CAMPBELL, M.P. Folio. paper, pp. 308. 1874. £1 11s. 6d.

Clarke.—RESEARCHES IN PRE-HISTORIC AND PROTO-HISTORIC COMPARATIVE PHILOLOGY, MYTHOLOGY, AND ARCHÆOLOGY. See page 56.

Cust.—LANGUAGES OF THE EAST INDIES. See page 3.

Cust.—LANGUAGES OF AFRICA. See page 6.

Edkins.—CHINA'S PLACE IN PHILOLOGY. An Attempt to show that the Languages of Europe and Asia have a Common Origin. By the Rev. JOSEPH EDKINS. Crown 8vo. cloth, pp. xxiii. and 403. 10s. 6d.

Ellis.—ETRUSCAN NUMERALS. By R. ELLIS, B.D. 8vo. pp. 52. 2s. 6d.

Ellis.—THE ASIATIC AFFINITIES OF THE OLD ITALIANS. By ROBERT ELLIS, B.D., Fellow of St. John's College, Cambridge, and author of "Ancient Routes between Italy and Gaul." Crown 8vo. pp. iv. 156, cloth. 1870. 5s.

Ellis.—ON NUMERALS, as Signs of Primeval Unity among Mankind. By ROBERT ELLIS, B.D., Late Fellow of St. John's College, Cambridge. Demy 8vo. cloth, pp. viii. and 94. 3s. 6d.

Ellis.—SOURCES OF THE ETRUSCAN AND BASQUE LANGUAGES. By ROBERT ELLIS, B.D., Late Fellow of St. John's College, Cambridge. Demy 8vo. pp. viii.-166. 1886. 7s. 6d.

Ellis.—Peruvia Scythica. The Quichua Language of Peru: its derivation from Central Asia with the American languages in general, and with the Turanian and Iberian languages of the Old World, including the Basque, the Lycian, and the Pre-Aryan language of Etruria. By Robert Ellis, B.D. 8vo. cloth, pp. xii. and 219. 1875. 6s.

Geiger.—Contributions to the History of the Development of the Human Race. Lectures and Dissertations. By Lazarus Geiger. Translated from the Second German Edition by David Asher, Ph.D. Post 8vo. cloth, pp. x. and 156. 1880. 6s.

Grey.—Handbook of African, Australian, and Polynesian Philology, as represented in the Library of His Excellency Sir George Grey, K.C.B., Her Majesty's High Commissioner of the Cape Colony. Classed, Annotated, and Edited by Sir George Grey and Dr. H. I. Bleek.

    Vol. I. Part 1.—South Africa. 8vo. pp. 186. 20s.
    Vol. I. Part 2.—Africa (North of the Tropic of Capricorn). 8vo. pp. 70. 4s.
    Vol. I. Part 3.—Madagascar. 8vo. pp. 24. 2s.
    Vol. II. Part 1.—Australia. 8vo. pp. iv. and 44. 3s.
    Vol. II. Part 2.—Papuan Languages of the Loyalty Islands and New Hebrides, comprising those of the Islands of Nengone, Lifu, Aneitum, Tana, and others. 8vo. p. 12. 1s.
    Vol. II. Part 3.—Fiji Islands and Rotuma (with Supplement to Part II., Papuan Languages, and Part I., Australia). 8vo. pp. 34. 2s.
    Vol. II. Part 4.—New Zealand, the Chatham Islands, and Auckland Islands. 8vo. pp. 76. 7s.
    Vol. II. Part 4 (continuation).—Polynesia and Borneo. 8vo. pp. 77-154. 7s.
    Vol. III. Part 1.—Manuscripts and Incunables. 8vo. pp. viii. and 24. 2s.
    Vol. IV. Part 1.—Early Printed Books. England. 8vo. pp. vi. and 266. 12s.

Gubernatis.—Zoological Mythology; or, the Legends of Animals. By Angelo de Gubernatis, Professor of Sanskrit and Comparative Literature in the Instituto di Studii Superiori e di Perfezionamento at Florence, etc. In 2 vols. 8vo. pp. xxxvi. and 432, vii. and 442. 28s.

Hoernle.—A Comparative Grammar of the Gaudian Language, with Special Reference to the Eastern Hindi. With Language Map and Table of Alphabets. By A. F. R. Hoernle. Demy 8vo. pp. 474. 1880. 18s.

Kilgour.—The Hebrew or Iberian Race, including the Pelasgians, the Phenicians, the Jews, the British, and others. By Henry Kilgour. 8vo. sewed, pp. 76. 1872. 2s. 6d.

March.—A Comparative Grammar of the Anglo-Saxon Language; in which its forms are illustrated by those of the Sanskrit, Greek, Latin, Gothic, Old Saxon, Old Friesic, Old Norse, and Old High-German. By Francis A. March, LL.D. Demy 8vo. cloth, pp. xi. and 253. 1877. 10s.

Notley.—A Comparative Grammar of the French, Italian, Spanish, and Portuguese Languages. By Edwin A. Notley. Crown oblong 8vo. cloth, pp. xv. and 396. 7s. 6d.

Oppert.—On the Classification of Languages. A Contribution to Comparative Philology. By Dr. G. Oppert. 8vo. paper, pp. vi. and 146. 1879. 7s. 6d.

Oriental Congress.—Report of the Proceedings of the Second International Congress of Orientalists held in London. 1874. Roy. 8vo. paper, pp. 76. 5s.

Oriental Congress.—Transactions of the Second Session of the International Congress of Orientalists, held in London in September, 1874. Edited by Robert K. Douglas, Honorary Secretary. Demy 8vo. cloth, pp. viii. and 456. 21s.

Pezzi.—Aryan Philology, according to the most recent Researches (Glottologia Aria Recentissima), Remarks Historical and Critical. By Domenico Pezzi, Membro della Facolta de Filosofia e lettere della R. Universit. di Torino. Translated by E. S. Roberts, M.A., Fellow and Tutor of Gonville and Caius College. Crown 8vo. cloth, pp. xvi. and 199. 6s.

Sayce.—An Assyrian Grammar for Comparative Purposes. By A. H. Sayce, M.A. 12mo. cloth, pp. xvi. and 188. 1872. 7s. 6d.

Sayce.—The Principles of Comparative Philology. By A. H. Sayce, Fellow and Tutor of Queen's College, Oxford. Second Edition. Cr. 8vo. cl., pp. xxxii. and 416. 10s. 6d.

Schleicher.—Compendium of the Comparative Grammar of the Indo-European, Sanskrit, Greek, and Latin Languages. By August Schleicher. Translated from the German by H. Bendall, B.A., Chr. Coll. Camb. 8vo. cloth. Part I. Grammar. pp. 184. 1874. 7s. 6d. Part II. Morphology. pp. viii. and 104. 1877. 6s.

Trübner's Collection of Simplified Grammars of the principal Asiatic and European Languages. Edited by Reinhold Rost, LL.D., Ph.D. Crown 8vo. cloth, uniformly bound.

    I.—Hindustani, Persian, and Arabic. By the late E. H. Palmer, M.A. Pp. 112. 5s.
    II.—Hungarian. By I. Singer, of Buda-Pesth. Pp. vi. and 88. 4s. 6d.
    III.—Basque. By W. Van Eys. Pp. xii. and 52. 3s. 6d.
    IV.—Malagasy. By G. W. Parker. Pp. 66. 5s.
    V.—Modern Greek. By E. M. Geldart, M.A. Pp. 68. 2s. 6d.
    VI.—Roumanian. By M. Torceanu. Pp. viii. and 72. 5s.
    VII.—Tibetan. By H. A. Jaschke. Pp. viii. and 104. 5s.
    VIII.—Danish. By E. C. Otté. Pp. viii. and 66. 2s. 6d.
    IX.—Turkish. By J. W. Redhouse. Pp. xii. and 204. 10s. 6d.
    X.—Swedish. By E. C. Otté. Pp. xii. and 70. 2s. 6d.
    XI.—Polish. By W. R. Morfill, M.A. Pp. viii. and 64. 3s. 6d.
    XII.—Pali. By E. Müller, Ph.D. Pp. xvi. and 144. 7s. 6d.
    XIII.—Sanskrit. By H. Edgren. Pp. xii.-178. 10s. 6d.
    XIV.—Grammaire Albanaise. Par P. W. Pp. x. and 170. 7s. 6d.
    XV.—Japanese. By B. H. Chamberlain. Pp. viii. and 108. 5s.
    XVI.—Serbian. By W. R. Morfill, M.A. Pp. viii. and 72. 4s. 6d.
    XVII.—Cuneiform. By G. Bertin. Pp. viii-118. 5s.

(Others in Preparation.)

Trübner's Catalogue of Dictionaries and Grammars of the Principal Languages and Dialects of the World. Considerably enlarged and revised, with an Alphabetical Index. A Guide for Students and Booksellers. Second Edition, 8vo. pp. viii. and 170, cloth. 1882. 5s.

⁎ The first edition, consisting of 64 pp., contained 1,100 titles; the new edition consists of 170 pp., and contains 3,000 titles.

Trumpp.—Grammar of the Pashto, or Language of the Afghans, compared with the Iranian and North-Indian Idioms. By Dr. Ernest Trumpp. 8vo. sewed, pp. xvi. and 412. 21s.

Weber.—Indian Literature. See "Trübner's Oriental Series," p. 3.

Wedgwood.—On the Origin of Language. By Hensleigh Wedgwood, late Fellow of Christ's College, Cambridge. Fcap. 8vo. pp. 172, cloth. 3s. 6d.

Whitney.—LANGUAGE AND ITS STUDY, with especial reference to the Indo-European Family of Languages. Seven Lectures by W. D. WHITNEY, Professor of Sanskrit, Yale College. Edited with Introduction, Notes, Grimm's Law with Illustration, Index, etc., by the Rev. R. MORRIS, M.A., LL.D. Second Edition. Cr. 8vo. cl., pp. xxii. and 318. 1881. 5s.

Whitney.—LANGUAGE AND THE STUDY OF LANGUAGE: Twelve Lectures on the Principles of Linguistic Science. By W. D. WHITNEY. Fourth Edition, augmented by an Analysis. Crown 8vo. cloth, pp. xii. and 504. 1884. 10s. 6d.

Whitney.—ORIENTAL AND LINGUISTIC STUDIES. By W. D. WHITNEY, Cr. 8vo. cl. 1874. Pp. x. and 418. 12s.
First Series. The Veda; the Avesta; the Science of Language.
Second Series.—The East and West—Religion and Mythology—Orthography and Phonology—Hindú Astronomy. Pp. 446. 12s.

GRAMMARS, DICTIONARIES, TEXTS, AND TRANSLATIONS.

AFRICAN LANGUAGES.

Bentley.—DICTIONARY AND GRAMMAR OF THE KONGO LANGUAGE, AS Spoken at San Salvador, the Ancient Capital of the Old Kongo Empire, West Africa. Compiled by the Rev. W. HOLMAN BENTLEY, Missionary of the Baptist Missionary Society on the Kongo. With an Introduction by R. N. Cust, Hon. Secretary of the Royal Asiatic Society. Demy 8vo, pp. xxiv. and 718, with Table of Concords, cloth. 1888. £1 1s.

Bleek.—A COMPARATIVE GRAMMAR OF SOUTH AFRICAN LANGUAGES. By W. H. I. BLEEK, Ph.D. Volume I. I. Phonology. II. The Concord. Section 1. The Noun. 8vo. pp. xxxvi. and 322, cloth. 1869. £4 4s.

Bleek.—A BRIEF ACCOUNT OF BUSHMAN FOLK LORE AND OTHER TEXTS. By W. H. I. BLEEK, Ph.D., etc., etc. Folio sd., pp. 21. 1875. 2s. 6d.

Bleek.—REYNARD THE FOX IN SOUTH AFRICA; or, Hottentot Fables. Translated from the Original Manuscript in Sir George Grey's Library. By Dr. W. H. I. BLEEK, Librarian to the Grey Library, Cape Town, Cape of Good Hope. Post. 8vo., pp. xxxi. and 94, cloth. 1864. 3s. 6d.

Callaway.—IZINGANEKWANE, NENSUMANSUMANE, NEZINDABA, ZABANTU (Nursery Tales, Traditions, and Histories of the Zulus). In their own words, with a Translation into English, and Notes. By the Rev. H. CALLAWAY, M.D.

Callaway. — THE RELIGIOUS SYSTEM OF THE AMAZULU.
Part I.—Unkulunkulu; or, the Tradition of Creation as existing among the Amazulu and other Tribes of South Africa, in their own words, with a translation into English, and Notes. By the Rev. Canon CALLAWAY, M.D. 8vo. pp. 128 sewed. 1868. 4s.
Part II.—Amatongo; or, Ancestor Worship, as existing among the Amazulu, in their own words, with a translation into English, and Notes. By the Rev. CANON CALLAWAY, M.D. 1869. 8vo. pp. 127, sewed. 1869. 4s.
Part III.—Izinyanga Zokubula; or, Divination, as existing among the Amazulu, in their own words. With a Translation into English, and Notes. By the Rev. Canon CALLAWAY, M.D. 8vo pp. 150. sewed. 1870. 4s.
Part IV.—Abatakati, or Medical Magic and Witchcraft. 8vo. pp. 40, sewed. 1s. 6d.

Christaller.—A Dictionary, English, Tshi, (Asante), Akra; Tshi (Chwee), comprising as dialects Akán (Asànté, Akém, Akuapém, etc.) and Fànté; Akra (Accra), connected with Adangme; Gold Coast, West Africa.

   Enyiresi, Twi né Ǹkraṅ | Eṅliši, Otšǔi ke Gã
   nsem - asekyere - ṅhōma. | wiemǫi - aṅišitšōmǫ- wolo.

By the Rev. J. G. Christaller, Rev. C. W. Locher, Rev. J. Zimmermann. 16mo. 7s. 6d.

Christaller.—A Grammar of the Asante and Fante Language, called Tshi (Chwee, Twi): based on the Akuapem Dialect, with reference to the other (Akan and Fante) Dialects. By Rev. J. G. Christaller. 8vo. pp. xxiv. and 203. 1875. 10s. 6d.

Christaller.—Dictionary of the Asante and Fante Language, called Tshi (Chwee, Twi). With a Grammatical Introduction and Appendices on the Geography of the Gold Coast, and other Subjects. By Rev. J. G. Christaller. Demy 8vo. pp. xxviii. and 672, cloth. 1882. £1 5s.

Cust.—Sketch of the Modern Languages of Africa. See "Trübner's Oriental Series," page 6.

Döhne.—The Four Gospels in Zulu. By the Rev. J. L. Döhne, Missionary to the American Board C.F.M. 8vo. pp. 208, cloth. 1866. 5s.

Döhne.—A Zulu-Kafir Dictionary, etymologically explained, with copious Illustrations and examples, preceded by an introduction on the Zulu-Kafir Language. By the Rev. J. L. Döhne. Royal 8vo. pp. xlii. and 418, sewed. Cape Town, 1857. 21s.

Grey.—Handbook of African, Australian, and Polynesian Philology. See page 49.

Grout.—The Isizulu: a Grammar of the Zulu Language; accompanied with an Historical Introduction, also with an Appendix. By Rev. Lewis Grout. 8vo. pp. lii. and 432, cloth. 21s.

Hahn.—Tsuni-||Goam. See "Trübner's Oriental Series," page 5.

Kolbe.—A Language Study Based on Bantu; or, An Inquiry into the Laws of Root-Formation, the Original Plural, the Sexual Dual, and the Principles of Word-Comparison; with Tables Illustrating the Primitive Pronominal System restored in the African Bantu Family of Speech. By the Rev. F. W. Kolbe, of the London Missionary Society, formerly of the Rhenish Herero Mission, Author of "An English-Herero Dictionary." Post 8vo. pp. viii. and 97, with Four Tables, cloth. 1888. 6s.

Krapf.—Dictionary of the Suahili Language. Compiled by the Rev. Dr. L. Krapf, Missionary C.M.S. in East Africa. With an Outline of Suahili Grammar. Royal 8vo. pp. xl.-434, cloth. 1882. 30s.

Steere.—Short Specimens of the Vocabularies of Three Unpublished African Languages (Gindo, Zaramo, and Angazidja). Collected by Edward Steere, LL.D. 12mo. pp. 20. 6d.

Steere.—Collections for a Handbook of the Nyamwezi Language, as spoken at Unyanyembe. By E. Steere, LL.D. Fcap. pp. 100, cloth. 1s. 6d.

Tindall.—A Grammar and Vocabulary of the Namaqua-Hottentot Language. By Henry Tindall, Wesleyan Missionary. 8vo. pp. 124, sewed. 6s.

Zulu Izaga; That is, Proverbs, or Out-of-the-Way Sayings of the Zulus. Collected, Translated, and interpreted by a Zulu Missionary. Crown 8vo. pp. iv. and 32, sewed. 2s. 6d.

ALBANIAN.

Grammaire Albanaise.—Par P. W. Crown 8vo. pp. viii. 170, cloth. 1887. 7s. 6d.

AMERICAN LANGUAGES.

Aboriginal American Literature, Library of. Edited by D. G. BRINTON, M.D. 8vo. cloth. 1. The Chronicles of the Mayas. pp. 280. £1 1s. (Or if with Set, 12s.) 2. The Iroquois Book of Rites. Edited by H. HALE. pp. 222. 12s. 3. The Comedy-Ballet of Güegüence. pp. 146. 10s. 4. A Migration Legend of the Creek Indians. By A. S. GATSCHET. pp. 252. 12s. 5. The Lenape and their Legends. By D. G. BRINTON, M.D. 8vo. pp. 262. 12s. 6. The Annals of the Cakchiquels. The Text, with a Translation, Notes and Introduction, by D. G. BRINTON, M.D. pp. 240. 12s. 7. Ancient Nahuatl Poetry. Text and Translation by D. G. BRINTON, M.D. pp. 182. 12s.

Byington.—GRAMMAR OF THE CHOCTAW LANGUAGE. By the Rev. CYRUS BYINGTON. Edited from the Original MSS. in Library of the American Philosophical Society, by D. G. BRINTON, M.D. Cr. 8vo. sewed, pp. 56. 7s. 6d.

Ellis.—PERUVIA SCYTHICA. See page 49.

Howse.—A GRAMMAR OF THE CREE LANGUAGE. With which is combined an analysis of the Chippeway Dialect. By JOSEPH HOWSE, Esq., F.R.G.S. 8vo. pp. xx. and 324, cloth. 7s. 6d.

Markham.—OLLANTA: A DRAMA IN THE QUICHUA LANGUAGE. Text, Translation, and Introduction. By CLEMENTS R. MARKHAM, F.R.G.S. Crown 8vo., pp. 128, cloth. 1871. 7s. 6d.

Markham.—A MEMOIR OF THE LADY ANA DE OSORIO, Countess of Chinchon, and Vice-Queen of Peru, A.D. 1629-39. With a Plea for the correct spelling of the Chinchona Genus. By C. R. MARKHAM, C.B., Member of the Imperial Academy Naturæ Curiosorum, with the Cognomen of Chinchon. Small 4to. pp. xii. and 100. With two Coloured Plates, Map and Illustrations. Handsomely bound. 1874. 28s.

Matthews.—ETHNOLOGY AND PHILOLOGY OF THE HIDATSA INDIANS. By WASHINGTON MATTHEWS, Assistant Surgeon, U.S. Army. 8vo. cloth. £1 11s. 6d.
CONTENTS:—Ethnography, Philology, Grammar, Dictionary, and English-Hidatsa Vocabulary.

Nodal.—LOS VINCULOS DE OLLANTA Y CUSI-KCUYLLOR. DRAMA EN QUICHUA. Obra Compilada y Espurgada con la Version Castellana al Frente de su Testo por el Dr. JOSÉ FERNANDEZ NODAL, Abogado de los Tribunales de Justicia de la República del Perú. Bajo los Auspicios de la Redentora Sociedad de Filántropos para Mejoror la Suerte de los Aborijenes Peruanos. Roy. 8vo. bds. pp. 70. 1874. 7s. 6d.

Nodal.—ELEMENTOS DE GRAMÁTICA QUICHUA Ó IDIOMA DE LOS YNCAS. Bajo los Auspicios de la Redentora. Sociedad de Filántropos para mejorar la suerte de los Aborijenes Peruanos. Por el Dr. Jose FERNANDEZ NODAL, Abogado de los Tribunales de Justicia de la República del Perú. Royal 8vo. cloth, pp. xvi. and 441. Appendix, pp. 9. £1 1s.

Ollanta: A DRAMA IN THE QUICHUA LANGUAGE. See under MARKHAM and under NODAL.

Pimentel.—Cuadro descriptivo y comparativo de las Lenguas Indigenas de México, o Tratado de Filologia Mexicana. Par Francisco Pimentel. 2 Edicion unica completa. 3 Volumes 8vo. *Mexico*, 1875. £2 2s.

Thomas.—The Theory and Practice of Creole Grammar. By J. J. Thomas. Port of Spain (Trinidad), 1869. 1 vol. 8vo. bds. pp. viii. and 135. 12s.

ANGLO-SAXON.

Harrison and Baskervill.— A Handy Dictionary of Anglo-Saxon Poetry. Based on Groschopp's Grein. Edited, Revised, and Corrected, with Grammatical Appendix, List of Irregular Verbs, and Brief Etymological Features. By J. A. Harrison, Prof. of English and Modern Languages in Washington and Lee University, Virginia; and W. Baskervill, Ph.D. Lips., Prof. of English Language and Literature in Vanderbilt University, Nashville, Ten. Square 8vo. pp. 318, cloth. 1886. 12s.

March.—A Comparative Grammar of the Anglo-Saxon Language; in which its forms are illustrated by those of the Sanskrit, Greek, Latin, Gothic, Old Saxon, Old Friesic, Old Norse, and Old High-German. By Francis A. March, LL.D. Demy 8vo. cloth, pp. xi. and 253. 1877. 10s.

March.—Introduction to Anglo-Saxon. An Anglo-Saxon Reader. With Philological Notes, a Brief Grammar, and a Vocabulary. By F. A. March, LL.D. 8vo. pp. viii. and 166, cloth. 1870. 7s. 6d.

Rask.—A Grammar of the Anglo-Saxon Tongue. From the Danish of Erasmus Rask, Professor of Literary History in, and Librarian to, the University of Copenhagen, etc. By B. Thorpe. Third edition, corrected and improved, with Plate. Post 8vo. pp. vi. and 192, cloth. 1879. 5s. 6d.

Wright.—Anglo-Saxon and Old-English Vocabularies. See page 79.

ARABIC.

Ahlwardt.—The Diváns of the Six Ancient Arabic Poets, Ennábiga, 'Antara, Tarafa, Zuhair, 'Alqama, and Imruolqais; chiefly according to the MSS. of Paris, Gotha, and Leyden, and the collection of their Fragments: with a complete list of the various readings of the Text. Edited by W. Ahlwardt. 8vo. pp. xxx. 340, sewed. 1870. 12s.

Alif Lailat wa Lailat.—The Arabian Nights. 4 vols. 4to. pp. 495, 493, 142, 434. Cairo, A.H. 1279 (1862). £3 3s.

This celebrated Edition of the Arabian Nights is now, for the first time, offered at a price which makes it accessible to Scholars of limited means.

Athar-ul-Adhár—Traces of Centuries; or, Geographical and Historical Arabic Dictionary, by Selim Khuri and Selim Sh-hade. Geographical Parts I. to V., Historical Parts I. and II. 4to. pp. 980 and 384. Price 7s. 6d. each part. [*In course of publication.*

Badger.—An English-Arabic Lexicon, in which the equivalents for English words and Idiomatic Sentences are rendered into literary and colloquial Arabic. By G. P. Badger, D.C.L. 4to. cloth, pp. xii. and 1248. 1880. £4.

Butrus-al-Bustány.—كتاب دائرة المَعَارِف. An Arabic Encylopædia of Universal Knowledge, by BUTRUS-AL-BUSTÁNY, the celebrated compiler of Mohit ul Mohit (محيط المحيط), and Katr el Mohit (قطر المحيط). This work will be completed in from 12 to 15 Vols., of which Vols. I. to VII. are ready, Vol. I. contains letter ا to اب; Vol. II. اب to ار; Vol. III. ار to اخ Vol. IV. اخ to اي Vol. V. با to بي Vol. VI با to حر. Vol. VII. حر to دم. Vol. VIII. دم to رو. IX. رو to سا. Small folio, cloth, pp. 800 each. £1 11s. 6d. per Vol.

Carletti.—MÉTHODE THÉORICO-PRATIQUE DE LANGUE ARABE. Par P. V. CARLETTI. 4to. pp. 318, wrapper. 10s.

Cotton.—ARABIC PRIMER. Consisting of 180 Short Sentences containing 30 Primary Words prepared according to the Vocal System of Studying Language. By General SIR A. COTTON, K.C.S.I. Cr. 8vo. cloth, pp. 38. 2s.

Hassoun.—THE DIWAN OF HATIM TAI, an Old Arabic Poet of the Sixth Century of the Christian Era. Edited by R. HASSOUN. With Illustrations. 4to. pp. 43. 3s. 6d.

Jami, Mulla.—SALAMAN U ABSAL. An Allegorical Romance; being one of the Seven Poems entitled the Haft Aurang of Mullá Jámí, now first edited from the Collation of Eight Manuscripts in the Library of the India House, and in private collections, with various readings. by FORBES FALCONER, M.A., M.R.A.S. 4to. cloth, pp. 92. 1850. 7s. 6d.

Koran (The). Arabic text, lithographed in Oudh, A.H. 1284 (1867). 16mo. pp. 942. 6s.

Koran.—EXTRACTS FROM THE CORAN IN THE ORIGINAL, WITH ENGLISH RENDERING. Compiled by Sir WILLIAM MUIR, K.C.S.I., LL.D., Author of the "Life of Mahomet." Second Edition. Crown 8vo. pp. 72, cloth. 1885. 2s. 6d.

Koran.—See Wherry, page 5.

Ko-ran (Selections from the).—See "Trübner's Oriental Series," p. 3.

Leitner.—INTRODUCTION TO A PHILOSOPHICAL GRAMMAR OF ARABIC. Being an Attempt to Discover a Few Simp'e Principles in Arabic Grammar. By G. W. LEITNER. 8vo. sewed, pp. 52. *Lahore.* 4s.

Morley.—A DESCRIPTIVE CATALOGUE of the HISTORICAL MANUSCRIPTS in the ARABIC and PERSIAN LANGUAGES preserved in the Library of the Royal Asiatic Society of Great Britain and Ireland. By WILLIAM H. MORLEY, M.R.A.S. 8vo. pp. viii. and 160, sewed. London, 1854. 2s. 6d.

Muhammed.—THE LIFE OF MUHAMMED. Based on Muhammed Ibn Ishak. By Abd El Malik Ibn Hisham. Edited by Dr. FERDINAND WÜSTENFELD. The Arabic Text. 8vo. pp. 1026, sewed. Price 21s. Introduction, Notes, and Index in German. 8vo. pp. lxxii. and 266, sewed. 7s. 6d. Each part sold separately.

The text based on the Manuscripts of the Berlin, Leipsic, Gotha and Leyden Libraries, has been carefully revised by the learned editor, and printed with the utmost exactness.

Newman.—A HANDBOOK OF MODERN ARABIC, consisting of a Practical Grammar, with numerous Examples, Dialogues, and Newspaper Extracts, in a European Type. By F. W. NEWMAN, Emeritus Professor of University College, London. Post 8vo. pp. xx. and 192, cloth. 1866. 6s.

Newman.—A Dictionary of Modern Arabic —1. Anglo-Arabic Dictionary. 2. Anglo-Arabic Vocabulary. 3. Arabo-English Dictionary. By F. W. Newman, Emeritus Professor of University College, London. In 2 vols. crown 8vo., pp. xvi. and 376—464, cloth. £1 1s.

Palmer.—The Song of the Reed; and other Pieces. By E. H. Palmer, M.A., Cambridge. Crown 8vo. cloth, pp. 208. 1876. 5s.

Among the Contents will be found translations from Hafiz, from Omer el Kheiyám, and from other Persian as well as Arabic poets.

Palmer.—Hindustani, Persian, and Arabic Grammar Simplified. By E. H. Palmer, M.A., Cambridge. Second Edition. Crown 8vo. pp. viii.-104, cloth. 1885. 5s.

Rogers.—Notice on the Dinars of the Abbasside Dynasty. By Edward Thomas Rogers, late H.M. Consul, Cairo. 8vo. pp. 44, with a Map and four Autotype Plates. 5s.

Schemeil.—El Mubtaker; or, First Born. (In Arabic, printed at Beyrout). Containing Five Comedies, called Comedies of Fiction, on Hopes and Judgments, in Twenty-six Poems of 1092 Verses, showing the Seven Stages of Life, from man's conception unto his death and burial. By Emin Ibrahim Schemeil. In one volume, 4to. pp. 166, sewed. 1870. 5s.

Syed Ahmad.—Life of Mohammed. See Muhammed.

Wherry.—Commentary on the Quran. See page 5.

ASSAMESE.

Bronson.—A Dictionary in Assamese and English. Compiled by M. Bronson, American Baptist Missionary. 8vo. calf, pp. viii. and 609. £2 2s.

*** Catalogue of Assamese Books to be had of Messrs. Trübner & Co., Post free for one penny stamp.

ASSYRIAN (Cuneiform, Accad, Babylonian).

Bertin.—Abridged Grammars of the Languages of the Cuneiform Inscriptions. By G. Bertin, M.R.A.S. I. A Sumero-Akkadian Grammar. II. An Assyro-Babylonian Grammar. III. A Vannic Grammar. IV. A Medic Grammar. V. An Old Persian Grammar. Crown 8vo. pp. viii.-118, cloth. 1888. 5s.

Budge.—Assyrian Texts, Selected and Arranged, with Philological Notes. By E. A. Budge, B.A., Assyrian Exhibitioner, Christ's College, Cambridge. Crown 4to. cloth, pp. viii. and 44. 1880. 7s. 6d.

Budge.—The History of Esarhaddon. See "Trübner's Oriental Series," p. 4.

Catalogue (A) of leading Books on Egypt and Egyptology, and on Assyria and Assyriology, to be had at the affixed prices, of Trübner and Co. pp. 40. 1880. 1s.

Clarke.—Researches in Pre-historic and Proto-historic Comparative Philology, Mythology, and Archæology, in connexion with the Origin of Culture in America and the Accad or Sumerian Families. By Hyde Clarke. Demy 8vo. sewed, pp. xi. and 74. 1875. 2s. 6d.

Cooper.—An Archaic Dictionary, Biographical, Historical and Mythological; from the Egyptian and Etruscan Monuments, and Papyri. By W. R. Cooper. London, 1876. 8vo. cloth. 15s.

Hincks.—Specimen Chapters of an Assyrian Grammar. By the late Rev. E. Hincks, D.D., Hon. M.R.A.S. 8vo., sewed. pp. 44. 1s.

Lenormant (F.)—Chaldean Magic; its Origin and Development. Translated from the French. With considerable Additions by the Author. London, 1877. 8vo. pp. 440. 12s.

Luzzatto.—Grammar of the Biblical Chaldaic Language and the Talmud Babylonical Idioms. By S. D. Luzzatto. Translated from the Italian by J. S. Goldammer. Cr. 8vo. cl., pp. 122. 7s. 6d.

Rawlinson.—Notes on the Early History of Babylonia. By Colonel Rawlinson, C.B. 8vo. sd., pp. 48. 1s.

Rawlinson.—A Commentary on the Cuneiform Inscriptions of Babylonia and Assyria, including Readings of the Inscription on the Nimrud Obelisk, and Brief Notice of the Ancient Kings of Nineveh and Babylon, by Major H. C. Rawlinson. 8vo. pp. 84. sewed. London, 1850. 2s. 6d.

Rawlinson.—Inscription of Tiglath Pileser I., King of Assyria, B.C. 1150, as translated by Sir H. Rawlinson, Fox Talbot, Esq., Dr. Hincks. and Dr. Oppert. Published by the Royal Asiatic Society. 8vo. sd., pp. 74. 2s.

Rawlinson.—Outlines of Assyrian History, from the Inscriptions of Nineveh. By Lieut. Col. Rawlinson, C.B., followed by some Remarks by A. H. Layard, Esq., D.C.L. 8vo., pp. xliv., sewed. London, 1852. 1s.

Records of the Past: being English Translations of the Assyrian and the Egyptian Monuments. Published under the sanction of the Society of Biblical Archæology. Edited by S. Birch. Vols. 1 to 12. 1874 to 1879. £1 11s. 6d. or 3s. 6d. each vol.

Renan.—An Essay on the Age and Antiquity of the Book of Nabathæan Agriculture. To which is added an Inaugural Lecture on the Position of the Shemitic Nations in the History of Civilization. By M. Ernest Renan, Membre de l'Institut. Crown 8vo., pp. xvi. and 148, cloth. 3s. 6d.

Sayce.—An Assyrian Grammar for Comparative Purposes. By A. H. Sayce, M.A. 12mo. cloth, pp. xvi. and 188. 1872. 7s. 6d.

Sayce.—An Elementary Grammar and Reading Book of the Assyrian Language, in the Cuneiform Character: containing the most complete Syllabary yet extant, and which will serve also as a Vocabulary of both Accadian and Assyrian. London, 1875. 4to. cloth. 9s.

Sayce.—Lectures upon the Assyrian Language and Syllabary. London, 1877. Large 8vo. 9s. 6d.

Sayce.—Babylonian Literature. Lectures. London, 1877. 8vo. 4s.

Smith.—The Assyrian Eponym Canon; containing Translations of the Documents of the Comparative Chronology of the Assyrian and Jewish Kingdoms, from the Death of Solomon to Nebuchadnezzar. By E. Smith. London, 1876. 8vo. 9s.

AUSTRALIAN LANGUAGES.

Grey.—Handbook of African, Australian, and Polynesian Philology. See page 49.

BASQUE.

Ellis.—Sources of the Basque and Etruscan Languages. See p. 48.

Van Eys.—Outlines of Basque Grammar. By W. J. Van Eys. Crown 8vo. pp. xii. and 52, cloth. 1883. 3s. 6d.

BENGALI.

Catalogue of Bengali Books, sold by Messrs. Trübner & Co., post free for penny stamp.

Browne.—A Bángálí Primer, in Roman Character. By J. F. Browne, B.C.S. Crown 8vo. pp. 32, cloth. 1881. 2s.

Charitabali (The); or, Instructive Biography by Isvarachandra Vidyásagara. With a Vocabulary of all the Words occurring in the Text, by J. F. Blumhardt, Bengali Lecturer University College, London; and Teacher of Bengali Cambridge University. 12mo. pp. 120-iv.-48, cloth. 1884. 5s.

Mitter.—Bengali and English Dictionary for the Use of Schools. Revised and improved. 8vo. cloth. Calcutta, 1860. 7s. 6d.

Sykes.—English and Bengali Dictionary for the Use of Schools. Revised by Gopee Kissen Mitter. 8vo. cloth. Calcutta, 1874. 7s. 6d.

Yates.—A Bengálí Grammar. By the late Rev. W. Yates, D.D. Reprinted, with improvements, from his Introduction to the Bengálí Language. Edited by I. Wenger. Fcap. 8vo. bds, pp. iv. and 150. Calcutta, 1864. 4s.

BIHARI.

Catalogue of Bihari Books, sold by Messrs. Trübner & Co., post free for penny stamp.

Grierson.—Seven Grammars of the Dialects and Sub-Dialects of the Bihárí Language Spoken in the Province of Bihár, in the Eastern Portion of the N. W. Provinces, and in the Northern Portion of the Central Provinces. Compiled under orders of the Government of Bengal. By George E. Grierson, B.C.S., Joint Magistrate of Patna. Part 1. Introductory; 2. Bhojpúri; 3. Magadhí; 4. Maithil-Bhojpuri; 5. South Maithili; 6. South Maithil-Magadhi; 7. Not yet Published. Fcap. 4to. cloth. Price 2s. 6d. each.

Hoernle and Grierson.—Comparative Dictionary of the Bihari Language. Compiled by A. F. R. Hoernle, of the Bengal Educational Service, and G. A. Grierson, of Her Majesty's Bengal Civil Service. (Published under the Patronage of the Government of Bengal.) Part I. From A to Ag'mani. 4to. pp. 106, wrapper. 1885. 5s.

BRAHOE (Brahui).

Bellew.—From the Indus to the Tigris. A Narrative; together with Synoptical Grammar and Vocabulary of the Brahoe language. See p. 19.

Duka.—An Essay on the Bráhúí Grammar. By Dr. T. Duka. Demy 8vo. pp. 78, paper. 1887. 3s. 6d.

BURMESE.

Hough's GENERAL OUTLINES OF GEOGRAPHY (in Burmese). Re-written and enlarged by Rev. JAS. A. HASWELL. Large 8vo. pp. 368. Rangoon, 1874. 9s.

Judson.—A DICTIONARY, English and Burmese, Burmese and English. By A. JUDSON. 2 vols. 8vo. pp. iv. and 968, and viii. and 786. 25s. each.

Judson.—A GRAMMAR OF THE BURMESE LANGUAGE. 8vo. pp. 52, boards. *Rangoon*, 1883. 3s.

Sloan.—A PRACTICAL METHOD with the Burmese Language. By W. H. SLOAN. Second Edition. Large 8vo. pp. 232. Rangoon, 1887. 12s. 6d.

We-than-da-ya, THE STORY OF, A BUDDHIST LEGEND. Sketched from the Burmese Version of the Pali Text. By L. ALLAN GOSS, Inspector of Schools, Burma. With five Illustrations by a native artist. 4to. pp. x.—80, paper. 1886. 5s.

CHINESE.

Acheson.—AN INDEX TO DR. WILLIAMS'S "SYLLABIC DICTIONARY OF THE CHINESE LANGUAGE." Arranged according to Sir THOMAS WADE's System of Orthography. Royal 8vo. pp. viii. and 124. Half bound. Hongkong. 1879. 18s.

Baldwin.—A MANUAL OF THE FOOCHOW DIALECT. By Rev. C. C. BALDWIN, of the American Board Mission. 8vo. pp. viii.-256. 18s.

Balfour.—TAOIST TEXTS. See page 41.

Balfour.—THE DIVINE CLASSIC OF NAN-HUA. Being the Works of Chuang-Tsze, Taoist Philosopher. With an Excursus, and copious Annotations in English and Chinese. By H. BALFOUR, F.R.G.S. Demy 8vo. pp. xxxviii. and 426, cloth. 1881. 14s.

Balfour.—WAIFS AND STRAYS FROM THE FAR EAST; being a Series of Disconnected Essays on Matters relating to China. By F. H. Balfour. 8vo. pp. 224, cloth. 1876. 10s. 6d.

Balfour.—LEAVES FROM MY CHINESE SCRAP BOOK. See page 6.

Ball.—THE CANTONESE-MADE-EASY VOCABULARY. A small Dictionary in English and Cantonese, containing only Words and Phrases used in the Spoken Language, with the Classifiers Indicated for each Noun, and Definitions of the Different Shades of Meaning; as well as Notes on the Different Uses of some of the Words where Ambiguity might Otherwise Arise. By J. DYER BALL, M.R.A.S., etc., of H.M.C.S., Hong Kong. Royal 8vo. pp. 6—27, wrappers. 5s.

Ball.—EASY SENTENCES IN THE CANTONESE DIALECT, WITH A VOCABULARY. Being the Lessons in "Cantonese-made-easy" and "The Cantonese-made-easy Vocabulary." By J. DYER BALL, M.R.A.S., etc., of H.M.C.S., Hong Kong. Royal 8vo. pp. 74, paper. 7s. 6d.

Ball.—AN ENGLISH-CANTONESE POCKET VOCABULARY. Containing Common Words and Phrases, Printed without the Chinese Characters, or Tonic Marks, the Sounds of the Chinese Words being Represented by an English Spelling as far as Practicable. By J. DYER BALL, M.R.A.S., etc., Author of "Cantonese-made-easy." Crown 8vo. pp. 8—24, cloth. 4s.

Beal.—THE BUDDHIST TRIPITAKA, as it is known in China and Japan. A Catalogue and Compendious Report. By SAMUEL BEAL, B.A. Folio, sewed, pp. 117. 7s. 6d.

Beal.—The Dhammapada. See "Trübner's Oriental Series," page 3.

Beal.—Buddhist Literature. See pages 6, 41 and 42.

Bretschneider.—See page 27.

Chalmers.—The Origin of the Chinese; an Attempt to Trace the connection of the Chinese with Western Nations, in their Religion, Superstitions, Arts, Language, and Traditions. By John Chalmers, A.M. Foolscap 8vo. cloth. pp. 78. 5s.

Chalmers.—A Concise Khang-hsi Chinese Dictionary. By the Rev. J. Chalmers, LL.D., Canton. Three Vols. Royal 8vo. bound in Chinese style, pp. 1000. £1 10s.

Chalmers.—The Structure of Chinese Characters, under 300 Primary Forms; after the Shwoh-wan, 100 A.D., and the Phonetic Shwoh-wan 1833. By John Chalmers, M.A., LL.D. 8vo. pp. x-199, with a plate, cloth. 1882. 12s. 6d.

China Review; or, Notes and Queries on the Far East. Published bi-monthly. Edited by E. J. Eitel. 4to. Subscription, £1 10s. per volume.

Dennys.—A Handbook of the Canton Vernacular of the Chinese Language. Being a Series of Introductory Lessons, for Domestic and Business Purposes. By N. B. Dennys, M.R.A.S., Ph.D. 8vo. cloth, pp. 4, 195, and 31. £1 10s.

Dennys.—The Folk-Lore of China, and its Affinities with that of the Aryan and Semitic Races. By N. B. Dennys, Ph.D., author of "A Handbook of the Canton Vernacular," etc. 8vo. cloth, pp. 168. 10s. 6d.

Douglas.—Chinese-English Dictionary of the Vernacular or Spoken Language of Amoy, with the principal variations of the Chang-Chew and Chin-Chew Dialects. By the Rev. Carstairs Douglas, M.A., LL.D., Glasg. High quarto, cloth, double columns, pp. 632. 1873. £3 3s.

Douglas.—Chinese Language and Literature. Two Lectures delivered at the Royal Institution, by R. K. Douglas, of the British Museum, and Prof. of Chinese at King's College. Cr. 8vo. pp. 118, cl. 1875. 5s.

Douglas.—The Life of Jenghiz Khan. Translated from the Chinese, with an Introduction, by R. K. Douglas, of the British Museum. Crown 8vo. pp. xxxvi.-106, cloth. 1877. 5s.

Edkins.—A Grammar of Colloquial Chinese, as exhibited in the Shanghai Dialect. By J. Edkins, B.A. Second edition, corrected. 8vo. half-calf, pp. viii. and 225. Shanghai, 1868. 21s.

Edkins.—A Vocabulary of the Shanghai Dialect. By J. Edkins. 8vo. half-calf, pp. vi. and 151. Shanghai, 1869. 21s.

Edkins.—Religion in China. A Brief Account of the Three Religions of the Chinese. By Joseph Edkins, D.D. Post 8vo. cloth. 7s. 6d.

Edkins.—A Grammar of the Chinese Colloquial Language, commonly called the Mandarin Dialect. By Joseph Edkins. Second edition. 8vo. half-calf, pp. viii. and 279. Shanghai, 1864. £1 10s.

Edkins.—Introduction to the Study of the Chinese Characters. By J. Edkins, D.D., Peking, China. Roy. 8vo. pp. 340, paper boards. 18s.

Edkins.—CHINA'S PLACE IN PHILOLOGY. An attempt to show that the Languages of Europe and Asia have a common origin. By the Rev. JOSEPH EDKINS. Crown 8vo., pp. xxiii.—403, cloth. 10s. 6d.

Edkins.—CHINESE BUDDHISM. See "Trübner's Oriental Series," p. 4.

Edkins.—PROGRESSIVE LESSONS IN THE CHINESE SPOKEN LANGUAGE, with Lists of Common Words and Phrases, and an Appendix containing the Laws of Tones in the Pekin Dialect. Fourth Edition, 8vo. Shanghai, 1881. 12s.

Edkins.—THE EVOLUTION OF THE CHINESE LANGUAGE, as exemplifying the origin and growth of Human Speech. By JOSEPH EDKINS, D.D. Author of "Religion in China;" "Chinese Buddhism;" etc. Reprinted from the Journal of the Peking Oriental Society. 1887. 8vo. pp. xvi.—96. 3s. 6d.

Eitel.—CHINESE DICTIONARY IN THE CANTONESE DIALECT. By ERNEST JOHN EITEL, Ph.D. Tubing. I. to IV. 8vo. sewed, 12s. 6d. each.

Eitel.—HANDBOOK FOR THE STUDENT OF CHINESE BUDDHISM. By the Rev. E. J. EITEL, of the London Missionary Society. Cr. 8vo. pp. viii., 224, cl. 18s.

Eitel.—FENG-SHUI: or, The Rudiments of Natural Science in China. By Rev. E. J. EITEL, M.A., Ph.D. Demy 8vo. sewed, pp. vi. and 84. 6s.

Faber.—A SYSTEMATICAL DIGEST OF THE DOCTRINES OF CONFUCIUS, according to the Analects, Great Learning, and Doctrine of the Mean, with an Introduction on the Authorities upon Confucius and Confucianism. By ERNST FABER, Rhenish Missionary. Translated from the German by P. G. von Möllendorff. 8vo. sewed, pp. viii. and 131. 1875. 12s. 6d.

Faber.—INTRODUCTION TO THE SCIENCE OF CHINESE RELIGION. A Critique of Max Müller and other Authors. By E. FABER. 8vo. paper, pp. xii. and 154. Hong Kong, 1880. 7s. 6d.

Faber.—MIND OF MENCIUS. See "Trübner's Oriental Series," p. 5.

Ferguson.—CHINESE RESEARCHES. First Part: Chinese Chronology and Cycles. By T. FERGUSON. Cr. 8vo. pp. vii. and 274, sd. 1880. 10s. 6d.

Giles.—A DICTIONARY OF COLLOQUIAL IDIOMS IN THE MANDARIN DIALECT. By HERBERT A. GILES. 4to. pp. 65. £1 8s.

Giles.—THE SAN TZU CHING; or, Three Character Classic; and the Ch'Ien Tsu Wen; or, Thousand Character Essay. Metrically Translated by HERBERT A. GILES. 12mo. pp. 28. 2s. 6d.

Giles.—SYNOPTICAL STUDIES IN CHINESE CHARACTER. By HERBERT A. GILES. 8vo. pp. 118. 15s.

Giles.—CHINESE SKETCHES. By HERBERT A. GILES, of H.B.M.'s China Consular Service. 8vo. cl., pp. 204. 10s. 6d.

Giles.—A GLOSSARY OF REFERENCE ON SUBJECTS CONNECTED WITH THE Far East. By H. A. GILES, of H.M. China Consular Service. 8vo. sewed, pp. v.–183. 7s. 6d.

Giles.—CHINESE WITHOUT A TEACHER. Being a Collection of Easy and Useful Sentences in the Mandarin Dialect. With a Vocabulary. By HERBERT A. GILES. 12mo. pp. 60. 6s.

Hernisz.—A GUIDE TO CONVERSATION IN THE ENGLISH AND CHINESE LANGUAGES, for the use of Americans and Chinese in California and elsewhere. By STANISLAS HERNISZ. Square 8vo. pp. 274, sewed. 10s. 6d.

The Chinese characters contained in this work are from the collections of Chinese groups engraved on steel, and cast into moveable types, by Mr. Marcellin Legrand, engraver of the Imperial Printing Office at Paris. They are used by most of the missions to China.

Kidd.—Catalogue of the Chinese Library of the Royal Asiatic Society. By the Rev. S. Kidd. 8vo. pp. 58, sewed. 1s.

Kwong.—Kwong's Educational Series. By Kwong Ki Chiu, late Member of the Chinese Educational Commission in the United States, &c. In English and Chinese. All Post 8vo. cloth. First Reading Book. Illustrated with Cuts. pp. 162. 1885. 4s. First Conversation Book. pp. xxxii. and 248. 10s. Second Conversation Book. pp. xvi. and 406. 12s. Manual of Correspondence and Social Usages. pp. xxvi. and 276. 12s.

Legge.—The Chinese Classics. With a Translation, Critical and Exegetical Notes, Prolegomena, and Copious Indexes. By James Legge, D.D., of the London Missionary Society. 7 vols. Royal 8vo. cloth.
Vol. I. Confucian Analects, the Great Learning, and the Doctrine of the Mean. pp. 526. £2 2s. Vol. II. Works of Mencius. pp. 634. £2 2s. Vol. III. Part I. First Part of the Shoo-King, or the Books of Tang, the Books of Yu, the Books of Hea, the Books of Shang, and the Prolegomena. pp. viii. and 280. £2 2s. Vol. III. Part II. Fifth Part of the Shoo-King, or the Books of Chow, and the Indexes. pp. 281—736. £2 2s. Vol. IV. Part I. First Part of the She-King, or the Lessons from the States; and the Prolegomena. pp. 182-244. £2 2s. Vol. IV. Part II. The 2nd, 3rd and 4th Parts of the She-King, or the Minor Odes of the Kingdom, the Greater Odes of the Kingdom, the Sacrificial Odes and Praise-Songs, and the Indexes. pp. 540. £2 2s. Vol. V. Part I. Dukes Yin, Hwan, Chwang, Min, He, Wan, Seuen, and Ch'ing; and the Prolegomena. pp. xii, 148 and 110. £2 2s. Vol. V. Part II. Dukes Seang, Ch'aon, Ting, and Gai, with Tso's Appendix, and the Indexes. pp. 526. £2 2s.

Legge.—The Chinese Classics. Translated into English. With Preliminary Essays and Explanatory Notes. By James Legge, D.D., LL.D. Crown 8vo. cloth. Vol. I. The Life and Teachings of Confucius. pp. vi. and 338. 10s. 6d. Vol. II. The Life and Works of Mencius. pp. 412. 12s. Vol. III. The She King, or The Book of Poetry. pp. viii. and 432. 12s.

Legge.—Inaugural Lecture on the Constituting of a Chinese Chair in the University of Oxford, 1876, by Rev. James Legge, M.A., LL.D., Professor of Chinese at Oxford. 8vo. pp. 28, sewed. 6d.

Legge.—Confucianism in Relation to Christianity. A Paper Read before the Missionary Conference in Shanghai, on May 11, 1877. By Rev. James Legge, D.D., LL.D. 8vo. sewed, pp. 12. 1877. 1s. 6d.

Legge.—A Letter to Professor Max Müller, chiefly on the Translation into English of the Chinese Terms *Tî* and *Shang Tî*. By J. Legge, Professor of Chinese, Oxford. Crown 8vo. sewed, pp. 30. 1880. 1s.

Leland.—Fusang; or, the Discovery of America by Chinese Buddhist Priests in the Fifth Century. By Charles G. Leland. Cr. 8vo. cloth, pp. xix and 212. 1875. 7s. 6d.

Leland.—Pidgin-English Sing-Song; or Songs and Stories in the China-English Dialect. With a Vocabulary. By Charles G. Leland. Crown 8vo. pp. viii. and 140, cloth. 1876. 5s.

Lobscheid.—English and Chinese Dictionary, with the Punti and Mandarin Pronunciation. By the Rev. W. Lobscheid, Knight of Francis Joseph, etc. Folio, pp. viii. and 2016. In Four Parts. £8 8s.

Lobscheid.—Chinese and English Dictionary, Arranged according to the Radicals. By the Rev. W. Lobscheid, Knight of Francis Joseph, etc. Imp. 8vo. double columns, pp. 600, bound. £2 8s.

M'Clatchie.—CONFUCIAN COSMOGONY. A Translation (with the Chinese Text opposite) of section 49 (Treatise on Cosmogony) of the "Complete Works" of the Philosopher Choo-Foo-Tze, with Explanatory Notes. By the Rev. THOMAS M'CLATCHIE, M.A. Small 4to. pp. xviii. and 162. 1874. £1 1s.

Macgowan.—A MANUAL OF THE AMOY COLLOQUIAL. By Rev. J. MACGOWAN, of the London Missionary Society. Second Edition. 8vo. half-bound, pp. 206. Amoy, 1880. £1 10s.

Macgowan.—ENGLISH AND CHINESE DICTIONARY OF THE AMOY DIALECT. By Rev. J. MACGOWAN, London Missionary Society. Small 4to. half-bound, pp. 620. Amoy, 1883. £3 3s.

Maclay and Baldwin.—AN ALPHABETIC DICTIONARY OF THE CHINESE LANGUAGE IN THE FOOCHOW DIALECT. By Rev. R. S. MACLAY, D.D., of the Methodist Episcopal Mission, and Rev. C. C. BALDWIN, A.M., of the American Board of Mission. 8vo. half-bound, pp. 1132. Foochow, 1871. £4 4s.

Mayers.—THE ANGLO-CHINESE CALENDAR MANUAL. A Handbook of Reference for the Determination of Chinese Dates during the period from 1860 to 1879. With Comparative Tables of Annual and Mensual Designations, etc. Compiled by W. F. MAYERS, Chinese Secretary, H.B.M.'s Legation, Peking. 2nd Edition. Sewed, pp. 28. 7s. 6d.

Mayers.—THE CHINESE GOVERNMENT. A Manual of Chinese Titles, Categorically arranged, and Explained with an Appendix. By W. F. MAYERS, Chinese Secretary to H.B.M.'s Legation at Peking. Second Edition, with additions by G. M. H. Playfair, H.B.M. Vice-Consul, Shanghai. 8vo. cloth, pp. lxiv-158. 1886. 15s.

Medhurst.—CHINESE DIALOGUES, QUESTIONS, and FAMILIAR SENTENCES, literally translated into English, with a view to promote commercial intercourse and assist beginners in the Language. By the late W. H. MEDHURST, D.D. A new and enlarged Edition. 8vo. pp. 226. 18s.

Möllendorff.—MANUAL OF CHINESE BIBLIOGRAPHY, being a List of Works and Essays relating to China. By P. G. and O. F. VON MÖLLENDORFF, Interpreters to H.I.G.M.'s Consulates at Shanghai and Tientsin. 8vo. pp. viii. and 378. £1 10s.

Morrison.—A DICTIONARY OF THE CHINESE LANGUAGE. By the Rev. R. MORRISON, D.D. Two vols. Vol. I. pp. x. and 762; Vol. II. pp. 828, cloth. Shanghae, 1865. £6 6s.

Peking Gazette.—Translation of the Peking Gazette for 1872 to 1885, 8vo. cloth. 10s. 6d. each.

Piry.—LE SAINT EDIT, Etude de Littérature Chinoise. Préparée par A. THEOPHILE PIRY, du Service des Douanes Maritimes de Chine. Chinese Text with French Translation. 4to. cloth, pp. xx. and 320. 21s.

Playfair.—CITIES AND TOWNS OF CHINA. 25s. See page 37.

Ross.—A MANDARIN PRIMER. Being Easy Lessons for Beginners, Transliterated according to the European mode of using Roman Letters. By Rev. JOHN ROSS, Newchang. 8vo. wrapper, pp. 122. 7s. 6d.

Rudy.—THE CHINESE MANDARIN LANGUAGE, after Ollendorff's New Method of Learning Languages. By CHARLES RUDY. In 3 Volumes. Vol. I. Grammar. 8vo. pp. 248. £1 1s.

Scarborough.—A COLLECTION OF CHINESE PROVERBS. Translated and Arranged by WILLIAM SCARBOROUGH, Wesleyan Missionary, Hankow. With an Introduction, Notes, and Copious Index. Cr. 8vo. pp. xliv. and 278. 10s.6d.

Stent.—A CHINESE AND ENGLISH VOCABULARY IN THE PEKINESE DIALECT. By G. E. STENT. Second Edition, 8vo. pp. xii.-720, half bound. 1877. £2.

Stent.—A CHINESE AND ENGLISH POCKET DICTIONARY. By G. E. STENT. 16mo. pp. 250. 1874. 15s.

Vaughan.—The Manners and Customs of the Chinese of the Straits Settlements. By J. D. VAUGHAN. Royal 8vo. boards. Singapore, 1879. 7s. 6d.

Vissering.—ON CHINESE CURRENCY. Coin and Paper Money. With a Facsimile of a Bank Note. By W. Vissering. Royal 8vo. cloth, pp. xv. and 219. Leiden, 1877. 18s.

Williams.—A SYLLABIC DICTIONARY OF THE CHINESE LANGUAGE, arranged according to the Wu-Fang Yuen Yin, with the pronunciation of the Characters as heard in Peking, Canton, Amoy, and Shanghai. By S. WELLS WILLIAMS. 4to. cloth, pp. lxxiv. and 1252. 1874. £5 5s.

Wylie.—NOTES ON CHINESE LITERATURE; with introductory Remarks on the Progressive Advancement of the Art; and a list of translations from the Chinese, into various European Languages. By A. WYLIE, Agent of the British and Foreign Bible Society in China. 4to. pp. 296, cloth. Price, £1 16s.

COREAN.

Ross.—A COREAN PRIMER. Being Lessons in Corean on all Ordinary Subjects. Transliterated on the principles of the Mandarin Primer by the same author. By the Rev. JOHN ROSS, Newchang. Demy 8vo. stitched. pp. 90. 10s.

DANISH.

Otté.—HOW TO LEARN DANO-NORWEGIAN. A Manual for Students of Dano-Norwegian, and especially for Travellers in Scandinavia. Based upon the Ollendorffian System of teaching languages, and adapted for Self-Instruction. By E. C. OTTÉ. Second Edition. Crown 8vo. pp. xx.-338, cloth. 1884. 7s. 6d. (Key to the Exercises, pp. 84, cloth, price 3s.)

Otté.—SIMPLIFIED GRAMMAR OF THE DANISH LANGUAGE. By E. C. OTTÉ. Crown 8vo. pp. viii.-66, cloth. 1884. 2s. 6d.

EGYPTIAN (COPTIC, HIEROGLYPHICS).

Birch.—EGYPTIAN TEXTS: I. Text, Transliteration and Translation —II. Text and Transliteration.—III. Text dissected for analysis.—IV. Determinatives, etc. By S. Birch. London, 1877. Large 8vo. 12s.

Catalogue (C) of leading Books on Egypt and Egyptology on Assyria and Assyriology. To be had at the affixed prices of Trübner and Co. 8vo., pp. 40. 1880. 1s.

Chabas.—LES PASTEURS EN ÉGYPTE.—Mémoire Publié par l'Académie Royale des Sciences à Amsterdam. By F. CHABAS. 4to. sewed, pp. 56. Amsterdam, 1868. 6s.

Clarke.—Memoir on the Comparative Grammar of Egyptian, Coptic, and Ude. By Hyde Clarke, Cor. Member American Oriental Society; Mem. German Oriental Society, etc., etc. Demy 8vo. sd., pp. 32. 2s.

Egyptologie.—(Forms also the Second Volume of the First Bulletin of the Congrès Provincial des Orientalistes Français.) 8vo. sewed, pp. 604, with Eight Plates. Saint-Etiene, 1880. 8s. 6d.

Lieblein.—Recherches sur la Chronologie Egyptienne d'après les listes Généalogiques. By J. Lieblein. Roy. 8vo. sewed, pp. 147, with Nine Plates. Christiana, 1873. 7s. 6d.

Mariette-Bey.—The Monuments of Upper Egypt; a translation of the "Itinéraire de la Haute Egypte" of Auguste Mariette-Bey. Translated by Alphonse Mariette. Crown 8vo. pp. xvi. and 262, cloth. 1877. 7s. 6d.

Records of the Past. Being English Translations of the Assyrian and the Egyptian Monuments. *Published under the Sanction of the Society of Biblical Archæology.* Edited by Dr. S. Birch.
Vols. I. to XII., 1874-79. 3s. 6d. each. (Vols. I., III., V., VII., IX., XI., contain Assyrian Texts.)

Renouf.—Elementary Grammar of the Ancient Egyptian Language, in the Hieroglyphic Type. By Le Page Renouf. 4to., cloth. 1875. 12s.

ENGLISH (Early and Modern English and Dialects).

Ballad Society (The).—Subscription—Small paper, one guinea, and large paper, three guineas, per annum. List of publications on application.

Barnes.—Glossary of the Dorset Dialect, with a Grammar of its Word Shapening and Wording. By W. Barnes, B.D. Demy 8vo. pp. viii.—126, sewed. 1886. 6s.

Boke of Nurture (The). By John Russell, about 1460-1470 Anno Domini. The Boke of Keruynge. By Wynkyn de Worde, Anno Domini 1513. The Boke of Nurture. By Hugh Rhodes, Anno Domini 1577. Edited from the Originals in the British Museum Library, by Frederick J. Furnivall, M.A., Trinity Hall. Cambridge, Member of Council of the Philological and Early English Text Societies. 4to. half-morocco, gilt top, pp. xix. and 146, 28, xxviii. and 56. 1867. 1l. 11s. 6d.

Burne.—Shropshire Folk-Lore; A Sheaf of Gleanings. Edited by C. S. Burne from the Collections of G. F. Jackson. Demy 8vo. pp xvi.—664, cloth. 1886. 25s.

Charnock.—Verba Nominalia; or Words derived from Proper Names. By Richard Stephen Charnock, Ph.Dr, F.S.A., etc. 8vo. pp. 326, cloth. 14s.

Charnock.—Ludus Patronymicus; or, the Etymology of Curious Surnames. By Richard Stephen Charnock, Ph.D., F.S.A., F.R.G.S. Crown 8vo. pp. 182, cloth. 7s. 6d.

Charnock.—A Glossary of the Essex Dialect. By R. S. Charnock. 8vo. cloth, pp. x. and 64. 1880. 3s. 6d.

Chaucer Society (The).—Subscription, two guineas per annum. *List of Publications on application.*

Eger and Grime; an Early English Romance. Edited from Bishop Percy's Folio Manuscript, about 1650 A.D. By J. W. HALES, M.A., and F. J. FURNIVALL, M.A., of Trinity Hall, Cambridge. 4to., pp. 64 (only 100 copies printed), bound in the Roxburghe style. 10s. 6d.

Early English Text Society's Publications. Subscription, one guinea per annum. All demy 8vo. in wrappers.

1. EARLY ENGLISH ALLITERATIVE POEMS. In the West-Midland Dialect of the Fourteenth Century. Edited by R. MORRIS, Esq., from an unique Cottonian MS. 16s.
2. ARTHUR (about 1440 A.D.). Edited by F. J. FURNIVALL, Esq., from the Marquis of Bath's unique MS. 4s.
3. ANE COMPENDIOUS AND BREUE TRACTATE CONCERNYNG YE OFFICE AND DEWTIE OF KYNGIS, etc. By WILLIAM LAUDER. (1556 A.D.) Edited by F. HALL, Esq., D.C.L. 4s.
4. SIR GAWAYNE AND THE GREEN KNIGHT (about 1320-30 A.D.). Edited by R. MORRIS, Esq., from an unique Cottonian MS. 10s.
5. OF THE ORTHOGRAPHIE AND CONGRUITIE OF THE BRITAN TONGUE; a treates, noe shorter than necessarie, for the Schooles, be ALEXANDER HUME. Edited for the first time from the unique MS. in the British Museum (about 1617 A.D.), by HENRY B. WHEATLEY, Esq. 4s.
6. LANCELOT OF THE LAIK. Edited from the unique MS. in the Cambridge University Library (ab. 1500), by the Rev. WALTER W. SKEAT, M.A. 8s.
7. THE STORY OF GENESIS AND EXODUS, an Early English Song, of about 1250 A.D. Edited for the first time from the unique MS. in the Library of Corpus Christi College, Cambridge, by R. MORRIS, Esq. 8s.
8. MORTE ARTHURE; the Alliterative Version. Edited from ROBERT THORNTON's unique MS. (about 1440 A.D.) at Lincoln, by the Rev. GEORGE PERRY, M.A., Prebendary of Lincoln. 7s.
9. ANIMADVERSIONS UPPON THE ANNOTACIONS AND CORRECTIONS OF SOME IMPERFECTIONS OF IMPRESSIONES OF CHAUCER'S WORKES, reprinted in 1598; by FRANCIS THYNNE. Edited from the unique MS. in the Bridgewater Library. By G. H. KINGSLEY, Esq., M.D., and F. J. FURNIVALL, Esq., M.A. 10s.
10. MERLIN, OR THE EARLY HISTORY OF KING ARTHUR. Edited for the first time from the unique MS. in the Cambridge University Library (about 1450 A.D.), by HENRY B. WHEATLEY, Esq. Part I. 2s. 6d.
11. THE MONARCHE, and other Poems of Sir David Lyndesay. Edited from the first edition by JOHNE SKOTT, in 1552, by FITZEDWARD HALL, Esq., D.C.L. Part I. 3s.
12. THE WRIGHT'S CHASTE WIFE, a Merry Tale, by Adam of Cobsam (about 1462 A.D.), from the unique Lambeth MS. 306. Edited for the first time by F. J. FURNIVALL, Esq., M.A. 1s.
13. SEINTE MARHERETE, ÞE MEIDEN ANT MARTYR. Three Texts of ab. 1200, 1310, 1330 A.D. First edited in 1862, by the Rev. OSWALD COCKAYNE, M.A., and now re-issued. 2s.
14. KYNG HORN, with fragments of Floriz and Blauncheflur, and the Assumption of the Blessed Virgin. Edited from the MSS. in the Library of the University of Cambridge and the British Museum, by the Rev. J. RAWSON LUMBY. 3s. 6d.

15. POLITICAL, RELIGIOUS, AND LOVE POEMS, from the Lambeth MS. No. 306, and other sources. Edited by F. J. FURNIVALL, Esq., M.A. 7s. 6d.
16. A TRETICE IN ENGLISH breuely drawe out of þ book of Quintis essencijs in Latyn, þ Hermys þ prophete and king of Egipt after þ flood of Noe, fader of Philosophris, hadde by reuelacioun of an aungil of God to him sente. Edited from the Sloane MS. 73, by F. J. FURNIVALL, Esq., M.A. 1s.
17. PARALLEL EXTRACTS from 29 Manuscripts of PIERS PLOWMAN, with Comments, and a Proposal for the Society's Three-text edition of this Poem. By the Rev. W. SKEAT, M.A. 1s.
18. HALI MEIDENHEAD, about 1200 A.D. Edited for the first time from the MS. (with a translation) by the Rev. OSWALD COCKAYNE, M.A. 1s.
19. THE MONARCHE, and other Poems of Sir David Lyndesay. Part II., the Complaynt of the King's Papingo, and other minor Poems. Edited from the First Edition by F. HALL, Esq., D.C.L. 3s. 6d.
20. SOME TREATISES BY RICHARD ROLLE DE HAMPOLE. Edited from Robert of Thornton's MS. (ab. 1440 A.D.), by Rev. GEORGE G. PERRY, M.A. 1s.
21. MERLIN, OR THE EARLY HISTORY OF KING ARTHUR. Part II. Edited by HENRY B. WHEATLEY, Esq. 4s.
22. THE ROMANS OF PARTENAY, OR LUSIGNEN. Edited for the first time from the unique MS. in the Library of Trinity College, Cambridge, by the Rev. W. W. SKEAT. M.A. 6s.
23. DAN MICHEL'S AYENBITE OF INWYT, or Remorse of Conscience, in the Kentish dialect, 1340 A.D. Edited from the unique MS. in the British Museum, by RICHARD MORRIS, Esq. 10s. 6d.
24. HYMNS OF THE VIRGIN AND CHRIST; THE PARLIAMENT OF DEVILS, and Other Religious Poems. Edited from the Lambeth MS. 853, by F. J. FURNIVALL, M.A. 3s.
25. THE STACIONS OF ROME, and the Pilgrim's Sea-Voyage and Sea-Sickness, with Clene Maydenhod. Edited from the Vernon and Porkington MSS., etc., by F. J. FURNIVALL, Esq., M.A. 1s.
26. RELIGIOUS PIECES IN PROSE AND VERSE. Containing Dan Jon Gaytrigg's Sermon; The Abbaye of S. Spirit; Sayne Jon, and other pieces in the Northern Dialect. Edited from Robert of Thorntone's MS. (ab. 1460 A.D.), by the Rev. G. PERRY, M.A. 2s.
27. MANIPULUS VOCABULORUM: a Rhyming Dictionary of the English Language, by PETER LEVINS (1570). Edited, with an Alphabetical Index by HENRY B. WHEATLEY. 12s.
28. THE VISION OF WILLIAM CONCERNING PIERS PLOWMAN, together with Vita de Dowel, Dobet et Dobest. 1362 A.D., by WILLIAM LANGLAND. The earliest or Vernon Text; Text A. Edited from the Vernon MS., with full Collations, by Rev. W. W. SKEAT, M.A. 7s.
29. OLD ENGLISH HOMILIES AND HOMILETIC TREATISES. (Sawles Warde and the Wohunge of Ure Lauerd: Ureisuns of Ure Louerd and of Ure Lefdi, etc.) of the Twelfth and Thirteenth Centuries. Edited from MSS. in the British Museum, Lambeth, and Bodleian Libraries; with Introduction, Translation, and Notes, by RICHARD MORRIS. First Series. Part 1. 7s.

30. PIERS, THE PLOUGHMAN'S CREDE (about 1394). Edited from the MSS. by the Rev. W. W. SKEAT, M.A. 2s.

31. INSTRUCTIONS FOR PARISH PRIESTS. By JOHN MYRC. Edited from Cotton MS. Claudius A. II., by EDWARD PEACOCK, Esq., F.S.A., etc., etc. 4s.

32. EARLY ENGLISH MEALS AND MANNERS; John Russell's Boke of Nuture, Wynkyn de Worde's Boke of Keruynge, The Boke of Curtasye, R. Weste's Booke of Demeanor, Seager's Schoole of Vertue, The Babees Book, Aristotle's A B C, Urbanitatis, Stans Puer ad Mensam, The Lytille Childrenes Lytil Boke, For to serve a Lord, Old Symon, The Birched School-Boy, etc. With some Forewords on Education in Early England. Edited by F. J. FURNIVALL, M.A., Trin. Hall, Cambridge. 15s.

33. THE BOOK OF THE KNIGHT DE LA TOUR LANDRY, 1372. A Father's Book for his Daughters, Edited from the Harleian MS. 1764, by THOMAS WRIGHT Esq., M.A., and Mr. WILLIAM ROSSITER. 8s.

34. OLD ENGLISH HOMILIES AND HOMILETIC TREATISES. (Sawles Warde, and the Wohunge of Ure Lauerd: Ureisuns of Ure Louerd and of Ure Lefdi, etc.) of the Twelfth and Thirteenth Centuries. Edited from MSS. in the British Museum, Lambeth, and Bodleian Libraries; with Introduction, Translation, and Notes, by RICHARD MORRIS. First Series. Part 2. 8s.

35. SIR DAVID LYNDESAY'S WORKS. PART 3. The Historie of ane Nobil and Wailzeand Sqvyer, WILLIAM MELDRUM, umqvhyle Laird of Cleische and Bynnis, compylit be Sir DAUID LYNDESAY of the Mont alias Lyoun King of Armes. With the Testament of the said Williame Meldrum, Sqyyer, compylit alswa be Sir Dauid Lyndesay, etc. Edited by F. HALL, D.C.L. 2s.

36. MERLIN, OR THE EARLY HISTORY OF KING ARTHUR. A Prose Romance (about 1450-1460 A.D.), edited from the unique MS. in the University Library, Cambridge, by HENRY B. WHEATLEY. With an Essay on Arthurian Localities, by J. S. STUART GLENNIE, Esq. Part III. 1869. 12s.

37. SIR DAVID LYNDESAY'S WORKS. Part IV. Ane Satyre of the thrie estaits, in commendation of vertew and vitvperation of vyce. Maid be Sir DAVID LINDISAY, of the Mont, alias Lyon King of Armes. At Edinbvrgh. Printed be Robert Charteris, 1602. Cvm privilegio regis. Edited by F. HALL, Esq., D.C.L. 4s.

38. THE VISION OF WILLIAM CONCERNING PIERS THE PLOWMAN, together with Vita de Dowel, Dobet, et Dobest, Secundum Wit et Resoun, by WILLIAM LANGLAND (1377 A.D.). The "Crowley" Text; or Text B. Edited from MS. Laud Misc. 581, collated with MS. Rawl. Poet. 38, MS. B. 15. 17. in the Library of Trinity College, Cambridge, MS. Dd. 1. 17. in the Cambridge University Library, the MS. in Oriel College, Oxford, MS. Bodley 814, etc. By the Rev. WALTER W. SKEAT, M.A., late Fellow of Christ's College, Cambridge. 10s. 6d.

39. THE "GEST HYSTORIALE" OF THE DESTRUCTION OF TROY. An Alliterative Romance, translated from Guido De Colonna's "Hystoria Troiana." Now first edited from the unique MS. in the Hunterian Museum, University of Glasgow, by the Rev. GEO A. PANTON and DAVID DONALDSON. Part I. 10s. 6d.

40. ENGLISH GILDS. The Original Ordinances of more than One Hundred Early English Gilds: Together with the olde usages of the cite of Wynchestre; The Ordinances of Worcester; The Office of the Mayor of Bristol; and the Customary of the Manor of Tettenhall-Regis. From

Original MSS. of the Fourteenth and Fifteenth Centuries. Edited with Notes by the late Toulmin Smith, Esq., F.R.S. of Northern Antiquaries (Copenhagen). With an Introduction and Glossary, etc., by his daughter, Lucy Toulmin Smith. And a Preliminary Essay, in Five Parts, On the History and Development of Gilds, by Lujo Brentano, Doctor Juris Utriusque et Philosophiæ. 21s.

41. The Minor Poems of William Lauder, Playwright, Poet, and Minister of the Word of God (mainly on the State of Scotland in and about 1568 A.D., that year of Famine and Plague). Edited from the Unique Originals belonging to S. Christie-Miller, Esq., of Britwell, by F. J. Furnivall, M.A., Trin. Hall, Camb. 3s.

42. Bernardus de Cura rei Famuliaris, with some Early Scotch Prophecies, etc. From a MS., KK 1. 5, in the Cambridge University Library. Edited by J. Rawson Lumby, M.A., late Fellow of Magdalen College, Cambridge. 2s.

43. Ratis Raving, and other Moral and Religious Pieces, in Prose and Verse. Edited from the Cambridge University Library MS. KK 1. 5, by J. Rawson Lumby, M.A., late Fellow of Magdalen College, Cambridge. 3s.

44. Joseph of Arimathie: otherwise called the Romance of the Seint Graal, or Holy Grail: an alliterative poem, written about A.D. 1350, and now first printed from the unique copy in the Vernon MS. at Oxford. With an appendix, containing "The Lyfe of Joseph of Armathy," reprinted from the black-letter copy of Wynkyn de Worde; "De sancto Joseph ab Arimathia," first printed by Pynson, A.D. 1516; and "The Lyfe of Joseph of Arimathia," first printed by Pynson, A.D. 1520. Edited, with Notes and Glossarial Indices, by the Rev. Walter W. Skeat, M.A. 5s.

45. King Alfred's West-Saxon Version of Gregory's Pastoral Care. With an English translation, the Latin Text, Notes, and an Introduction Edited by Henry Sweet, Esq., of Balliol College, Oxford. Part I. 10s.

46. Legends of the Holy Rood; Symbols of the Passion and Cross-Poems. In Old English of the Eleventh, Fourteenth, and Fifteenth Centuries. Edited from MSS. in the British Museum and Bodleian Libraries: with Introduction, Translations, and Glossarial Index. By Richard Morris, LL.D. 10s.

47. Sir David Lyndesay's Works. Part V. The Minor Poems of Lyndesay. Edited by J. A. H. Murray, Esq. 3s.

48. The Times' Whistle: or, A Newe Daunce of Seven Satires, and other Poems: Compiled by R. C., Gent. Now first Edited from MS. Y. 8. 3. in the Library of Canterbury Cathedral; with Introduction, Notes, and Glossary, by J. M. Cowper. 6s.

49. An Old English Miscellany, containing a Bestiary, Kentish Sermons, Proverbs of Alfred, Religious Poems of the 13th century. Edited from the MSS. by the Rev. R. Morris, LL.D. 10s.

50. King Alfred's West-Saxon Version of Gregory's Pastoral Care. Edited from 2 MSS., with an English translation. By Henry Sweet, Esq., Balliol College, Oxford. Part II. 10s.

51. Þe Liflade of St. Juliana, from two old English Manuscripts of 1230 A.D. With renderings into Modern English, by the Rev. O. Cockayne and Edmund Brock. Edited by the Rev. O. Cockayne, M.A. Price 2s.

52. Palladius on Husbondrie, from the unique MS., ab. 1420 A.D., ed. Rev. B. Lodge. Part I. 10s.

53. OLD ENGLISH HOMILIES, Series II., from the unique 13th-century MS. in Trinity Coll. Cambridge, with a photolithograph; three Hymns to the Virgin and God, from a unique 13th-century MS. at Oxford, a photo-lithograph of the music to two of them, and transcriptions of it in modern notation by Dr. RIMBAULT, and A. J. ELLIS, Esq., F.R.S.; the whole edited by the Rev. RICHARD MORRIS, LL.D. 8s.

54. THE VISION OF PIERS PLOWMAN, Text C (completing the three versions of this great poem), with an Autotype; and two unique alliterative Poems: Richard the Redeles (by WILLIAM, the author of the *Vision*); and The Crowned King; edited by the Rev. W. W. SKEAT, M.A. 18s.

55. GENERYDES, a Romance, edited from the unique MS., ab. 1440 A.D., in Trin. Coll. Cambridge, by W. ALDIS WRIGHT, Esq., M.A., Trin. Coll. Cambr. Part I. 3s.

56. THE GEST HYSTORIALE OF THE DESTRUCTION OF TROY, translated from Guido de Colonna, in alliterative verse; edited from the unique MS. in the Hunterian Museum, Glasgow, by D. DONALDSON, Esq., and the late Rev. G. A. Panton. Part II. 10s. 6d.

57. THE EARLY ENGLISH VERSION OF THE "CURSOR MUNDI," in four Texts, from MS. Cotton, Vesp. A. iii. in the British Museum; Fairfax MS. 14. in the Bodleian; the Göttingen MS. Theol. 107; MS. R. 3, 8, in Trinity College, Cambridge. Edited by the Rev. R. Morris, LL.D. Part I. with two photo-lithographic facsimiles by Cooke and Fotheringham. 10s. 6d.

58. THE BLICKLING HOMILIES, edited from the Marquis of Lothian's Anglo-Saxon MS. of 971 A.D., by the Rev. R. MORRIS, LL.D. (With a Photolithograph). Part I. 8s.

59. THE EARLY ENGLISH VERSION OF THE "CURSOR MUNDI;" in four Texts, from MS. Cotton Vesp. A. iii. in the British Museum; Fairfax MS. 14. in the Bodleian; the Göttingen MS. Theol. 107; MS. R. 3, 8, in Trinity College, Cambridge. Edited by the Rev. R. Morris, LL.D. Part II. 15s.

60. MEDITACYUNS ON THE SOPER OF OUR LORDE (perhaps by ROBERT OF BRUNNE). Edited from the MSS. by J. M. COWPER, Esq. 2s. 6d.

61. THE ROMANCE AND PROPHECIES OF THOMAS OF ERCELDOUNE, printed from Five MSS. Edited by Dr. JAMES A. H. MURRAY. 10s. 6d.

62. THE EARLY ENGLISH VERSION OF THE "CURSOR MUNDI," in Four Texts. Edited by the Rev. R. MORRIS, M.A., LL.D. Part III. 15s.

63. THE BLICKLING HOMILIES. Edited from the Marquis of Lothian's Anglo-Saxon MS. of 971 A.D., by the Rev. R. MORRIS, LL.D. Part II. 4s.

64. FRANCIS THYNNE'S EMBLEMES AND EPIGRAMS, A.D. 1600, from the Earl of Ellesmere's unique MS. Edited by F. J. FURNIVALL, M.A. 4s.

65. BE DOMES DAEGE (Bede's De Die Judicii) and other short Anglo-Saxon Pieces. Ed. from the unique MS. by the Rev. J. RAWSON LUMBY, B.D. 2s.

66. THE EARLY ENGLISH VERSION OF THE "CURSOR MUNDI," in Four Texts. Edited by Rev. R. MORRIS, M.A., LL.D. Part IV. 10s.

67. NOTES ON PIERS PLOWMAN. By the Rev. W. W. SKEAT, M.A. Part I. 21s.

68. The Early English Version of the "CURSOR MUNDI," in Four Texts. Edited by Rev. R. MORRIS, M.A., LL.D. Part V. 25s.

69. ADAM DAVY'S FIVE DREAMS ABOUT EDWARD II. THE LIFE OF SAINT ALEXIUS. Solomon's Book of Wisdom. St. Jerome's 15 Tokens before Doomsday. The Lamentation of Souls. Edited from the Laud MS. 622, in the Bodleian Library, by F. J. FURNIVALL, M.A. 5s.
70. GENERYDES, a Romance. Edited by W. ALDIS WRIGHT, M.A. Part II. 4s.
71. THE LAY FOLK'S MASS-BOOK, 4 Texts. Edited by Rev. Canon SIMMONS. 25s.
72. PALLADIUS ON HUSBONDRIE, englisht (ab. 1420 A.D.). Part II. Edited by S. J. HERRTAGE, B.A. 5s.
73. THE BLICKLING HOMILIES, 971 A.D. Edited by Rev. Dr. R. MORRIS. Part III. 8s.
74. ENGLISH WORKS OF WYCLIF, hitherto unprinted. Edited by F. D. MATTHEW. 20s.
75. CATHOLICON ANGLICUM, an early English Dictionary, from Lord Monson's MS, A.D. 1483. Edited with Introduction and Notes by S. J. HERRTAGE, B.A.; and with a Preface by H. B. WHEATLEY. 20s.
76. AELFRIC'S METRICAL LIVES OF SAINTS, in MS. Cott. Jul. E. 7. Edited by Rev. Prof. SKEAT, M.A. Part I. 10s.
77. BEOWULF. The unique MS. Autotyped and Transliterated. Edited by Professor ZUPITZA. Ph.D. 25s.
78. THE FIFTY EARLIEST ENGLISH WILLS in the Court of Probate, 1387-1439. Edited by F. J. FURNIVALL, M.A. 7s.
79. KING ALFRED'S OROSIUS FROM LORD TOLLEMACHE'S 9TH CENTURY MS. Part I. Edited by H. SWEET, M.A. 13s.
  Extra Volume. Facsimile of the Epinal Glossary, 8th Century, edited by H. SWEET. 15s.
80. THE ANGLO-SAXON LIFE OF ST. KATHERINE AND ITS LATIN ORIGINAL. Edited by Dr. EINENKEL. 12s.
81. PIERS PLOWMAN. Notes, Glossary, etc., Part IV., Section II., completing the Work. Edited by Rev. Prof. SKEAT, M.A. 18s.
82. AELFRIC'S METRICAL LIVES OF SAINTS, MS. Cott. Jul. E. 7. ed. Rev. Prof. SKEAT, M.A., LL.D. Part II. 12s.
83. THE OLDEST ENGLISH TEXTS. Charters, etc., ed. H. SWEET, M.A. 20s.
84. ADDITIONAL ANALOGS TO "THE WRIGHT'S CHASTE WIFE." No. 12. By W. A. CLOUSTON. 1s.
85. THE THREE KINGS OF COLOGNE. 2 English Texts and 1 Latin. ed. Dr. C. HORSTMANN. 17s.
86. PROSE LIVES OF WOMEN SAINTS, ab. 1610 A.D., from the unique MS, by Dr. C. HORSTMANN. 12s.

Extra Series. Subscriptions—Small paper, one guinea; large paper two guineas, per annum.

1. THE ROMANCE OF WILLIAM OF PALERNE (otherwise known as the Romance of William and the Werwolf). Translated from the French at the command of Sir Humphrey de Bohun, about A.D. 1350, to which is added a fragment of the Alliterative Romance of Alisaunder, translated from the

Latin by the same author, about A.D. 1340; the former re-edited from the unique MS. in the Library of King's College, Cambridge, the latter now first edited from the unique MS. in the Bodleian Library, Oxford. By the Rev. WALTER W. SKEAT, M.A. 8vo. sewed, pp. xliv. and 328. 13s.

2. ON EARLY ENGLISH PRONUNCIATION, with especial reference to Shakspere and Chaucer; containing an investigation of the Correspondence of Writing with Speech in England, from the Anglo-Saxon period to the present day, preceded by a systematic Notation of all Spoken Sounds by means of the ordinary Printing Types; including a re-arrangement of Prof. F. J. Child's Memoirs on the Language of Chaucer and Gower, and reprints of the rare Tracts by Salesbury on English, 1547, and Welsh, 1567, and by Barcley on French, 1521. By ALEXANDER J. ELLIS, F.R.S. Part I. On the Pronunciation of the XIVth, XVIth, XVIIth, and XVIIIth centuries. 8vo. sewed, pp. viii. and 416. 10s.

3. CAXTON'S BOOK OF CURTESYE, printed at Westminster about 1477–8, A.D., and now reprinted, with two MS. copies of the same treatise, from the Oriel MS. 79, and the Balliol MS. 354. Edited by FREDERICK J. FURNIVALL, M.A. 8vo. sewed, pp. xii. and 58. 5s.

4. THE LAY OF HAVELOK THE DANE; composed in the reign of Edward I., about A.D. 1280. Formerly edited by Sir F. MADDEN for the Roxburghe Club, and now re-edited from the unique MS. Laud Misc. 108, in the Bodleian Library, Oxford, by the Rev. WALTER W. SKEAT, M.A. 8vo. sewed, pp. lv. and 160. 10s.

5. CHAUCER'S TRANSLATION OF BOETHIUS'S "DE CONSOLATIONE PHILOSOPHIE." Edited from the Additional MS. 10,340 in the British Museum. Collated with the Cambridge Univ. Libr. MS. Ii. 3. 21. By RICHARD MORRIS. 8vo. 12s.

6. THE ROMANCE OF THE CHEVELERE ASSIGNE. Re-edited from the unique manuscript in the British Museum, with a Preface, Notes, and Glossarial Index, by HENRY H. GIBBS, Esq., M.A. 8vo. sewed, pp. xviii. and 38. 3s.

7. ON EARLY ENGLISH PRONUNCIATION, with especial reference to Shakspere and Chaucer. By ALEXANDER J. ELLIS, F.R.S., etc., etc. Part II. On the Pronunciation of the XIIIth and previous centuries, of Anglo-Saxon, Icelandic, Old Norse and Gothic, with Chronological Tables of the Value of Letters and Expression of Sounds in English Writing. 10s.

8. QUEENE ELIZABETHES ACHADEMY, by Sir HUMPHREY GILBERT. A Booke of Precedence, The Ordering of a Funeral, etc. Varying Versions of the Good Wife, The Wise Man, etc., Maxims, Lydgate's Order of Fools, A Poem on Heraldry, Occleve on Lords' Men, etc., Edited by F. J. FURNIVALL, M.A., Trin. Hall, Camb. With Essays on Early Italian and German Books of Courtesy, by W. M. ROSSETTI, Esq., and E. OSWALD Esq. 8vo. 13s.

9. THE FRATERNITYE OF VACABONDES, by JOHN AWDELEY (licensed in 1560-1, imprinted then, and in 1565) from the edition of 1575 in the Bodleian Library. A Caveat or Warening for Commen Cursetors vulgarely called Vagabones, by THOMAS HARMAN, ESQUIERE. From the 3rd edition of 1567, belonging to Henry Huth, Esq., collated with the 2nd edition of 1567, in the Bodleian Library, Oxford, and with the reprint of the 4th edition of 1573. A Sermon in Praise of Thieves and Thievery, by PARSON HABEN or HYBERDYNE, from the Lansdowne MS. 98, and Cotton Vesp. A. 25. These

parts of the Groundworke of Conny-catching (ed. 1592), that differ from *Harman's Caueat*. Edited by EDWARD VILES & F. J. FURNIVALL. 8vo. 7s. 6d.

10. THE FYRST BOKE OF THE INTRODUCTION OF KNOWLEDGE, made by Andrew Borde, of Physycke Doctor. A COMPENDYOUS REGYMENT OF A DYETARY OF HELTH made in Mountpyllier, compiled by Andrewe Boorde, of Physycke Doctor. BARNES IN THE DEFENCE OF THE BERDE: a treatyse made, answerynge the treatyse of Doctor Borde upon Berdes. Edited, with a life of Andrew Boorde, and large extracts from his Breuyary, by F. J. FURNIVALL, M.A., Trinity Hall, Camb. 8vo. 18s.

11. THE BRUCE; or, the Book of the most excellent and noble Prince, Robert de Broyss, King of Scots: compiled by Master John Barbour, Archdeacon of Aberdeen, A.D. 1375. Edited from MS. G 23 in the Library of St. John's College, Cambridge, written A.D. 1487; collated with the MS. in the Advocates' Library at Edinburgh, written A.D. 1489, and with Hart's Edition, printed A.D. 1616; with a Preface, Notes, and Glossarial Index, by the Rev. WALTER W. SKEAT, M.A. Part I. 8vo. 12s.

12. ENGLAND IN THE REIGN OF KING HENRY THE EIGHTH. A Dialogue between Cardinal Pole and Thomas Lupset, Lecturer in Rhetoric at Oxford. By THOMAS STARKEY, Chaplain to the King. Edited, with Preface, Notes, and Glossary, by J. M. COWPER. And with an Introduction, containing the Life and Letters of Thomas Starkey, by the Rev. J. S. BREWER, M.A. Part II. 12s.

13. A SUPPLICACYON FOR THE BEGGARS. Written about the year 1529, by SIMON FISH. Now re-edited by FREDERICK J. FURNIVALL. With a Supplycacion to our moste Souersigne Lorde Kynge Henry the Eyght (1544 A.D.), A Supplication of the Poore Commons (1546 A.D.), The Decaye of England by the great multitude of Shepe (1550-3 A.D.). Edited by J. MEADOWS COWPER. 6s.

14. ON EARLY ENGLISH PRONUNCIATION, with especial reference to Shakspere and Chaucer. By A. J. ELLIS, F.R.S., F.S.A. Part III. Illustrations of the Pronunciation of the xivth and xviith Centuries. Chaucer, Gower, Wycliffe, Spenser, Shakspere, Salesbury, Barcley, Hart, Bullokar, Gill. Pronouncing Vocabulary. 10s.

15. ROBERT CROWLEY'S THIRTY-ONE EPIGRAMS, Voyce of the Last Trumpet, Way to Wealth, etc., 1550-1 A.D. Edited by J. M. COWPER, Esq. 12s.

16. A TREATISE ON THE ASTROLABE; addressed to his son Lowys, by Geoffrey Chaucer, A.D. 1391. Edited from the earliest MSS. by the Rev. WALTER W. SKEAT, M.A., late Fellow of Christ's College, Cambridge. 10s.

17. THE COMPLAYNT OF SCOTLANDE, 1549, A.D., with an Appendix of four Contemporary English Tracts. Edited by J. A. H. MURRAY, Esq. Part I. 1s.

18. THE COMPLAYNT OF SCOTLANDE, etc. Part II. 8s.

19. OURE LADYES MYROURE, A.D. 1530, edited by the Rev. J. H. BLUNT, M.A., with four full-page photolithographic facsimiles by Cooke and Fotheringham. 24s.

20. LONELICH'S HISTORY OF THE HOLY GRAIL (ab. 1450 A.D.), translated from the French Prose of SIRES ROBIERS DE BORRON. Re-edited from the Unique MS. in Corpus Christi College, Cambridge, by F. J. Furnivall, Esq. M.A. Part I. 8s.

21. BARBOUR'S BRUCE. Edited from the MSS. and the earliest printed edition by the Rev. W. W. SKEAT, M.A. Part II. 4s.
22. HENRY BRINKLOW'S COMPLAYNT OF RODERYCK MORS, somtyme a gray Fryre, unto the Parliament Howse of Ingland his naturall Country, for the Redresse of certen wicked Lawes, euel Customs, and cruel Decreys (ab. 1542); and THE LAMENTACION OF A CHRISTIAN AGAINST THE CITIE OF LONDON, made by Roderigo Mors, A.D. 1545. Edited by J. M. COWPER, Esq. 9s.
23. ON EARLY ENGLISH PRONUNCIATION, with especial reference to Shakspere and Chaucer. By A. J. ELLIS, Esq., F.R.S. Part IV. 10s.
24. LONELICH'S HISTORY OF THE HOLY GRAIL (ab. 1450 A.D.), translated from the French Prose of SIRES ROBIERS DE BORRON. Re-edited from the Unique MS. in Corpus Christi College, Cambridge, by F. J. FURNIVALL, Esq., M.A. Part II. 10s.
25. THE ROMANCE OF GUY OF WARWICK. Edited from the Cambridge University MS. by Prof. J. ZUPITZA, Ph.D. Part I. 20s.
26. THE ROMANCE OF GUY OF WARWICK. Edited from the Cambridge University MS. by Prof. J. ZUPITZA, Ph.D. (The 2nd or 15th century version). Part II. 14s.
27. THE ENGLISH WORKS OF JOHN FISHER, Bishop of Rochester (died 1535). Edited by Professor J. E. B MAYOR, M.A. Part I., the Text. 16s.
28. LONELICH'S HISTORY OF THE HOLY GRAIL. Edited by F. J. FURNIVALL, M.A. Part III. 10s.
29. BARBOUR'S BRUCE. Edited from the MSS. and the earliest Printed Edition, by the Rev. W. W. SKEAT, M.A. Part III. 21s.
30. LONELICH'S HISTORY OF THE HOLY GRAIL. Edited by F. J. FURNIVALL, Esq., M.A. Part IV. 15s.
31. ALEXANDER AND DINDIMUS. Translated from the Latin about A.D. 1340-50. Re-edited by the Rev. W. W. SKEAT, M.A. 6s.
32. STARKEY'S "ENGLAND IN HENRY VIII.'S TIME." Part I. Starkey's Life and Letters. Edited by S. J. HERRTAGE, B.A. 8s.
33. GESTA ROMANORUM: the Early English Versions. Edited from the MSS. and Black-letter Editions, by S. J. HERRTAGE, B.A. 15s.
34. CHARLEMAGNE ROMANCES: No. I. Sir Ferumbras. Edited from the unique Ashmole MS. by S. J. HERRTAGE, B.A. 15s.
35. CHARLEMAGNE ROMANCES: II. The Sege off Malayne, Sir Otuell, etc. Edited by S. J. HERRTAGE, B.A. 12s.
36. CHARLEMAGNE ROMANCES: III. Lyf of Charles the Grete, Pt. 1. Edited by S. J. HERRTAGE, B.A. 16s.
37. CHARLEMAGNE ROMANCES: IV. Lyf of Charles the Grete, Pt. 2. Edited by S. J. HERRTAGE, B.A. 15s.
38. CHARLEMAGNE ROMANCES: V. The Sowdone of Babylone. Edited by Dr. HAUSKNECHT. 15s.
39. CHARLEMAGNE ROMANCES: VI. The Taill of Rauf Colyear, Roland, Otuel, etc. Edited by SYDNEY J. HERRTAGE, B.A. 15s.
40. CHARLEMAGNE ROMANCES: VII. Houn of Burdeux. By Lord Berners. Edited by S. L. LEE, B.A. Part I. 15s.

41. CHARLEMAGNE ROMANCES: VIII. Huon of Burdeux. By Lord BERNERS. Edited by S. L. LEE, B.A. Part II. 15s.
42. GUY OF WARWICK. Two Texts (Auchinleck MS. and Caiu's MS.). Edited by Prof. ZUPITZA. Part I. 15s.
43. CHARLEMAGNE ROMANCES: IX. Huon of Burdeux, by Lord BERNERS. Edited by S. L. LEE, B.A. Part III. 15s.
44. CHARLEMAGNE ROMANCES: X. The Four Sons of Aymon. Edited Miss O. RICHARDSON. Part I. 15s.
45. CHARLEMAGNE ROMANCES: XI. The Four Sons of Aymon. Edited by O. RICHARDSON. Part II. 20s.
46. SIR BEVIS OF HAMPTON, from the Auchinleck and other MSS. Edited by Prof. E. KOLBING. Part I. 10s.
47. THE WARS OF ALEXANDER. Edited by Prof. SKEAT, Litt.D., LL.D. 20s.
48. SIR BEVIS OF HAMTON, ed. Prof. E. KOLBING. Part II. 10s.
49. GUY OF WARWICK, 2 texts (Auchinleck and Caius MSS.). Part 2. Edited by Prof. J. ZUPITZA. 15s.
50. CHARLEMAGNE ROMANCES: Huon of Burdeux. By Lord BERNERS. Edited by S. L. LEE, B.A. Part IV. 5s.

English Dialect Society's Publications. Subscription, 1873 to 1876, 10s. 6d. per annum; 1877 and following years, 20s. per annum. All demy 8vo. in wrappers.

1. Series B. Part I. Reprinted Glossaries, I.-VII. Containing a Glossary of North of England Words, by J. H.; Glossaries, by Mr. MARSHALL; and a West-Riding Glossary, by Dr. WILLAN. 7s. 6d.
2. Series A. Bibliographical. A List of Books illustrating English Dialects. Part I. Containing a General List of Dictionaries, etc.; and a List of Books relating to some of the Counties of England. 4s. 6d.
3. Series C. Original Glossaries, Part I. Containing a Glossary of Swaledale Words. By Captain HARLAND. 4s.
4. Series D. The History of English Sounds. By H. SWEET, Esq. 4s. 6d.
5. Series B. Part II. Reprinted Glossaries. VIII.-XIV. Containing seven Provincial English Glossaries, from various sources. 7s.
6. Series B. Part III. Reprinted Glossaries. XV.-XVII. Ray's Collection of English Words not generally used, from the edition of 1691; together with Thoresby's Letter to Ray, 1703. Re-arranged and newly edited by Rev. WALTER W. SKEAT. 8s.
6*. Subscribers to the English Dialect Society for 1874 also receive a copy of 'A Dictionary of the Sussex Dialect.' By the Rev. W. D. PARISH.
7. Series D. Part II. The Dialect of West Somerset. By F. T. ELWORTHY, Esq. 3s. 6d.
8. Series A. Part II. A List of Books Relating to some of the Counties of England. Part II. 6s.
9. Series C. A Glossary of Words used in the Neighbourhood of Whitby. By F. K. ROBINSON. Part 1. A—P. 7s. 6d.

10. Series C. A Glossary of the Dialect of Lancashire. By J. H. NODAL and G. MILNER. Part I. A—E. 3s. 6d.
11. On the Survival of Early English Words in our Present Dialects. By Dr. R. MORRIS. 6d.
12. Series C. Original Glossaries. Part III. Containing Five Original Provincial English Glossaries. 7s.
13. Series C. A Glossary of Words used in the Neighbourhood of Whitby. By F. K. Robinson. Part II. P—Z. 6s 6d.
14. A Glossary of Mid-Yorkshire Words, with a Grammar. By C. CLOUGH ROBINSON. 9s.
15. A GLOSSARY OF WORDS used in the Wapentakes of Manley and Corringham, Lincolnshire. By EDWARD PEACOCK, F.S.A. 9s. 6d.
16. A Glossary of Holderness Words. By F. Ross, R. STEAD, and T. HOLDERNESS. With a Map of the District. 7s. 6d.
17. On the Dialects of Eleven Southern and South-Western Counties, with a new Classification of the English Dialects. By Prince LOUIS LUCIEN BONAPARTE. With Two Maps. 1s.
18. Bibliographical List. Part III. completing the Work, and containing a List of Books on Scottish Dialects, Anglo-Irish Dialect, Cant and Slang, and Americanisms, with additions to the English List and Index. Edited by J. H. NODAL. 4s. 6d.
19. An Outline of the Grammar of West Somerset. By F. T ELWORTHY, ESQ. 5s.
20. A Glossary of Cumberland Words and Phrases. By WILLIAM DICKINSON, F.L.S. 6s.
21. Tusser's Five Hundred Pointes of Good Husbandrie. Edited with Introduction, Notes and Glossary, by W. PAINE and SIDNEY J. HERRTAGE, B.A. 12s. 6d.
22. A Dictionary of English Plant Names. By JAMES BRITTEN, F.L.S., and ROBERT HOLLAND. Part I. (A to F). 8s. 6d.
23. Five Reprinted Glossaries, including Wiltshire, East Anglian, Suffolk, and East Yorkshire Words, and Words from Bishop Kennett's Parochial Antiquities. Edited by the Rev. Professor SKEAT, M.A. 7s.
24. Supplement to the Cumberland Glossary (No. 20). By W. DICKINSON, F.L.S. 1s.
25. Specimens of English Dialects. First Volume. I. Devonshire; Exmoor Scolding and Courtship. Edited, with Notes and Glossary, by F. T. ELWORTHY. II. Westmoreland; Wm. de Worfat's Bran New Wark. Edited by Rev. Prof. SKEAT. 8s. 6d.
26. A Dictionary of English Plant Names. By J. BRITTEN and R. HOLLAND. Part II. (G to O). 1880. 8s. 6d.
27. Glossary of Words in use in Cornwall. I. West Cornwall. By Miss M. A. COURTNEY. II. East Cornwall. By THOMAS Q. COUCH. With Map. 6s.
28. Glossary of Words and Phrases in use in Antrim and Down. By WILLIAM HUGH PATTERSON, M.R.I.A. 7s.

29. An Early English Hymn to the Virgin. By F. J. FURNIVALL, M.A., and A. J. ELLIS, F.R.S. 6d.
30. Old Country and Farming Words. Gleaned from Agricultural Books. By JAMES BRITTEN, F.L.S. 10s. 6d.
31. The Dialect of Leicestershire. By the Rev. A. B. EVANS, D.D., and SEBASTIAN EVANS, LL.D. 10s. 6d.
32. Five Original Glossaries. Isle of Wight, Oxfordshire, Cumberland, North Lincolnshire and Radnorshire. By various Authors. 7s. 6d.
33. George Eliot's Use of Dialect. By W. E. A. AXON. (Forming No. 4 of "Miscellanies.") 6d.
34. Turner's Names of Herbes, A.D. 1548. Edited (with Index and Indentification of Names) by JAMES BRITTEN, F.L.S. 6s. 6d.
35. Glossary of the Lancashire Dialect. By J. H. NODAL and GEO. MILNER. Part II. (F to Z). 6s.
36. West Worcester Words. By MRS. CHAMBERLAIN. 4s. 6d.
37. Fitzherbert's Book of Husbandry, A.D. 1534. Edited with Introduction, Notes, and Glossarial Index. By the REV. PROFESSOR SKEAT. 8s. 6d.
38. Devonshire Plant Names. By the REV. HILDERIC FRIEND. 5s.
39. A Glossary of the Dialect of Aldmondbury and Huddersfield. By the Rev. A. EASHER, M.A., and the Rev. THOS. LEES, M.A. 8s. 6d.
40. HAMPSHIRE WORDS AND PHRASES. Compiled and Edited by the Rev. Sir WILLIAM H. COPE, Bart. 6s.
41. NATHANIEL BAILEY'S ENGLISH DIALECT WORDS OF THE 18TH CENTURY. Edited by W. E. A. AXON. 9s.
41.* THE TREATYSE OF FYSSHINGE WITH AN ANGLE. By JULIANA BARNES. An earlier form (circa 1450) edited with Glossary by THOMAS SATCHELL, and by him presented to the subscribers for 1883.
42. UPTON-ON-SEVERN WORDS AND PHRASES. By the Rev. Canon LAWSON. 2s. 6d.
43. ANGLO-FRENCH VOWEL SOUNDS. A Word List Illustrating their Correspondence with Modern English. By Miss B. M. SKEAT. 4s.
44. GLOSSARY OF CHESHIRE WORDS. By R. HOLLAND. Part I. (A–F.) 7s.
45. ENGLISH PLANT NAMES. Part III. completing the work. 10s.
46. GLOSSARY OF CHESHIRE WORDS. By ROBERT HOLLAND. Part 2. (G Z), completing the vocabulary. 9s.
47. BIRD NAMES. By the Rev. CHARLES SWAINSON. 12s.
48. FOUR DIALECT WORDS—Clem, Lake, Oss, Nesh. By THOMAS HALLAM. 4s.
49. REPORT ON DIALECTAL WORK, From May '85 to May '86. By A. J. ELLIS, F.R.S. (Miscellanies, No. 5). 2s.
50. GLOSSARY OF WEST SOMERSET WORDS. By F. T. ELWORTHY. 20s.
51. CHESHIRE GLOSSARY. By. R. HOLLAND. Part III. completing the work. 6s.
52. S.W. LINCOLNSHIRE GLOSSARY (Wapentake of Graffoe). By the Rev. R. E. COLE. 7s. 6d.

53. THE FOLK SPEECH OF SOUTH CHESHIRE. By THOMAS DARLINGTON. 15s.
54. A DICTIONARY OF THE KENTISH DIALECT. By the Rev. W. D. PARISH and the Rev. W. FRANK SHAW. 10s.
55. SECOND REPORT ON DIALECTAL WORK. From May '86 to May '87. By A. J. ELLIS, F.R.S. (Miscellanies, No. 6). 2s.

Freeman.—ON SPEECH FORMATION AS THE BASIS FOR TRUE SPELLING. By H. FREEMAN. Crown 8vo. pp. viii.-88, cloth. 3s. 6d.

Furnivall.—EDUCATION IN EARLY ENGLAND. Some Notes used as Forewords to a Collection of Treatises on "Manners and Meals in the Olden Time," for the Early English Text Society. By F. J. FURNIVALL, M.A. 8vo. sewed, pp. 74. 1s.

Garlanda.—THE FORTUNES OF WORDS. Letters to a Lady. By FEDERICO GARLANDA, Ph.D. Crown 8vo. pp. vi.-226, cloth. 1888. 5s.

Garlanda.—THE PHILOSOPHY OF WORDS. A Popular Introduction to the Science of Language. By FEDERICO GARLANDA, Ph.D. Crown 8vo. pp. vi.-294, cloth. 1888. 5s.

Gould.—GOOD ENGLISH; or, Popular Errors in Language. By E. S. GOULD. Revised Edition. Crown 8vo. cloth, pp. xii. and 214. 1880. 6s.

Hall.—ON ENGLISH ADJECTIVES IN -ABLE, with Special Reference to RELIABLE. By FITZEDWARD HALL, C.E., M.A., Hon. D.C.L. Oxon. Crown 8vo. cloth, pp. viii. and 238. 1877. 7s. 6d.

Hall.—MODERN ENGLISH. By FITZEDWARD HALL, M.A., Hon. D.C.L., Oxon. Cr. 8vo. cloth, pp. xvi. and 394. 1873. 10s. 6d.

Jackson.—SHROPSHIRE WORD-BOOK; A Glossary of Archaic and Provincial Words, etc., used in the County. By GEORGINA F. JACKSON. 8vo. pp. xcvi. and 524. 1881. 31s. 6d.

Manipulus Vocabulorum.—A Rhyming Dictionary of the English Language. By Peter Levins (1570). Edited, with an Alphabetical Index, by HENRY B. WHEATLEY. 8vo. pp. xvi. and 370, cloth. 14s.

Manning.—AN INQUIRY INTO THE CHARACTER AND ORIGIN OF THE POSSESSIVE AUGMENT in English and in Cognate Dialects. By the late JAMES MANNING, Q.A.S., Recorder of Oxford. 8vo. pp. iv. and 90. 2s.

Percy.—BISHOP PERCY'S FOLIO MANUSCRIPTS—BALLADS AND ROMANCES. Edited by John W. Hales, M.A., Fellow and late Assistant Tutor of Christ's College, Cambridge; and Frederick J. Furnivall, M.A., of Trinity Hall, Cambridge; assisted by Professor Child, of Harvard University, Cambridge, U.S.A., W. Chappell, Esq., etc. In 3 volumes. Vol. 1, pp. 610; Vol. 2, pp. 681; Vol. 3, pp. 640. Demy 8vo. half-bound. £4 4s. Extra demy 8vo. half-bound, on Whatman's ribbed paper, £6 6s. Extra royal 8vo., paper covers, on Whatman's best ribbed paper, £10 10s. Large 4to., paper covers, on Whatman's best ribbed paper, £12.

Philological Society. Transactions of the, contains several valuable Papers on Early English. For contents see page 24.

Shakespeare Notes.—By F. A. LEO. Demy 8vo. pp. viii. and 120, cloth. 1885. 6s.

Stratmann.—A DICTIONARY OF THE OLD ENGLISH LANGUAGE. Compiled from the writings of the XIIIth, XIVth, and XVth centuries. By FRANCIS HENRY STRATMANN. 3rd Edition. 4to. with Supplement. In wrapper. £1 16s.

Stratmann.—AN OLD ENGLISH POEM OF THE OWL AND THE NIGHTINGALE Edited by FRANCIS HENRY STRATMANN. 8vo. cloth, pp. 60. 3s.

Turner.—THE ENGLISH LANGUAGE. A Concise History of the English Language, with a Glossary showing the Derivation and Pronunciation of the English Words. By R. TURNER. In German and English on opposite pages. 18mo, sewed, pp. viii. and 80. 1884. 1s. 6d.

Wedgwood.—A DICTIONARY OF ENGLISH ETYMOLOGY. By HENSLEIGH WEDGWOOD. Third revised Edition. With an Introduction on the Formation of Language. Imperial 8vo., double column, pp. lxxii. and 746. 21s.

Wright.—FEUDAL MANUALS OF ENGLISH HISTORY. A Series of Popular Sketches of our National History, compiled at different periods, from the Thirteenth Century to the Fifteenth, for the use of the Feudal Gentry and Nobility. (In Old French). Now first edited from the Original Manuscripts. By THOMAS WRIGHT, Esq., M.A. Small 4to. cloth, pp. xxiv. and 184. 1872. 15s.

Wright.—ANGLO-SAXON AND OLD-ENGLISH VOCABULARIES, Illustrating the Condition and Manners of our Forefathers, as well as the History of the Forms of Elementary Education, and of the Languages Spoken in this Island from the Tenth Century to the Fifteenth. Edited by THOMAS WRIGHT, Esq., M.A., F.S.A., etc. Second Edition, edited and collated, by RICHARD WULCKER. 2 vols. 8vo. pp. xx.-408, and iv.-486, cloth. 1884. 28s.

Wright.—CELT, ROMAN, AND SAXON. See page 41.

FRISIAN.

Cummins.—A GRAMMAR OF THE OLD FRIESIC LANGUAGE. By A. H. CUMMINS, A.M. Second Edition, with Reading Book, Glossary, etc. Crown 8vo. cloth, pp. xvi. and 130. 1887. 6s.

Oera Linda Book, from a Manuscript of the Thirteenth Century, with the permission of the Proprietor, C. Over de Linden, of the Helder The Original Frisian Text, as verified by Dr. J. O. OTTEMA; accompanied by an English Version of Dr. Ottema's Dutch Translation, by WILLIAM R. SANDBACH. 8vo. cl. pp. xxvii. and 223. 5s.

GAUDIAN (See under "HOERNLE," page 42.)

OLD GERMAN.

Kroeger.—THE MINNESINGER OF GERMANY. By A. E. KROEGER. 12mo. cloth, pp. vi. and 284. 7s.

CONTENTS.—Chapter I. The Minnesinger and the Minnesong.—II. The Minnelay.—III. The Divine Minnesong.—IV. Walther von der Vogelweide.—V. Ulrich von Lichtenstein.—VI. The Metrical Romances of the Minnesinger and Gottfried von Strassburg's ' Tristan and Isolde."

GIPSY.

Leland.—THE ENGLISH GIPSIES AND THEIR LANGUAGE. By CHARLES G. LELAND. Second Edition. Crown 8vo. cloth, pp. 276. 7s. 6d.

Leland.—THE GYPSIES.—By C. G. LELAND. Crown 8vo. pp. 372, cloth. 1882. 10s. 6d.

Paspati.—Études sur les Tchinghianés (Gypsies) ou Bohémiens de l'Empire Ottoman. Par Alexandre G. Paspati, M.D. Large 8vo. sewed, pp. xii. and 652. Constantinople, 1871. 28s.

GOTHIC.

Skeat.—A Moeso-Gothic Glossary, with an Introduction, an Outline of Moeso-Gothic Grammar, and a List of Anglo-Saxon and Modern English Words etymologically connected with Moeso-Gothic. By the Rev. W. W. Skeat. Small 4to. cloth, pp. xxiv. and 342. 1868. 9s.

GREEK (Modern and Classic).

Bizyenos.—ΑΤΟΙΔΕΣ ΑΥΡΑΙ Poems. By M. Bizyenos. With Frontispiece Etched by Prof. A. Legros. Royal 8vo. pp. viii.-312. Printed on hand-made paper, and richly bound. 1884. £1 11s. 6d.

Buttmann.—A Grammar of the New Testament Greek. By A. Buttmann. Authorized translation by Prof J. H. Thayer, with numerous additions and corrections by the author. Demy 8vo. cloth, pp. xx. and 474. 187 . 14s.

Byrne.—Origin of the Greek, Latin and Gothic Roots. By James Byrne, M.A. Demy 8vo. pp. viii. and 360, cloth. 1887. 18s.

Contopoulos.—A Lexicon of Modern Greek-English and English Modern Greek. By N. Contopoulos. In 2 vols. 8vo. cloth. Part I. Modern Greek-English, pp. 460. Part II. English-Modern Greek, pp. 582. £1 7s.

Contopoulos.—Handbook of Greek and English Dialogues and Correspondence. Fcap. 8vo. cloth, pp. 258. 1879. 2s. 6d.

Edmonds.—Greek Lays, Idylls, Legends, etc. A Selection from Recent and Contemporary Poets. Translated by E. M. Edmonds. With Introduction and Notes. Crown 8vo. pp. xiv. and 264, cloth. 1885. 6s. 6d.

Gaster.—Ilchester Lectures on Greeko-Slavonic Literature, and its Relation to the Folk-lore of Europe during the Middle Ages. With two Appendices and Plates. By M. Gaster, Ph.D. Crown 8vo. pp. x. and 280, cloth. 1887. 7s. 6d.

Geldart.—A Guide to Modern Greek. By E. M. Geldart. Post 8vo. cloth, pp. xii. and 274. 1883. 7s. 6d. Key, cloth, pp. 28. 2s. 6d.

Geldart.—Simplified Grammar of Modern Greek. By E. M. Geldart, M.A. Crown 8vo. pp. 68, cloth. 1883. 2s. 6d.

Lascarides.—A Comprehensive Phraseological English-Ancient and Modern Greek Lexicon. Founded upon a manuscript of G. P. Lascarides, Esq., and Compiled by L. Myrianthieus, Ph. D. In 2 vols. foolscap 8vo. pp. xiv. and 1,338, cloth. 1882. £1 10s.

Murdoch.—A Note on Indo-European Phonology. With Especial Reference to the True Pronunciation of Ancient Greek. By D. B. Murdoch, L.R.C.P., etc. Demy 8vo. pp. 40, wrapper. 1887. 1s. 6d.

Newman.—Comments on the Text of Æschylus. By F. W. Newman. Demy 8vo. pp. xii. and 144, cloth. 1884. 5s.

Sophocles.—Romaic or Modern Greek Grammar. By E. A. Sophocles. 8vo. pp. xxviii. and 196. 10s. 6d.

Sophocles.—Greek Lexicon of the Roman and Byzantine Periods (From B.C. 146 to A.D. 1100). By E. A. Sophocles. Super-royal 8vo. pp. xvi.-1188, half-bound, cloth sides. 52s. 6d.

GUJARATI.

Catalogue of Gujarati Books sold by Messrs. Trübner and Co. post free for penny stamp.

Minocheherji.—Pahlavi, Gujarâti and English Dictionary. By Jamaspji Dastur Minochehekji Jamasp Asana. 8vo. Vol. I., pp. clxii. and 1 to 168. Vol. II., pp. xxxii and pp. 169 to 440. 1877 and 1879. Cloth. 14s. each. (To be completed in 5 vols.)

Shápurjí Edaljí.—A Grammar of the Gujarátí Language. By Shápurjí Edaljí. Cloth, pp. 127. 10s. 6d.

Shápurjí Edaljí.—A Dictionary, Gujarati and English. By Shápurjí Edaljí. Second Edition. Crown 8vo. cloth, pp. xxiv. and 874. 21s.

GURMUKHI (Punjabi).

Adi Granth (The); or, The Holy Scriptures of the Sikhs, translated from the original Gurmuki, with Introductory Essays, by Dr. Ernest Trumpp, Munich. Roy. 8vo. pp. 866, cloth. £2 12s. 6d.

Singh.—Sakhee Book; or, The Description of Gooroo Gobind Singh's Religion and Doctrines, translated from Gooroo Mukhi into Hindi, and afterwards into English. By Sirdar Attar Singh, Chief of Bhadour. With the author's photograph. 8vo. pp. xviii. and 205. 15s.

HAWAIIAN.

Andrews.—A Dictionary of the Hawaiian Language, to which is appended an English-Hawaiian Vocabulary, and a Chronological Table of Remarkable Events. By Lorrin Andrews. 8vo. pp. 500, cloth. £1 11s. 6d.

HEBREW.

Bickell.—Outlines of Hebrew Grammar. By Gustavus Bickell, D.D. Revised by the Author; Annotated by the Translator, Samuel Ives Curtiss, junior, Ph.D. With a Lithographic Table of Semitic Characters by Dr. J. Euting. Cr. 8vo. sd., pp. xiv. and 140. 1877. 3s. 6d.

Collins.—A Grammar and Lexicon of the Hebrew Language, entitled Sefer Hassohám. By Rabbi Moseh Ben Yitshak, of England. Edited from a MS. in the Bodleian Library of Oxford, and collated with a MS. in the Imperial Library of St. Petersburg, with Additions and Corrections. By G. W. Collins, M.A., Corpus Christi College, Camb., Hon. Hebrew Lecturer, Keble College, Oxford. Part I. 4to. pp. 112, wrapper. 1884. 7s. 6d.

Gesenius.—Hebrew and English Lexicon of the Old Testament, including the Biblical Chaldee, from the Latin. By Edward Robinson. Fifth Edition. 8vo. cloth, pp. xii. and 1160. £1 16s.

Gesenius.—HEBREW GRAMMAR. Translated from the Seventeenth Edition. By Dr. T. J. CONANT. With Grammatical Exercises, and a Chrestomathy by the Translator. 8vo. cloth, pp. xvi.–364. £1.

Hebrew Literature Society (Publications of the).

First Series.

Vol. I. Miscellany of Hebrew Literature. Demy 8vo. cloth, pp. viii. and 228. 10s.
Vol. II. The Commentary of Ibn Ezra on Isaiah. Edited from MSS., and Translated with Notes, Introductions, and Indexes, by M. FRIEDLÄNDER, Ph.D. Vol. I. Translation of the Commentary. Demy 8vo. cloth, pp. xxviii. and 332. 10s. 6d.
Vol. III. The Commentary of Ibn Ezra. Vol. II. The Anglican Version of the Book of the Prophet Isaiah amended according to the Commentary of Ibn Ezra. Demy 8vo. cloth, pp. 112. 4s. 6d.

Second Series.

Vol. I. Miscellany of Hebrew Literature. Vol. II. Edited by the Rev. A. LÖWY. Demy 8vo. cloth, pp. vi. and 276. 10s. 6d.
Vol. II. The Commentary of Ibn Ezra. Vol. III. Demy 8vo. cloth, pp. 172. 7s.
Vol. III. Ibn Ezra Literature. Vol. IV. Essays on the Writings of Abraham Ibn Ezra. By M. FRIEDLANDER, Ph.D. Demy 8vo. cloth, pp. x.–252 and 78. 12s. 6d.

Third Series.

Vols. I.–III. The Guide of the Perplexed of Maimonides. Translated from the original text and annotated by M. Friedländer, Ph.D. Demy 8vo. pp. lxxx.–370, and x.–226, and xxviii.–328, cloth. £1 11s. 6d.

Hershon.—TALMUDIC MISCELLANY. See "Trübner's Oriental Series," page 4.

Jastrow.—A DICTIONARY OF THE TARGUMIM, THE TALMUD BABLI AND Yerushalmi, and the Midrashic Literature. Compiled by M. JASTROW, Ph.D. Demy 4to. boards. Part I. pp. 100. 5s. Part II. pp. 96. 5s.

Land.—THE PRINCIPLES OF HEBREW GRAMMAR. By J. P. N. LAND, Professor of Logic and Metaphysic in the University of Leyden. Translated from the Dutch by REGINALD LANE POOLE, Balliol College, Oxford. Part I. Sounds. Part II. Words. Crown 8vo. pp. xx. and 220, cloth. 7s. 6d.

Mathews.—ABRAHAM BEN EZRA'S UNEDITED COMMENTARY ON THE CANTICLES, the Hebrew Text after two MS., with English Translation by H. J. MATHEWS, B.A., Exeter College, Oxford. 8vo. cl. limp, pp. x., 34, 24. 2s. 6d.

Nutt.—TWO TREATISES ON VERBS CONTAINING FEEBLE AND DOUBLE LETTERS by R. Jehuda Hayug of Fez, translated into Hebrew from the original Arabic by R. Moses Gikatilia, of Cordova; with the Treatise on Punctuation by the same Author, translated by Aben Ezra. Edited from Bodleian MSS. with an English Translation by J. W. NUTT, M.A. Demy 8vo. sewed, pp. 312. 1870. 7s. 6d.

Semitic (Songs of the). In English Verse. By G. E. W. Cr. 8vo. cloth, pp. 140. 5s.

Weber.—System der altsynagogalen Palästinischen Theologie. By Dr. FERD. WEBER. 8vo. sewed. Leipzig, 1880. 7s.

HINDI.

Catalogue of Hindi Books sold by Messrs. Trübner and Co. post free for penny stamp.

Ballantyne.—ELEMENTS OF HINDÍ AND BRAJ BHÁKÁ GRAMMAR. By the late JAMES R. BALLANTYNE, LL.D. Second edition, revised and corrected. Crown 8vo., pp. 38, cloth. 1868. 5s.

Bate.—A DICTIONARY OF THE HINDEE LANGUAGE. Compiled by J. D. BATE. 8vo. cloth, pp. 806. £2 12s. 6d.

Beames.—NOTES ON THE BHOJPURÍ DIALECT OF HINDÍ, spoken in Western Behar. By JOHN BEAMES, Esq., B.C.S., Magistrate of Chumparun. 8vo. pp. 26, sewed. 1868. 1s. 6d.

Browne.—A HINDI PRIMER. In Roman Character. By J. F. BROWNE, B.C.S. Crown 8vo. pp. 36, cloth. 1882. 2s. 6d.

Hoernle.—Hindi Grammar. See page 49.

Kellogg.—A GRAMMAR OF THE HINDI LANGUAGE, in which are treated the Standard Hindi, Braj, and the Eastern Hindi of the Ramayan of Tulsi Das; also the Colloquial Dialects of Marwar, Kumaon, Avadh, Baghelkhand, Bhojpur, etc., with Copious Philological Notes. By the Rev. S. H. KELLOGG, M.A. Royal 8vo. cloth, pp. 400. 21s.

Mahabharata. Translated into Hindi for MADAN MOHUN BHATT, by KRISHNACHANDRADHARMADHIKARIN of Benares. (Containing all but the Harivansá.) 3 vols. 8vo. cloth, pp. 574, 810, and 1106. £2 2s.

Mathuráprasáda Misra.—A TRILINGUAL DICTIONARY, being a Comprehensive Lexicon in English, Urdú, and Hindi, exhibiting the Syllabication, Pronunciation, and Etymology of English Words, with their Explanation in English, and in Urdú and Hindi in the Roman Character. By MATHURAPRASADA MISRA, Second Master, Queen's College, Benares. 8vo. cloth, pp. xv. and 1330. Benares, 1865. £1 10s.

HINDUSTANI.

Catalogue of Hindustani Books sold by Messrs. Trübner and Co. post free for penny stamp.

Ballantyne.—HINDUSTANI SELECTIONS in the Naskhi and Devanagari Character. With a Vocabulary of the Words. Prepared for the use of the Scottish Naval and Military Academy, by JAMES R. BALLANTYNE. Royal 8vo. cloth, pp. 74. 3s. 6d.

Craven.—The Popular Dictionary in English and Hindustani and Hindustani and English. with a Number of Useful Tables. By the Rev. T. CRAVEN, M.A. Fcap. 8vo. pp. 214, cloth. 1882. 3s. 6d.

Dowson.—A GRAMMAR of the Urdu or Hindustani Language. By J. DOWSON. Second Edition. Crown 8vo. pp. xvi. and 264, cloth. 1887. 10s. 6d.

Dowson.—A HINDUSTANI EXERCISE BOOK. Containing a Series of Passages and Extracts adapted for Translation into Hindustani. By JOHN DOWSON, M.R.A.S. Crown 8vo. pp. 100, limp cloth. 2s. 6d.

Eastwick.—KHIRAD AFROZ (The Illuminator of the Understanding). By Maulaví Hafízu'd-dín. A New Edition of Hindústání Text, carefully revised, with Notes, Critical and Explanatory. By EDWARD B. EASTWICK, F.R.S., Imperial 8vo. cloth, pp. xiv. and 319. Re-issue, 1867. 18s.

Fallon.—A NEW HINDUSTANI-ENGLISH DICTIONARY. With Illustrations from Hindustani Literature and Folk-lore. By S. W. FALLON, Ph.D. Halle Roy. 8vo. cloth, pp. xxviii. and 1216 and x Benares, 1879. £3 10s.

Fallon.—ENGLISH-HINDUSTANI DICTIONARY. With Illustrations from English Literature and Colloquial English Translated into Hindustani. By S. W. FALLON. Roy. 8vo. pp. iv.-674, sewed. £1 10s.

Fallon.—A HINDUSTANI-ENGLISH LAW AND COMMERCIAL DICTIONARY. By S. W. FALLON. 8vo. cloth, pp. ii. and 284. Benares, 1879. 12s. 6d.

Ikhwánu-s Safá; or, BROTHERS OF PURITY. Describing the Contention between Men and Beasts as to the Superiority of the Human Race. Translated from the Hindústání by Professor J. DOWSON, Staff College, Sandhurst. Crown 8vo. pp. viii. and 156, cloth. 7s.

Khirad-Afroz (The Illuminator of the Understanding). By Maulaví Hafizu'd din. A new edition of the Hindú-táni Text, carefully revised, with Notes, Critical and Explanatory. By E. B. EASTWICK, M.P., F.R.S. 8vo. cloth, pp. xiv. and 321. 18s.

Lutaifi Hindee (The); or, HINDOOSTANEE JEST-BOOK, containing a Choice Collection of Humorous Stories in the Arabic and Roman Characters; to which is added a Hindoostanee Poem by MEER MOOHUMMUD TUQUEE. 2nd edition, revised by W. C. Smyth. 8vo. pp. xvi. and 160. 1840. 10s. 6d.; reduced to 5s.

Mathuráprasáda Misra.—A TRILINGUAL DICTIONARY, being a comprehensive Lexicon in English, Urdú, and Hindi. See under Hindi, page 83.

Palmer.—HINDUSTANI GRAMMAR. See page 56.

HUNGARIAN.

Singer.—SIMPLIFIED GRAMMAR OF THE HUNGARIAN LANGUAGE. By I. SINGER, of Buda-Pesth. Crown 8vo. cloth, pp. vi. and 88. 1884. 4s. 6d.

ICELANDIC.

Anderson—NORSE MYTHOLOGY, or the Religion of our Forefathers. Containing all the Myths of the Eddas carefully systematized and interpreted, with an Introduction, Vocabulary and Index. By R. B. ANDERSON, Prof. of Scandinavian Languages in the University of Wisconsin. Crown 8vo. cloth. Chicago, 1879. 12s. 6d.

Anderson and Bjarnason.—VIKING TALES OF THE NORTH. The Sagas of Thorstein, Viking's Son, and Fridthjof the Bold. Translated from the Icelandic by R. B. Anderson, M.A., and J. Bjarnason. Also, Tegner's Fridthjof's Saga. Translated into English by G. Stephens. Crown 8vo. cloth, pp. xviii. and 370. Chicago, 1877. 10s.

Cleasby.—AN ICELANDIC-ENGLISH DICTIONARY. Based on the MS. Collections of the late Richard Cleasby. Enlarged and completed by G. VIGFUSSON. With an Introduction, and Life of Richard Cleasby, by G. WEBBE DASENT, D.C.L. 4to. £3 7s.

Cleasby.—APPENDIX TO AN ICELANDIC-ENGLISH DICTIONARY. See Skeat.

Edda Saemundar Hinns Froda—The Edda of Saemund the Learned. From the Old Norse or Icelandic. By BENJAMIN THORPE. Part II, with Index of Persons and Places. 12mo. pp. viii. and 172, cloth. 1866. 4s.

Publications of the Icelandic Literary Society of Copenhagen. For Numbers 1 to 54, see " Record," No. 111, p. 14.

55. SKÍRNER TÍDINDI. Hins Islenzka Bókmentafélags, 1878. 8vo. pp. 176. Kaupmannahöfn, 1878. Price 5s.
56. UM SIDBÓTINA Á ISLANDI eptir Þorkel Bjarnason, prest á Reynivöllum. Utgefid af Hinu Islenzka Bókmentafélagi. 8vo. pp. 177. Reykjavik, 1878. Price 7s. 6d.
57. BISKUPA SÖGUR, gefnar út af Hinu Íslenzka Bókmentafélagi. Annat Bindi III. 1878. 8vo. pp. 509 to 804. Kaupmannahöfn. Price 10s.
58. SKÝRSLUR OG REIKNÍNGAR Hins Islenzka Bókmentafélags, 1877 to 1878. 8vo. pp. 28. Kaupmannahöfn, 1878. Price 2s.
59. FRJETTIR FRA ISLANDI, 1877, eptir V. Briem. 8vo. pp. 50. Reykjavik, 1878. Price 2s. 6d.
60. ALÞÍNGISSTADUR HINN FORNI VID Öxara, med Uppdrattum eptir Sigurd Gudmundsson. 8vo. pp. 66, with Map. Kaupmannahöfn, 1878. Price 6s.

Skeat.—A LIST OF ENGLISH WORDS, the Etymology of which is illustrated by Comparison with Icelandic. Prepared in the form of an Appendix to Cleasby and Vigfusson's Icelandic-English Dictionary. By the Rev. WALTER W. SKEAT, M.A., English Lecturer and late Fellow of Christ's College, Cambridge; and M.A. of Exeter College, Oxford; one of the Vice-Presidents of the Cambridge Philological Society; and Member of the Council of the Philological Society of London. 1876. Demy 4to. sewed. 2s.

Tegner.—FRIDTHJOF'S SAGA, A NORSE ROMANCE. By ESAIAS TEGNÉR, Bishop of Wexiö. Translated from the Swedish by THOMAS A. E. HOLCOMB and MARTHA A. LYON HOLCOMB. Crown 8vo. pp. viii.-214, cloth. 1883. 6s. 6d.

Thorhelson, Pall.—DICTIONNAIRE ISLANDAIS-FRANCAIS. Vol. I. Part I. 8vo. pp. 32. To be completed in about 50 parts. Price 1s. each.

JAPANESE.

Aston.—A GRAMMAR OF THE JAPANESE WRITTEN LANGUAGE. By W. G. ASTON, M.A., Assistant Japanese Secretary, H B.M.'s Legation, Yedo, Japan. Second edition, Enlarged and Improved. Royal 8vo. pp. 306. 28s.

Aston.—A SHORT GRAMMAR OF THE JAPANESE SPOKEN LANGUAGE. By W. G. ASTON, M.A., H. B. M.'s Legation, Yedo, Japan. Third edition. 12mo. cloth, pp. 96. 12s.

Black.—YOUNG JAPAN, YOKOHAMA AND YEDO. A Narrative of the Settlement and the City, from the Signing of the Treaties in 1858 to the close of the Year 1879. With a Glance at the Progress of Japan during a period of Twenty-one Years. By J. R. BLACK. Two Vols., demy 8vo. pp. xviii. and 418 ; xiv. and 522, cloth. 1881. £2 2s.

Chamberlain. — A ROMANISED JAPANESE READER. Consisting of Japanese Anecdotes, Maxims, etc., in Easy Written Style ; with English Translation and Notes. By B. H. CHAMBERLAIN, Professor of Japanese at l Philology in the Imperial University of Tokyo. 12mo. pp. xlii.—346, cloth. 1886. 6s.

Chamberlain.—SIMPLIFIED JAPANESE GRAMMAR. See page 50.
Chamberlain.—CLASSICAL POETRY OF THE JAPANESE. See page 4.
Dickins.—THE OLD BAMBOO-HEWER'S STORY (Taketori no Okina no Monogatari). The Earliest of the Japanese Romances, written in the Tenth Century. Translated, with Observations and Notes, by F. VICTOR DICKINS. With Three Chromo-Lithographic Illustrations taken from Japanese Makimonos, to which is added the Original Text in Roman, with Grammar, Analytical Notes and Vocabulary. 8vo. cl., pp. 118. 1888. 7s. 6d.
Hepburn.—A JAPANESE AND ENGLISH DICTIONARY. With an English and Japanese Index. By J. C. HEPBURN, M.D., LL.D. Second edition. Imperial 8vo. cloth, pp. xxxii., 632 and 201. 18s.
Hepburn.—A JAPANESE-ENGLISH AND ENGLISH-JAPANESE DICTIONARY. By J. C. HEPBURN, M.D., LL.D. Third Edition, demy 8vo. pp. xxxiv.—964, half-morocco. 1887. £1 10s.
Hepburn.—A JAPANESE-ENGLISH AND ENGLISH-JAPANESE DICTIONARY. By J. C. HEPBURN, M.D., LL.D. Abridged by the Author. Second Edition, Revised and Enlarged. 16mo. cloth, pp. viii. and 1033. 1887. 14s.
Hoffmann, J. J.—A JAPANESE GRAMMAR. Second Edition. Large 8vo. cloth, pp. viii. and 368, with two plates. £1 1s.
Hoffmann.—SHOPPING DIALOGUES, in Japanese, Dutch, and English. By Professor J. HOFFMANN. Oblong 8vo. pp. xiii. and 44, sewed. 5s.
Hoffmann (Prof. Dr. J. J.)—JAPANESE-ENGLISH DICTIONARY.—Published by order of the Dutch Government. Elaborated and Edited by Dr. L. SERRURIER. Vols. 1 and 2. Royal 8vo. Brill, 1881. 12s. 6d.
Imbrie.— HANDBOOK OF ENGLISH-JAPANESE ETYMOLOGY. By W. IMBRIE. 8vo. pp. xxiv. and 208, cloth. Tôkiyô, 1880. £1 1s.
Metchnikoff.—L'Empire Japonais, texte et dessins, par L. METCHNIKOFF. 4to. pp. viii. and 694. Illustrated with maps, coloured plates and woodcuts. cloth. 1881. £1 10s.
Pfoundes.—FU SO MIMI BUKURO. See page 37.
Satow.—AN ENGLISH JAPANESE DICTIONARY OF THE SPOKEN LANGUAGE. By ERNEST MASON SATOW, Japanese Secretary to H.M. Legation at Yedo, and ISHIBASHI MASAKATA, of the Imperial Japanese Foreign Office. Second edition. Imp. 32mo., pp. xvi. and 416, cloth. 12s. 6d.
Suyematz.—GENJI MONOGATARI. The most celebrated of the Classical Japanese Romances. Translated by K. SUYEMATZ. Crown 8vo. pp. xvi. and 254, cloth. 1882. 7s. 6d.

KABAIL.

Newman.—KABAIL VOCABULARY. Supplemented by Aid of a New Source. By F. W. NEWMAN, Emeritus Professor of University College, London. Crown 8vo., pp. 124, cloth. 1888. 5s.

KANARESE.

Garrett.—A MANUAL ENGLISH AND KANARESE DICTIONARY, containing about Twenty-three Thousand Words. By J. GARRETT. 8vo. pp. 908, cloth. Bangalore, 1872. 18s.

KAYATHI.

Grierson.—A HANDBOOK TO THE KAYATHI CHARACTER. By G. A. GRIERSON, B.C.S., late Subdivisional Officer, Madhubani, Darbhanga. With Thirty Plates in Facsimile, with Translations. 4to. cloth, pp. vi. and 4. Calcutta, 1881. 18s.

KELTIC (CORNISH, GAELIC, WELSH, IRISH).

Bottrell.—TRADITIONS AND HEARTHSIDE STORIES OF WEST CORNWALL. By WILLIAM BOTTRELL. With Illustrations by Mr. JOSEPH BLIGHT. Crown 8vo. cloth. Second Series, pp. iv. and 300. 6s. Third Series, pp. viii. and 200, cloth. 1880. 6s.

Evans.—DICTIONARY OF THE WELSH LANGUAGE. By the Rev. D. SILVAN EVANS, B.D., Rector of Llanwrin, N. Wales. Part 1, A—AWYS. Royal 8vo. pp. 420, paper. 1887. 10s. 6d.

Rhys.—LECTURES ON WELSH PHILOLOGY. By JOHN RHYS, M.A., Professor of Celtic at Oxford. Second revised and enlarged edition. Crown 8vo. cloth, pp. xiv. and 468. 1879. 15s.

Spurrell.—A GRAMMAR OF THE WELSH LANGUAGE. By WILLIAM SPURRELL. 3rd Edition. Fcap. cloth, pp. viii.-206. 1870. 3s.

Spurrell.—A WELSH DICTIONARY. English-Welsh and Welsh-English. With Preliminary Observations on the Elementary Sounds of the English Language, a copious Vocabulary of the Roots of English Words, a list of Scripture Proper Names and English Synonyms and Explanations. By WILLIAM SPURRELL. Third Edition. Fcap. cloth, pp. xxv. and 732. 8s. 6d.

Stokes.—GOIDELICA—Old and Early-Middle Irish Glosses: Prose and Verse. Edited by WHITLEY STOKES. Second edition. Medium 8vo. cloth, pp. 192. 1872. 18s.

Stokes.—TOGAIL TROI; The Destruction of Troy. Transcribed from the fascimile of the Book of Leinster, and Translated, with a Glossarial Index of the Rare Words, by W. STOKES. 8vo. pp. xv.-188, boards. 1882. 18s. A limited edition only, privately printed, Calcutta.

Stokes.—THE BRETON GLOSSES AT ORLEANS. By W. STOKES. 8vo. pp. x.-78, boards. 1880. 10s. 6d. A limited edition only, privately printed, Calcutta.

Stokes.—THREE MIDDLE-IRISH HOMILIES on the Lives of Saints Patrick, Brigit, and Columba. By W. STOKES. 8vo. pp. xii.-140, boards. 1877. 10s. 6d. A limited edition only privately printed, Calcutta.

Stokes.—BEUNANS MERIASEK. The Life of Saint Meriasek, Bishop and Confessor. A Cornish Drama. Edited, with a Translation and Notes, by WHITLEY STOKES. Medium 8vo. cloth, pp. xvi.-280, and Facsimile. 1872. 15s.

Stokes.—THE OLD-IRISH GLOSSES AT WÜRZBURG AND CARLSRUHE. Edited, with a Translation and Glossarial Index, by WHITLEY STOKES, D.C.L., Part I. The Glosses and Translation. Demy 8vo. pp. viii. and 342, paper. 10s. 6d.

Wright's Celt, Roman, and Saxon. See page 41.

KONKANI.

Maffei.—A Konkani Grammar. By Angelus F. X. Maffei. 8vo. pp. xiv. and 438, cloth. Mangalore, 1882. 18s.

Maffei.—An English-Konkani and Konkani-English Dictionary. 8vo. pp. xii. and 546; xii. and 158. Two parts in one. Half bound. £1 10s.

LIBYAN.

Newman.—Libyan Vocabulary. An Essay towards Reproducing the Ancient Numidian Language, out of Four Modern Languages. By F. W. Newman, Emeritus Professor of University College, London. Crown 8vo. pp. vi. and 204, cloth. 1882. 10s. 6d.

MAHRATTA (Marathi).

Catalogue of Marathi Books sold by Messrs. Trübner & Co. post free for penny stamp.

Æsop's Fables.—Originally Translated into Marathi by Sadashiva Kashinath Chhatre. Revised from the 1st ed. 8vo. cloth. Bombay, 1877. 5s. 6d.

Ballantyne.—A Grammar of the Mahratta Language. For the use of the East India College at Haileybury. By James R. Ballantyne, of the Scottish Naval and Military Academy. 4to. cloth, pp. 56. 5s.

Bellairs.—A Grammar of the Marathi Language. By H. S. K. Bellairs, M.A., and Laxman Y. Ashkedkar, B.A. 12mo. cloth, pp. 90. 5s.

Molesworth.—A Dictionary, Márathi and English. Compiled by J. T. Molesworth, assisted by George and Thomas Candy. Second Edition, revised and enlarged. By J. T. Molesworth. Royal 4to. pp. xxx and 922, boards. Bombay, 1857. £2 2s.

Molesworth.—A Compendium of Molesworth's Marathi and English Dictionary. By Baba Padmanji. Second Edition. Revised and Enlarged. Demy 8vo. pp. xx. and 624, cloth. 15s.

Navalkar.—The Student's Maráthi Grammar. By G. R. Navalkar. New Edition. 8vo. cloth, pp. xvi. and 342. Bombay, 1879. 18s.

Tukarama.—A Complete Collection of the Poems of Tukárama (the Poet of the Mahárashtra). In Marathi. Edited by Vishnu Parashuram Shastri Pandit, under the supervision of Sankar Pandurang Pandit, M.A. With a complete Index to the Poems and a Glossary of difficult Words. To which is prefixed a Life of the Poet in English, by Janárdan Sakhárám Gádgil. 2 vols. in large 8vo. cloth, pp. xxxii. and 742, and pp. 728, 18 and 72. Bombay 1873. £1 1s. each vol.

MALAGASY.

Catalogue of Malagasy Books sold by Messrs. Trübner & Co. post free for penny stamp.

Parker.—A Concise Grammar of the Malagasy Language. By G. W. Parker. Crown 8vo. pp. 66, with an Appendix, cloth. 1883. 5s.

Van der Tuuk.—Outlines of a Grammar of the Malagasy Language. By H. N. van der Tuuk. 8vo., pp. 28, sewed. 1s.

MALAY.

Catalogue of Malay Books sold by Messrs. Trübner & Co. post free for penny stamp.

Dennys.—A HANDBOOK OF MALAY COLLOQUIAL, as spoken in Singapore, Being a Series of Introductory Lessons for Domestic and Business Purposes. By N. B. DENNYS, Ph.D., F.R.G.S., M.R.A.S, etc , Author of "The Folklore of China," etc. 8vo. pp. 204, cloth. 1878. £1 1s.

Maxwell.—A MANUAL OF THE MALAY LANGUAGE. With an Introductory Sketch of the Sanskrit Element in Malay. By W. E. MAXWELL, Assistant Resident, Perak, Malay Peninsula. Crown 8vo. cloth, pp. viii.-184. 1882. 7s. 6d.

Miscellaneous Papers relating to Indo-China and the Indian Archipelago. See page 7.

Swettenham.—VOCABULARY OF THE ENGLISH AND MALAY LANGUAGES. With Notes. By F. A. SWETTENHAM. 2 Vols. Vol. I. English-Malay Vocabulary and Dialogues. Vol. II. Malay-English Vocabulary. Small 8vo. boards. Singapore, 1881. £1.

The Traveller's Malay Pronouncing Handbook, for the Use of Travellers and New-comers to Singapore. 32mo. pp. 251, boards. *Singapore*, 1886. 5s.

Van der Tuuk.—SHORT ACCOUNT OF THE MALAY MANUSCRIPTS BELONGING TO THE ROYAL ASIATIC SOCIETY. By H. N. VAN DER TUUK. 8vo. pp. 52. 2s. 6d.

MALAYALIM.

Gundert.—A MALAYALAM AND ENGLISH DICTIONARY. By Rev. H. GUNDERT, D. Ph. Royal 8vo. pp. viii. and 1116. £2 10s.

MAORI.

Grey.—MAORI MEMENTOS: being a Series of Addresses presented by the Native People to His Excellency Sir George Grey, K.C.B., F.R.S. With Introductory Remarks and Explanatory Notes; to which is added a small Collection of Laments, etc. By CH. OLIVER B. DAVIS. 8vo. pp. iv. and 228, cloth, 12s.

Williams.—FIRST LESSONS IN THE MAORI LANGUAGE. With a Short Vocabulary. By W. L. WILLIAMS, B.A. Fcap. 8vo. pp. 98, cloth. 5s.

PALI.

D'Alwis.—A DESCRIPTIVE CATALOGUE of Sanskrit, Pali, and Sinhalese Literary Works of Ceylon. By JAMES D'ALWIS, M.R.A.S., etc., Vol. I. (all published), pp. xxxii. and 244. 1870. 8s. 6d.

Beal.—DHAMMAPADA. See "Trübner's Oriental Series," page 3.

Bigandet.—GAUDAMA. See "Trübner's Oriental Series," page 4.

Buddhist Birth Stories. See "Trübner's Oriental Series," page 4.

Bühler.—THREE NEW EDICTS OF AŚOKA. By G. BÜHLER. 16mo. sewed, with Two Facsimiles. 2s. 6d.

Childers.—A PALI-ENGLISH DICTIONARY, with Sanskrit Equivalents, and numerous Quotations, Extracts, and References. Compiled by the late Prof. R. C. CHILDERS, late of the Ceylon C. S. Imperial 8vo., double columns, pp. xxii. and 622, cloth. 1875. £3 3s. The first Pali Dictionary ever published.

Childers.—THE MAHÂPARINIBBÂNASUTTA OF THE SUTTA-PITAKA. The Pali Text. Edited by the late Professor R. C. CHILDERS. 8vo. cloth, pp. 72. 5s.

Childers.—ON SANDHI IN PALI. By the late Prof. R. C. CHILDERS. 8vo. sewed, pp. 22. 1s.

Coomára Swamy.—SUTTA NIPÁTA; or, the Dialogues and Discourses of Gotama Buddha. Translated from the Pali, with Introduction and Notes. By Sir M. COOMARA SWAMY. Cr. 8vo. cloth, pp. xxxvi. and 160. 1874. 6s.

Coomára Swamy.—THE DATHÁVANSA; or, the History of the Tooth-Relic of Gotama Buddha. The Pali Text and its Translation into English, with Notes. By Sir M. COOMARA SWAMY, Mudeliár. Demy 8vo. cloth, pp. 174. 1874. 10s. 6d. English Translation only, with Notes. Pp. 100, cloth. 6s.

Davids.—See BUDDHIST BIRTH STORIES, "Trübner's Oriental Series," page 4.

Davids.—SIGIRI, THE LION ROCK, NEAR PULASTIPURA, AND THE 39TH CHAPTER OF THE MAHÁVAMSA. By T. W. RHYS DAVIDS. 8vo. pp. 30. 1s. 6d.

Dickson.—THE PÁTIMOKKHA, being the Buddhist Office of the Confession of Priests. The Pali Text, with a Translation, and Notes, by J. F. DICKSON. 8vo. sd., pp. 69. 2s.

Fausböll.—JÁTAKA. See under JÁTAKA.

Fausböll.—THE DASARATHA-JÁTAKA, being the Buddhist Story of King Ráma. The original Pali Text, with a Translation and Notes by V. FAUSBÖLL. 8vo. sewed, pp. iv. and 48. 2s. 6d.

Fausböll.—FIVE JÁTAKAS, containing a Fairy Tale, a Comical Story, and Three Fables. In the original Páli Text, accompanied with a Translation and Notes. By V. FAUSBÖLL. 8vo. sewed, pp. viii. and 72. 6s.

Fausböll.—TEN JÁTAKAS. The Original Páli Text, with a Translation and Notes. By V. FAUSBÖLL. 8vo. sewed, pp. xiii. and 128. 7s. 6d.

Fryer.—VUTTODAYA. (Exposition of Metre.) By SAṄGHARAKKHITA THERA. A Pali Text, Edited, with Translation and Notes, by Major G. E. FRYER. 8vo. pp. 44. 2s. 6d.

Haas.—CATALOGUE OF SANSKRIT AND PALI BOOKS IN THE LIBRARY OF THE BRITISH MUSEUM. By Dr. ERNST HAAS. Printed by Permission of the Trustees of the British Museum. 4to. cloth, pp. 200. £1 1s.

Jataka (The); together with its Commentary. Being Tales of the Anterior Birth of Gotama Buddha. For the first time Edited in the original Pali by V. FAUSBÖLL. Demy 8vo. cloth. Vol. I. pp. 512. 1877. 28s. Vol. II., pp. 452. 1879. 28s. Vol. III. pp. viii.-544. 1883. 28s. Vol. IV. pp. x.-450. 1887. 28s. For Translation see under "Buddhist Birth Stories," page 4.

The "Jataka" is a collection of legends in Pali, relating the history of Buddha's transmigration before he was born as Gotama. The great antiquity of this work is authenticated by its forming part of the sacred canon of the Southern Buddhists, which was finally settled at the last Council in 246 B.C. The collection has long been known as a storehouse of ancient fables, and as the most original attainable source to which almost the whole of this kind of literature, from the Panchatantra and Pilpay's fables down to the nursery stories of the present day, is traceable; and it has been considered desirable, in the interest of Buddhistic studies as well as for more general literary purposes, that an edition and translation of the complete work should be prepared. The present publication is intended to supply this want.—*Athenæum*.

Mahawansa (The)—THE MAHAWANSA. From the Thirty-Seventh Chapter. Revised and edited, under orders of the Ceylon Government, by H. SUMANGALA, and DON ANDRIS DE SILVA BATUWANTUDAWA. Vol. I. Pali Text in Sinhalese character, pp. xxxii. and 436. Vol. II. Sinhalese Translation, pp. lii. and 378 half-bound. Colombo, 1877. £2 2s.

Mason.—THE PALI TEXT OF KACHCHAYANO'S GRAMMAR, WITH ENGLISH ANNOTATIONS. By FRANCIS MASON, D.D. I. The Text Aphorisms, 1 to 673. II. The English Annotations, including the various Readings of six independent Burmese Manuscripts, the Singalese Text on Verbs, and the Cambodian Text on Syntax. To which is added a Concordance of the Aphorisms. In Two Parts. 8vo. sewed, pp. 208, 75, and 28. Toongoo, 1871. £1 11s. 6d.

Minayeff.—GRAMMAIRE PALIE. Esquisse d'une Phonétique et d'une Morphologie de la Langue Palie. Traduite du Russe par St. Guyard. By J. MINAYEFF. 8vo. pp. 128. Paris, 1874. 8s.

Müller.—SIMPLIFIED GRAMMAR OF THE PALI LANGUAGE. By E. MÜLLER, Crown 8vo. cloth, pp. xvi. and 144. 1884. 7s. 6d.

Senart.—KACCĀYANA ET LA LITTÉRATURE GRAMMATICALE DU PÂLI. Ire Partie. Grammaire Palie de Kaccâyana, Sutras et Commentaire, publiés avec une traduction et des notes par E. SENART. 8vo. pp. 338. Paris, 1871. 12s.

PAZAND.

Maino-i-Khard (The Book of the).—The Pazand and Sanskrit Texts (in Roman characters) as arranged by Neriosengh Dhaval, in the fifteenth century. With an English translation, a Glossary of the Pazand texts, containing the Sanskrit, Rosian, and Pahlavi equivalents, a sketch of Pazand Grammar, and an Introduction. By E. W. WEST. 8vo. sewed, pp. 484. 1871. 16s.

PEGUAN.

Haswell.—GRAMMATICAL NOTES AND VOCABULARY OF THE PEGUAN LANGUAGE. To which are added a few pages of Phrases, etc. By Rev. J. M. HASWELL. 8vo. pp. xvi. and 160. 15s.

PEHLEWI.

Dinkard (The).—The Original Pehlwi Text, the same transliterated in Zend Characters. Translations of the Text in the Gujrati and English Languages; a Commentary and Glossary of Select Terms. By PESHOTUN DUSTOOR BEHRAMJEE SUNJANA. Vols. I. and II. 8vo. cloth. £2 2s.

Haug.—AN OLD PAHLAVI-PAZAND GLOSSARY. Ed., with Alphabetical Index, by DESTUR HOSHANGJI JAMASPJI ASA, High Priest of the Parsis in Malwa. Rev. and Enl., with Intro. Essay on the Pahlavi Language, by M. HAUG, Ph.D. Pub. by order of Gov. of Bombay. 8vo. pp. xvi. 152, 268, sd. 1870. 28s.

Haug.—A LECTURE ON AN ORIGINAL SPEECH OF ZOROASTER (Yasna 45), with remarks on his age. By MARTIN HAUG, Ph.D. 8vo. pp. 28, sewed. Bombay, 1865. 2s.

Haug.—THE PARSIS. See "Trübner's Oriental Series," page 3.

Haug.—An Old Zand-Pahlavi Glossary. Edited in the Original Characters, with a Transliteration in Roman Letters, an English Translation, and an Alphabetical Index. By Destur Hoshengji Jamaspji. High-priest of the Parsis in Malwa, India. Rev. with Notes and Intro. by Martin Haug, Ph.D. Publ. by order of Gov. of Bombay. 8vo. sewed, pp. lvi. and 132. 15s.

Haug.—The Book of Arda Viraf. The Pahlavi text prepared by Destur Hoshangji Jamaspji Asa. Revised and collated with further MSS., with an English translation and Introduction, and an Appendix containing the Texts and Translations of the Gosht-i Fryano and Hadokht Nask. By Martin Haug, Ph.D., Professor of Sanskrit and Comparative Philology at the University of Munich. Assisted by E. W. West, Ph.D. Published by order of the Bombay Government. 8vo. sewed, pp. lxxx., v., and 316. £1 5s.

Minocheherji.—Pahlavi, Gujarâti and English Dictionary. By Jamaspji Dastur Minocherji, Jamasp Asana. 8vo. Vol. I. pp. clxii. and 1 to 168, and Vol. II. pp. xxxii. and pp. 169 to 440. 1877 and 1879. Cloth. 14s. each. (To be completed in 5 vols.)

Sunjana.—A Grammar of the Pahlvi Language, with Quotations and Examples from Original Works and a Glossary of Words bearing affinity with the Semitic Languages. By Peshotun Dustoor Behramjee Sunjana, Principal of Sir Jamsetjee Jejeeboy Zurthosi Madressa. 8vo. cl., pp. 18-457. 25s.

Thomas.—Early Sassanian Inscriptions, Seals and Coins, illustrating the Early History of the Sassanian Dynasty, containing Proclamations of Ardeshir Babek, Sapor I., and his Successors. With a Critical Examination and Explanation of the Celebrated Inscription in the Hâjiâbad Cave, demonstrating that Sapor, the Conqueror of Valerian, was a Professing Christian. By Edward Thomas, F.R.S. Illustrated. 8vo. cloth, pp. 148. 7s. 6d.

Thomas.—Comments on Recent Pehlvi Decipherments. With an Incidental Sketch of the Derivation of Aryan Alphabets, and Contributions to the Early History and Geography of Tabaristán. Illustrated by Coins. By Edward Thomas, F.R.S. 8vo. pp. 56, and 2 plates, cloth, sewed. 3s. 6d.

West.—Glossary and Index of the Pahlavi Texts of the Book of Arda Viraf, The Tale of Gosht-I Fryano, The Hadokht Nask, and to some extracts from the Dîn-Kard and Nirangistan; prepared from Destur Hoshangji Asa's Glossary to the Arda Viraf Namak, and from the Original Texts, with Notes on Pahlavi Grammar. By E. W. West, Ph.D. Revised by Martin Haug, Ph.D. Published by order of the Government of Bombay. 8vo. sewed, pp. viii. and 352. 25s.

PENNSYLVANIA DUTCH.

Haldeman. — Pennsylvania Dutch: a Dialect of South Germany with an Infusion of English. By S. S. Haldeman, A.M., Professor of Comparative Philology in the University of Pennsylvania, Philadelphia. 8vo. pp. viii. and 70, cloth. 1872. 3s. 6d.

PERSIAN.

Ballantyne.—Principles of Persian Caligraphy, illustrated by Lithographic Plates of the TA"LIK characters, the one usually employed in writing the Persian and the Hindûstani. Second edition. Prepared for the use of the Scottish Naval and Military Academy, by James R. Ballantyne. 4to. cloth, pp. 14, 6 plates. 2s. 6d.

Blochmann.—THE PROSODY OF THE PERSIANS, according to Saifi, Jami, and other Writers. By H. BLOCHMANN, M.A., Assistant Professor, Calcutta Madrasah. 8vo. sewed, pp. 166. 10s. 6d.

Blochmann.—A TREATISE ON THE RUBA'I entitled Risalah i Taranah. By AGHA AHMAD 'ALI. With an Introduction and Explanatory Notes, by H. BLOCHMANN, M.A. 8vo. sewed, pp. 11 and 17. 2s. 6d.

Blochmann.—THE PERSIAN METRES BY SAIFI, and a Treatise on Persian Rhyme by Jami. Edited in Persian, by H. BLOCHMANN, M.A. 8vo. scarce, pp. 62. 3s. 6d.

Eastwick.—THE GULISTAN. See "Trübner's Oriental Series," page 4.

Finn.—PERSIAN FOR TRAVELLERS. By A. FINN, H.B.M. Consul at RESHT. Part I. Rudiments of Grammar. Part II. English-Persian Vocabulary. Oblong 32mo, pp. xiii.—232, cloth. 1884. 5s.

Griffith.—YUSUF AND ZULAIKHA. See "Trübner's Oriental Series," p. 5.

Gulshan-i-Raz.—THE DIALOGUE OF THE GULSHAN-I-RAZ; or, Mystical Garden of Roses of Mahmoud Shabistari. With Selections from the Rubaiyat of Omar Khayam. Crown 8vo. pp. vi.-64, cloth. 1888. 3s.

Háfiz of Shíráz.—SELECTIONS FROM HIS POEMS. Translated from the Persian by HERMAN BICKNELL. With Preface by A. S. BICKNELL. Demy 4to., pp. xx. and 384, printed on fine stout plate-paper, with appropriate Oriental Bordering in gold and colour, and Illustrations by J. R. HERBERT, R.A. £2 2s.

Haggard and Le Strange.—THE VAZIR OF LANKURAN. A Persian Play. A Text-Book of Modern Colloquial Persian, for the use of European Travellers, Residents in Persia, and Students in India. Edited, with a Grammatical Introduction, a Translation, copious Notes, and a Vocabulary giving the Pronunciation of all the words. By W. H. HAGGARD and GUY LE STRANGE. Crown 8vo. pp. xl.-176 and 56 (Persian Text), cloth. 1882. 10s. 6d.

Mirkhónd.—THE HISTORY OF THE ATÁBEKS OF SYRIA AND PERSIA. By MUHAMMED BEN KHÁWENDSHÁH BEN MAHMUD, commonly called MÍRKHÓND. Now first Edited from the Collation of Sixteen MSS., by W. H. MORLEY, Barrister-at-law, M.R.A.S. To which is added a Series of Facsimiles of the Coins struck by the Atábeks, arranged and described by W. S. W. VAUX, M.A., M.R.A.S. Roy. 8vo. cloth, 7 Plates, pp. 118. 1848. 7s. 6d.

Morley.—A Descriptive Catalogue of the Historical Manuscripts in the Arabic and Persian Languages preserved in the Library of the Royal Asiatic Society of Great Britain and Ireland. By WILLIAM H. MORLEY, M.R.A.S. 8vo. pp. viii. and 160, sewed. London, 1854. 2s. 6d.

Palmer.—THE SONG OF THE REED. See page 56.

Palmer.—A CONCISE PERSIAN-ENGLISH DICTIONARY By E. H. PALMER, M.A., Professor of Arabic in the University of Cambridge. Second Edition. Royal 16mo. pp. viii. and 364, cloth. 1883. 10s. 6d.

Palmer.—A CONCISE ENGLISH-PERSIAN DICTIONARY. Together with a Simplified Grammar of the Persian Language. By the late E. H. PALMER, M.A., Lord Almoner's Reader and Professor of Arabic, Cambridge. Completed and Edited from the MS. left imperfect at his death. By G. LE STRANGE. Royal 16mo. pp. xii. and 546, cloth. 1883. 10s. 6d.

Palmer.—SIMPLIFIED PERSIAN GRAMMAR. See page 56.

Redhouse.—THE MESNEVI. See "Trübner's Oriental Series," page 4.

Rieu.—Catalogue of the Persian Manuscripts in the British Museum. By Charles Rieu, Ph.D., Keeper of the Oriental MSS. 4to. cloth. Vol. I. pp. 432. 1879. 25s. Vol. II. 1881. 25s. Vol. III. 1883. 25s.

Whinfield.—Gulshan-i-Raz; The Mystic Rose Garden of Sa'd ud din Mahmud Shabistani. The Persian Text, with an English Translation and Notes, chiefly from the Commentary of Muhammed Bin Yahya Lahiji. By E. H. Whinfield, M.A., late of H.M.B.C.S. 4to. pp. xvi., 94, 60, cloth. 1880. 10s 6d

Whinfield.—Quatrains of Omar Khayyám. See page 5.

PIDGIN-ENGLISH.

Leland.—Pidgin-English Sing-Song; or Songs and Stories in the China-English Dialect. With a Vocabulary. By Charles G. Leland. Fcap. 8vo. cl., pp. viii. and 140. 1876. 5s.

POLISH.

Baranowski.—Anglo-Polish Lexicon. By J. J. Baranowski, formerly Under-Secretary to the Bank of Poland, in Warsaw. Fcap. 8vo. pp. viii. and 492, cloth. 1883. 12s.

Baranowski.—Slownik Polsko-Angielski. (Polish-English Lexicon.) By J. J. Baranowski. Fcap. 8vo. pp. iv.-402, cloth. 1884. 12s.

Morfill.—A Simplified Grammar of the Polish Language. By W. R. Morfill, M.A. Crown 8vo. pp. viii.—64, cloth. 1884. 3s. 6d.

PRAKRIT.

Cowell.—A short Introduction to the Ordinary Prakrit of the Sanskrit Dramas. With a List of Common Irregular Prakrit Words. By Prof. E. B. Cowell. Cr. 8vo. limp cloth, pp. 40. 1875. 3s. 6d.

Cowell.—Prakrita-Prakasa; or, The Prakrit Grammar of Vararuchi, with the Commentary (Manorama) of Bhamaha; the first complete Edition of the Original Text, with various Readings from a collation of Six MSS. in the Bodleian Library, etc., with Notes, English Translation, and Index of Prakrit Words, an Easy Introduction to Prakrit Grammar. By E. B. Cowell, Professor of Sanskrit at Cambridge. New Edition, with New Preface, etc. Second Issue. 8vo. cloth, pp. xxxi. and 204. 1868. 14s.

PUKSHTO (Pakkhto, Pashto).

Bellew.—A Grammar of the Pukkhto or Pukshto Language, on a New and Improved System. Combining Brevity with Utility, and Illustrated by Exercises and Dialogues. By H. W. Bellew, Assistant Surgeon, Bengal Army. Super-royal 8vo., pp. xii. and 156, cloth. 21s.

Bellew.—A Dictionary of the Pukkhto, or Pukshto Language, on a New and Improved System. With a reversed Part, or English and Pukkhto. By H. W. Bellew, Assistant Surgeon, Bengal Army. Super-royal 8vo. pp. xii. and 356, cloth. 42s.

Plowden.—Translation of the Kalid-i-Afghani, the Text Book for the Pakkhto Examination, with Notes, Historical, Geographical, Grammatical, and Explanatory. By Trevor Chichele Plowden, Captain H.M. Bengal Infantry, and Assistant Commissioner, Panjab. Small 4to. cloth, pp. xx. and 395 and ix. With Map. *Lahore,* 1875. £2 10s.

Thorburn.—Bannú; or, Our Afghan Frontier. By S. S. Thorburn, I.C.S., Settlement Officer of the Bannú District. 8vo. cloth, pp. x. and 480. 1876. 18s.

    pp. 171 to 230: Popular Stories, Ballads and Riddles, and pp. 231 to 413: Pashto Proverbs Translated into English. pp. 414 to 473: Pashto Proverbs in Pashto.

Trumpp.—Pašto Grammar. See page 50.

ROUMANIAN.

Torceanu.—Simplified Grammar of the Roumanian Language. By R. Torceanu. Crown 8vo. pp. viii.-72, cloth. 1883. 5s.

RUSSIAN.

Freeth.—A Condensed Russian Grammar for the Use of Staff Officers and others. By F. Freeth, B.A., late Classical Scholar of Emmanuel College, Cambridge. Crown 8vo. pp. iv.-76, cloth. 1886. 3s. 6d.

Lermontoff.—The Demon. By Michael Lermontoff. Translated from the Russian by A. Condie Stephen. Crown 8vo. pp. 88, cloth. 1881. 2s. 6d.

Riola.—A Graduated Russian Reader, with a Vocabulary of all the Russian Words contained in it. By H. Riola. Crown 8vo. pp. viii. and 314. 1879. 10s. 6d.

Riola.—How to Learn Russian. A Manual for Students of Russian, based upon the Ollendorfian system of teaching languages, and adapted for self instruction. By Henry Riola, Teacher of the Russian Language. With a Preface by W. R. S. Ralston, M.A. Second Edition. Crown 8vo. cloth, pp. 576. 1884. 12s.

    Key to the above. Crown 8vo. cloth, pp. 126. 1878. 5s.

Thompson.—Dialogues, Russian and English. Compiled by A. R. Thompson. Crown 8vo. cloth, pp. iv.-132. 1882. 5s.

Wilson.—Russian Lyrics in English Verse. By the Rev. C. T. Wilson, M.A., late Chaplain, Bombay. Crown 8vo. pp. xvi. and 244, cloth. 1887. 6s.

SAMARITAN.

Nutt.—A Sketch of Samaritan History, Dogma, and Literature. Published as an Introduction to "Fragments of a Samaritan Targum." By J. W. Nutt, M.A. Demy 8vo. cloth, pp. viii. and 172. 1874. 5s.

Nutt.—Fragments of a Samaritan Targum. Edited from a Bodleian MS. With an Introduction, containing a Sketch of Samaritan History, Dogma, and Literature. By J. W. Nutt, M.A. Demy 8vo. cloth, pp. viii. 172, and 84. With Plate. 1874. 15s.

SAMOAN.

Pratt.—A GRAMMAR AND DICTIONARY of the Samoan Language. By Rev. GEORGE PRATT, Forty Years a Missionary of the London Missionary Society in Samoa. Second Edition. Edited by Rev. S. J. Whitmee, F.R.G.S. Crown 8vo. cloth, pp. viii. and 380. 1878. 18s.

SANSKRIT.

Aitareya Brahmanam of the Rig Veda. 2 vols. See under HAUG.

D'Alwis.—A DESCRIPTIVE CATALOGUE OF SANSKRIT, PALI, AND SINHALESE LITERARY WORKS OF CEYLON. By JAMES D'ALWIS, M.R.A.S., Advocate of the Supreme Court, &c., &c. In Three Volumes. Vol. I., pp. xxxii. and 244, sewed. 1870. 8s. 6d.

Apastambíya Dharma Sutram.—APHORISMS OF THE SACRED LAWS OF THE HINDUS, by APASTAMBA. Edited, with a Translation and Notes, by G. Bühler. By order of the Government of Bombay. 2 parts. 8vo. cloth, 1868-71. £1 4s. 6d.

Arnold.—THE SONG CELESTIAL; or, Bhagavad-Gítá (from the Mahábhárata). Being a Discourse between Arjuna, Prince of India, and the Supreme Being under the form of Krishna. Translated from the Sanskrit Text by Sir E. ARNOLD, M.A., K.C.I.E., etc. Second edition. Crown 8vo. pp. 192, cloth. 1885. 5s.

Arnold.—THE SECRET OF DEATH: being a Version, in a Popular and Novel Form, of the Katho Upanishad, from the Sanskrit, with some Collected Poems. By Sir E. Arnold, M.A., K.C.I.E. Third Edition. Crown 8vo. pp. 430, cloth. 1885. 7s. 6d.

Arnold.—LIGHT OF ASIA. See page 41.

Arnold.—INDIAN POETRY. See "Trübner's Oriental Series," page 4.

Arnold.—THE ILIAD AND ODYSSEY OF INDIA. By Sir EDWIN ARNOLD, M.A., K.C.I.E., etc. Fcap. 8vo. sd., pp. 24. 1s.

Apte.—THE STUDENT'S GUIDE TO SANSKRIT COMPOSITION. Being a Treatise on Sanskrit Syntax for the use of School and Colleges. 8vo. boards. Poona 1881. 6s.

Apte.—THE STUDENT'S ENGLISH-SANSKRIT DICTIONARY. Roy. 8vo. pp. xii. and 526, cloth. Poona, 1884. 16s.

Atharva Veda Prátiçákhya.—See under WHITNEY.

Auctores Sanscriti. Vol. I. The Jaiminíya-Nyáya-Mála-Vistara. Edited for the Sanskrit Text Society under the supervision of THEODOR GOLDSTÜCKER. Parts I. to VII., pp. 582, large 4to. sewed. 10s each part. Complete in one vol., cloth, £3 13s. 6d. Vol. II. The Institutes of Gautama. Edited with an Index of Words, by A. F. STENZLER, Ph.D. Professor of Oriental Languages in the University of Breslau. 8vo. cloth, pp. iv. 78. 1876. 4s. 6d. Vol. III. Vaitána Sútra. The Ritual of the Atharva Veda. Edited with Critical Notes and Indices, by DR. RICHARD GARBE. 8vo. sewed, pp. 119. 1878. 5s. Vols. IV. and V. Vardhamána's Ganaratnamahodadhi, with the Author's Commentary. Edited, with Critical Notes and Indices, by J. EGGELING, Ph.D. 8vo. wrapper. Part I., pp. xii. and 240. 1879. 6s. Part II., pp. 240. 1881. 6s.

Avery.—CONTRIBUTIONS TO THE HISTORY OF VERB-INFLECTION IN SANSKRIT. By J. AVERY. 8vo. paper, pp. 106. 4s.
Ballantyne.—SANKHYA APHORISMS OF KAPILA. See page 6.
Ballantyne.—FIRST LESSONS IN SANSKRIT GRAMMAR; together with an Introduction to the Hitopadésa. Fourth edition. By JAMES R. BALLANTYNE, LL.D., Librarian of the India Office. 8vo. pp. viii. and 110, cloth. 1884. 3s. 6d.
Benfey.—A PRACTICAL GRAMMAR OF THE SANSKRIT LANGUAGE, for the use of Early Students. By THEODOR BENFEY, Professor of Sanskrit in the University of Göttingen. Second, revised and enlarged, edition. Royal 8vo. pp. viii. and 296, cloth. 10s. 6d.
Benfey.—VEDICA UND VERWANDTES. By THEOD. BENFEY. Crown 8vo. paper, pp. 178. Strassburg, 1877. 7s. 6d.
Benfey.—VEDICA UND LINGUISTICA.—By TH. BENFEY. Crown 8vo. pp. 254. 10s. 6d.
Bibliotheca Indica.—A Collection of Oriental Works published by the Asiatic Society of Bengal. Old Series. Fasc. 1 to 235. New Series. Fasc. 1 to 408. (Special List of Contents to be had on application.) Each Fasc. in 8vo., 2s.; in 4to., 4s.
Bibliotheca Sanskrita.—See TRÜBNER.
Bombay Sanskrit Series. Edited under the superintendence of G. BÜHLER, Ph. D., Professor of Oriental Languages, Elphinstone College, and F. KIELHORN, Ph. D., Superintendent of Sanskrit Studies, Deccan College. 1868-84.

1. PANCHATANTRA IV. AND V. Edited, with Notes, by G. BÜHLER, Ph.D. Pp. 84, 16. 3s.
2. NÁGOJÍBHATTA'S PARIBHÁSHENDUŚEKHARA. Edited and explained by F. KIELHORN, Ph. D. Part I., the Sanskrit Text and Various Readings. pp. 116. 4s.
3. PANCHATANTRA II. AND III. Edited, with Notes, by G. BÜHLER, Ph. D. Pp. 86, 14, 2. 3s.
4. PANCHATANTRA I. Edited, with Notes, by F. KIELHORN, Ph.D. Pp. 114, 53. 3s. 6d.
5. KÁLIDÁSA'S RAGHUVAMŚA. With the Commentary of Mallinátha. Edited, with Notes, by SHANKAR P. PANDIT, M.A. Part I. Cantos I.-VI. 4s.
6. KÁLIDÁSA'S MÁLAVIKÁGNIMITRA. Edited, with Notes, by SHANKAR P. PANDIT, M.A. 4s. 6d.
7. NÁGOJÍBHATTA'S PARIBHÁSHENDUŚEKHARA. Edited and explained by F. KIELHORN, Ph.D. Part II. Translation and Notes. (Paribháshás, i.-xxxvii.) pp. 184. 4s.
8. KÁLIDÁSA'S RAGHUVAMŚA. With the Commentary of Mallinátha. Edited, with Notes, by SHANKAR P. PANDIT, M.A. Part II. Cantos VII.-XIII. 4s.
9. NÁGOJÍBHATTA'S PARIBHÁSHENDUŚEKHARA. Edited and explained by F. KIELHORN. Part II. Translation and Notes. (Paribháshás xxxviii.-lxix.) 4s.
10. DANDIN'S DASAKUMARACHARITA. Edited with critical and explanatory Notes by G. Bühler. Part I. 3s.
11. BHARTRIHARI'S NITISATAKA AND VAIRAGYASATAKA, with Extracts from Two Sanskrit Commentaries. Edited, with Notes, by KASINATH T. TELANG. 4s. 6d.
12. NÁGOJIBHATTA'S PARIBHÁSHENDUŚEKHARA. Edited and explained by F. KIELHORN. Part II. Translation and Notes. (Paribháshás lxx.-cxxii.) 4s.

13. KALIDASA'S RAGHUVAMSA, with the Commentary of Mallinátha. Edited, with Notes, by SHANKAR P. PANDIT. Part III. Cantos XIV.–XIX. 4s.
14. VIKRAMÁNKADEVACHARITA. Edited, with an Introduction, by G. BÜHLER. 3s.
15. BHAVABHÚTI'S MÁLATI-MÁDHAVA. With the Commentary of Jagaddhara, edited by RAMKRISHNA GOPAL BHANDARKAR. 14s.
16. THE VIKRAMORVASÍYAM. A Drama in Five Acts. By KÁLIDÁSA. Edited with English Notes by Shankar P. Pandit, M.A. pp. xii. and 129 (Sanskrit Text) and 148 (Notes). 1879. 6s.
17. HEMACHDRA'S DESÍNÁMÁLÁ, with a Glossary by Dr. PISCHEL and Dr. BÜHLER. Part I. 10s.
18—22 and 26. PATANJALI'S VYAKARANAMAHABHÁSHYA. By Dr. KIELHORN. Part I–IV. Vol. I. II. Part II. Each part 5s.
23. THE VÁSISHTHADHARMASASTRAM. Aphorisms on the Sacred Law of the Aryas, as taught in School of Vasishtha. Edited by Rev. A. A. FUHRER. 8vo. sewed. 1883. 2s. 6d.
24. KADAMBARI. Edited by PETER PETERSON. 8vo. sewed. 1883. 15s.
25. KIRTIKAUMUDI. SRI SOMESVARADEVA, and edited by ABAJI VISHNU KATHAVATI. 8vo. sewed. 1883. 3s. 6d.
27. MUDRARAKSHASA. By VISAKHADATTA. With the Commentary of Dhundhiraj. Edited with critical and explanatory notes by K. T. Telang. 8vo. sewed. 1884. 6s.
28, 29, and 30. PATANJALI'S VYAKARANAMAHABHÁSHYA. By Dr. KIELHORN. Vol III., Parts I., II., and III. Each Part 5s.
31. VALLABHADEVA'S SUBHÁSHITÁVALI. Edited by Dr. P. PETERSON and PANDIT DURGAR PRASAD. 12s. 6d.
32. LAUGÁKSHI BHASKAR'S SARKA-KAUMUDI. Edited by Prof. M. N. DVIVEDI. 1s. 6d.
33. HITOPADESA BY NARAYANA. Edited by Prof. P. Peterson. 4s. 6d.

Borooah.—A COMPANION TO THE SANSKRIT-READING UNDERGRADUATES of the Calcutta University, being a few notes on the Sanskrit Texts selected for examination, and their Commentaries. By ANUNDORAM BOROOAH. 8vo. pp. 64. 3s. 6d.

Borooah.—A PRACTICAL ENGLISH-SANSKRIT DICTIONARY. By ANUNDORAM BOROOAH, B.A., B.C.S., of the Middle Temple, Barrister-at-Law. Vol. I. A to Falseness. pp. xx.–580-10. Vol. II. Falsification to Oyster, pp. 581 to 1060. With a Supplementary Treatise on Higher Sanskrit Grammar or Gender and Syntax, with copious illustrations from standard Sanskrit Authors and References to Latin and Greek Grammars, pp. vi. and 296. 1879. Vol. III. £1 11s. 6d. each.

Borooah.—BHAVABHUTI AND HIS PLACE IN SANSKRIT LITERATURE. By ANUNDORAM BOROOAH. 8vo. sewed. pp. 70. 5s.

Brhat-Sanhita (The).—See under Kern.

Brown.—SANSKRIT PROSODY AND NUMERICAL SYMBOLS EXPLAINED. By CHARLES PHILIP BROWN, Author of the Telugu Dictionary, Grammar, etc., Professor of Telugu in the University of London. Demy 8vo. pp. 64, cloth. 3s. 6d.

Burnell.—RIKTANTRAVYÁKARANA. A Prátiçákhya of the Samaveda. Edited, with an Introduction, Translation of the Sutras, and Indexes, by A. C. BURNELL, Ph.D. Vol. I. Post 8vo. boards, pp. lviii. and 84. 10s. 6d.

Burnell.—A CLASSIFIED INDEX to the Sanskrit MSS. in the Palace at Tanjore. Prepared for the Madras Government. By A. C. BURNELL, Ph.D. In 4to. Part I. pp. iv. and 80, stitched, stiff wrapper. Vedic and Technical Literature. Part II. pp. iv. and 80. Philosophy and Law. 1879. Part III. Drama, Epics, Purānas and Tantras, Indices, 1880. 10s. each part.

Burnell.—CATALOGUE OF A COLLECTION OF SANSKRIT MANUSCRIPTS. By A. C. BURNELL, M.R.A.S., Madras Civil Service. PART 1. *Vedic Manuscripts.* Fcap. 8vo. pp. 64, sewed. 1870. 2s.

Burnell.—DAYADAÇAÇLOKI. TEN SLOKAS IN SANSKRIT, with English Translation. By A. C. BURNELL. 8vo. pp. 11. 2s.

Burnell.—ON THE AINDRA SCHOOL OF SANSKRIT GRAMMARIANS. Their Place in the Sanskrit and Subordinate Literatures. By A. C. BURNELL. 8vo. pp. 120. 10s. 6d.

Burnell.—THE SĀMAVIDHĀNABRĀHMANA (being the Third Brāhmaṇa) of the Sāma Veda. Edited, together with the Commentary of Sāyaṇa, an English Translation, Introduction, and Index of Words, by A. C. BURNELL. Volume I.—Text and Commentary, with Introduction. 8vo. pp. xxxviii. and 104. 12s. 6d.

Burnell.—THE ARSHEYABRAHMANA (being the fourth Brāhmana) OF THE SAMA VEDA. The Sanskrit Text. Edited, together with Extracts from the Commentary of Sayana, etc. An Introduction and Index of Words. By A. C. BURNELL, Ph D. 8vo, pp. 51 and 109. 10s. 6d.

Burnell.—THE DEVATĀDHYĀYABRĀHMANA (being the Fifth Brāhmaṇa) of the Sama Veda. The Sanskrit Text edited, with the Commentary of Sāyaṇa, an Index of Words, etc., by A. C. BURNELL, M.R.A.S. 8vo. and Trans., pp. 34. 5s.

Burnell.—THE JAIMINĪYA TEXT OF THE ARSHEYABRĀHMAṆA OF THE Sāma Veda. Edited in Sanskrit by A. C. BURNELL, Ph. D. 8vo. sewed, pp. 56. 7s. 6d.

Burnell. — THE SAMHITOPANISHADBRĀHMANA (Being the Seventh Brāhmaṇa) of the Sāma Veda. The Sanskrit Text. With a Commentary, an Index of Words, etc. Edited by A. C. BURNELL, Ph.D. 8vo. stiff boards, pp. 86. 7s. 6d.

Burnell.—THE VAMÇABRĀHMANA (being the Eighth Brāhmaṇa) of the Sāma Veda. Edited, together with the Commentary of Sāyaṇa, a Preface and Index of Words, by A. C. BURNELL, M.R.A.S., etc. 8vo. sewed, pp. xliii., 12, and xii., with 2 coloured plates. 10s. 6d.

Burnell.—The Ordinances of Manu. See page 6.

Catalogue OF SANSKRIT WORKS PRINTED IN INDIA, offered for Sale at the affixed nett prices by TRÜBNER & Co. 16mo, pp. 52. 1s.

Chintamon.—A COMMENTARY ON THE TEXT OF THE BHAGAVAD-GĪTĀ; or, the Discourse between Krishna and Arjuna of Divine Matters. A Sanscrit Philosophical Poem. With a few Introductory Papers. By HURRYCHUND CHINTAMON, Political Agent to H. H. the Guicowar Mulhar Rao Maharajah of Baroda. Post 8vo. cloth, pp. 118. 6s.

Clark.—MEGHADUTA, THE CLOUD MESSENGER. Poem of Kalidasa. Translated by the late REV. THOMAS CLARK, M.A. Fcap. 8vo. pp. 64. wrapper. 1882. 1s.

Colebrooke.—The Life and Miscellaneous Essays of Henry Thomas Colebrooke. See page 29.

Cowell and Eggeling.—CATALOGUE OF BUDDHIST SANSKRIT MANUSCRIPTS in the Possession of the Royal Asiatic Society (Hodgson Collection). By Professors E. B. COWELL and J. EGGELING. 8vo. sd., pp. 56. 2s. 6d.

Cowell.—SARVA DARSANA SAMGRAHA. See page 5.

Da Cunha.—THE SAHYADRI KHANDA OF THE SKANDA PURANA; a Mythological, Historical and Geographical Account of Western India. First edition of the Sanskrit Text, with various readings. By J. GERSON DA CUNHA, M.R.C.S. and L.M. Eng., L.R.C.P. Edinb., etc. 8vo. bds. pp. 580. £1 1s.

Davies.—HINDU PHILOSOPHY. See page 4.

Davies.—BHAGAVAD GITA. See "Trübner's Oriental Series," page 5.

Dutt.—KINGS OF KÁSHMIRA: being a Translation of the Sanskrita Work Rajataranggini of Kahlana Pandita. By J. CH. DUTT. 12mo. paper, pp. v. 302, and xxiii. 4s.

Edgren.—A COMPENDIOUS SANSKRIT GRAMMAR. With a brief Sketch of Scenic Prakrit. By H. EDGREN, Ph.D., Professor of Sanskrit in the University of Nebraska, U.S.A. Crown 8vo. pp. xii.—178, cloth. 1885. 10s. 6d.

Gautama.—THE INSTITUTES OF GAUTAMA. See *Auctores Sanscriti*.

Goldstücker.—A DICTIONARY, SANSKRIT AND ENGLISH, extended and improved from the Second Edition of the Dictionary of Professor H. H. WILSON, with his sanction and concurrence. Together with a Supplement, Grammatical Appendices, and an Index, serving as a Sanskrit-English Vocabulary. By THEODOR GOLDSTÜCKER. Parts I. to VI. 4to. pp. 400. 1856-1863. 6s. each

Goldstücker.—PANINI: His Place in Sanskrit Literature. An Investigation of some Literary and Chronological Questions which may be settled by a study of his Work. A separate impression of the Preface to the Facsimile of MS. No. 17 in the Library of Her Majesty's Home Government for India, which contains a portion of the MANAVA-KALPA-SUTRA, with the Commentary of KUMARILA-SWAMIN. By THEODOR GOLDSTÜCKER. Imperial 8vo. pp. 268, cloth. £2 2s.

Gough.—PHILOSOPHY OF THE UPANISHADS. See page 6.

Griffith.—SCENES FROM THE RAMAYANA, MEGHADUTA, ETC. Translated by RALPH T. H. GRIFFITH, M.A., Principal of the Benares College. Second Edition. Crown 8vo. pp. xviii, 244, cloth. 6s.

CONTENTS.—Preface—Ayodhya—Ravan Doomed—The Birth of Rama—The Heir apparent—Manthara's Guile—Dasaratha's Oath—The Step-mother—Mother and Son—The Triumph of Love—Farewell!—The Hermit's Son—The Trial of Truth—The Forest—The Rape of Sita—Rama's Despair—The Messenger Cloud—Khumbakarna—The Suppliant Dove—True Glory—Feed the Poor—The Wise Scholar.

Griffith.—THE RÁMÁYAN OF VÁLMIKI. Translated into English verse. By RALPH T. H. GRIFFITH, M.A., Principal of the Benares College. 5 vols. Demy 8vo. cloth. Vol. I., pp. xxxii. 440. 1870. Out of print. II., pp. 504. Out of print. III., pp. v. and 371. 1872. IV., pp. viii. and 432. 1873. V., pp. 368. 1875. Complete Sets £7 7s.

Griffith.—KÁLIDÁSA'S BIRTH OF THE WAR GOD. See page 3.

Haas.—Catalogue of Sanskrit and Pali Books in the Library of the British Museum. By Dr. ERNST HAAS. 4to. pp. 200, cloth. 1876. £1 1s.

Haug.—THE AITAREYA BRAHMANAM OF THE RIG VEDA: containing the Earliest Speculations of the Brahmans on the meaning of the Sacrificial Prayers, and on the Origin, Performance, and Sense of the Rites of the Vedic Religion. Edited, Translated, and Explained by MARTIN HAUG, Ph.D. 2 vols. Cr. 8vo. Map of the Sacrificial Compound at the Soma Sacrifice. pp. 312 and 544. £2 2s.

Hunter.—CATALOGUE OF SANSKRIT MANUSCRIPTS (Buddhist) Collected in Nepâl by B. H. HODGSON, late Resident at the Court of Nepâl. Compiled from Lists in Calcutta, France, and England. By Sir W. W. HUNTER, K.S.S.F., LL.D., &c. 8vo. pp. 28, wrapper. 1880. 2s.

Jacob.—HINDU PANTHEISM. See "Trübner's Oriental Series," page 4.

Jaiminiya-Nyâya-Mâlâ-Vistara.—See under AUCTORES SANSCRITI.

Kâśikâ.—A COMMENTARY ON PÂNINI'S GRAMMATICAL APHORISMS. By PANDIT JAYÂDITYA. Edited by PANDIT BÂLA SÂSTRÎ, Prof. Sansk. Coll., Benares. First part, 8vo. pp. 490. Part II. pp. 474. 16s. each part.

Kern.—THE ÂRYABHATIYA, with the Commentary Bhatadipikâ of Paramadiçvara, edited by Dr. H. KERN. 4to. pp. xii. and 107. 9s.

Kern.—THE BRHAT-SANHITÁ; or, Complete System of Natural Astrology of Varâha-Mihira. Translated from Sanskrit into English by Dr. H. KERN, Professor of Sanskrit at the University of Leyden. Part I. 8vo. pp. 50, stitched. Parts 2 and 3 pp. 51–154. Part 4 pp. 155–210. Part 5 pp. 211–266. Part 6 pp. 267–330. Price 2s. each part. [*Will be completed in Nine Parts.*

Kielhorn.—A GRAMMAR OF THE SANSKRIT LANGUAGE. By F. KIELHORN, Ph.D., Superintendent of Sanskrit Studies in Deccan College. Registered under Act xxv. of 1867. Demy 8vo. pp. xvi. 260. cloth. 1870. 10s. 6d.

Kielhorn.—KÂTYÂYANA AND PATANJALI. Their Relation to each other and to Panini. By F. KIELHORN, Ph. D., Prof. of Orient. Lang. Poona. 8vo. pp. 64. 1876. 3s. 6d.

Laghu Kaumudí. A Sanskrit Grammar. By Varadarâja. With an English Version. Commentary, and References. By JAMES R. BALLANTYNE, LL.D. Third Edition. 8vo. pp. xxxiv. and 424, cloth. 1881. £1 5s.

Lanman.—On Noun-Inflection in the Veda. By R. LANMAN, Associate Prof. of Sanskrit in Johns Hopkins University. 8vo. pp. 276, wrapper. 1880. 10s.

Lanman.—A SANSKRIT READER, with Vocabulary and Notes. By C. R. LANMAN, Prof. of Sanskrit in Harvard College. Part I. and II.—Text and Vocabulary. Imp. 8vo. pp. xx.—294, cloth. 1884. 10s. 6d.

Mahabharata.—TRANSLATED INTO HINDI for Madan Mohun Bhatt, by KRISHNACHANDRADHARMADHIKARIN, of Benares. Containing all but the Harivansa. 3 vols. 8vo. cloth. pp. 574, 810, and 1106. £3 3s.

Mahábhárata (in Sanskrit), with the Commentary of Nilakantha. In Eighteen Books: Book I. Âdi Parvan, fol. 248. II. Sabhâ do. fol. 82. III. Vana do. fol. 312. IV. Virâta do. fol. 62. V. Udyoga do. fol. 180. VI. Bhíshma do. fol. 189. VII. Drona do. fol. 215. VIII. Karna do fol. 115. IX. Salya do. fol. 42. X. Sauptika do. fol. 19. XI. Strí do. fol. 19. XII. Sânti do.:— a. Râjadharma, fol. 128; b. Âpadharma, fol. 41; c. Mokshadharma, fol. 290. XIII. Anuśâsana Parvan, fol. 207. XIV. Aśwamedhika do. fol. 78. XV. Âsramavâsika do. fol. 26. XVI. Mausala do. fol. 7. XVII. Mâhâprasthânika do. fol. 3. XVIII. Swargarohana do. fol. 8. Printed with movable types. Oblong folio. Bombay, 1863. £12 12s.

Maha-Vira-Charita; or, the Adventures of the Great Hero Rama. An Indian Drama in Seven Acts. Translated into English Prose from the Sanskrit of Bhavabhúti. By J. PICKFORD, M.A. Crown 8vo. pp 192, cloth. 1871. 5s.

Maino-i-Khard (The Book of the).—The Pazand and Sanskrit Texts (in Roman characters) as arranged by Neriosengh Dhaval, in the fifteenth century. With an English translation, a Glossary of the Pazand texts, containing the Sanskrit, Rosian, and Pahlavi equivalents, a sketch of Pazand Grammar, and an Introduction. By E. W. WEST. 8vo. sewed, pp. 484. 1871. 16s.

Manava-Kalpa-Sutra; being a portion of this ancient Work on Vaidik Rites, together with the Commentary of KUMARILA-SWAMIN. A Facsimile of the MS. No. 17, in the Library of Her Majesty's Home Government for India. With a Preface by THEODOR GOLDSTÜCKER. Oblong folio, pp. 268 of letterpress and 121 leaves of facsimiles. Cloth. £4 4s.

Mandlik.—THE YÁJÑAVALKYA SMṚITI, Complete in Original, with an English Translation and Notes. With an Introduction on the Sources of, and Appendices containing Notes on various Topics of Hindu Law. By V. N. MANDLIK. 2 vols. in one. Roy. 8vo. pp. Text 177, and Transl. pp. lxxxvii. and 532. Bombay, 1880. £3.

Megha-Duta (The). (Cloud-Messenger.) By Kālidāsa. Translated from the Sanskrit into English verse, with Notes and Illustrations. By the late H. H. WILSON, M.A., F.R.S., etc. Vocabulary by F. JOHNSON, sometime Professor of Oriental Languages at the College of the Hon. the East India Company, Haileybury. New Edition. 4to. cloth, pp. xi. and 180. 10s. 6d.

Muir.—TRANSLATIONS from Sanskrit Writers. See page 3.

Muir.—ORIGINAL SANSKRIT TEXTS, on the History of the People of India, their Religion and Institutions. Collected, Translated, and Illustrated by JOHN MUIR, D.C.L., LL.D. Demy 8vo. cloth. Vol. I. Mythical Accounts of the Origin of Caste. Second Edition, pp. xx. 532. 1868. 21s. II. Trans-Himalayan Origin of the Hindus, and their Affinity with the Western Branches of the Aryan Race. Second Edition, pp. xxxii. and 512. 1871. 21s. III. The Vedas: Opinions of their Authors, and of later Indian Writers, on their Origin, Inspiration, and Authority. Second Edition, pp. xxxii. 312. 1868. 16s. IV. Comparison of the Vedic with the later representations of the principal Indian Deities. Second Edition. pp. xvi. and 524. 1873. 21s. V. The Cosmogony, Mythology, Religious Ideas, Life and Manners of the Indians in the Vedic Age. Third Edition. pp. xvi. 492. 1884. 21s.

Nagananda; OR THE JOY OF THE SNAKE-WORLD. A Buddhist Drama in Five Acts. Translated into English Prose, with Explanatory Notes, from the Sanskrit of Sri-Harsha-Deva. By PALMER BOYD, B.A., Sanskrit Scholar of Trinity College, Cambridge. With an Introduction by Professor COWELL. Crown 8vo., pp. xvi. and 100, cloth. 4s. 6d.

Nalopákhyánam.—STORY OF NALA; an Episode of the Mahá-Bhárata. The Sanskrit Text, with Vocabulary, Analysis, and Introduction. By Sir M. MONIER-WILLIAMS, K.C.I.E., M.A. The Metrical Translation by the Very Rev. H. H. MILMAN, D.D. 8vo. cloth. 15s.

Naradiya Dharma Sastram; OR, THE INSTITUTES OF NARADA. Translated for the First Time from the unpublished Sanskrit original. By Dr. JULIUS JOLLY, University, Wurzburg. With a Preface, Notes chiefly critical, an Index of Quotations from Narada in the principal Indian Digests, and a general Index. Crown 8vo., pp. xxxv. 144, cloth. 10s. 6d.

Oppert.—List of Sanskrit Manuscripts in Private Libraries of Southern India. Compiled, Arranged, and Indexed, by GUSTAV OPPERT, Ph.D. Vol. I. Royal 8vo. cloth, pp. 620, 1880. 21s.

Oppert.—ON THE WEAPONS, ARMY ORGANIZATION, AND POLITICAL MAXIMS of the Ancient Hindus. With Special Reference to Gunpowder and Fire Arms. By G. OPPERT. 8vo. sewed, pp. vi. and 162. Madras, 1880. 7s. 6d.

Patanjali.—THE VYÁKARANA-MAHÁBHÁSHYA OF PATANJALI. Edited by F. KIELHORN, Ph.D., Professor of Oriental Languages, Deccan College. Vol. I., Part I. pp. 200. 8s. 6d.

Perry.—A SANSKRIT PRIMER. Based on the "Leitfaden für den Elementar-Cursus des Sanskrit" of Prof. Georg Bühler, of Vienna. By E. D. PERRY, of Columbia Coll., New York. 8vo. pp. xii. and 230, cl. 1886. 7s. 6d.

Peterson.—THE AUCHITYALAMKARA OF KSHEMENDRA; with a Note on the Date of Patanjali, and an Inscription from Kotah. By P. PETERSON, Elphinstone Professor of Sanskrit, Bombay. Demy 8vo. pp. 54, sewed, 1885. 2s.

Rámáyan of Válmiki.—5 vols. See under GRIFFITH.

Ram Jasan.— A SANSKRIT AND ENGLISH DICTIONARY. Being an Abridgment of Professor Wilson's Dictionary. With an Appendix explaining the use of Affixes in Sanskrit. By Pandit RAM JASAN, Queen's College, Benares. Published under the Patronage of the Government, N.W.P. Royal 8vo. cloth, pp. ii. and 707. 28s.

Rig-Veda Sanhita.—A COLLECTION OF ANCIENT HINDU HYMNS. See page 45.

Rig-Veda-Sanhita: THE SACRED HYMNS OF THE BRAHMANS. Translated and explained by F. MAX MÜLLER, M.A., LL.D. See page 45.

Rig-Veda.—THE HYMNS OF THE RIG-VEDA in the Samhita and Pada Texts. By F. MAX MÜLLER, M.A., etc. See page 45.

Sabdakalpadruma, the well-known Sanskrit Dictionary of RAJÁH RADHAKANTA DEVA. In Bengali characters. 4to. Parts 1 to 40. (In course of publication.) 3s. 6d. each part.

Sáma-Vidhána-Bráhmana. With the Commentary of Sáyana. Edited, with Notes, Translation, and Index, by A. C. BURNELL, M.R.A.S. Vol. I. Text and Commentary. With Introduction. 8vo. cloth, pp. xxxviii. and 104. 12s. 6d.

Sakuntala.—A SANSKRIT DRAMA IN SEVEN ACTS. Edited by Sir M. MONIER-WILLIAMS, K.C.I.E., M.A. Second Edition. 8vo. cl. £1 1s.

Sakuntala.—KÁLIDÁSA'S ÇAKUNTALÁ. The Bengali Recension. With Critical Notes. Edited by RICHARD PISCHEL. 8vo. cloth, pp. xi. and 210. 14s.

Sarva-Sabda-Sambodhini; OR, THE COMPLETE SANSKRIT DICTIONARY. In Telugu characters. 4to. cloth, pp. 1078. £2 15s.

Surya-Siddhanta (Translation of the).—See WHITNEY.

Táittiríya-Pratiçakhya.—See WHITNEY.

Tarkavachaspati.—VACHASPATYA, a Comprehensive Dictionary, in Ten Parts. Compiled by TARANATHA TARKAVACHASPATI, Professor of Grammar and Philosophy in the Government Sanskrit College of Calcutta. An Alphabetically Arranged Dictionary, with a Grammatical Introduction and Copious Citations from the Grammarians and Scholiasts, from the Vedas, etc. Parts I. to XIII. 4to. paper. 1873-6. 18s. each Part.

Thibaut.—THE SÚLVASÚTRAS. English Translation, with an Introduction. By G. THIBAUT, Ph.D., Anglo-Sanskrit Professor Benares College. 8vo. cloth, pp. 47, with 4 Plates. 5s.

Thibaut.—CONTRIBUTIONS TO THE EXPLANATION OF JYOTISHA-VEDÁNGA By G. THIBAUT, Ph.D. 8vo. pp. 27. 1s. 6d.

Trübner's Bibliotheca Sanscrita. A Catalogue of Sanskrit Literature, chiefly printed in Europe. To which is added a Catalogue of Sanskrit Works printed in India; and a Catalogue of Pali Books. Constantly for sale by Trübner & Co. Cr. 8vo. sd., pp. 84. 2s. 6d.

Vardhamana.—See Auctores Sanscriti, page 96.

Vedarthayatna (The); or, an Attempt to Interpret the Vedas. A Marathi and English Translation of the Rig Veda, with the Original Saṁhitâ and Pada Texts in Sanskrit. Parts I. to XXVIII. 8vo. pp. 1—896. Price 3s. 6d. each.

Vishnu-Purana (The).—See page 45, and also "Wilson," page 105.

Weber.—ON THE RÁMÁYANA. By Dr. ALBRECHT WEBER, Berlin. Translated from the German by the Rev. D. C. Boyd, M.A. Reprinted from "The Indian Antiquary." Fcap. 8vo. sewed, pp. 130. 5s.

Weber.—INDIAN LITERATURE. See page 3.

Whitney.—ATHARVA VEDA PRÁTIÇÁKHYA; or, Çáunakíyá Caturádhyáyiká (The). Text, Translation, and Notes. By WILLIAM D. WHITNEY, Professor of Sanskrit in Yale College. 8vo. pp. 286, boards. £1 11s. 6d.

Whitney.—SURYA-SIDDHANTA (Translation of the): A Text-book of Hindu Astronomy, with Notes and an Appendix, containing additional Notes and Tables, Calculations of Eclipses, a Stellar Map, and Indexes. By the Rev. E. BURGESS. Edited by W. D. WHITNEY. 8vo. pp. iv. and 354, boards. £1 11s. 6d.

Whitney.—TÁITTIRÍYA-PRÁTIÇÁKHYA, with its Commentary, the Tribháshyaratna: Text, Translation, and Notes. By W. D. WHITNEY, Prof. of Sanskrit in Yale College, New Haven. 8vo. pp. 469. 1871. £1 5s.

Whitney.—Index Verborum to the Published Text of the Atharva-Veda. By William Dwight Whitney, Professor in Yale College. (Vol. XII. of the American Oriental Society). Imp. 8vo. pp. 384, wide margin, wrapper. 1881. £1 5s.

Whitney.—A SANSKRIT GRAMMAR, including both the Classical Language, and the Older Language, and the Older Dialects, of Veda and Brahmana. 8vo. cloth, pp. [*New Edition, in the Press.*

Whitney.—THE ROOTS, VERB-FORMS, AND PRIMARY DERIVATIVES OF THE SANSKRIT LANGUAGE. A Supplement to his Sanskrit Grammar. By WILLIAM DWIGHT WHITNEY. Demy 8vo. pp. xiv.—250, cloth. 1885. 7s. 6d.

Williams.—A DICTIONARY, ENGLISH AND SANSCRIT. By SIR MONIER MONIER-WILLIAMS, K.C.I.E., M.A. Published under the Patronage of the Hon East India Company. 4to. pp. xii. 862, cloth. 1851. £3 3s.

Williams.—A SANSKRIT-ENGLISH DICTIONARY, Etymologically and Philologically arranged, with special reference to Greek, Latin, German, Anglo-Saxon, English, and other cognate Indo-European Languages. By Sir MONIER MONIER-WILLIAMS, K.C.I.E., M.A., Boden Professor of Sanskrit. 4to. cloth, pp. xxv. and 1186. £4 14s. 6d.

Williams.—A PRACTICAL GRAMMAR OF THE SANSKRIT LANGUAGE, arranged with reference to the Classical Languages of Europe, for the use of English Students, by Sir MONIER MONIER-WILLIAMS, K.C.I.E., M.A. 1877. Fourth Edition, Revised. 8vo. cloth. 15s.

Wilson.—Works of the late HORACE HAYMAN WILSON, M.A., F.R.S., etc., and Boden Prof. of Sanskrit in the University of Oxford. 12 vols. Demy Vols. I. and II. ESSAYS AND LECTURES, chiefly on the Religion of the Hindus. Collected and Edited by Dr. R. ROST. 2 vols. pp. xiii. and 399, vi. and 416. 21s. Vols. III, IV. and V. ESSAYS ANALYTICAL, CRITICAL,

AND PHILOLOGICAL, ON SUBJECTS CONNECTED WITH SANSKRIT LITERATURE. Collected and Edited by Dr. R. Rost. 3 vols. pp. 408, 406, and 390. 36s. Vols. VI., VII., VIII., IX. and X., Part I. VISHNU PURÁNÁ, A SYSTEM OF HINDU MYTHOLOGY AND TRADITION. Vols. I. to V. Translated from the original Sanskrit, and Illustrated by Notes derived chiefly from other Puráṇás. Edited by F. HALL, M.A., D.C.L., Oxon. pp. cxl. and 200; 344; 344; 346. 2l. 12s. 6d. Vol. X., Part 2, containing the Index to, and completing the Vishnu Puráná, compiled by F. Hall. pp. 268. 12s. Vols. XI. and XII. SELECT SPECIMENS OF THE THEATRE OF THE HINDUS. Translated from the Original Sanskrit. 3rd corrected Ed. 2 vols. pp. lxi. and 384; and iv. and 418 21s.

Wilson.—SELECT SPECIMENS OF THE THEATRE OF THE HINDUS. Translated from the Original Sanskrit. By the late H. H. WILSON, M.A., F.R.S. Third corrected edition. 2 vols. 8vo., pp. lxxi. and 384; iv. and 418, cloth. 21s.

CONTENTS.—Vol. I.—Preface—Treatise on the Dramatic System of the Hindus—Dramas translated from the Original Sanskrit—The Mrichchakati, or the Toy Cart—Vikrama and Urvasi, or the Hero and the Nymph—Uttara Ráma Charitra, or continuation of the History of Ráma. Vol. II.—Dramas translated from the Original Sanskrit—Máláti and Mádhava, or the Stolen Marriage—Mudrá Rakshasa, or the Signet of the Minister—Ratnávalí, or the Necklace—Appendix, containing short accounts of different Dramas.

Wilson.—A DICTIONARY IN SANSKRIT AND ENGLISH. Translated, amended, and enlarged from an original compilation prepared by learned Natives for the College of Fort William by H. H. WILSON. The Third Edition edited by Jagunmohana Tarkalankara and Khettramohana Mookerjee. Published by Gyanendrachandra Rayachoudhuri and Brothers. 4to. pp. 1008. Calcutta, 1874. £3 3s.

Wilson (H. H).—See also Megha Duta, Rig-Veda, and Vishnu-Puráná.

Yajurveda.—THE WHITE YAJURVEDA IN THE MADHYANDINA RECENSION. With the Commentary of Mahidhara. Complete in 36 parts. Large square 8vo. pp. 571. £4 10s.

SERBIAN.

Morfill.—SIMPLIFIED SERBIAN GRAMMAR. By W. R. MORFILL, M.A., Crown 8vo. pp. viii. and 72, cloth. 1887. 4s. 6d.

SHAN.

Cushing.—GRAMMAR OF THE SHAN LANGUAGE. By the Rev. J. N. CUSHING. Large 8vo. pp. xii. and 60, boards. Rangoon, 1871. 9s.

Cushing.—Elementary Handbook of the Shan Language. By the Rev. J. N. CUSHING, M A. Small 4to. boards, pp. x. and 122. 1880. 12s. 6d.

Cushing.—A Shan and English Dictionary. By J. N. CUSHING, M.A. Demy 8vo. cloth, pp. xvi. and 600. 1881. £1 1s. 6d.

SINDHI.

Trumpp.—GRAMMAR OF THE SINDHI LANGUAGE. Compared with the Sanskrit, Prakrit, and the Cognate Indian Vernaculars. By Dr. ERNEST TRUMPP. Printed by order of Her Majesty's Government for India. Demy 8vo. sewed, pp. xvi. and 590. 15s.

SINHALESE.

Aratchy.—ATHETHA WAKYA DEEPANYA, or a Collection of Sinhalese Proverbs, Maxims, Fables, etc. Translated into English. By A. M. S. ARATCHY. 8vo. pp. iv. and 84, sewed. Colombo, 1881. 2s. 6d.

D'Alwis.—A DESCRIPTIVE CATALOGUE of Sanskrit, Pali, and Sinhalese Literary Works of Ceylon. By JAMES D'ALWIS, M.R.A.S. Vol. I. (all published) pp. xxxii. and 244, sewed. 1877. 8s. 6d.

Childers.—NOTES ON THE SINHALESE LANGUAGE. No. 1. On the Formation of the Plural of Neuter Nouns. By the late Prof. R. C. CHILDERS. Demy 8vo. sd., pp. 16. 1873. 1s.

Mahawansa (The)—THE MAHAWANSA. From the Thirty-Seventh Chapter. Revised and edited, under orders of the Ceylon Government, by H. Sumangala, and Don Andris de Silva Batuwantudawa. Vol. I. Pali Text in Sinhalese Character, pp. xxxii. and 436.—Vol. II. Sinhalese Translation, pp. lii. and 378, half-bound. Colombo, 1877. £2 2s.

Steele.—AN EASTERN LOVE-STORY. Kusa Jātakaya, a Buddhistic Legend. Rendered, for the first time, into English Verse (with notes) from the Sinhalese Poem of Alagiyavanna Mohottala, by THOMAS STEELE, Ceylon Civil Service. Crown 8vo. cloth, pp. xii. and 260. London, 1871. 6s.

SUAHILI.

Krapf.—DICTIONARY OF THE SUAHILI LANGUAGE. By the Rev. Dr. L. KRAPF. With Introduction, containing an outline of a Suahili Grammar. The Preface contains a most interesting account of Dr. Krapf's philological researches respecting the large family of African Languages extending from the Equator to the Cape of Good Hope, from the year 1843, up to the present time. Royal 8vo. pp. xl.-434, cloth. 1882. 30s.

SWEDISH.

Otte.—SIMPLIFIED GRAMMAR OF THE SWEDISH LANGUAGE. By E. C. OTTÉ. Crown 8vo. pp. xii.—70, cloth. 1884. 2s. 6d.

SYRIAC.

Gottheil.—A TREATISE ON SYRIAC GRAMMAR. By MÂR(I) ELIA OF SÔBHÂ. Edited and Translated from the Manuscripts in the Berlin Royal Library by R. J. H. Gottheil. Royal 8vo. pp. 174, cloth. 1887. 12s. 6d.

Kalilah and Dimnah (The Book of). Translated from Arabic into Syriac. Edited by W. WRIGHT, LL.D., Professor of Arabic in the University of Cambridge. 8vo. pp. lxxxii.-408, cloth. 1884. 21s.

Phillips.—THE DOCTRINE OF ADDAI THE APOSTLE. Now first Edited in a Complete Form in the Original Syriac, with an English Translation and Notes. By GEORGE PHILLIPS, D.D., President of Queen's College, Cambridge. 8vo. pp. 122, cloth. 7s. 6d.

Stoddard.—GRAMMAR OF THE MODERN SYRIAC LANGUAGE, as spoken in Oroomiah, Persia, and in Koordistan. By Rev. D. T. STODDARD, Missionary of the American Board in Persia. Demy 8vo. bds., pp. 190. 10s. 6d.

TAMIL.

Catalogue of Tamil Books sold by Messrs. Trübner & Co. post free for penny stamp.

Beschi.—CLAVIS HUMANIORUM LITTERARUM SUBLIMIORIS TAMULICI IDIOMATIS. Auctore R. P. CONSTANTIO JOSEPHO BESCHIO, Soc. Jesu, in Madurensi Regno Missionario. Edited by the Rev. K. IHLEFELD, and printed for A. Burnell, Esq., Tranquebar. 8vo. sewed, pp. 171. 10s. 6d.

Lazarus.—A TAMIL GRAMMAR, Designed for use in Colleges and Schools. By J. LAZARUS. 12mo. cloth, pp. viii. and 230. London, 1879. 5s. 6d.

TELUGU.

Catalogue of Telugu Books sold by Messrs. Trübner & Co. post free for penny stamp.

Arden.—A PROGRESSIVE GRAMMAR OF THE TELUGU LANGUAGE, with Copious Examples and Exercises. In Three Parts. Part I. Introduction.—On the Alphabet and Orthography.—Outline Grammar, and Model Sentences. Part II. A Complete Grammar of the Colloquial Dialect. Part III. On the Grammatical Dialect used in Books. By A. H. ARDEN, M.A., Missionary of the C. M. S. Masulipatam. 8vo. sewed, pp. xiv. and 380. 18s.

Arden.—A COMPANION Telugu Reader to Arden's Progressive Telugu Grammar. 8vo. cloth, pp. 130. Madras, 1879. 7s. 6d.

Carr.—ఒక్కొక్కడి సామెతలు. A COLLECTION OF TELUGU PROVERBS, Translated, Illustrated, and Explained; together with some Sanscrit Proverbs printed in the Devanâgarî and Telugu Characters. By Captain M. W. CARR, Madras Staff Corps. One Vol. and Supplement, roy. 8vo. pp. 488 & 148. 31s. 6d.

TIBETAN.

Csoma de Körös.—A DICTIONARY Tibetan and English (only). By A. CSOMA DE KÖRÖS. 4to. cloth, pp. xxii. and 352. Calcutta, 1834. £2 2s.

Csoma de Körös.—A GRAMMAR of the Tibetan Language. By A. CSOMA DE KÖRÖS. 4to. sewed, pp. xii. and 204, and 40. 1834. 25s.

Jaschke.—A TIBETAN-ENGLISH DICTIONARY. With special reference to the prevailing dialects; to which is added an English-Tibetan Vocabulary. By H. A. JASCHKE, late Moravian Missionary at Kijelang, British Lahoul. Compiled and published under the orders of the Secretary of State for India in Council. Royal 8vo. pp. xxii.-672, cloth. 30s.

Jaschke.—TIBETAN GRAMMAR. By H. A. JASCHKE. Crown 8vo. pp. viii. and 104, cloth. 1883. 5s.

Lewin.—A MANUAL of Tibetan, being a Guide to the Colloquial Speech of Tibet, in a Series of Progressive Exercises, prepared with the assistance of Yapa Ugyen Gyatsho, by Major THOMAS HERBERT LEWIN. Oblong 4to. cloth, pp. xi. and 176. 1879. £1 1s.

Schiefner.—Tibetan Tales. See "Trübner's Oriental Series," page 5.

TURKI.

Shaw.—A SKETCH OF THE TURKI LANGUAGE. As Spoken in Eastern Turkistan (Kàshgbar and Yarkand). By ROBERT BARKLAY SHAW, F.R.G.S., Political Agent. In Two Parts. With Lists of Names of Birds and Plants by J. SCULLY. Surgeon, H.M. Bengal Army. 8vo. sewed, Part I., pp. 130. 1875. 7s. 6d.

TURKISH.

Arnold.—A SIMPLE TRANSLITERAL GRAMMAR OF THE TURKISH LANGUAGE. Compiled from various sources. With Dialogues and Vocabulary. By Sir EDWIN ARNOLD, M.A., K.C.I.E., etc. Pott 8vo. cloth, pp. 80. 1877. 2s. 6d.

Gibb.—OTTOMAN POEMS. Translated into English Verse in their Original Forms, with Introduction, Biographical Notices, and Notes. Fcap. 4to. pp. lvi. and 272. With a plate and 4 portraits. Cloth. By E. J. W. GIBB. 1882. £1 1s.

Gibb.—THE STORY OF JEWÂD, a Romance, by Ali Aziz Efendi, the Cretan. Translated from the Turkish, by E. J. W. GIBB. 8vo. pp. xii. and 238, cloth. 1884. 7s.

Hopkins.—ELEMENTARY GRAMMAR OF THE TURKISH LANGUAGE. With a few Easy Exercises. By F. L. HOPKINS, M.A., Fellow and Tutor of Trinity Hall, Cambridge. Cr. 8vo. cloth, pp. 48. 1877. 3s. 6d.

Redhouse.—On the History, System, and Varieties of Turkish Poetry, Illustrated by Selections in the Original, and in English Paraphrase. With a notice of the Islamic Doctrine of the Immortality of Woman's Soul. By J. W. REDHOUSE. Demy 8vo. pp. 64, sewed. 1879. 1s. 6d.; cloth, 2s. 6d.

Redhouse.—THE TURKISH CAMPAIGNER'S VADE-MECUM OF OTTOMAN COLLOQUIAL LANGUAGE; containing a concise Ottoman Grammar; a carefully selected Vocabulary, alphabetically arranged, in two parts, English and Turkish, and Turkish and English; also a few Familiar Dialogues; the whole in English characters. By J. W. REDHOUSE, F.R.A.S. Third Edition. Oblong 32mo. pp. viii.-372, limp cloth. 1882. 6s.

Redhouse.—OTTOMAN-TURKISH GRAMMAR. See page 50.

Redhouse.—TURKISH AND ENGLISH LEXICON, showing in English the Significations of the Turkish Terms. By J. W. REDHOUSE, M.R.A.S., etc. Parts I. to III. Imperial 8vo. pp. 960, paper covers. 1885. 27s.

UMBRIAN.

Newman.—THE TEXT OF THE IGUVINE INSCRIPTIONS, with interlinear Latin Translation and Notes. By FRANCIS W. NEWMAN, late Professor of Latin at University College, London. 8vo. pp. xvi. and 54, sewed. 1868. 2s.

URIYA.

Browne.—AN URIYÁ PRIMER IN ROMAN CHARACTER. By J. F. BROWNE, B.C.S. Crown 8vo. pp. 32, cloth. 1882. 2s. 6d.

Maltby.—A PRACTICAL HANDBOOK OF THE URIYA OR ODIYA LANGUAGE. By THOMAS J. MALTBY, Madras C.S. 8vo. pp. xiii. and 201. 1874. 10s. 6d.

www.ingramcontent.com/pod-product-compliance
Lightning Source LLC
Chambersburg PA
CBHW020259240426
43673CB00039B/649